HUMAN SPIRITUALITY IN THE LIGHT OF THE ISLAMIC TRADITION

HUMAN SPIRITUALITY IN THE LIGHT OF THE ISLAMIC TRADITION

Shahzad Ahmed Ansari

RANDOM PUBLICATIONS

NEW DELHI - 110 002 (INDIA)

Human Spirituality in the Light of the Islamic Tradition

ISBN 978-93-51117-22-3

Published in 2015 in India by

RANDOM PUBLICATIONS

4376-A/4B, Gali Murari Lal, Ansari Road
New Delhi-110 002
Phone: +9111-43580356, 23289044
E-mail: randomexports@gmail.com; sales@randompublications.com; info@randompublications.com

Reprinted 2026

Type Setting by: Friends Media, Delhi-110089

Preface

Traditionally spirituality has been defined as a process of personal transformation in accordance with religious ideals. Since the 19th century spirituality is often separated from religion, and has become more oriented on subjective experience and psychological growth. It may refer to almost any kind of meaningful activity or blissful experience, but without a single, widely-agreed definition. The Pillars of Islam are five basic acts in Islam, considered obligatory for all believers. The Quran presents them as a framework for worship and a sign of commitment to the faith. They are (1) the shahadah (creed), (2) daily prayers (salat), (3) almsgiving (zakah), (4) fasting during Ramadan and (5) the pilgrimage to Mecca (hajj) at least once in a lifetime. The Shia and Sunni sects both agree on the essential details for the performance of these acts. The essence of Islamic spirituality is the realization of Unity as expressed in the Qur'an, on the basis of the prophetic model and with the aid of the Prophet".

Since the principle of Unity governs all facets of Islamic life, the quest for spirituality in Islam is therefore not restricted to some narrowly conceived domain, apart from the general life of the community; what distinguishes the spirituality of Islam from the religion taken as a whole, then, is "the dimension of depth or inwardness", so that the forms of the religion are interiorized, rather than opposed; and the journey from the form to the essence which it expresses can be conceived as the movement from the outward to the inward, the periphery to the centre, which is the locus of realized Unity. It is the elevation of the human condition to a plane where the mind is focused on the higher, non-material realities of a godly existence. The one who gives all his attention to worldly things and who centres his attention on mere appearances is regarded as being material-minded. Conversely, who rises above material things or appearances, who find his focus of interest in non material things, is regarded as being spiritual or godly. The latter is one who follows the injunction of the Quran: "Be devoted servants of God" (3:79). Spiritualism and humanism are the sources of origin in Islam. While Holy Scripture i.e. Qur'an is considered divine, other social systems are definitely man-made. Thus when the freedom of people to question the tenets of Islam is confronted with armed resistance, then as a religion it loses its universality and credibility as a divine revelation from God. Islam as a peaceful religion does not choose the path of violence to achieve any goal. Islam doesn't view 'spirituality' separately from everyday activities. In Islam everything is 'spiritual' because all actions must be in accordance with God's pleasure. This view comes from the Islamic creed and the Muslims' understanding of tawhid (the oneness of God). 'There is no deity worthy of worship except God' this conviction creates a world view, a perspective and a unique behaviour. It essential means that all actions – from having a shower to picking up litter from the floor – should be referred to the Creator. This establishes a constant awareness, mindfulness and consciousness of God in everything that the Muslim says or does. The understanding of spirituality in Islam is unlike the secular understanding. It is the constant reference to God and ensuring that everything he or she does is in accordance with God's pleasure.

Spanning the breadth of Islamic civilization from Morocco to Indonesia, this book demonstrates how Muslims have used the literary and visual arts in all their richness and diversity to communicate religious values.

I thank all members of my team who have helped in the preparation of the book. My special thanks go to "Random Publications" who have published the book.

— *Shahzad Ahmed Ansari*

Contents

Chapter 1

Basic Aspects of Islamic Philosophy

The basic philosophy of Islam revolves round a set of beliefs and concepts. The Unity of God, Prophethood and the Hereafter are the irreducible fundamentals of this creed. These concepts are rooted in the basic awareness of man and the realities of human experience. Human awareness springs from a sense of being which is inherent to man and his comtemplation of the physical universe. The Quran dwells on the reality of human consciousness generated by an interaction of the inner self of man and the outer world of nature. Sura Zariyat states:

> *"On earth, and in yourselves, there are signs for firm believers. Can you not see? Heaven holds your sustenance and all that you are promised. I swear by the Lord of heaven and earth that this is true, as true as you are speaking now"* *(51:20-23).*

The cardinal beliefs of Islam are not figments of imagination made sacrosanct by supernatural sanctions but emanate from deeper levels of human thought and experience. As man delves into his own self and contemplates about his whereabouts he is irresistibly drawn towards four basic realisations which point to the reality of God. The universe is a vast mechanism of infinite complexity but it is perfectly ordered and regulated. Man has a limited vision and potentialities.

Basic Issues

There are many areas of life and dimensions of the universe which defy his understanding. Man cannot comprehend the universe as a whole, much less control it. Sura Yunus states: "The unbelievers ask: Why has no sign been given him by his Lord? Say: Allah alone has knowledge of what is hidden. What if you will: I too am waiting. It is he who guides you by land and sea. You embark and as you set sail, rejoicing in a favourable wind, a raging tempest overtakes you. Billows surge upon you from every side and you fear that you are encompassed by death. You pray to Allah with all fervour. Deliver us from this peril and we will be truly thankful. Yet when he has delivered you, you commit evil in the land and act unjustly. Men, it is your own souls that you are corrupting" (10: 20-23).

Beneath the complex exterior of the universe lies a design, a pattern, a system. The Quran dilates on the impeccable order of the universe as a sign of divine being who presides over it. This is described being who presides over it. This is described as Hikmat Sura Yasin says:

> *"Let the once-dead earth be a sign to them. We gave it life and from it produced grain for their sustenance. We planted it with the palm and the vine and watered it with gushing springs, so that men might feed on its fruit. It was not their hands which made all this. Should they not give thanks?*

The night is another sign for men from the night We lifted the day—and they are plunged in darkness.

The sun hastens to its resting place: its course is laid for it by the Mighty One, the All-Knowing, We have ordained phases for the moon, which daily wanes and in the end appears like a bent and withered twig.

The Sun is not allowed to overtake the moon, nor does the night outpace the day. Each in its own orbits runs" (36: 36-43).

The Universe provides for man and caters to his purposes and requirements. This fact is epitomised by the Quranic term *Raboobiyat Sura Qaf* cogently states:

> *"We spread out the earth and set upon it immovable mountains. We brought forth in it all kinds of delectable plants. A lesson and an admonition to penitent men. We send down blessed water from the sky with which We bring forth gardens and the harvest grain, and tall palm trees laden with clusters of dates, a sustenance for men; thereby giving new life to some dead land. Such shall be the Resurrection." (50: 7-11).*

The universe holds out many benefits to man which are not accidental but form part of the cosmic design. This aspect of universal experience is embodied in the Quranic term *Naymat.* The mercy of God who has made the universe as the abode of man is not only unlimited but also continuous. The boundless mercy and munificence of God is described as *Rehman* while its continuity and timelessness as *Rahim. Sura Waqiah* states:

> *You surely know of the first creation. Why, then do you not reflect? Consider the seeds you grow. Is it you that give them growth or We? If We pleased We could turn your harvest into chaff.*

Consider the water that you drink. Was it you that poured it from the cloud or We? if We pleased We could turn it bitter. Why then do you not give thanks?

> *Observe the fire which you light. Is it you that create its wood or We? We have made it a reminder for man.*
>
> *(56: 58—74).*

The awareness generated by human contemplation of the universe underpins the reality of God. Deep down the recesses of human psyche lies the evidence of a reality higher than man himself. The objective universe offers many hints and clues for the existence of a mighty power.

The concept of Prophethood flows from the concept of God with irresistible logic. God, who is the creator and sustainer of man enjoins upon him a certain way of life. The values and principles of life which God has framed for the salvation of man are communicated through revelation. The prophets are the messengers of God and teachers among men. They convey by word and deed the infallible message of God. The message of God was conveyed to man gradually. Islam marked the perfection of Divine communication and its apostle Muhammad (peace be upon him); embodied the finality of prophethood.

Although the fundamental beliefs of Islam are rooted in the introspective reaches of human personality and the many splendoured reality of physical universe, there are many queries and questions which agitate the mind and require a satisfactory answer. The prophets disabused the minds of men of erratic beliefs and mistaken notions. Apart from this, history bears proof of many societies which were so sunk in abysmal ignorance and superstition as to disallow any opportunities of contemplation. The prophets admonished such people to the right path and exposed their misconceptions.

The prophets drew the attention of ignorant and confused men to the reality of God and offered for human weal a full-fledged system of life. They were not day-dreamers but men of action who braved with courage and steadfastness the opposition of the uninformed. They were dynamic persons who changed the destiny of man by conviction and consistency. They were not closeted away from the ordeal and challenge which their environment posed. The prophets brought despairing men a message of hope and infused them with a noble purpose. Sura *Araf* states:

> *Whenever, there come to you apostles from amongst you rehearsing my signs unto you. Those who follow them will be rewarded and those who reject them will be punished.*

Sura Mujadala bears out the dignity and stature of the prophets:

> *Believers, when you converse in private, do not speak with wickedness and enmity and disobedience towards the apostle, but with justice and piety. Have fear of Allah before whom you shall be brought together. Believers, when you confer with the apostle, give alms before such conference. That is best and purest for you. But if you lack the means, know that Allah is forgiving and merciful. (58:9-10).*

How would the prophets be recognised? The Quran states that the first man on earth was a prophet, therefore, he needed no proof of himself. Thereafter, every prophet foretold the signs of his successor. Jesus told his people that he was the messenger of God as proclaimed to them by Moses. The Bible contained many hints and references about the advent of the Prophet (peace be upon him). The chapter of New Testament captioned Matthew makes many statements about the prophet who would follow Jesus. Prophesy reached its perfection and came to fulfilment in Muhammad (peace be upon him).

Almighty's Superiority

The Quran guarantees the triumph of good represented by Prophet (peace be upon him) over evil embodied in ignorant persons whom he confronts with the divine message. The prophets over-came by faith in God and personal resilience the storm of opposition raised by vested interest they sought to abolish. Those who persisted in evil despite the warning and admonition of apostle were exterminated from the face of earth by natural calamity. The Quran is unambiguous on this fact.

Those that oppose Allah and His Apostle shall be brought low as have been before them. We have sent down clear revelations. A shameful punishment awaits the unbelievers.

Do you see those that have befriended people with whom Allah is angry? They belong neither to you nor to them. They knowingly swear to falsehood. Allah has prepared for them a grievous scourage. Evil indeed is that which they have done. They use their faith as a disguise and debar others from the path of Allah. A shameful scourage awaits them (58.5: 14— 16).

Akhrat (Hereafter) is another cardinal concept of Islam. It has a basis in sound human experience. Man has limitless desires and aspiration. His self craves for the infinite. He has a natural urge to transcend the confines of time and space and rise above the transitoriness of life. The belief in *Akhrat* fulfils human promptings for and eternal life; it provides a point of certainty in flux and unending change.

Secondly, human beings live in communities. Social life entails a system of rights and responsibilities. No society exists in a perfect form. Here men are being deprived of fundamental rights and there responsibilities are being shrugged aside. Exploitation of man by man is a fact of life. The short span of life and human ways of doing things preclude the possibility of dispensing perfect justice. How can a person responsible for massacre be punished in this life? These facts provide a rational basis for belief in the Hereafter.

Bounty of God

Picking up threads from the concept of God discussed above, emphasis was laid on the bounty of God. If God has offered men certain benefits and previleges, why should man not be accountable for it? *Sura Naba* recounts the gardens of luxurious growth given to man and draws attention to the day of sorting out. The Quran dwells on the concept of *Akhrat* at great length:

About what are they asking?

About the fateful tidings—the theme of their disputes.

But they shall know the truth; before long they shall know it.

Did we not spread the earth like a bed and raise the mountains like pillars?

We created you in pairs and gave you rest in sleep.

We made the night a mantle, and ordained the day for work. We built above you seven mighty heavens and placed in them a shining lamp. We sent down abundant water from the clouds, bringing forth grain and varied plants, and gardens thick with foliage.

Fixed is the Day of Judgement. On that day the Trumpet shall be sounded and you shall come in multitudes. The gates of heaven shall swing open and the mountains shall pass away like vapour (78: 1-12).

The *al-Qiyamah* is variously described by the Quran as Day of Judgement, Day of Reckoning, Day of Sorting Out.

A rational interpretation of fundamental beliefs of Islam has been attempted. The Quran makes a cogent and convincing statement of how concepts like unity of God, Prophethood and the hereafter are rooted in human observation and experience. It rejects the view that religion is based on the instinct of fear latent in man and demonstrates that the roots of religious faith in positive aspects of human life.

Islam has made unique contributions to human civilisation; and among these is the concept of the dignity of man. According to the Holy Quran man is the noblest of God's creation, as it says; "Certainly, We created man in the best make". (95: 4). At another place the Holy Quran declares: "And surely We have honoured the children of Adam and We carry them in the land and the sea, and We provide them with good things, and We have made them to excel highly most of those whom We have created". (17: 70). Man was made Allah's vicegerent on earth, and he was destined to rule everything around him. The Holy Quran says: "And when thy Lord said to the angels, I am going to place in the earth one who shall rule in it". (2: 30).

The idea of man being the ruler of the universe is repeated in many verses of the Holy Book: "And He has made subservient to you whatsoever is in the heavens and whatsoever is in the earth, all, from Himself. (45: 13). "Allah is He Who made subservient to you the sea that the ships may glide therein by His Grace, and that you may give thanks". (45: 12). "He has made subservient to you the sun and the moon; each pursues its course till an appointed time". (31: 29). "And He has made subservient to you the night and the day and the sun and the moon. And the stars are made subservient by His command. Surely there are signs in this for a people who understand" (16:12).

According to Islam, man's position in nature was that of a conqueror. He was created to control all the forces of nature and to rule in the earth and not to bow before them. But man degraded himself to the utmost when started worshipping the earth, rivers, trees, fire, the sun and the moon and the stars, and all those objects of nature which were made subservient to him. He even worshipped unhewn stones, and sometimes carved out idols with his own hands and worshipped them as if they were Divine, or as if they controlled good or evil for him. As the Holy Quran says: "Do you worship that which you knew not? And Allah has created you and what you make" (37: 95-96). And as Abraham asked his Sire: "Why dost thou worship that which neither hears, nor sees, nor does it avail thee in the least" (19:42).

The gravest of sins, according to the Holy Quran is *Shirk* or associating others with Allah. This is not due to feeling of jealousy on the part of Allah, but because *Shirk* demoralises man, while Divine unity brings about his moral elevation. That is why Islam has laid so much emphasis on *Tauheed* or oneness of God, which is the most fundamental principle of the Islamic faith.

Man was endowed with vast capabilities for attaining knowledge. In the first place, he was given knowledge by Allah as the Holy Quran says: "And he gave Adam knowledge of all things" (2: 31). The Arabs were an illiterate people, and reading and writing was so rare among them that it may be said not to have existed at all. The Holy Prophet (peace be upon him), himself did not know reading and writing and is called Unlettered Prophet (peace be upon him), as stated in the Quran: "And thou didst not recite before it any book, nor didst thou transcribe one with thy right hand (29: 48). Yet the first Divine message received by him was about reading and writing. As the Quran says: Read in the name of thy Lord who created. Creates man from a clot. Read and thy Lord is most bounteous, Who taught to write with the pen. He taught man what he knew not". (96: 1-5).

Read and write, was thus His first message; and to these two means of gaining knowledge of things, the faculty of observation was also granted to man. The Holy Quran has repeatedly invited the attention of man to the creation of this universe and the various phenomena working around him. He asked to observe and reflect. To quote one instance from the Quran: "In the creation of the heavens and the earth and the alternation of the night and the day, there are surely signs for men of understanding. Those who remember Allah standing and sitting and (lying) on their sides and reflect on the creation of the heavens and the earth.

Our Lord, thou hast not created this in vain"; (3: 189-90). The process of observing and reflecting convinces man that every thing made by God is perfect. He sees no incongruity in Allah's creation, and this naturally leads him to His glorification. "Glorify the name of the Lord, the Most High; Who creates things, then makes them complete: And who makes things according to a measure then guides them to their goal". (87: 1-3).

Man, before Islam, was at the lowest ebb of human civilisation. He was just a slave of nature's forces. The Holy Prophet (peace be upon him) raised him to the dignity of the master and the ruler, and it was due to this realisation of man's position to the universe that the Muslims in their very early history took vigorous strides towards the expansion of knowledge and the advancement of the sciences. Reading and writing was within a few years spread throughout the whole of Arabia and other countries which came under the influence of Islam and the Muslim State so encouraged the pursuit of study and scientific research, that centres of learning and universities sprang up throughout the empire of Islam.

According to Islam, every child is born in a state of sinlessness; and it is afterwards in life, that a person becomes a Jew or a Christian or anything else by following the religion of his parents. The Holy Prophet (peace be upon him) said: "Every child that is born conforms to the true religion (Allah's *fitrat;* and it is his parents who make him a Jew or a Christian or a Magian" *(Bukhari,* 32: 79). Every child is, thus, recognised by birth to be a Muslim, and the purity of human nature is not affected by his being born of non-Muslim parents.

The Holy Prophet (peace be upon him) once related a vision in which he had seen the Prophet Abraham in paradise with children all around him, and he added that those children were all the children that had died in the state of nature, i.e. before they attained the age of discretion. Some of the companions of the Holy Prophet (peace be upon him) asked him if the children of the polytheists were also included? The Holy Prophet (peace be upon him) replied: "Yes, the children of those who set up gods with God *(mushrikeen)* as well" *(Bokhari,* 91:48). The doctrine of the sinlessness of man by birth is an aid to his leading a sinless life. If a man does good and avoids evil, he is true to his nature. It further strengthens him to overcome sin, because he knows that nature had fitted him for this task. And step by step he can further rise to very high spiritual levels.

Not only that no impurity is attached to man by birth, but he also partakes of the Divine nature, for it was the Divine Spirit that was breathed into man, into every human child. As the Holy Quran says: "Who made beautiful everything that He created, and He began the creation of man from dust. Then He made his progeny of an extract of worthless water. Then He made him complete and breathed into him of His spirit" (32: 7-9). The Divine Spirit spoken of here is something distinct from the animal soul. It shows a mystic relation of the spirit of man with the Divine Spirit, and refers to the higher life of man. The destiny of man, according to Islam, is thus higher than mere conquest of nature, it is to seek union with the Divine Spirit. The goal of life is "Liqa Allah", or the meeting of God. In the language of the Holy Quran: "O man; thou must strive hard striving (to attain) to thy Lord until thou meet Him" (84: 6).

Islam encompasses entire human conduct. Justice is the *sine qua non* of Islam. Like other religions Islam is not satisfied with just transformation of the moral viewpoint of the individual or society, leaving man to his own sweet whim of what to obey and what not to obey as per the dictates of his convenience.

Islam is concerned with all sides, all sectors and all levels. As such, it aims at making a compact, homogenous, steel-cast *'Millat'* with definite laws of do's and don'ts and, what is more important, with a sovereign enforcing authority backed by all powers of reward and punishment. It gives laws in all sectors of human conduct at levels of family, society and polity, trade, politics, social manners, citizenship, agriculture, industry, foreign relations, health, public finance, public works, education, civilisation and what not. And it gives justice to see that they are practically enforced.

After declaration of prophethood, for full 13 years in Makkah, the Prophet of Islam (peace be upon him) preached the best principles of individual and social conduct, presented the best logic and arguments, demonstrated the best powers of oratory and persuasion, gave the best specimens of personal virtues, quoted the commandments of the Holy Quran, discussed the life-after-death. More than 95 per cent of the inhabitants of Makkah and of the places around remained infidels showing intenser enmity towards the Holy Prophet (peace be upon him), his Companions and Islam. When, however, the scene changed to Medina with Islam becoming a state, a government, a political and military force, new people came within its fold and Islam could set up a model in all sectors for all times and climes.

At Medina, the Prophet (peace be upon him) blended the ever-warring tribes into one compact fraternity, changed hearts, values and viewpoints, reformed society and polity, created an atmosphere of dependable safety, peace and goodwill and overthrew the governments of oppression and tyranny whose game was to play one set of people against another.

The Holy Quran puts all emphasis on the suppression of oppression and enforcement of justice.

"Verily Allah orders you to give the due to whomsoever it belongs and when you sit in judgement, be just and upright—" *(4: 58).*

"O people of Eimman *(Faith) give all support and perseverance to the cause of justice in the way of Allah. And do not trespass for fear of this nation or that. And catch full hold of justice as it is close to* Taqwa. *And fear none but Allah. Verily He knows every action of yours". (5: 8).*

"Tell them, O Prophet, that your Allah has commanded justice."

"Sure, we have sent to you this Book of Rights so that you may pronounce judgements between peoples as per the commandments of Allah. And do not be among those who unjustly take sides" *(4: 105).*

Only 227 verses of the Holy Quran discuss laws and they pertain to no more than 11 sectors of human activity. Of course, this is the core and kernel, the nucleus. All the remaining parts of the structure of the Islamic polity have been furnished by the *Sunnah,* the sayings and doings of the Prophet (peace be upon him).

As regards the two evil courses of bribe and recommen-dations the Holy Prophet (peace be upon him) said that he who gives and he who takes bribe will both go to Hell. He has cursed the giver and taker of bribe.

True Judge : The Holy Prophet (peace be upon him) had to deal with hundreds of cases between persons belonging to erstwhile opposite camps. The least favour or disfavour on his part would have broken the oneness and unity of *Millat.* But it was his impartial justice that gave no loophole of criticism to anyone that kept the *Millat* intact, that is the model par excellence to all posterity.

He has prescribed the special qualifications of the judge, the *Qazi.* Once he said: "Judges are of three kinds-one of which will go to Paradise, recognises the right of one *vis-a-vis* another and pronounces judgements accordingly.

The other is one who recognises the rights but due to any worldly consideration does not act accordingly. And the third kind is one who does not care to recognise the rights and acts unjustly".

"When a judge does his best to know the truth from untruth and finds the truth, he would get two rewards.

But one who does not find the truth in spite of his best efforts would get one reward only."

As regards the court-procedure, he said: "None is to pronounce judgement if he is in wrath and anger."

"Both the parties are to be present before the judge."

"I am but a human being. I try legal disputes. It is possible that one of the party is more adept in presenting his side of the case and under the impression of his being rightful, I judge in his favour. So if a party secures such a favour by trampling the right of another party, the former is taking nothing but a piece of Hellish Fire. It is for him to take it or leave it."

He has ordered the judge to hear equally attentatively both the parties and to deliver judgement only when the truth comes out. Similarly, the Holy Prophet (peace be upon him) has laid down the essential qualifications of the court witness.

He had refused to accept the evidence of (1) person guilty of breach of trust, (2) person guilty of immoral sex; (3) person who has previously been inflicted with court punishment; (4) person who harbours feelings of revenge or hate against his brother, including the party in question; (5) person who has been guilty of giving false evidence; (6) person who is related to or in service of one of the parties or is a flatterer to one of the parties.

He said that giving false evidence is equivalent to committing *Shirk.*

The Holy Prophet (peace be upon him) while awarding judgement took full notice of the condition of health, of finance and of other factors of the guilty and gave relaxations accordingly. He always pardoned whenever it could be. He always arranged for compromise and *Qasas* whenever it could be. He gave punishment only when it had to be. Islam considers the whole humanity as one family and treats mankind as one community. The Holy Prophet (peace be upon him) was first to demolish narrow visions of geographical and political nationhood, and taught the lesson of broadmindedness and international brotherhood to the world at large.

Paying his tribute to the Holy Prophet (peace be upon him) the French poet Lamartine wrote: "Muhammad is the one great man without whom the world would appear incomplete. Truly, Muhammad stands to this day, and for all time to come, at the peak of humanity.

Every nation at sometime or other, in its history, had its superman, the luminary who gave it light, the reformer who inspired it with noble ideals, and the Prophet who raised it morally, intellectually and spiritually on a high pedestal. But no other prophet of any religion has exercised so deep and lasting an influence in the religious, historical and social history of mankind as the Prophet of Islam (peace be upon him).

As a prophet and reformer, entrusted with the noble mission of raising mankind from the depths of degradation and the dungeons of moral, political, social and religious bankruptcy and decadence into which it had fallen in the sixth century, Prophet Muhammad (peace be upon him) could not be otherwise than a revolutionary in the fullest sense of the term. The lofty ideals he preached not only brought about a complete change in the political situation but also had an equally important and a more enduring bearing on the social conditions of the people. To consider that the advent of the Holy Prophet (peace be upon him) on the Arab horizon merely heralded the birth of a politically unified Arabia is to pay but poor tribute to him and confess shocking ignorance of the implications of the message and his dynamic personality which ushered in a revolution of considerable magnitude in the thought and actions not only of the Arabs but of mankind itself.

Islam, the religion the Holy Prophet (peace be upon him) preached, introduced the conception of the nation as a unit and a vital stage in the organisation of human society. It is lofty in the conception of the relationship of man to God and noble in its doctrine of duty of man to man to the lower creation. It was the first religion that preached and practised democracy in its true sense.

It was Islam which for the first time proclaimed liberty to mankind, and introduced universal brotherhood in humanity. It does not recognise differences of class, caste, race, nation, or geographical and political boundaries and territories of the world. No one in Islam is better because of creed or colour. "An Arab has no superiority over a non-Arab, nor a non-Arab over Arab except piety". Islam laid down the ideal that nobility depends not in belonging to a particular family or tribe but upon being noble in personal conduct and character. The Divine Message has come down to us in the form of the Holy Quran which is the basic source of guidance for humanity.

It is a great charter of the freedom of humanity. As a book of ethics, and a code of conduct, clear, concise and simple in terms, there is no other sacred book in the world to replace it. It is "a stupendous monument of solitary legislation", to quote the words of Washington Irving. No wonder it has exercised a most potent and powerful influence over mankind throughout the ages. Islam's institutions are unique: they do not compromise with materialistic dogmas. They stand firm on individual piety and individual freedom a close-knit family devoted to the welfare of a classless, benevolent society.

The principle of equality and brotherhood, justice and freedom which the Holy Prophet (peace be upon him) defined as integral elements of faith have engendered a righteous character and a noble spirit in society. Distinguishing the essence of piety from the mere form of ceremony of righteousness, the Holy Prophet (peace be upon him) made faith in Allah and benevolence towards man the essential features of religion. He brought to perfection the grand idea of unifying the whole human race and gathering it together under one banner.

His was "a life consecreted, from first to last, to the service of God and humanity". He preached that a true Muslim is one from the danger of whose tongue and hands all Muslims are immune and that the best occupation is service to mankind, that knowledge is a valuable legacy, manners and courtesy the various ornaments, and carefulness a clear and transparent mirror and that spiritual virtue consists in adoring Allah.

The Prophet of Islam (peace be upon him) denounced vehemently meanness and slander, hypocrisy and untruthfulness, superstition, gambling, drinking, oppression of the weak by the strong and other evils, and gave new light and guidance to mankind. The supreme place he gave in the faith to the duty of alms-giving and charity to the poor is another praiseworthy feature of religion he preached. He told us that every good act is a charity, an exhortation to your fellowmen to do virtuous deeds is equal to alms-giving; guiding the wanderer to the right path is charity; assisting the blind in crossing the street is charity; removing stones and thorns and other obstructions from the road is charity; giving water to the thirsty is charity, and so on. There is hardly a religious duty which is more sacred and benevolent to the Muslims than that of charity to the poor. The Holy Prophet (peace be upon him) preached that true poverty is not merely lack of wealth but lack of desire for wealth.

The strict observance by the Muslims of the daily prayers for five times is another testimony to the value of a living faith and the spirit of universal brotherhood. One should also witness the congregational prayers offered by the faithful to see for himself the atmosphere of equality, brotherhood and love. In the presence of Allah, all stand shoulder to shoulder, the rich and the powerful with the poor and the lowly, the master and the servant offering prayers and bowing themselves before Allah in abject submission. Can there be any more levelling influence in the world?

Universal Religion

The Holy Prophet (peace be upon him) upheld the dignity of women and gave them an honoured place in society. The economic and cultural position of women was raised to a high status, and recognition of women's right to property marked the beginning of a new era, which is now the recognised feature of every civilized society. With his far-sighted vision, the Holy Prophet (peace be upon him) laid down a complete social system containing minute regulations for man's conduct in all circumstances of life.

His love for, and human treatment of, animals are too well-known. According to a *Hadith,* the Holy Prophet (peace be upon him) is reported to have said: "If you behold three mounting an animal, stone them until one descends". The Prophet of Islam (peace be upon him) will for ever remain the symbol of the most exemplary human conduct. All his efforts were aimed at elevating man's mind and soul, and giving him an exalted position. He preached righteousness and toleration, and in his own self presented the most accomplished model of his teachings. In his own lifetime he moulded the character of his fellowmen, reformed them, changed their thoughts, put new ideals before them, elevated them to a higher plane and let them onwards, towards the path of progress and to the fullness of a better and nobler life.

With the passage of time, Western writers, in spite of their ignorance and prejudice, began to assess the position of the Holy Prophet (peace be upon him) and the revolution brought about by him. In the case of some honest and fair appraisal and objective considerations have been dominant. A case in illustration is that of Dozy where truth found to favour: "We see then that the Arab conquests of the seventh century have continued to play an important role in human history, down to present day. It is this unparalleled combination of secular and religious influence which I feel entitles Muhammad (peace be upon him) to be considered the most influential single figure in human history". (The 100*: A ranking of the Most Influential Persons in History*— Michael H. Hart). In this list the name of the Holy Prophet (peace be upon him) is on the top. Jesus Christ is number three.

Lamartine in his *"History* de *La Turquie",* Vol. II, says about the Holy Prophet (peace be upon him):

"No person in the world had ever willingly or unwillingly, independently or under duress kept before him an object or goal higher than the goal of Muhammad (peace be upon him).

Higher Goal

This goal was much higher than general human level, much above human intellect. What was this goal? To do away one by one with the curtains of superstition that were hung between God and man to fill the heart of man by his presence and dye man in colours of God's attributes, to present in the crowd of false deities the sacred and reasonable concept of God free of any defect. Up to now no man has dared to undertake such a stupendous and grand task, which is beyond human reach and then its sources should be so limited. This is so because neither when he conceived the idea of this responsibility, nor when practical steps were taken to implement it, he had only his person or a few residents of a corner of the desert at his disposal.

There were no sources, no support, nor necessary arrangements. With this sort of paucity of resources, no man in the world, up to now, has brought about such a glorious and splendid revolution.

"A revolution of such dimensions that within two hundred years, Islam practically as a religion ruled over Arabia. In the name of God, it had conquered Iran, Khorasan, Western India, Syria, Egypt, Ethiopia, territory of North Africa known at that time, many islands of Mediterranean and Spain. If the loftiness of the goal, absence of resources and brilliancy of results is the criterion of human genius, then where is the man who can dare present any other human being to compete with Muhammad (peace be upon him). Great men in the world have piled arms, codified laws and ruled over extensive empires. At the most they created material powers and resources which in most cases were reduced to ashes. But this man did not shake only the armies and battalions, legislative assemblies, big empires, nations and families but also the hearts of millions of people living in one-third area of the known world of that time.

"And more than that. This personality shook places of sacrifices, deities, religions and rituals, conceptions and convictions and as a matter of fact shook the very souls of men. On the basis of a book, whose every word has a legal significance, he built up a community which in its turn fused different languages and races into one single nation. This everlasting nation, rebellion and hatred against false gods and overflowing love for one God are the legacies of this great personality. In the midst of a plethora of false gods the proclamation of conception about one God in itself was such a miracle that as soon as these words were uttered by him all places of worship of false gods were destroyed. One-third of the world was set on fire.

"His life, his devotion, his relentless efforts against superstition and the great courage to scoff at the fury and anger of false gods is known. His life at Makkah and thirteen years' tribulations and severe opposition were met with supreme fortitude and courage. He gladly bore the ridicule and denial of the opponents. All these troubles and then migration by him, his continuous preaching and invitation, his supreme efforts, his full confidence in the success of his mission and in unfavourable circumstances his supernatural calm and collected disposition at the time of victory and success, amnesty and forgiveness not for the sake of statecraft, but for the success of his divine goal and object. His wishes and hopes in the world of deep strance, his regular prayers, his supplications, secret contacts with his God, his life, his death and his popularity and influence after his demise, all these facts provide evidence for what kind of life?

Do these facts show a life of a deceitful fabrication or the life of a person who had unshakable confidence and trust in his claims. It was his this very iron-clad confidence and faith generated in him a very strong current on power and strength by which he made his belief ever-living and everlasting.

What was this belief? "First Oneness of God and the second to explain what God is not. This *"illa"* and the other *"illa"*. One part to wipe away the false gods in the world (even use of sword if pressed by necessity) and the other part to lay out the carpet of one true God's majesty.

A great thinker, orator of a high order, prophet law-giver, military leader, victor of beliefs and convictions, responsible for presenting correct ideology of life with reason and clarity of vision; the founder of a system, in which false gods cannot enter man's mind; twenty worldly states and above them the sovereignty of One God. This is Muhammad (peace be upon him)."

> *"Bring all of your criteria, all of your tests by which the greatness of human beings is checked and measured and then reply if the world has produced any man greater than him?"*

The views of another Western author, viz., Pringle Kennedy should be taken into consideration. After dealing with the subject of social, religious and cultural condition of the world he says: "It is a matter of surprise that this new culture was born in Arabia at a time when it was urgently needed.

> *"For those among us who think man is everything, Muhammad (peace be upon him) is a great example of*

> *what a man can do. Those who believe that changes and revolutions in history are not the result of one man's efforts but are more dependent on the peculiarities of environments and the ability of human mind to accept them cannot deny that if a revolution had to come (as it came in Arabia) it could not take place without Muhammad (peace be upon him) and would have remained pending for an indefinite period". (Pringle Kennedy—*
>
> "In Arabian Society at the Time of Muhammad".

The Eclipse of Christianity in Islam by L. E. Brown bears testimony to the fact that: "Due to influence of Muhammad (peace be upon him), Arab clannish pride and exclusiveness came to an end. They became members of a brotherhood which they never knew. This link was the faith of Oneness of God. If brought them to a centre and conquests followed easily.

Hitti opines in his book *"History of the Arabs"* as under: "This was the first time that the Arabs were brought together not in the name of blood-relationship but in the name of religion. Allah was the supreme sovereign of this state. The Prophet (peace be upon him), throughout his life was His representative and ruler of the country. For this reason Muhammad (peace be upon him) in addition to his spiritual responsibilities, directed the affairs of the state like state officials. In his nation after forsaking all tribal preferences and old relationship became brothers."

The Reverend Stephenson is of the opinion: "It must be freely admitted at first that for his nation the personality of Muhammad (peace be upon him) was the source of many and great benefits. He was born in a country where political set-ups, reasonable beliefs and ethical behaviour were unknown. He brought about these three things. Through his mature intelligence, he reformed all these three simultaneously.

In place of different tribes he made them one nation, similarly he preached the Unity of God in place of deities and gods. All the major unwholesome practices were done away with. As Islam flowed out of old Arabia, barbarians were gathered in its fold and they became the possessors of the benefits of Islam. Islam is an instrument to lead human beings from darkness to light and from *Satan* to God.

The Reverend Bosworth Smith observes: "On account of such a good fortune which has not parallel in history, Muhammad (peace be upon him) is the founder of three elements. One nation, one state and one religion. The founder himself was unlettered but he gave the world a Book which has poetic and musical stance in it as also complete code of conduct and law. This is the miracle of Muhammad (peace be upon him), permanent miracle and actually a miracle."

Islam's Impact

They all write about an unprecedented revolution not only political but social, religious, moral, ethical and in short all matters covering life of man. They all pay tribute to Quran. At this stage it is necessary we should know what was there in the world at that time that was swept away to make room for higher and bright set up and a new world was created.

Pringle in his *"Arabian Society at the Time of Muhammad"* (peace be upon him) says that at that time it seemed that the grand edifice of civilisation which had been built during the last 4,000 years, was about to collapse and human beings were about to revert to the same barbaric state wherein every tribe was deadly enemy of the other and nobody had any knowledge or regard for institutions and regulated existence. Ancient tribal values had been lost, and on the lines of old methods kingship could no longer flourish. The institutions which Christianity introduced they did not inculcate spirit of discipline or unity but were being the cause of disunity estrangement and destruction. Time had come when all-round there was gross indiscipline, bloodshed and there was no horizon of man's life. It had gone down to the level of beasts of jungle.

The tall tree of civilisation whose green and flourishing branches provided shadow and comfort to the world and were laden with the golden fruits of art, science and literature was shaking about to fall. It no longer received the moisture of respect and attachment. Only the outer crust remained. The holocaust of wars and battles cut it down to pieces and these pieces were supported by old customs and ceremonies. It was feared that they would fall down any time. Was it possible under these conditions to create or introduce emotional culture which could bring round humanity to one central point and save civilisation. This culture had to be of a new pattern because all old customs and usages had finished and to resurrect them needed centuries.

Says Carlyle: "The humanity like a dry jungle was waiting for a spark. That spark of electricity appeared in the form of that great personality and ignited the universe."

This is the evaluation of great revolution brought about by the Holy Prophet (peace by upon him). They could not go further for two reasons. Firstly, the prejudice and opposition generated by Pope Urban II (1042—1099) who initiated the crusades. This prejudice still exists. Secondly, the West is devoting all its energy and deploying all scientific discoveries to destroy opponents besides exploiting the weak. Deadly arms are being manufactured and sold. Humanity today stands at the brink of mass destruction. For these reasons, the West has not been able to turn its attention towards higher values, and sanctity of human life.

Historic March : Islam has always faced challenges on its historical march. It faced its first crisis when the Holy Prophet (peace be upon him) passed away from this earthly scene. This was very close to the rise of Islam as a historical force. When the Holy Prophet (peace be upon him) died, the crucial point was whether there should be any Islamic history at all. Some of the then Muslims (e.g. the Beduins) felt that the affair was now over: they had taken a vow of fidelity to a leader, he was no more, and that was the end of the affairs. Others felt the need for restoring status quo and emphasising the recognition of urban and tribal realities. Besides, it was presumed that new religious faith should take its course on those basis. But this was rejected and it was decided that to keep the followers of the Holy Prophet (peace be upon him) united as a socio-political economic unit and as one that marches forward in the world to enforce and spread as unit the message of Islam. This decision was taken not without opposition which was finally crushed and silenced. This decision was of immense significance for the later history of Islam.

The decision to keep the community intact and choose a leader for itself in place of the Holy Prophet (peace be upon him) appeared to be more pertinent than the issue (which has received immeasurable attention) of who that leader should be. Then emerged the issue of the actual development of Islamic history on earth, having understood the significance of its last success and homogeneity. The early Muslims took the whole burden and opportunity of government as well as cultural creation in the widest sense. They completed this task significantly so that when they could presently look at this society that they had constructed, they felt satisfied that it led the world. God had enjoined upon men the way to live; those who followed the path were visibly receiving His blessings.

Great Debacle : History, however, has its own inner logic. Muslims feel it to be will of God on earth.

But this period of Islam's earthly glory did not last long. The early period of Islam primarily comprised Arab elements, it lost its vigour after spending its inherent force with the fall of Baghdad in 1258, the successful Arab rule came to its formal end. The Mughal invasion gave a death blow to the Arab ascendency of Islam. Many millions were massacred; whole cities were laid waste and political rules passed into the hands of infidel barbarians. This ended the classical period of Islamic history. This was a first great crisis of Islamic history. With the demise of the Arab Empire, Islamic history seemed to have lost its driving force. It appeared as if divine purpose as conceived by Islam was faltering, if it has not actually failed.

Great Survival

Despite this debacle, Islam on earth survived this crisis and it re-appeared in a new and rather different mould. With the drawing to a close of the European Middle Ages, Islam's mediaeval period—between its classical and modern eras—set in motion. Historians of Islam—whether Muslims or Westerns have taken much less interest in this mediaeval phase of Islam than that of the classical. In spite of it, there were new aspects which were not without significance. This phase of Islam produced constructive answers to the issues raised.

New Development

On the religious side, *Sufism* was a new major development. The *Sufi* or mystic interpretation of Islam has its germs even in the classical period. Yet at the time it was confined to an insignificant minority, comprising an elite of the pious withdrawn from the main stream of Islamic march. The mediaeval period bolstered its immensity throughout the Muslim world. The movement took an institutional form and gained popularity. There were additions also in interpretation; as for example, the *Masnavi* of Jalaluddin Roomi which was produced after the fall of Baghdad.

Besides, Islam converted the conquerors. After imposing on the Muslim alien rulers for 50 years, the Mughal dynasty which had subjugated the Muslim world, itself embraced Islam as a historical force soon asserted itself in Persian and Turkish forms. These forms were different from the preceding ones. New forms were different from the old in the government structure, social organisation and in cultural and aesthetic values. In this new era, Islam again began to march as a political force.

After its nadir in the Thirteenth Century, Islam began to touch a new zenith in the Sixteenth; which could be put forth as the Islam's greatest century uptil now. Then the Ottoman Empire was a most powerful state on earth; Europe shivered before its apparently unending series of conquests. At the same time, *Safuids* had established a family based on imperial power in Iran, the Mughals then had firmly entrenched themselves in India and constituted the greatest rule the subcontinent had seen for many a long time. This second revival of Islam was confined not only to the building of Empires, but it was a new expansion also in geographical and spiritual senses. The second great wave of military expansion and missionary fervour brought for Islam new converts: in the Northern Asia Minor and the Balkans and Central Asia, in the South Negro Africa and in the East Indonesia. Thus, classical Islam was doubled in area and numbers. Once again, it was evident that historical Islam was a power to be reckoned with.

However, the second flowering of Islam, with the possible exception of the Turkish, has not been generally regarded by the Muslims as fully consistent with the classical Islam. What the Muslims accomplished in it is not so keenly regarded as a complete example of Islam at work in the world, moulding into a divine pattern the flux, of historical development. But this tendency should not be overemphasised. The classical version of Islam has always remained official, and its social importance cannot be minimised. But even in this period Muslims never grudged to extol any individual who either successfully defended Islamic domain or extended it. Even then, there were many Muslims in the world who regarded conquest of Constantinople in 1453 as an example of God's power as well as Sultan Muhammad's effort. However, it is a fact that in the sixteenth century Muslim World was again a mighty force having wealth and splendour. Whatever opinion one may hold up of it, the Muslims of this period were victorious in a history expansive and successful.

But even this success did not last long. The second wave of Islamic Revival was more short-lived than the first. The advance of Muslim society ceased and by the eighteenth century it entered a period of decline. Its military and political power underwent serious reverses; its commercial and economic life enfeebled, its intellectual efforts stagnated, its artistic talent lost lustre and religious vitality ebbed. The writings of great masters were confined to commentaries and classical systems were used to congeal mental faculties rather than as an impetus for opening up new horizons of thought. On the *Sufi* side, the orders degenerated from mystic perception to exploitable superstition. Besides, it is a strange coincidence that this decay coincided with a new upsurge of Europe. At about the same time, Western civilisation set about its greatest venture of expansion that human history has ever seen. It accumulated vitality, skill, and power on a vast scale; with them the West was then refashioning its own life and soon the life of the globe.

Forces of West : The force of the West which was imbued with exploratory restlessness met the Muslim World in decline and subdued it. By 1800, the West subjugated such centres of Muslim power as remained on many areas and imposed its rule. During most of the nineteenth century many Muslim countries lost their freedom. The Dutch entrenched them in Indonesia; Iran and the Ottoman Empire, though formally independent, lost their freedom to act. Muslim society, once dignified was now everywhere despondent in spirit and prey to outside forces.

Muslims uphold that Islam essentially is a religion, and as such deeply personal and also conclusively surpassing all particularities and limits of this existence and all its affairs; despite this, it has the distinction of having a deep concern for these affairs. It was essential for a true Muslim to carry out in this world the divine obligation as to how mankind, individually and collectively, should live. If this is seen from another angle, it appears that Muslims should see how that ideal society is built. In short, Islamic history is the fulfilment, under divine guidance, of the purpose of human history.

It is a fact that actual Islamic history, for some centuries, approximated to this ideal. We have also observed that in actual fact, periods of decay and regeneration in Islamic history have alternated. Besides, we have also noticed that the mediaeval period of Islamic history has ended in disorder. Although, many Muslim countries had gained independence after World War II and their economic plight has considerably improved, yet the basic problem has persisted; and the issue of internal cohesion and fear of foreign interference remained. In this age of Super Power contention for the domination at the cost of the other, fears of foreign interference and internal disorder have not vanished and then a challenge to Islam's will to carve history according to its dynamism.

The basic malady of modern Islam lies in perception that something has gone wrong with Islamic history; hence the fundamental problem of meodern Muslim is how to restore that history; and set it working in full vigour again so that Islamic society may again be luxuriant as a divinely-guided society. In the twentieth century the basic spiritual crisis of Islam results from the realisation that something is discordant between God-ordained religion and the historical development of the world controlled by God. Muslims have failed to establish any tangible interconnection between these two factors—otherwise they would have long subjugated the contemporary historical situation to the requirements of their faith.

This is not to say that the Muslims have ignored this problem. Of course, men like Abdul Wahab Najdi (1703- 1887), Jamaluddin Afghany (1839-1897), Shah Waliullah (1703-1762), and many others have tried to analyse and solve this problem. Their efforts in this direction have immense value. But the problem still persists and the Muslim world despite its area, numerical strength and potential wealth had failed to shake of fears of internal disruption and foreign interference.

This is not to say, that the Muslims did not try to adopt suitable devices for the transportation of its worldly condition. Many attempts have been made to solve the problem; firstly, liberalism was tried, but it failed. From the late nineteenth century to the First World War, European liberalism was in great vogue in many Muslim countries, but Muslims soon realised that this internal Westernising of the Islamic community constituted subtler and more dangerous version of the same threat; subversion from within. Its inherent threat to Islamic history and society was enough to alarm those who fervently cherish the realisation and embodiment of classical divine precepts as the goal of Muslim endeavour. This attitude to Westernisation has in recent decades reappeared with new vigour and vehemence.

Above all, there has been despair in the particular ties between Islam and Western liberalism itself. In the early stages of contact of Muslim world and the Western liberalism, Muslims hoped that Western liberalism could assist them in their basic enterprise of reconstructing the Islamic society, and thereby setting Islamic history on road to progress. The resulting disenchantment had led Muslims to seek new ways of fulfilling Islamic mission on earth as the Islamic Revolution in Iran, the shift in Pakistan to a new search for Islamic solution of problems and revival of Islam-oriented parties in many Muslim countries. But behind this new trend lurks the danger of an emerging new dogmatism which in its old form severely blocked the progress of Muslims for centuries. The need remains for reconciling Islam with rational modes of thought and behaviour to reconstruct Islamic society. Islam is an Arabic word and like many Arabic words, has no single word equivalent in the English or any other language. As for the meaning of the word, it connotes profoundest security and, therefore, peace obtained through submission. And since such peace and security can be derived only through submission to the Will of God, it implies total Submission of God.

Such being the literal meaning of Islam, man's awareness of submission to God must not be dated as commencing with any particular era, philosopher, prophet or scripture. The Holy Quran itself clarified this beyond a shadow of doubt. All the prophets from Noah to Muhammad (peace be upon them) are the Messengers of God and therefore the prophets of True Religion *(Deen-i-Haq)*. Obviously, the best of media for learning the ways of such submission is the education imparted by those inspired from the Divine Source.

Lasting Notions

The reason why Orientalists and those we speak of as Muslims refer to Islam as the religion of the illustrious Prophet Muhammad (peace be upon him) is that he is the last in the lineage of the prophets, the Book revealed to him is the last revealed word of God, and his pattern of life is the only one worthy of being followed in practice, because far more is known about him than about any other prophet and therefore it can be said with authenticity that every act and deed of his is the matchless example of piety and righteousness. This finality, both of the Book and prophethood has established the fact beyond any shadow of doubt that Islam and Islam alone shows the Light of Allah to the entire humanity which has been groping in pitch darkness.

Some great Western thinkers, for instance Thomas Carlyle in his *"Hero and Hero Worship"* looks upon the Prophet of Islam (peace be upon him) as his idea! of a true prophet and Islam equated with submission to God as the ideal religion. Goethe believed the same, though it is not on record that he subscribed to the same estimate of the Holy Prophet (peace be upon him). To his question: "If this be Islam, do we not all live in Islam?" Carlyle answers, " yet we that have any moral faith, we all live so." So much for the literal meaning of the word Islam, and it is this sense that the Quran and its Prophet (peace be upon him) use the word. Having established the meaning of Islam, we proceed to the implication of the word submission. Submission is obedience-in-action. There is no such thing as believing in submission but no submitting in action. Ignorance of this simple logic—or wilful evasion of it—underlies the tragedy of those who pretend to be Muslims but just as the implications of Islam are ignored so also are those of being Muslim. The general belief conveniently developed is that if you recite the words " There is no god save Allah and Muhammad is the messenger of Allah" you are a Muslim, and you need trouble yourself no more about deeds or misdeeds, the fire of hell being now forbidden on you. There could be no greater mistake.

Oath of Allegiance : During the Holy Prophet's (peace be upon him) lifetime and for at least some decades after him, the recital of these words was no more than an equivalent to an oath of allegiance, and it was understood by the convert that having conceded and acknowledged the Holy Prophet's (peace be upon him) Divine-messenger status, the convert would do as the messenger bade him do. For instance, as long as the authority of the messenger was not acknowledged he could not reasonably expect one to demolish one's idols, but once that authority was acknowledged, his orders and counsels were acted upon in word and spirit in all matters. It was never taken for granted that having accepted the validity of his Messenger-of-Allah status there was no change required in deeds and practices. If it were otherwise his claim to prophethood would have been acknowledged by everyone the first day he made the announcement.

On the contrary, we find that he is offered immense bribes of wealth, position, and beautiful women, if only he would let them continue to do as they wished to do. But this condition was not acceptable to him. The objective of his mission was not to get himself acknowledged but to get humanity do the right things.

But today, it is regrettable indeed, the Holy Quran, its arguments, words and spirit have all been modified to suit the conveniences of those having vested interests. The *'kalima'* has been given a technical significane, made a magical chanting and regard to the practice of the Holy Prophet's (peace be upon him) councils has been consigned to oblivion. In not a single instance does the Holy Quran commend belief or acknowledgement of its Prophet (peace be upon him) without action. The words repeated again and again are:

> *"Those who believe and do good work, for them are gardens below which rivers flow...." Paradise is never held out to those who merely believe or recite* 'kalima'.

"Forgiveness" says the Holy Quran is incumbent on Allah only towards those why do evil in ignorance and then turn quickly in repentence to Allah. These are the ones toward whom Allah relenteth. Allah is ever Knower, Wise. Forgiveness is not for those who do ill deeds until when death attends one of them, he says I repent (4:17-18). "He who does wrong will have the recompense thereof and he will not find against Allah any protecting friend or helper. And who does good works, whether male or female and is a believer, such will enter paradise" (4: 123-124). "For those who do good is the best reward and more thereto. Neither ignominy nor dust cometh near their faces. Such are rightful owners of the garden" (10:26).

That a believer is not necessarily a Muslim the Holy Quran clarifies:

> *"O you who believe; observe your duty to Allah with right observance and do not die save as Muslims: (4: 102). Here the Holy Quran is directly addressing those who already believe, not disbelievers, in the Messenger-of-God status of the Holy Prophet (peace be upon him) telling them that such belief or acknowledgement is not necessarily to be equated with Islam. To be Islamic they shall have to be performers of submission to God even unto death; Again the Prophets Ibrahim and Yaqub (peace be upon them) are quoted as advising their sons not to die except as performers of submission (2: I 32). The sons of Ibrahim and grandson Yaqub and the latter's many sons were always believers in the unity of God and the messengership of their prophet-fathers, yet their belief or assumption was not enough. What was still required and would be constantly and always required was submission-in-action. The advice quoted was a reminder to them and is to all others.*

Not Mere Belief : It is clear that mere belief is not looked upon by the Holy Quran as qualifying one to the status of being Muslim. There is a good reason for this. Belief unaccompanied by action can be very deceptive, a person may think quite sincerely that he believes while he really does not believe. True, genuine belief is a state of the mind that firmly grips the substrata and conscious levels of it. When belief comes into total possession, it becomes impossible for the mind so possessed to do anything but what the belief directs. The validity of belief can be tested only by deeds. If the deeds are not right, the belief too is not right. People who assume that though they are habitual sinners, they do have *Iman,* only victims of self-deception. Faith and deeds cannot contradict one another.

There are not a few people today who observe the five daily prayers, fast and even perform *Haj.* At the same time, if they are Government servants, they live on bribe-accumulated wealth, even after retirement. Or, if in business, they may be smugglers, or land-lords, and in *every* case live in violation of the Quranic injunctions in respect of *Riba,* their excuse being that since they perform the elementary prescribed rituals and offer contributions to various *mazars* (shrines), salvation is assured to them. Not content with the sins of their own bribes they try to bribe the souls of dead saints.

The Holy Prophet (peace be upon him) like the Quran, does not offer any assurance to mere observer of ritualistic prayers, fasting or pilgrimage *(Haj)* but he does guarantee paradise for him from whose preserves his modesty.

He commends giving water to a thirsty dog, and declares that the acquisition of learning or keeping a night's watch at the frontier is better than many a night of prayers. All this is not to say that prayers, fasting or the Annual Pilgrimage to Makkah are valueless. They are of immense value but like priceless pearls, are fragile and quickly demolished by the stroke of wrong deeds. Helped by good deeds they are polished imbued with lustre and become meaningful. Deeds and rituals act and react on one another. Wrong deeds indicate that the rituals are not being effective.

Of course, there are levels of submission, surrender. Human nature being what it is, weaknesses being inherently compulsive, it is not to be expected that one may never stray off the straight and narrow path. God does not expect the same calibre of devotion, say, from a man of humble capacity and means with modest ambitions, of common pursuits and little learning as He does from one capable of high thinking and commanding greater resources and leisure. The level of Islam or Submission differs from man to man. Thus, the Holy Quran tells certain Bedouins who came to the Holy Prophet (peace be upon him) declaring they had *Iman* (faith):

> *"Do not say that you have faith* (Iman) *because faith has not entered your hearts yet: but say rather: We have acknowledged with preliminary submission. Yet if you act in obedience to Allah and His Messenger, He will not withhold from you the reward of your deeds. Allah is Forgiving, Merciful."*

And the Book goes on to define faith:

> *"The full of faith are those only who believe in God and His Messenger and afterwards do not waver but strive with their wealth and their lives for the cause of God. Such are the sincere."* *(49:14-15).*

The test of true faith, that is striving with one's wealth and even life. Money is the anvil on which *'Iman'* is hammered out.

On one occasion, while sitting in the company of his companions the Holy Prophet (peace be upon him) exclaimed:

> *"Who is it that will carry out four behests?"*

Abu Huraira said, "I will, O Messenger of Allah". Then the Holy Prophet (peace be upon him) grasped his hand and said:

> *"If you are content with what you have, you will be rich. If you do good to your neighbours, you will be a* momin *(truly imbued with faith); and if you wish for others what you wish for yourself, you will be a Muslim. And do not laugh much, for oo much laughter dulls a man's intellect."*

Test of a Muslim

The Supreme Being in one instance tells us that the test of a man being a true Muslim is that he spends his wealth and his life according to the revealed commandments, and in the other, the Holy Prophet (peace be upon him) defines a Muslim as one who makes no difference between what he desires for himself and what he desires for his fellowmen. Salvation is elevated to a superordinary level namely doing to others what one would have others do to him. The highest submission is that of the Prophets (peace be upon him).

Just as doing god has levels, so has doing evil. There is the evil that God forgives. This is what might be called a slip. A man going along the *sirat-i-mustaqim,* the straight path, strays off but realising his error, returns immediately to it. Misdeeds that are planned and persisted in do not fall in the category of forgivable sins. Sins that are crimes which corrupt society victimise millions of human beings. A judge or police officer, for instance, who takes a bribe, primarily deprives someone of his right. This is the first wrong. But the fact that he sets an example for corruption, that he becomes an abettor in the economic inflation—to note but one result— thereby causing prices to rise and, consequently bringing hardship to the poor in short, becoming a corrupter of social conditions, the extent of his misdeed is surely not one that God overlooks.

Their professions have the sanctity of law behind them. But does the Holy Quran justify their activities? Does the Holy Quran justify or condemn profiteering? Does the Holy Prophet (peace be upon him) countenance the renting out of land or building property? Does the Holy Quran forbid turning any wealth into a commodity of circulation among the rich? It is permissible to market the free gifts of nature, pre-eminently land? Is exploiting labour Islamic? Is dividing humanity into wealth-based classes not against the words and spirit of the Holy Quran and the *Sunnah* of its Holy Prophet (peace be upon him)?

Finally, what then is our religion? The religion of wrong-doers is wrong-doing, not Islam. Such people take shelter behind the shield of the slogan that religion is a personal affair. In the present day world this has become the rule rather than the exception. You may claim to be a Muslim, well and good. But whether you offer your prayers or not, whether you observe fasting during *Ramazan* or not, whether you pay *Zakat* or not, whether you perform *Haj* or not, no one bothers. It is presumed to be your personal affair. None has a right to interfere in the personal affairs of others. This is the prevailing situation the world over. But has this the sanction of Islam? Nothing that the slogan: " Religion is a personal affair" is a creation of the anti-Islamic forces, let us examine this attitude in the light of Islamic teachings.

Scientific Thinking

Contrary to the hostile propaganda Islam of all the religions of the world, is perhaps the most tolerant though not compromising religion. There is no compulsion in matters of faith is its basic proclamation of Human Rights. It not only proclaims the human right of freedom, but extends to all mankind the fullest freedom of thought, of action, of speech and expression. "Say, O people; Truth has reached you from your Lord, so whosoever seeks guidance, does so for his own benefit, and whosoever goes astray is himself responsible for it and I am not a supervisor on you" (10:108). Again, "Say, Truth is from your Lord, So whosoever wishes may believe and whosoever wishes may disbelieve." (18:29). Also, "Act as you please, verily Allah sees what you do" (41:40).

Islam preaches without being in the least coercive. It brings to light the inherent weak-spots in various systems of thought. It lays bare before our eyes the final outcome of the right or wrong ways of life. It distinguishes for us what is good and what is bad. It unfolds the mysteries of the universe and holds before our eyes a unified view of cosmos. It urges us to observe, to think to mediate to infer and to do justice to ourselves not deceiving ourselves by making false decisions knowingly not to be misled by biases, prejudices, self-interests.

Everything has been made as clear as day. Yet there is no compulsion. You choose the right path, well and good. You feel inclined to tread the wrong path? Well that is your own outlook and choice, Islam gives you the basic freedom. But please have the courage to declare your faith or your faithlessness. Be clear in your mind. Do nt mix up things. Do not hesitate. Choose any system and stick to it. Own it boldly. Let there be no hypocrisy, no showing off, no lip-service, no contradiction in your thought and action.

But once you have exercised your option, your choice is automatically curtailed. You are bound to act in a specified way you have no option to claim to have certain faith and to disobey the injunctions of your faith. "Where God and His Apostle have decisively laid down (the course) in any matter, it does not behove a believer man or woman to act on their own sweet will in that matter" (33:36). This is for Muslims, for the Jews and the Christians a similar law has been laid down. "And whosoever does not decide (his affairs) according to what God has laid down, he is an unbeliever" (544: 5.47).

Here your choice is curtailed. Option is still there, but in one direction only. You may offer prayers night and day, but you cannot cut them down to less than five times a day. You may observe fasting for most of the year, but you cannot disregard fasting during the month of *Ramazan.* You may give away all your wealth to the poor and the needy, but you cannot withhold *Zakat,* if it is due from you. You may perform *Haj* as many times in your lifetimes as convenient, but you cannot forego it altogether if you are liable under *Shariah.* The option you see, is now on the positive constructive side only. There is no option on the negative, destructive or regressive side.

Practising your religion is no more your personal affair. It becomes a state affair as well. Now that practice of religion becomes partly a State affair, let us see how an Islamic State should deal with it. According to the Holy Quran, there are four classes of people to deal with by a State internally. First there are True Muslims, the *Mo'minin.* These are the people who have willingly accepted Islam as their religion and practice it faithfully out of a love for it. This class seldom causes any trouble to the State.

True Muslim : Next come the Muslims—ordinary Muslims who profess Islam mainly through inheritance to some extent consciously. Before preoccupied with worldly affairs, they often neglect to observe the injunctions of Islam meticulously, mostly because of their preoccupations, lassitude or heedlessness or even ignorance, with no intention of repudiating such injunctions. How should the State deal with them? Islam's preferred course seems to be educative rather than coercive. Islam believes in inner self-discipline more than an outer imposed discipline through legal measures.

The Holy Prophet (peace be upon him) is said to have expressed his indignation at those who do not fast in *Ramazan* by saying, "Were it not for children and the sick ones, I have an urge to set fire to those houses from which smoke rises during daytime in *Ramadan".* Imam Abu Hanifa has labelled those who give up their prayers intentionally as expelled from Islam. Similar expressions of wrath, indignation and dislike are met with against those who show laxity in the observance of Islamic injunctions. However, if non-observance of Islamic injunctions become massive and widespread and poses a threat to true religious thinking by setting up bad example for the masses, the State may take suitable steps to ensure that religious injunctions are followed faithfully or at least not flouted publicly. No punishment has been prescribed by the Holy Quran for drinking, but Hazrat Omar prescribed 80 lashes for drinking perhaps with a view to nipping the evil in the bud.

Thirdly there are the Hypocrites. These are a dangerous class. They follow no rules except the dictates of their self-interest. They claim to be Muslims not out of any love for Islam, but because of a likelihood of sharing the benefits accruing to the Muslims. Should tables turn on Muslims, they will not hesitate to join anti-Islamic and anti-State forces. For these the course to be followed by the State has been laid down in the Holy Quran. "O Prophet; fight against the infidels and the hypocrites and be stern with them". (66:9). Muslim history provides examples of tackling these people. In the days of Caliph Abu Bakr (God be pleased with him), for example, some tribes made an open attempt to make the practice of religion a personal affair by refusing to pay *Zakat*.

Hazrat Abu Bakr's keen foresight saw in this attitude a danger for the State and decided to wage a war against them disregarding their observance of prayers and other injunctions of Islam. This example provides a hint for an Islamic State to interfere in the so-called personal affairs of the Muslims to ensure that Islam is followed by the Muslims in its entirety and not piecemeal. But State intervention is warranted only when non-observance of Islamic injunctions becomes massive and widespread and poses a threat to Islam or State. Short of that the preferred course is one of educating the masses in religious teachings and setting right patterns of behaviour at the top levels of society from where they shall automatically percolate to the levels of the masses.

Fourthly, there are the minorities. As hinted earlier, they too are expected to follow faithfully their own religious injunctions. Islamic State can provide them help by proper legal administrative and organisational measures.

Holy Quran, the Guide

Islamic polity in modern times will always be guided and inspired by the teachings of the Holy Quran and by the sayings and traditions, acts and deeds of the greatest benefactor mankind has known, the Holy Prophet Muhammad (peace be upon him). Blessed by and chosen of God, his was a divine mission, one of lifting humanity from the depths of moral and spiritual degeneration and guiding its steps towards a new destiny, a new life of peace, equality and brotherhood. All world historians are agreed that there has been no revolution greater than the one the Holy Prophet (peace be upon him) brought about. If there has ever been a total revolution it was this.

Unlike so many incomplete ideologies of later ages, it at once gave its followers moral elevation, economic emancipation and political freedom. It brought peace; it brought equality; it banished racism, it ended exploitation; and it founded a society which by its orderliness, discipline and progress dazzled the entire world. There is for the modern man the beautifully worded but largely ignored U.N. Charter. But Islam gave a much more comprehensive charter of human freedom some 1400 years ago and, what is more, unlike the present day got it fully implemented wherever it held sway. Islam has played a pioneering role in the evolution of human civilisation in the sense that it was the first to rise above the considerations of race, colour, language and ationality—problems that still afflict humanity—and did not just give a call but actually established a world brotherhood, based on its lofty ideals.

Holy Quran

The first source of Islamic law is the Holy Quran which is the revelation of Allah and the Book in which His Message to mankind is contained. It is the word of Allah revealed to Prophet Muhammad (PBUH) through the angel Jibbrail. It is the foundation of Islamic Law and a Book of exalted power. The Quran contains a set of moral and juridical injunctions which are the basis of Islamic law and which concern the life of human beings in every detail.

The early revelations received in Mecca deal largely with questions of beliefs and morals. It was later, after the Prophet's (PBUH) migration to Medina when Muslims lived in an organised society that the principles regarding contracts, succession, crime, constitutional law and international law were revealed. Many of these revelations were very short. The principle contained in a simple sentence could be the foundation on which a whole structure of law could be built, for example:

> *"Give full measure when you measure and weigh with a balancethat is straight."* *(17: 35)*
>
> *"Those who unjustly eat up the property of orphans ea up afire into their own bodies."* *(4: 10)*

The place of the Holy Quran as a source of law is due to its being a source of guidance not only to the spiritual good of the Hereafter but also towards the spiritual, physical and social good attainable in this world. It attends to minimum details for the refinement of the individual or for peaceful and congenial relations among human beings. It calls for lowering the voice when talking and modesty in walking. In order not to accumulate wealth in a few hands and to avoid disputes and quarrels, a fair plan is provided for the distribution of wealth left behind by a deceased person. Human dignity is to be respected, injustice even to an enemy is prohibited and the rights and properties of others are to be protected. Parents are instructed to inculcate in their children Islamic virtues and good manners. Children have to treat their parents with reverence, obedience and tenderness. A ruler is to be aware of his duties and responsibilities. He is to be obeyed for the smooth running of the State and for peace and tranquillity.

The Quranic law is everlasting and perpetual. It does not change with the passage of time. It should be studied with the object of acting in accordance with its teachings and moulding our lives accordingly. The Quran is addressed to the entire humanity, above all barriers and limitations of race, religion and time. It contains directives for the head of the state as well as a common person, for the rich as well as the poor, for peace as well as for war, for spiritual as well as material prosperity. Its laws guide human beings to perfection. It appeals to the reason of man and invites him to exercise his purpose in life.

Compilation of Quran

The task of recording the revelations received by the Holy Prophet (PBUH) was undertaken during his lifetime. He entrusted the duty of recording the Quran in writing to a number of his companions particularly the four Khalifas and Zaid bin Sabit, Khalid bin Walid, Sabit bin Qais etc.

Whenever a chapter or a verse was revealed, it was written down. The Holy Prophet (PBUH) also indicated the proper place of a verse in a relevant chapter. One of his companions had reported: One day I was sitting in the company of the Holy Prophet (PBUH). During my presence, the Holy Prophet (PBUH) raised his eyes to the sky and then lowering them said:

> *"Jibbrail had come to inform me of the proper place of the verse."*

The arrangement of the chapters was done by the prophet himself, under Divine guidance. In this way the Quran was recorded in scriptural form and learnt by heart during the lifetime of the Holy Prophet (PBUH). The Quran was written on thin and flat tablets of stone, wood, branches of palm trees, bones of camels and goats and on pieces of leather. It was not compiled in a book form during the lifetime of the Holy Prophet (PBUH). According to the scribe Zaid bin Sabit:

> *"The Holy Prophet (PBUH) departed from this world and the Quran had not been collected and compiled on anything so far."*

The work of recording the text of the Quran in writing was, therefore, completed during the Prophet's (PBUH) lifetime but not its compilation. After the death of the Holy Prophet (PBUH) his companions felt the necessity to collect and compile the text of the Quran. Hadrat Abu Bakr, the first Khalifa in consultation with Hadrat Umar undertook this noble task, which was completed during his rule and under his supervision. A large number of people who had learnt the Quran by heart had died in the battle of Yamama. Hadrat Umar therefore pointed out to Hadrat Abu Bakr that if more people who had memorised Quran died in future battles, Muslims would be deprived of a great part of the Quran. He suggested that the Quran should be compiled.

Hadrat Abu Bakr however, hesitated and said that he would not do the job left undone by the Holy Prophet (PBUH). Hadrat Umar argued that under the circumstances the compilation of the Quran had become an absolute necessity. According to Hadrat Abu Bakr:

> *"Umar went on persuading me to accept his suggestion till I was convinced that he was right so I accepted his suggestion."*

Hadrat Abu Bakr then directed Zaid bin Sabit to collect the Quranic verses from every part of the Islamic Empire and compile them into book form. Zaid expressed his feelings in these words:

> *"By Allah, if I had been asked to uproot a mountain and put it in another place it would not have been so hard a task for me as the compilation of the Holy Quran. I objected whyAbu Bakr and Umar wanted a thing done, which was left undone by the Holy Prophet (PBUH). ButAbu Bakr insisted that getting the Quran compiled was necessary. He persuaded me every now and then till my opinion also changed and became identical with that ofAbu Bakr and Umar. I started the work and traced out and collected the Quran from every corner and every person who was in possession of any part of it. I collected*

it from palm leaves, white stones, small pieces of wood and people who had committed it to memory."

Zaid bin Sabit was not content just finding a written piece of the Quran. He also verified it from those people who had heard it from the Holy Prophet (PBUH) and committed it to memory. Though Zaid himself was a Hafiz of th Quran, he always tried to find a verse in writing before including it in his manuscript, so that the version of the Quran he recorded was the one heard from and written under the supervision of the Holy Prophet (PBUH). The script prepared by Zaid remained with the first Khalifa and after his death was transferred to the custody of Hadrat Umar. After the death of Hadrat Umar, this script was transferred to Hadrat Hafsa.

Imam Bukhari has narrated on the authority of Anas that after the conquest of Syria and Iraq, the people of these countries recited the Quran in different ways. This disturbed Hadrat Anas who went to Hadrat Uthman and requested him to take immediate action for the removal of these differences, otherwise it might create rifts among the Muslims. Accordingly, Hadrat Uthman acquired the copy of the Quran prepared by Hadrat Zaid bin Sabit, from Hadrat Hafsa and appointed scribes to make copies of it. Copies of the Quran were prepared and sent to the capital city of every province of the Muslim state. Hadrat Uthman also ordered that all existing copies of the Quran with the exception of the authentic ones be burnt. Thus, the Quran that is being read now is the same as in the time of Hadrat Abu Bakr. Nothing has been deleted or added to it. The arrangement of the chapters and verses is the same as ordered by the Holy Prophet (PBUH), in accordance with instructions received from Hadrat Jibbrail.

The fact that the Holy Prophet (PBUH) used to recite the Quran by this very arrangement has been established by traditions reported from him through different people. It also stands established by the opinion of the companions that the present form of compilation and arrangement of the Quran is the same as that ordered by the Holy Prophet (PBUH) under Divine guidance.

It is no new tale of fiction, but a confirmation of previous scriptures, and an explanation of all things, and a guidance and mercy to those who believe.

(Quran: Sura 12: III Joseph)

Three voices God Loves:

The voice of the cock

The voice of one reading the Quran

The voice of one seeking pardon in the early morning.

Tradition of the Prophet Muhammad

Quoted by Al-Ghazzali:

The guide on the road of life is the Holy Quran.

The revelations that came to the Prophet Muhammad were written down by his Companions, put in order under his instructions, and finally compiled by the third Caliph 'Uthman, less than ten years after the Prophet's death. The text is exactly the same now as it was then.

In one book it ranges the whole of life: the worship of God, the nature of man, and the way he should live. It gives both a portrait of creation and instructions by which the individual, the family and the community should conduct their affairs.

The western reader, faced with an English "interpretation", finds himself at a disadvantage. The transition from the original has stripped away its beauty. The unsurpassed music of its language is gone and the Quran is meant to be *heard.* The vivid word pictures it paints raise no such response as they do in the mind of an Arab reader. Moreover, while it is divided into chapter *(sura)* and verse, it does not provide a sequence easy to read or to tabulate. It calls for an effort of imagination and study which is difficult to make. The orthodox view that the Quran cannot be translated becomes quickly understandable to anyone who tries to enter into the truth and the experience it conveys.

Nevertheless, from early times the effort at interpretation has been essential for Muslims whose language is other than Arabic. It is the duty of every Muslim to read, and to the best of his ability to understand, the Holy Book. For example, a manuscript centuries old, in the library of Aligarh Muslim University, shows a Persian commentary painstakingly written under the Arabic text in Mughal times. In Istanbul, the "Book Market" has numbers of editions on sale - some of them having the original Arabic transliterated into the modern Turkish script, with a version in Turkish alongside. Translations are appearing in languages ranging from Swahili to Russian and Chinese, including the European languages, with the aim of bringing the Quran to believer and unbeliever alike.

Language of the Quran

The language of the Quran, with its dignity, its rhythm, its range and the depth of its meaning, is to the Muslim a part of the miracle of its revelation.

In the remote deserts and tribal communities of Arabia, a rich linguistic vehicle developed, ready to carry a prophetic message to millions and to become the means of expression of a great civilisation.

The Arabic language is built on simple three-letter "roots" which each convey a basic idea and which are developed into an intricate pattern of words covering many shades of meaning. There are only about a thousand of these roots. Human personality enters into each original concept: acting, demanding, cooperating, suffering, seeking and being sought, intense or relaxed. The result is a structure that gives infinite flexibility.

Many of these roots are common to all the Semitic languages. Before Muhammad's day they had already served mankind well, as the linguistic basis of the early Mesopotamian civilisation, and as the means of expressing the grandeur of Old Testament prophecy. In Arabia the development of language was far richer and more complex. Pre-Islamic poetry used words that convey heroism, joy and sorrow, deep feelings and high ideals — words that were there prepared and ready to carry the inspiration of the Prophet of Arabia to the world.

The dynamic of Arabic is still active. The same original roots are being used to serve the needs of modern science and technology. And while colloquial speech diverges, the classical Arabic - simplified, but in essence the language of the Quran - is heard and understood all over the Arab World. It is the vehicle of radio, television and cinema, and is read in newspapers that may be bought on the streets of any world capital.

What the Quran means to a practising Muslim is explained here by two scholars, one a political scientist and the other a sociologist.

Muslim Lives by the Quran : "The Muslim lives by the Quran," says Professor Yusuf K. Ibish, Professor of Islamic Political Theory and Institutions in the American University of Beirut. He comes from Damascus, has a Harvard Ph.D., and is a trusted authority on Sufism.

I have not yet come across a western man who understands what the Quran is. It is not a book in the ordinary sense, nor is it comparable to the Bible, either the Old or New Testaments. It is an expression of Divine Will. If you want to compare it with anything in Christianity, you must compare it with Christ Himself. Christ was the expression of the Divine among men, the revelation of the Divine Will. That is what the Quran is. If you want a comparison for the role of Muhammad, the better one in that particular respect would be Mary. Muhammad was the vehicle of the Divine, as she was the vehicle. His illiteracy was comparable with her virginity, symbolic of purity. There are western orientalists who have devoted their life to the study of the Quran, its text, the analysis of its words, discovering that this word is Abyssinian, that word is Greek by origin. The Bible and other literary works have also been subjected to this treatment. But all this is immaterial. The Quran was divinely inspired, then it was compiled, and what we have now is the expression of God's Will among men. That is the important point.

One has to make an effort to understand. Like the bride behind the veil the Holy Quran does not lend itself easily to the seeker. You can read it as you would read any book, and you will gather certain things from it. But to grasp its message truly, you have to penetrate from the external appearance to the inner reality, from the exoteric to the esoteric meaning. It is a two-level process, and of course one needs the guidance of those who know.

The Muslim lives by the Quran. From the first rituals of birth to the principal events of life and death, marriage, inheritance, business contracts: all are based on the Quran. A man can live and die decently if he seeks inspiration from the Quran. Most people from outside look on it as a small book containing limited instruction about conduct and life. This is not so. There are guiding principles, and you can unfold any number of valid interpretations.

Professor Yusuf Ibish, Beirut

Motivator of Thought: Dr Ali Issa Uthman is one of a Palestinian family coming from a village near Jerusalem, one of those divided by the armistice-line of 1948. He was educated in Chicago, where he took a Doctorate in Sociology. He was for some years Adviser to UNRWA on Education, and in particular on social studies. His book, *The Concept of Man in Islam, in the writings of Al-Ghazzali,* was published in Cairo in 1960. He says:

The Quran is organic in ideas - not in structure. Get away from the idea of a book that starts and develops. When you have read it all, then you have everything. You can pick it up and start reading it anywhere.

It appeals to common people as well as scholars. My mother is illiterate and she has an enjoyment of the Quran that I perhaps do not have the music of it. My understanding can get in the way. She and my father always used to pray. They were disturbed if they could not get their ablutions done in time to pray the evening prayer before the sun set, or if ever they slept after the sun had risen. As a child,

I used to open my eyes every morning in our Palestine village and see them at prayer. The younger generation who have been to school know and understand the words, but miss the feeling my parents had.

We cannot see Muslim thought in the right perspective unless we appreciate and understand the Quran as a motivator of thought and an end of knowledge. Without such understanding, the student of Muslim thought must continue to work in the dark. It is in the direct impact of the Quran on the Muslim mind that we may discover those unwritten, but perhaps most important and fundamental, orientations towards truth and human ends. In these orientations lie the Muslims' general sense of history and change, their peculiar sense of time, and their peculiar sense of purpose in seeking knowledge.

Truth in itself and outside man's knowledge does not have a biography of development. Only the individual's understanding of it has. Thus there is permanence in truth and change in understanding. The history of Muslim thought in general cannot be fully understood by an "evolutionary" approach to the history of ideas. The truth which is essential for happiness is supposed by Muslims to be all there and complete - in the Quran and the *Sunna,* (the tradition and practice of the Prophet).

Dr Ali Issa Uthman, Palestine and Beirut

Towards Understanding the Quran

One of the most influential Twentieth Century commentaries on the Quran is that by Sayyid Abul Ala Mawdudi (1903-1979). Written in Urdu, this massive work of scholarship was produced in the midst of the struggles for independence and the early years of Pakistan. It is entitled *Tafhim Al-Quran* (Towards Understanding the Quran). He undertook the task in 1941 and completed it in 1973, six volumes and thirty years later, strenuous years of leadership and controversy. A full English translation is appearing.

The following extracts from Mawdudi's Preface are taken from *Translations from The Quran,* made on the basis of Mawdudi's work by Altaf Gauhar, author and Editor-in-Chief of *South* magazine and *Third World Quarterly,* published from London. "These translations were undertaken at a time when the only book to which I had access was the Quran," he says.

Tafhim al-Quran is not a literal translation of the original text. It is an attempt to present the meanings of the Quran in plain language keeping the historical perspective in view. The Quran speaks to you in the language of life, vividly and melodiously: by comparison the language of translation is a poor echo of the glorious original one is left cold and begins to wonder whether this is indeed the Book which has no equal. The Quran is great literature as it is great instruction. Its words go straight to the heart and it is this quality which, like a crack of lightning, shook the length and breadth of Arabia.

The Quran presents an arrangement which is completely contrary to our expectations. We find beliefs, precepts, orders, criticisms, warnings, promises, arguments, evidence, historical illustrations and references to natural phenomena following one another in rapid succession without any apparent regard for logic ... It talks of the origin of man, the structure of the earth and the heavens ... It recalls the beliefs and criticizes the conduct of different nations, analyses metaphysical problems and refers to many other things. The object however is not to give lessons in metaphysics, philosophy, history or any other science, but to remove misunderstandings about reality ... to acquaint (man) with the result of actions which conflict with its underlying principles.

Whether one is a believer or not, as a rational person one must read this book *by* taking into account the fundamental assumptions made in the book itself, and by the Prophet who presented it to the world.

Holy Quran and the Prophets

No less than eight chapter headings in the Quran recall figures in the Old and New Testaments. Moses and Jesus, founders of Judaism and Christianity, are prophets like Muhammad with the title of *Rasool* (apostle), greater than *nabi* (announcer). In the course of the Quran, David and Solomon receive no less than thirty-three mentions, and Nuh appears some thirty times, as well as heading a chapter. The Sura of Joseph is the longest narrative given. Jonah, "the Man of the Fish", and Sheba, whose famous Queen visits Solomon, are both names of Suras.

Many of the stories are allusive rather than narratory. Evidently the facts were well known to the hearers, and the commentators fill in the details. Some of the information given is found in Jewish sources other than the Old Testament, and in the case of Jesus in the Apocryphal Gospels. The lives of the prophets were current knowledge in Muhammad's day, as they have continued to be throughout the Muslim world.

In one chapter of the Quran (Sura *6:* 83-86 *Cattle)* eighteen prophets are named. The authoritative modern commentary by

Abdullah Yusuf Ali analyses these in four groups. They cover, he says, the great teachers accepted among the three religions based on Moses, Jesus and Muhammad. First come Ibrahim, Ishaq and Jacob. Then follow those who "led active lives and are called 'doers of good'." These are Nuh, David and Solomon, Job and Joseph, Moses and Aaron. In contrast, the next group were not men of action but preachers of truth who led solitary lives. They include Zachariah and his son John (the Baptist), Jesus and Elias (Elijah), and their designation is "the righteous". Finally come four who were concerned in the clash of nations, and who through conflict and personal misfortune kept to the path of God: Ismail, Elisha, Jonah and Lot.

The chapter headed *The Prophets* (Sura 21) has a similar passage. Elsewhere over and over again the historic sequence is repeated - a warning, followed by either repentance or destruction, as God sends His messengers to one nation after another. The view of history in the Muslim mind is a prophetic one.

According to the Quran, the succession of prophets has been completed — sealed — by the mission of Muhammad. The truth necessary for man to live by has been revealed. There is no need for more. But if men do not presume to claim the stature of the prophets, there is still plenty of scope for humbly following their example. Muhammad's own constant emphasis that he was only a man like other men lays stress on the responsibility carried by all believers.

Here is one of many passages which show the heritage of prophetic inspiration common to Muslim, Jew and Christian.

We inspire thee [Muhammad] as We inspired Nuh and the prophets after him, as We inspired Ibrahim and Ismail and Ishaq and Jacob and the tribes, and Jesus and Job and Jonah and Aaron and Solomon, and as We imparted unto David the Psalms; And messengers We have mentioned unto thee before, and messengers We have not mentioned unto thee; and Allah spake direct unto Moses;

> *Messengers of good cheer and of warning, in order that mankind might have no argument against Allah after the messengers. Allah was ever Mighty, Wise.*
>
> *(Quran: Sura 4: 163-165)*

Holy Tradition (Sunnah)

The Prophet (PBUH) as the founder of Islam and the messenger of Allah's revelation to mankind is the best interpreter of the Book of Allah and his Hadith and the Sunnah; his sayings and actions are, after the Quran, the most important source of Islamic law.

The word *Sunnah* means literally a manner of acting, a rule of conduct, a mode of life. Applied to the life of the Prophet (PBUH), this meant, therefore, a rule deduced from the sayings or conduct of the Prophet. Such sayings and conduct could take the form of an utterance of the Prophet (PBUH) an action or practice of the Prophet (PBUH), or the approval by the Prophet (PBUH) of the action or practice of someone else.

The Hly Quran being the word of Allah, treats major issues and often deals with subjects in brief terms, leaving the details to beexplained by the Holy Prophe (PBUH) of Allah. It says:

> *"—-and We have sent down unto thee the Message: that thou mayest explain clearly to men what is sent for them." (16:44)*

In the Quran we are commanded to pray and pay *Zakat,* but there isno explanation of the frequency of prayers or the number of Rakat in each prayer. Neither is there an explanation given as to the amount on which the duty of *Zakat* applies or the percentage which has to be paid. All these details were learnt either from the Prophet's deeds or words or from both. The Holy Quran commands that we should be good to our neighbour; a number o *Ahadith* further stress this duty. The same applies to many other situations; hence the vital connection between the Quran and the practice and sayings of the Prophet (PBUH).

Many verses of the Holy Qurandeal with questions of law but not all the injunctions of the Shariah are clearly stated in it. There are many statements which needed furher explanations before they could become guides for human actions. This explanation and clarification was provided by the Holy Prophet (PBUH) who himself participated in the formation of the Shariah.

When the Islamic commonwealth was founded in Medina in 622 A.D., the Prophet was not only the spiritual leader but also the supreme judge of the Islamic community. Cases would be referred by his followers to the Prophet (PBUH) for his judgement. The underlying principle applied was the word of Allah from the Quran; but if the Quran was silent, or needed interpretation, the Prophet (PBUH), as the messenger of Allah would be the authority for reaching a decision.

The Holy Quran itself commands that the Prophet's (PBUH) teachings should be obeyed. It says:

> *"So take what the Messenger assigns to you, and deny yourselves that which he withholds from you." (59:7)*

It also says:

"He who obeys the Messenger obeys Allah." *(4: 80)*

The Quran frequently commands:

"O ye who believe ! obey Allah and obey the Messenger." *(4: 59)*

"Obey Allah and obey His Messenger. " *(3: 32, 5: 92, 64: 12)*

Thus, after the Quran, the Prophet's (PBUH) *Sunnah* and *Hadith* are the most precious sources of guidance which Islamic society possesses and along with the Quran, they are the fountainhead of all Islamic laws and thought. The Prophet (PBUH) was a *Nabi* and a *Rasool* who brought the cycle of Prophecy to an end. So, after hi there will be no new *Shariah* or Divine Law brought into the world until the end of time.

Compilation of Hadith : Tradtion in Arabic means Sunnah or Hadith. The difference between the two is that while Sunnah indicates the doings of the Holy Prophet (PBUH, Ahadith indicates his sayings.

The word *Hadith* is derived from 'Tahdis' which means to inform. There is another finding by the researchers of the word *Hadith.* Acording to them, this word is derived from a root which means to be new ormodern, the opposite of which is ancient. Thus by ancient is meant the Holy Quran and by new or modern is meant the *Hadith* of the Holy Prophet (PBUH). It is reported by Abdullah bin Masud that the Holy Prophet (PBUH) had said:

"Only two things carry importance, one is speech and the other is the method of action. So the words of Allah are the best of speech and the best method is the deeds of the Holy Prophet (PBUH)."

From the beginning of the birth of Islam, Muslims were interested in what the Holy Prophet (PBUH) said and did. After his death, when Islam had spread widely, new converts wanted to hear about him from his Companions and close associates. These people were the best authority for a knowledge of *Hadith* as they had listened to the Prophet (PBUH) and witnessed his actions. Thousands of Companions adhered to the Prophet's commandment:

"Preach what you hear me say. Also let those who see and hear me, take upon themselves to communicate my words to others and preach to their children, relatives and friends."

The Companions therefore considered it their duty to preach the Traditions of the Prophet (PBUH) to those who had not seen and listened to him. After their death, Muslims had to rely on the communications of the successors people of the first generation after Prophet Muhammad (PBUH) who had received their information from the Companions, and in the following generations, with the accounts of the "successors of the successors", that is, people of the second generation who had been associated with the successors and so on.

In those days, to recite and to memorize the Traditions was considered to be a great privilege. They were preserved in writing as well. In due course of time, a great amount of *Hadith* literature was collected.

Some writers headed by William Muir and Goldzhier put forth the argument that the collection and compilation *of Ahadith* was started some ninety years after the death of the Holy Prophet (PBUH). However, there is ample testimony to the fact that such records existed much earlier. During the time of the Holy Prophet (PBUH) and his Companions, more than ten thousand *Ahadith* were collected out of which 5,374 were attributed to Abu Hurrayrah. It has been verified from different sources that Abu Hurrayrah used to write down what he heard from the Holy Prophet (PBUH). Another Companion, Hadrat Abdullah bin Umar, on the order of the Holy Prophet (PBUH) used to write down every word of the Prophet's (PBUH) speech. This compilation was known as Sadiqa. These Companions persuaded their children and relatives to follow their instance. For example, Hadrat Anas used to stress upon his children:

> *"O my children, write down the text of Hadith."*

Hadrat Ali used to keep a booklet with him which contained many traditions mainly concerning the orders and instructions issued from time to time by the Holy Prophet (PBUH).

Imam Zohri, who was born in a Quraish family had preserved the Prophet's (PBUH) utterances in such detail that historians have remarked :

> *"Zohri would go to any soul in Medina and record from him or her about the Prophet's life events."*

Soon after the death of the Prophet (PBUH), the need for some authoritative guidance in Quranic interpretation was felt. The need was felt all the more because of the political and religious divisions. Also because of the expansion of Islam from a small community in

Central Arabia to a mighty empire due to which Muslim rulers faced all kinds of political, economic, legal and social problems quite unknown during the days of the Prophet (PBUH). The problem was to apply the Prophet's (PBUH) teachings and way of life to conditions which were never thought of before. It was solved by recording and placing in the appropriate context a large number of sayings and practices of the Holy Prophet (PBUH).

Numerous collections of *Hadith* were prepared by many scholars from various angles, and different methods were adopted in the arrangement of the material. Two models were mainly adopted. In the first category, *Hadith* traced to each Companion was put together under his name, no matter what their theme might be. Such a collection is called Musnad. Therefore, the titles of the chapters are Musnad of Abu Bakr, Musnad of Abu Hurrayrah, Musnad of Aishah, etc.

The most famous compilation in this category is Musnad of Imam Ahmad bin Hanbal, founder of the fourth school of law. It contains 40,000 Ahadith of which 10,000 have occurred more than once.

The second category of *Ahadith* are grouped into chapters and sub-chapters according to their theme. For instance we find chapters on *purity, prayers, fasting, Zakat, pilgrimage, marriage,* so on. The best known work of this type is Al-Muwatta which contains 1,720 *Ahadith* compiled by Imam Malik bin Anas, founder of the Maliki school of law. Another compilation of this category is Al-Musannaf of Imam Abd Al-Razzaq Al-Sanani (126-211 A.H.) which has been published in eleven volumes. It contains 11,033 *Ahadith.*

Hadith compilers introduced each *Hadith* with its own Isnad which means the series of authorities who may be called narrators or transmitters or Muhaddis. These authorities can be as few as two. Imam Malik, for example, in some *Ahadith* related from his teacher Nafi, who related from his teacher Abdullah bin Umar, a distinguished Companion of the Holy Prophet (PBUH). Yet the number could be three, four, five and even six, depending on how far the compiler's time was from the time of the Prophet.

The early authorities of *Hadith* who scrutinized each *Hadith,* both the text and the *isnad,* included in their compilations only those which they believed to be genuine, and rejected those which they suspected as fabricated. Yet, they graded each Hadith in terms of the degree of reliability. A *Hadith* could be authentic, Sahih, or less than authentic, although it was not false or a fabrication but a weak or

Zaeef Hadith which resulted from some weakness in the text or in the *Isnad.* The authorities on *Hadith* said that the text should have no conflict with the Quran or with a more reliable *Hadith.* The *Isnad* must be full and unbroken and each narrator mentioned in it must be known for his knowledge, piety and memory. Upto the beginning of the third century of Islam, compilations of *Hadith* did not discriminate between authentic *Hadith* and others lesser than authentic so the *Ahadith* were mixed up.

Imam Muhammad ibn Ismail-al-Bukhari (194-256 A.H.), was the first to conceive the idea of compiling the authentic *Ahadith* and therefore, he called his compilations as Sahih, "the authentic compilations". It took him sixteen years to compile this work which contains 7,397 *Ahadith* including four thousand repeated ones. He selected these *Ahadith* from amongst 600,000 *Ahadith* which he gathered in long and repeated journeys around the capitals of the world of Islam. On account of the strict conditions that he laid down for accepting a *Hadith* as *Sahih,* his work was acknowledged as one of the most authentic books on *Hadith* literature.

The example of Imam Bukhari was also followed by a number of other leading scholars. Eminent among them was Imam Muslim ibn Hajjaj (202-261 A.H.), whose compilation contains 12,000 *Ahadith* including 4,000 repetitions. The collections by *Bukhari* and *Muslim* are held in high esteem and are known as the two Sahihs i.e., the two collections recognized as authentic. Only those traditions which are recognized as absolutely correct are included in these works.

Among some others authors who followed them were Abu Daud (205-275 A.H.), author of *Al-Sunan; Al-Tirmidhi* (210-279 A.H.), author of *Al-Jami; Al-Nasai* (215-303 A.H.), author of *Kitab al-Sunnah;* and *Ibn Majah,* author of Kitab al-Sunnah. These four works along with those of *Bukhari* and *Muslim* became widely recognized in the Muslim world as the six leading Books *Al-Kutub al-Sitta* or *the six Sahihs,* i.e., *the sound, correct and reliable collections.*

At a later period, new collections were compiled by many scholars. In these works, contents were taken from the 'Six Books' and arranged in different ways until about the end of the fourth century of the age of Islam it was felt that all *Ahadith* circulating orally had been reduced to writing. Therefore, *Hadith* literature became exceedingly rich, and we as Muslims are very fortunate to have for our benefit such a great intellectual and religious wealth from which guidance can be derived.

Process of Reasoning (Ijtihad)

The Holy Quran is the fundamental source of the Shariah. It is the last and final revelation therefore its teachings shall always remains the source of Shariah for all times.

The Sunnah of the Holy Prophet (PBUH) comes next which sometimes elaborates and explains what has been mentioned in the Holy Quran and sometimes adds something to its commandments. In the latter case, it becomes the basis for legislation in Islam. The Quran and the Sunnah arc thus the eternal sources of law for Muslims and the basic principles of legislation in Islam.

However when sometimes the Quran and the Sunnah are silent about a matter, then it is a clear indication by the Supreme Law giver that the matter should be decided by the people concerned, in accordance with the needs of time and place. In all such matters, there is no alternative for a Muslim but to resort to Ijtihad which is the process of reasoning based on the Quran and the Sunnah. The Muslims are free to strive and endeavour to find solutions by using their own independent judgement Ijtihad in the light of the Quran and the Sunnah.

The main purpose of Ijtihad is to find ways and means to preserve and safeguard the principles of Islam in an ever changing and developing human society and to find solutions to new problems which have not been directly or clearly discussed or decided by the Quran and the Sunnah. The literal meaning of the word 'Ijtihad' is effort and it comes from a Hadith of the Prophet (PBUH) in which the Holy Prophet (PBUH) asked Muaz whom he had appointed governor of Yemen, by what criteria would he govern the regions assigned to him. 'According to the book of Allah', he answered. "And if you find nothing therein", the Prophet (PBUH) asked. Muaz answered, "According to the Sunnah of the Prophet (PBUH)." "And if you find nothing therein?" the Prophet (PBUH) asked again. "Then I will exert myself to form my own judgement", Muaz answered. And this the Prophet (PBUH) approved. Umar bin Aas was told by the Holy Prophet (PBUH) that if by exercising Ijtihad, he took a correct decision, he would get the reward of ten good deeds and if he took a wrong decision, he would get the reward of one good deed.

The most outstanding contributions in the field of Ijtihad have been made by Hadrat Umar. Less than twelve years after the Holy Prophet's (PBUH) death, he found it necessary to exercise Ijtihad. His first Ijtihad was with regard to the interpretation of the word 'thief in the Quranic verse:

"As to the thief, male or female, cut off his or her hands."
(5:38)

He excluded from the definition of thief all those who stole because of hunger or during famine.

Hadrat Umar also exercised Ijtihad in awarding punishments for theft. For example, the hands of a slave who had stolen a mirror from his master's wife were not cut on the ground that he himself, being the property of the master, could not be considered to have stolen. Similarly, he acquitted a man who had stolen from Bait-ul-Mal. Once, during Ramadan, he broke his fast on a cloudy day in the mistaken belief that dusk had fallen. But soon the sun started shining. Hadrat Umar said:

"It does not matter. We pondered over the matter according to our lights."

A well-known incident is his interpretation of verse 60 of Surah Taubah regarding charity. It says:

"Alms are for those whose hearts have been (recently) reconciled (to the truth)." *(9:60)*

Among others, who received a share from both Zakat and war booty were the Quraish chiefs like Abu Sufyan and Safwan bin Umayyah. They used to get one hundred camels each. Hadrat Abu Bakr gave them additional authority for land grants. But Hadrat Abu Bakr passed away before the grants could be awarded.

When the chiefs approached Hadrat Umar for implementation of the grants he not only tore those orders, but also stopped giving them the hundred camels which they used to get. His reason was that such a grant was a political necessity, when Islam was weak. But since Islam had become powerful during the time of Hadrat Umar, the old practice was no longer justified.

In the early centuries of Islam, there were jurists who developed and advocated Ijtihad. But in the later centuries, with the influence of different schools of law that had evolved and developed, this faculty of Ijtihad gave way to Taqlid that is, an acceptance of what the great scholars of fiqh have held in the past.

There are many problems facing Muslim society today in political, economic and social spheres - that can only be solved by Ijtihad, specially, in those matters where no distinct and direct command is found either in the Quran or the Sunnah. Some of these problems are, the current commercial transactions including insurance, the right of private ownership, nationalisation, tax system, the method of election to assemblies and election of the Head of the State, and the problems concerning international law particularly on the points of nationality and domicile, in different Muslim countries in the context of the concept of Dar-ul-Harb.

Ijtihad is concerned with matters, relating to human actions. It has no concern with one's faith, beliefs or religious convictions. The reason for this distinction is that in worldly matters we may ourselves discover the right way by using our intelligence. But intelligence alone cannot guide us in the field of religion.

Furthermore, Ijtihad should not be against any command or principle of the Holy Quran. People qualified for Ijtihad must not only possess vast religious knowledge, but must also be men of Taqwa that is, piety who can rise above their own personal ambitions and weaknesses. Although Islam does not believe in priesthood yet it does not give the right to everyone to undertake the difficult task of ijtihad. This right is limited to those only who fulfil all the basic and essential conditions of Ijtihad, in both religious knowledge and piety.

Ijtihad is meant to make the legal system of Islam dynamic and effective it should encourage a steady growth and development in Islam according to the needs and social circumstances of different times and places which will make Islam forceful and vigorous and prevent stagnation and decay.

It is only through the use of Ijtihad that we will be able to meet the challenges of modern civilization. It will contribute immensely to the intellectual revival of Islam in modern times and give a new force and vitality to Muslim society. It will also help to bring the Muslims all over the world close to one another.

Analogy (Qiyas)

The fourth source of Islamic law is Qiyas which, literally, means "judging or comparing with a thing." Qiyas means essentially to use human reasoning to compare an existing situation with one for which legislation already exists.

If the Quran has banned wine, it means that by reasoning, it has also banned all forms of alcoholic drinks, whose effect is like wine or something that causes intoxication.

The death of Prophet Muhammad (PBUH) deprived the Muslim community of the means of obtaining revelation and at the same time of his guidance in political and religious matters. The expansion of the Muslim Empire and the spread of Islam outside Arabia raised questions previously unknown, the answers to which could not be found in the Quran or the *Sunnah.*

Thus, they found themselves forced to take decisions or to regulate their conduct from their own opinion and reasoning.

Such resort to reasoning is often traced back to the conversation between the Prophet (PBUH) and Muaz ibn Jabal, the Governor of Yemen. When the Prophet (PBUH) appointed Muaz ibn Jabal as Governor and Judge in Yemen, the Prophet (PBUH) asked him:

"According to what will you judge?"

"According to the book of Allah."

"And if you find nothing therein ? "

"According to the Sunnah of the Prophet (PBUH)."

"And if you find nothing therein?"

"Then I will exert myself to form my own judgement." ibn Jabal replied.

According to another *Hadith,* the Prophet (PBUH) is reported to have told Abu Musa Ashari:

"Judge upon the Book of Allah. If you do not find in it what you need, upon the Sunnah of the Prophet (PBUH) and if you do not find in that also, then use your personal opinion."

Imam Abu Hanifa, one of the four great Imams was the first to give prominence to the doctrine of *Qiyas,* although as a principle of law, it was in practice even before him.

Consensus of Opinion (Ijma)

Ijma is the third source of Islamic law. Literally, Ijma means agreeing upon or uniting in opinion. It means the consensus of the Islamic community on some point of law. It can operate only where the Quran and the *Hadith* have not clarified a cerain aspect of the law. It is a gradual process through which the community over a period of time comes to a consensus over a question of law. The view of Muslims over the centuries has been that giving opinion on problems of law should be the function of Ulama who alone are well-versed in the science of law which is ver complex and requires deep study before we can claim to be an authority over them.

The laws of the Quran and the *Sunnah* were, no doubt, supreme but there was no bar to making laws according to the needs of the people as long as they did not go against the spirit of the revealed law and the *Sunnah.* These laws were, however, to be made in consultation. It is reported from the Holy Prophet (PBUH):

> *"If anything comes to you for decision, decide according to the Book of Allah. If anything comes to you which is not in the Book of Allah, then look to the Sunnah of the Prophet (PBUH). If anything comes to you which is not in the Sunnah of the Prophet (PBUH) then look to what people unanimously agree upon."*

In reply to Hadrat Ali as to how to proceed in cases where there was no definite direction in the Holy Quran or the *Sunnah,* the Prophet (PBUH) is reported to have said:

> *"Gather together the righteous from among my community and decide the matter by their counsel and do not decide it by any man's opinion."(Abu Daud).*

And again:

> *"My nation will not agree unanimously in error."*

Counsel was freely resorted to by the Prophet (PBUH) himself in all important matters. Medina was attacked thrice by the Quraish, and every time the Prophet (PBUH) held consultations with his followers about the best way to repel the enemy. On one of these occasions, he acted upon the opinion of the mjority and marched out of Medina to meet the enemy, althoughhis own opinion was that the Muslim army should not leave the town.

The Holy Prophet (PBUH) has said:

> *"Whatever the Muslims hold to be good is good before Allah. It is incumbent upon you to follow the most numerous body. Whoever separates himself from the main body will go to Hell. If you yourselves do not know, then question those who do."*

These traditions of the Holy Prophet (PBUH) are a sanction of *Ijma.*

Ijma is of three types:

1. *Ijma* or consensus of the Companions of the Holy Prophet (PBUH) which is also universally accepted and binding and is therefore, unchangeable.
2. *Ijma* of the jurists.
3. *Ijma of* the people, i.e., general body of the Muslim community.

As regards the last two, the jurists, particularly Imam Abu Hanifa, are of the view that they cannot be confined or limited to any particular age or country, and therefore, *Ijma* of one age can be modified by *Ijma* of the same or subsequent age.

Fundamental Elements

Islamic Faiths

The fundamental beliefs, which serve as the foundation of a religion, are called its doctrines or articles of faith. All th prophets of Allah, in their attempts to reform mankind, concentrated mainly on transferring their beliefs to their followers. The Holy Prophet (PBUH), too, began propagating his message by focusing attention on these beliefs.

These beliefs are stated in Iman-e-Mufassal which says:

> *"I believe in Allah, in His angels, in His books, in His messengers, in the Last Day and in the fact that everything, good or bad, is decided by Allah, the Almighty, and in life after Death."*

The Holy Quran says:

> *"O you who believe! Believe in Allah and His messenger and the scripture which He hath sent to His messenger and the scripture which He sent to those before (him). Any who denieth Allah, His angels, His books, His messengers and the Day of Judgement hath gone far, far astray. "* *(4:136)*

And also:

> *"... It is righteousness to believe in Allah and the Last Day and the angels and the book and the messengers." (2:177)*

The fundamental eliefs or articles of faith are:

1. Unity or Oneness of Allah
2. Angels
3. Revealed books
4. Prophets
5. Life after death.

Oneness of God (Tauheed)

Belief in the Unity and Oneness of Allah - Tauhid is the first and main principle of the Islamic faith. It means that Allah is te Supreme

Being, the Creator, Sustainer and Master of the universe, the highest authority and hence exclusively worthy of worship. he first Surah of the Holy Quran begins with the words:

> *"Praise be to Allah, the Cherisher and Susainer of the worlds."* *(1:2)*

Tauhid is the belief in Allah with all His powers. Allah is All-knowing, All-wise, and All-powerful. He is and will alays be. He has no beginning and no end.

He is the First and the Last. He has no parents or son. He has no partners of any sort in His attributes, power, wor and dominion. The Quran says:

> *" Say, praise be to Allah, Who begets no son and has no partner in (His) dominion ..."* *(17:11)*

And also:

> *"No son has He bgotten, nor has He a partner in His dominion..."* *(25:2)*

The Quran has laid the greatest emphasis on Allah's absolute Unity and Oneess, The concept has been summed up in Surah Ikhlas of the Holy Quran, which says:

> *Say He is Allah, the One and Only Allah, the Eternal, the Absolute. He begetteth not, nor is He begotten. And there is none like unto Him."* *(112:1-4)*

At another place, we are told:

> *"Allah! There is no god but H the Living, the Self-subsisting, Eternal."* *(2:255)*

And again:

> *"There is nothing hatever like unto Him and H is the One that hears and sees (all things)."* *(42:11)*

Islam emphatically proclaims that Allah, the Creator is not bound by any of the limitations of human beings or of anything else He has created. He has no body, nor form, no physical attributes, nor characteristics. He is he Originator and Fashioner of the universe with its vast and perfect system, the One Who sustains it and keeps it functioning according to His laws and plans.

Allah is beyond anything which the mind or senses of man can grasp or comprehend or imagine. He is above having any similarity to any of His creations for He alone is te Creator and everythingelse is created by Him. He alone is Divine and no other human being or any other creature can share His Divinity or His unique attributes. Allah isalways concerned and involved with every single part of His creation. All His creations exist and fulfil their functions by His command and will. For His concern is not only in creating, but also in sustaining and providing for Hs creatures, in guiding, regulating and maintaining them.

The vast universe with its flawless system clearly indicates that there is one Creator and one Controller. The sun, the moon, the galaxy and the whole universe obey the laws of the Supreme Authority. There is complete harmony and everything is set perfectly in the system. There is no flawand no need for improvement in it. Had there been more than one Creator and Controller, there would have been chaos and confusion as the Quran says:

> *"If there were in the heavens and the earth other gods besides Allah, there would have been confusion in both."*
> *(21:22)*

But there is no conflict and disorder in the universe. This pefect order and combination is the proof of the presence of one powerful Creator and Regulator. Allah has created everything in the earth and heavens for the service of mankind. When a person surrenders himself to Allah's commands, he gains superiority over all other creatures in the universe.

Tauhid shapes and regulates the entire course of a Muslim's life. A believer in Tauhid is sure that Allah knows and sees everything, so he is restrained from committing a sin either secretly or in the darkness of the night because of his firm conviction that Allah sees everything all the time.

A person who truly and whole heartedly believes that Allah alone is the Master of the universe, the sole Authority and Law-giver and he himself is a humble servant before Him, will not obey or give his dvotion or allegiance to other deities besides Allah. He would reject them all and submit himself to Allah alone and strive with all his might and energies against serving any deities other than Allah.

Significance ofAngels

Allah conveyed His revelation to prophets including Hadrat Muhammad (PBUH) through an angel, Hadrat Jibbrail. In the Holy Quran, angels are spoken of as 'messengers' which denotes their spiritual function of Divine messengers. The Quran says:

> *"He doth send down His angels with inspiration f His command to such of His servants as He pleaseth ...."*
>
> *(16:2)*

Because of this important role of angels as bringers of Divine revelation to prophets, the elief in them is so important as to form a fundamental article of faith in Islam.

Angels ct as Allah's agents and serve Him in many ways. They are created of light and unlike jinn and men have not been endowed with a free will. They are absolutely obedient to Allah's commands and are enaged in worship and service to Him. They are sent to potect men, to administer Allah's punishments, to carry His messages and to perform various othr functions.

Angels are heaveny beings not visible to ordinary mortals and thus, belong to the category of the unseen unless they appear in human form. They were sent by Allah to bring messages to Hadrat Zakriya and to Hadrat Maryam before whom the angels appeared in human form. Angels also appeared in human form before Hadrat Ibrahim to give him the glad tidings of the birth of a son. Hadrat Lut was also warned by angels in human form of the impending doom of his wicked people and told to leave the town that was going to be destroyed.

Angels are one of Allah's creation. They have been given the necessary qualities and powers to carry out their duties They are not His daughters nor are they objects of worship. They have no knowledge except what Allah has taught them, they obey Allah and act on His commands. They prostrated befoe Adam when Allah commanded them to do so. Angels glorify and praise Allah. They never get tired. They do not need sleep, nor do they require the things needed by human beings.

Angels have various functions and duties. They act as Allah's messengrs but do not descend except by Allah's command. They strengthen the hearts of the righteous believers and are their protectors. At the Battle of Badr, they helped and strengthened the hearts of the believers and put terror into the hearts of the unbelievers. They implore forgiveness for the believers but they can offer no intercession for them. They send blessings on the Holy Prophet (PBUH) and the believers.

Angels are the guardians of Hell-fire. They will welcome in Heaven all those who obey Allah's commands and will throw the wrong doers into Hell.

Angels record man's wors and deeds. Each human is attendd by two angels who record all his deeds upto the moment of his dath. This record will be presented to him on the Day of Jdgement. They are called the 'respected recorders.' The Quran says:

> *"But verily, over you (are appointed angels) to protect you kind and honourable, writing down (your deeds)." (82:10-11)*

There are many angels, the prominent among them are:

(1) Hadrat Jibbrail who brought revelations from Allah to the prophets including Hadrat Muhammad (PBUH).

(2) Hadrat Israil, also called the angel of death is responsible for taking our souls upon death.

(3) Hadrat Israfil who will blow the trumpet at the time of the end of the world, that is, on the Day of Judgement.

Human beings are the servants of Allah and His agents on earth who need guidance to carry out their various duties and responsibilities. This guidance is contained in the books of revelation sent to mankind through prophets and messengers. Belief in the reality of Allah's guidance to mankind in the form of revealed books is another basic article of faith in Islam.

Allah, who has created for man all things that are on the earth and has made subservient to him all that is in the heavens and on the earth, has provided everything for man's physical needs, has also provided him with spiritual guidance.

Revelation is the name given to the mean of communication employed by Allah for conveying His command and messages to prophets and apostles. Revelation is not due to the prophet's own thoughts, intelligence or knowledge, it is not acquired through study or learning nor is it earned through labour but it is a special gift from Allah.

About th various methods employed by Allah for communicating His commandments to His apostles, the Quran says:

> *"It is not fitting for a man that Allah should speak to him except by inspiration, or from behind a veil or by the sending of a messenger to reveal with Allah's permission what Allah wills: ...." (42:51)*

The guidance sent by Alah from time to time to His messengers was basically the same. The principles of religion relating the unity of Allah, His attributes, prayer, belief in prophethood, the Day of

Judgement and the concept of reward and punishment for one's deeds in the life Hereafter are common to all the revealed books. Howeer, as the needs of the people differed in different periods, the details of the Shariat laws given in these books also varied.

Each of the previous apostles and prophets was sent to some particular nation, people or tribe and therefore, the revelation sent o each was intended for the guidance of his eople. It was not intended to be universal because humanity had not yet reached the stage of readiness for suh a comprehensive and final guidance from Allah. This is clear from what the Quran states concerning the messages given to various prophets.

Moeover, by the time of the advent of the Holy Prohet (PBUH), the books revealed upto that time had either been totally lost, or their original message distorted. Th time had, therefore, come for Allah to send a final and complete revelation in the form of the Holy Quran.

The Holy Quran is the only revealed scripture, which has been preserved to the present time in its exact, original form and language. Although parts of the earlier revelations still survive, they are so intermixed with additions and alterations that it is very difficult to determine what part of them actually forms the original message sent by Allah.

The Holy Quran does not mention all the prophets nor all the revealed books. It only mentions revelations sent to Hadrat Nuh, Hadrat Ibrahim, Hadrat Ismail, Hadrat Ishaq, Hadrat Daud, HadratMusa, Hadrat Isa and the Holy Prophet Muhammad (PBUH).

The revealed books mentioned by name in the Holy Quran are:

(1) Sahuf-e-Ibrahim

(2) Zabur, granted to Hadrat Daud.

(3) Taurat, revealed to Hadrat Musa. About it, the Quran says:

"And before this was the book of Moses as a guide and a mercy. (46:12)

Thus, according to the Holy Quran, the book that Allah revealed to Hadrat Musa contained guidance, Allah's commands and warnings for the Bani Israel who failed to act according to its teachings. They distorted and perverted Allah's word. No copy of the original Taurat is now available.

(4) Injeel, granted to Hadrat Isa. About this book, the Quran says:

"And in their footsteps we sent Jesus the son of Mary cnfirming the law that had come before him: we sent

him the gospel therein was guidance and light, and confirmation of the law that had come before him: a guidance and an adomonition to those who fear Allah.“
(5:46)

The Injeel confirmed the Taurat and contained guidance and light for the Bani Israel. According to the Holy Quran, Allah took a covenant from those who call themselves Christians, but they forgot the message that was sent to them and failed to act according to its teachings.

(5) The Holy Quran is the last and the most comprehensive book rvealed by Allah to His last messenger, Hadrat Muhammad (PBUH), through Hadrat Jibbrail. It was not sent down by Allah all at once. Its revelation to the Holy Prophet (PBUH) was spread over a period of twenty-three years. The Holy Quran confirms the previous revelations, and points out and corrects some of the errors that had crept into the earlier revealed books. Thus, the Holy Quran perfects and completes Divine Revelation.

The Quran speaks of the attributes of Allah and His power, of man's relationship and responsibility to Him, of the certainty of thecoming of the Last Day and the life hereafter. It contains instructions about the principle of Islam and the method of worship and uides mankind to the right path.

It lays down moral and ethical principles to govern all aspects of human life, both individual and collective. It narrates the stories of some of the earlier prophets and nations as an example and encou-agement to the Prophet and his community and as a warning to those who deny Allah. Its main theme, rpeated again and again is the reality of Allah's Supreme Power and man's position as His slave and vicegerent who is accountable to Him in everything. About the Holy Quran Allah says:

"This is the Book; in it is guidance sure, without doubt, to those who fear Allah; who believe in the Unseen, are steadfast in prayer and spend out of what we have provied for them; and who believe in the revelation sent to thee and sent before thy time, and (in their hearts) have the assurance of the Hereafter; They are on (true guidance) from their Lord, and it is these who will prosper.“ (2:2-5)

Quran is undoubtedly the only book in the world that remains in the same form today as it was fourteen hundred years ago. This is because Allah Himself promised to safeguard it from corruption and change. Allah says:

" We have, without doubt, sent down the message and
We will assuredly guard it (from corrption)" *(15:9)*

The Holy Quran is a book for reading, reciting and learning in fact, prayers cannot be complete without the recitation of some parts of the Quran.

The Holy Prophet (PBUH) laid great mphasis on memorizing the Holy Quran. There is authentic proof to show that as soon as te Holy Prophet (PBUH) received a revelation, he would ask his scribes to write it down. Thc Quran was committed to memory as well as written down during the lifetime of the Holy Prophet (PBUH). The Quran was complete with the same arrangement of chapters and verses that we have now, at the time of the death of the Holy Prophet (PBUH).

The Quran is not only a blessed book, but also a complete code of life. We must, therefore, study it with the object of acting n all matters according to its teachings. We must mould our lives acording to the guidance contained in the Holy Quran and abstain from whatever is against its teachings.

The success of human beings on this earth and in the life after death depends on obedience to the Quranic teachings and principles which are as valid and binding today as at the time when they were revealed; for although the style and mode of human life have changed, the ultimate realities, the nature of good and evil and man's own nature are unalterable and permanent and are not affected by the passing of time or changes in the world.

Messengers of God

Since the beginning of creation, Allah has sent guidance for mankind through His selected people known as prophets or messengers. Belief in prophets forms the fourth ingredient of faith.

The Islamic concept of the role and function of prophethood is different from that of the other religions.

In Islam, the word prophet - Nabi - denotes one who is very near to Allah through the total surrender of his entire being to Him and who receives revelation from Him which serve as a source of guidance for men. If the revelation is in the form of a scripture, the prophet is, in addition, a messenger -Rasool-as well.

Islam holds that a prophet possesses the following characteristics: he is absolutely truthful, he is free of all kinds of sins, he delivers the messages from Allah without any omission or concealment and he has the highest order of intelligence and mental ability.

According to the Quran, all the apostles and prophets sent by Allah were en, had wives and children and were mortal. All of them taught in the language of the people to whom they were sent. At the same time, the Quran tells us that they were good and truthful, Allah favoured them above all others, chose them and guided them and conferred His grace upon them. He gave them the Book and prophethood andsent them for the guidance of their people. The unbelievers scoffed at them and persecuted them but they bore it patiently.

Some of them were endowed with more gifts than the others, but Muslims are asked to believe in all of them, to respect them and to make no·distinction amongst them. The Quran says:

> *"We make no distinction between one and another of His messengers."* *(2:285)*

And also:

> *"Those who deny Allah and His messengers and (those who) wish to separate Allah from His messengers, saying: "we believe in some but reject others": and (those who) wish to take a coure midway - They are in truth (equally), unbelievers;"* *(4:150-151)*

The Quran tells us that Allah always helped His apostles and prophets and punished and destroyed the wicked unbelievers. The apostle and prophets will be questioned on the Day of Judgement about the response of their people to their mission.

Allah sent prophets to mankind from amongst themselves for their guidance and reformation because a man can best serve as an example and a guide for his own race. The message could have been conveyed by the angels, but they belong to a different class of beings and cannot serve as models for men. The Quran says:

> *"If there were settled on earth, angels walking about in peace and quiet, we should certainly have sent them down from the hevens an angel for a messenger."*
>
> *(17:95)*

All the prophet who preceded Hadrat Muhammad (PBUH) were sent with a message of warning and guidance to a particular people. None of their messages was intended to be universal, until the last messenger, Hadrat Muhamad (PBUH) was entrusted with the final and complete guidance for the whole of humanity for all times to come.

The Quran says that Allah sent a warner and guide to every nation and it mentions the names of many of them.At the beginning of the line was HadratAdam, who was also the first human being. Allah bestowed prophethood on him and gave him guidance for himself and his descendants.

The first human beings on earth were true believers in one Allah, who submitted to His guidance. But, gradually over a period of time, they became idolators, until Allah raised a new messenger from amongst them to recall them to the truth. The Quran mentions Hadrat Nuh, who brought a message of warning to his peoples. They refused to listen and were destroyed by the flood. The next major prophet whose history is narrated in the Quran is Hadrat Ibrahim. Although he grew up among idolators, he surrendered himself to Allah with such total submission that Allah made him an example for people of all times. From Hadrat Ibrahim came a long line of prophts through his two sons - Hadrat Ismail and Hadrat Ishaq. From Hadrat Ishaq a number of prophets came which included Hadrat Yaqub, Hadrat Yusuf, Hadrat Musa, Hadrat Daud, Hdrat Sulaiman, Hadrat Yahya and Hadrat Isa. Hadrat Ismail was the ancestor of the Arabs and Hadrat Muhammad (PBUH) was among his descendants.

The Hol Quran proclaims that Hadrat Muhammad (PBUH) is the last messenger of Allah, 'The seal of the prophets.'He was born in Mecca, Arabia, nearly six hundred years after Hadrat Isa. It was the time when the Arabs practiced idolatory and the society was in a state of extreme corruption and decay. When Hadrat Muhammad (PBUH) called people to Islam and to a noble and righteous path he was met with intense hostility. At first he was ridiculed and opposed and then ith his small group of followers exposd to abuse, torture, boycott and ultimately the threat of assassination. But all of them remained firm and constant because they were sure of the truth of the message that was delivered to them. At last, after thirteen years of preaching and bearing patiently all the trials, the Holy Prophet (PBUH) with his followers migrated to Medina where he was able to establish the first Islamic state based upon the teachings of the Quran.

Soon, the Muslim community although initially small in nmber and poorly equipped was able to subdue the unbelievers. The Holy Prophet (PBUH) then returned to the city of Mecca from where he had migrated several years ago. He forgave his bitterest enemies and thus, the conquest of Mecca was a peaceful one. Prophet Muhammad (PBUH) died about a year later. He left behind for all times to come two permanent and unchangeable sources of guidance, the Holy Quran and his Sunnah - that is his own example and practice.

A complete and detailed account of thc lifc of thc Holy Prophet (PBUH) has been preserved by his followers. Hence the narrations preserved in the books of Hadith-sayings of the Holy Prophet (PBUH) deal with all aspects of life from the most personal matters to the conduct of war and affairs of the state. The Muslims have before them in every aspect of their lives the living example of the best of human beings as the Quran says:

> *"We have indeed in the Messenger of Allah a beautiful pattern (of conduct) for anyone whose hope is in Allah and the Final Day, and who engages much in the praise of Allah." (33:21)*

His wif, Aishah said about him that his conduct was the Quran. The Holy Prophet (PBUH) was very close to Allah, but he lived an extremely active and complete life. He was a devoted husband, father, a kind and responsible kinsman, a faithful and affectionate friend, a leader in worship as well as in battle and an excellent ruler and statesman. For the Muslims of his time as well as for the present and the future generations, he was and will always be the model, the teacher, the guide, the leader and the conveyor of Divine Guidance to mankind.

Belief in life after death, the Day of Judgement, bodily resurrection and Heaven and Hell is one of the articles of faith in Islam. Death is an absolute certainty. According to the Holy Quran, every soul shall have a tasteof death, and must pass away. A man's life on this earth ends with is death, after which another life begins. The Qiyamat-e-Sughraor lesser judgement takes place immediately after death. The word 'Barzakh' occurs in verse 100 of Surah al-Mominun:

> *"Beforethem is a partition (Barzakh) till the day they are raised up." (23:100)*

Abdullah Yusuf Ali has explained Barzakh: "Barzakh is the place or state in which people will be after death and before judgement. Behind them is the barrier of death and in front of them is the Barzakh, partition, a quiescent state until the judgement comes." Barzakh is therefore, the intermediate state in which the soul is placed after death till the resurrection.

The Holy Quran informs man of the reality of another life of infinite duration which will be very different from the life of this world. For Allah is easily able to transform His creatures from one state of being to another. The Quran speaks again and again of examples of such transformations: the coming to life again of the earth which lies dead and barren in winter or drought; the development of a sperm in the mother's womb into a human being with all the faculties of thinking and feeling. The Quran says:

> *"And among His signs is this: thou seest the earth barren and desolate; but when We send down rain to it, it is stirred to life and yields increase. Truly, He who gives life to the (dead) earth can surely give life to (men) who are dead. For He has power over all things."*
>
> *(41:39)*

Those who denied Allah and rejected His guidance and did evil deeds will be thrown into a fearsome and terrible abode, where they with their companions will be in a state of torment and agony. They will long to have another chance to return to the world to live thei lives differently but it will be too late. For such people, the Quran says:

> *"And on the day that the unbelievers will be placed before the fire (they will be asked) "Is this not the Truth?" they will say "Yea, by our Lord!" (One will say)*
>
> *"Then taste ye the penalty for that ye were wont to deny (Truth)! "* *(46:34)*

And also :

> *"The sinners will be in the punishment of hell, to dwell therein ..."*
>
> *Nowise shall We be unjust to them: But it is they who have been unjust themselves."* *(43:74, 76)*

As for the people who believed in Allah, who obeyed and submitted to Him and lived their lives for His pleasure, and who died in a state of surrender to Him, the Holy Quran sas:

> *"My devotees! No fear shall be on you that Day; nor shall ye grieve - (Being those) who have believed in Our signs and bowed (their will to Ours) in Islam. Enter ye the garden, ye and your wives in (beauty and) rejoicing."*
>
> *(43:68-70)*
>
> *"Those who have faith and do righteous deeds - they are the best of creatures.*
>
> *Their reward is with Allah; gardens of Eternity, beneath which rivers flows; they will dwell therein for ever;...."*
>
> *(8:7-8)*

The two states of Heaven and Hell are not spiritual. They will be experienced in physical forms by the new bodies with which Allah will raise men up. The Quran describes Hell as a state of intense, fearful burning and agony without respite, among the most horrifying surroundings and companions. For its inhabitants, it will be a tmporary or permanent state of torture depending upon the nature and extent of their sins. The worst part of their suffering will be the awareness that they have brought about this punishment upon themselves by rejecting Allah and ignoring the guidance and the clear warnings which He had conveyed to them through His messengers. The Quran says:

> *"Those who have earned evil will have a reward of like evil: ignominy will cover their (faces): No defender will they have from (the wrah of) Allah: ... they are companions of the fire: they will abide therein." (10:27)*

The Quran tells us that the inhabitants of Heaven will experience happiness and joy that will far exceed anything one can imagine. The ultimate trumph and bliss for these people will be their nearness to Allah. The Quran says:

> *"To those who do right is a goodly (reward) -yea, more (than in measure)! No darkness nor shame shall cover their faces! They are companions of the garden; they will abide therein." (10:26)*

The Quran describes the outline of the events of the Last Day in a very clear and awe-inspiring language. It says that at a time which is known only to Alah, the hour of judgement will come all of a sudden; and it will be like the twinkling of an eye. When the first trumpet of Resurrection is sounded, the earth will be split apart, it will be shaken to its depths, it will be in violent commotion and become as a level sretch.

The mountains will crumble to dust and will fly here and there like wool. The sun will be folded up, the moon will be in darkness, the stars will become dim and fall. The oceans will boil over and burst forth.

Human souls will be dazed and lose all consciousness of time andplace. The world will cease to be in the form which we see now and there will be a new heaven and a new earth. The Quran says:

> *"When the sky is rent asunder, and hearkens to (The command of) its Lord and it must needs (Do so) - and when the earth is flattened out, and casts forth what is within it and becomes (clean) empty." (84: 1-4)*

On that day, the bodies of te dead will be rejoined with their souls, while those who are alive on earth at that time will die and be joined to this assembly.

All men will stand before Allah, each one, alone and helpless, to give an account of their deeds. They will be given their book of deeds, which they will be asked to read.

The good will be given their record in their right hands and the sinners in their left hands or from behind their backs. No injustice will be done on that day.

People's hands, feet and tongues will bear witness against them. No one shall speak except by Allah's leave, no ransom or compensation will be accepted, there will be no bargaining or friendship and there will be no intercession except by Allah's permission. Parents, children, spouses and relatives will be of no avail.

The Quran says:

> *"Then he who is given his record in his right hand, soon will his account be taken by an easy reckoning, and he will turn to his people, rejoicing! But he who is given his record behind his back- soon will he cry for perdition, and he will enter a blazing fire."* *(84: 7-12)*

Ad also:

> *"At length, when there comes the deafening noise - that Day shall a man flee from his own brother, and from his mother and his father, and from his wife and his children. Each one of them, that Day, will have enough concern (of his own) to make him indifferent to the others. "* *(80:33-37)*

Islam lays the greatest stress on the individual's accountability to Allah. The human being's life in this world is a trial, an examination period, during which he prepares himself, either for reward or punishment, for the next life which is ever lasting.

It is obvious that a person who has lived his life in submission to Allah is in an entirely different state from the one who has lived all his life in rebellion and ingratitude to Allah.

Those who do not believe in a future life become immoral and irresponsible because, for them the short life on this earth is everything. On the other hand, those who have a firm belief in life after death fear Allah, follow the straight path, do good deeds and abstain from all evil deeds.

Chapter 2

Treasure of Wisdom in Islam

Man has the ability of prying into secret realities and into the causes of things. With this ability he is able to analyse situations, to have knowledge of individual and social life, and to put everything in its prper place and proper context. This is a reflection of God's Attribute: the Possessor of Knowledge and Wisdom. Thus the Quran speaks again and again of God as the Knower and the Wise and the Knower of the Secrets of the Hearts:

He granteth wisdom
To whom H pleaseth;
And he to whom wisdom
Is granted receiveth
Indeed a benefit overflowing; *(II - 269)*

Comprehensiveness

his virtue enlarges the horizons of the mind. It helps man to understand things and to extend his grasp and reach. It is a reflection of God's Attribute of being All-Encompassing in Knowledge. The Quran says:

Nor shallthey compass
Aught of His Knowledge
Except as He willeth. *(II - 255)*

The Matchless

Owing to this virtue, the individual develops his unique individuality, which makes him like nobody else. This is a reflection of God's Absolute Uniqueness, and Attribute about which the Quran says:

there is nothing
Whatever like unto Him, *(XLII - 11)*

The above argument indicates the measure of human character in the Islamic scheme of cultural reconstruction; it indicates the kind of human character which should be regarded as the essential and the ideal one.

Concept of Family

Disintegration of the Family in the West : Individual life is constructed in the context of social life, and social life begins in the family which is its unit. In western culture, the institution of the family has been disintegrated, resulting in the freezing of feelings of affections, love and sympathy. There, every person feels that nobody is his or hers, and that he is alone in an alien world.

Insistence on Affection Through Family in Cultural Reconstruction : In the scheme of cultural reconstruction, the institution of the family is the basis of the life of the community. For maintaining this institution mutual love, affection and sympathy have been insisted on. The Quran speaks of these things in various ways:

Reverence God, through Whom
Ye demend your mutual (rights),
And (reverence) the wombs
(that bore you) *(IV - 1)*

AlArham (wombs) is the plural of the Arabic word *Rahm* womb which literally means the womb of a woman. But figuratively it means family relationship and bounds of kindship—the English word 'kindness', in its original and wider meaning is the closest synonyms for the Arabic terms. *Tajul 'uroos* says:

> Rahm *means the womb of a woman. Since the various members of family come from the same womb, the term has been used in the sense of kinship. The figurative meaning of* rahm *is kinship. When an Arab says that such and such persons have* rahm *between them he means they are very closely-related.*

Rahm includes close relations which may be both intimate and non-intimate: *"Rahm* is the term used for all relations, without distinction whether they are intimate or non-intimate" (Qurtubi). The above Quranic verse (IV -I) insists on rewarding kinsfolk and condemns the rejection of kinship bonds, Abu Bakr Jassas says: '

The Verse insists on the right of familial relationships and prohibits their severence'. (Jassas Razi, Ahkamul Quran) *Ibn-e-Hayyan says: Juxtaposing God with the 'womb' indicates that violation of the bonds of kinship is a great sin (*Al Bahrul Muheet).

Importance of Bonds of Kinship in Other Quranic Verses: The implications of Sympathy for, and doing good to one another because of familial bonds of kinship are not confined to this life. They extend beyond this life too. The distribution of inheritance is based on such an idea:

But kindered by blood
Have prior rights
Against each other
In the Book of God. *(VII-75)*

The bond of kinship is so strong that even differences of religion do not break it; and the claim for affection and love remains inspite of them. Thus, the Holy Prophet said to his kinsfolk:

Say: 'No reward do I
Ask of you for this
Except the love
Of others near to kin. *(XLII-23)*

Those who violate the bond of kinship have been regarded by the Quran as transgressors:

But He causes not to stray,
Except those who forsake (the path),
Those who break God's Covenant
After it is ratified,
And who sunder what God
Has ordered to be joined,
And do mischief on earth: *(II-26-27)*

Prophet's Teachings

The Holy Prophet has interpreted the reverence to kinship or wombs in various ways. He always spoke of the excellence of this virtue and insisted on the importance of maintaining it. For example, he says:

God said: 'I am Allah, I am the One. I created mercy and derived it from my own name. He who joins the bond of mercy, I shall join him (with blessings).

He who breaks this bond, I shall break him (into damnation).

(Abu Daud, Mishkat, *Babul Birre Was-Sila)*

Mercy is a twig entwined with the Merciful One. Allah said: 'He who joins it, I shall join him. He who severes it, I shall severe him. *(Bukhari, Muslim,* Kitabul Birre Wal-Sila)

Allah created all the creatures. After He has finished this work Mercy stood up and got hold of the Merciful One by the waist. The Merciful One said: 'Stop!

Mercy said: "This is the place of him who seeks refuge with thee. The Merciful One said: Art thou not satisfied with the decree that I burnt him who burnt thee and I severed him who severes thee? At this Mercy replied: 'I am satisfied'.

(Mishkat, *Babul Birra Wal-Sala)*

Rahm or Mercy is related to the throne of God. Mercy says: He who joins e, Allah shall join him; and He who severs me, Allah shall severe him *(Op cit).*

In the West Children and Parents are not Responsible for Mutual Care : In Western culture, parents and children have become burdens on one another. The relation between them has been broken down and so have th bonds and rights of kinship. The children are brought up in nurseries and the old parents are taken care of by houses for the ol, which are separately and specially built for them. Eventually in such a position the natural feelings which are related to blood kinship are suppressed and vitiated. Feelings of affection and love should not be looked for or expected in such a situation.

Natural Feelings and Rights in the Scheme of Islamic Cultural Reconstruction: In the Islamic scheme of cultural reconstruction due consideration is given to natural family feelings. The bond of kinship between persons has been emphasised very muchand the rights and duties associated with ithave been spelled out and insisted on. Various Verses of the Quran insisted on doing good to parents. Often this command comes after the command regarding faith in one God and His worship, which, perhaps, implies that the efficient cause of man's birth (God) and the material cause (parents) both must be considered and one must give what is due to both of them.

The difference is only with regard to what is primary and what is secondary. Here are some Verses of the Quran:

The Lord hath decreed
That ye worship none but Him,
And that ye be kind
To parents. Whether one
Or both of them attain
Old age in thy life,
Say not to them a word
Of contempt, nor repel them,
But address them
In terms of honour.
And, out of kindness, lower to them the wing
Of humility, and say:
'My Lord! bestow on them
The Mercy even as they
Cherished me in childhood'. (XVII - 23.24)
Serve God, and join not
Any partners with Him:
'Do good — to parents, kinsfold *(IV- 36)*
Say: 'Come, I will rechearse
What God hath (really)
Prohibited you from'; join not
Anything as equal with Him;
Be good to your parents; *(VI - 151)*

Since in bringing up children the mother has to suffer more of trouble, priority is given to her in the matter of doing good to parents. The Quran says:

Any We have enjoined on man
(To be good) to his parents:
In travail upon travail
Did his mother bare him,
And in years twain
Was his weaning: (hear

The command), 'show gratitude
to Me and to thy parents:
To me is (thy final) Goal. *(XXXI - 14)*
We have enjoined on man
Kindness to his parents:
In pain did his mother
Bare him, and in pain
Did she give him birth. *(XLVI - 15)*

Regarding doing good to parents there are certain Traditions. Once a man asked the Holy Prophet: 'What duty is enjoined on children towards their parents.' The Holy Prophet said: 'Both of them are thy paradise or hell'.

Another Tradition says: "The pleasure of God depends on the pleasure of the parents, and the displeasure of God is the displeasure of the parents. Still another Tradition says: 'May his nose be laid in the dust! May his nose be laid in the dust! May his nose be laid in the dust! (May he suffer abjection and humiliation). The audience asked: 'Whose nose, O Prophet of Allah?' The Holy Prophet replied:

> *'He who finds his parents or one of his parents and does not enter paradise'. The traditions, like the Quran, also command the giving of priority to the mother. Once a man asked the Holy Prophet who was most worthy of his good treatment. The Holy Prophet said: 'Thy mother'. He asked: 'Who next?' The reply was: 'Thy mother'. He once again asked: 'Who next?' The reply was 'Thy Mother'. At this he asked for the fourth time: 'Who next?' This time the reply was: 'Thy father'. Another person asked the Holy Prophet about the treatment to the memory of the parents after their death. The Holy Prophet said: 'Pray for their salvation; fulfil their vows and pacts; do good to your kinsfolk, keeping the parents in mind; and respect the words of your parents'. Doing good to parents is commanded even if their religion is different. When Abu Bakr's daughter Asma asked the Holy Prophet regardng her infidel mother, the Holy Prophet advised doing good to her out of human kindness.*
>
> (Bukhari, Muslim, *Kitabul Birre Wal Silah)*.

Cherishing is the Foremost Duty of Parents towards Children **:** In the scheme of cultural reconstruction, just as there are the duties of children towards parents in the same way there are the duties of parents towards children. Among them the foremost duty is that of cherishing and bringing up the children. The Quran speaks of the desire and the prayers of parents before the birth of the child as follows:

And if Thou givest us
A goodly child,
We vow we shall
(ever) be grateful' *(VII - 189)*

By the word 'goodly' are meant particular traits of character. But the word keeps changing its meaning according to the context. In this context 'goodly' has been explained by exegetes as follows:

A healthy child, one whose body should be alright; healthy in the sense that his limbs should be intact; perfectly healthy in the sense of having the capability to do good deeds for the benefit of humanity.

Children should be brought up According to Their Needs : The bringing up of children should be done in such way as to ensure their proper development and to provide them with the things they need according to their age. Thus, the Quran speaks of breast-feeding the child as follows:

The mother shall give suck
To their offspring
For two whole years,
If the father desires
To complete the term. *(II- 233)*

The relation established by giving suck to a child is reverenced so much that if another woman gives suck to the child instead of the mother, the child and that woman have the same relation between them as would obtain in the case of the real mother. This relation is Holy and not to be violated. Hence the Quran prohibits marriage with:

foster-mothers
(Who gave you suck), foster sisters: *(IV- 23)*

The father is entrusted with supporting the woman who gave suck to the children, be she a real mother or a foster mother:

But he shall bear the cost
Of their fooding and clothing
On equitable terms. *(II-233)*

Several Traditions speak of the affection of the Holy Prophet for children. Once a rustic Arab said to the Holy Prophet: 'Do you kiss your Child? I have never done it myself. At this the Holy Prophet said: 'If Allah has taken off all mercy from your heart, what can I do'. In another Tradition the name of this rustic arab is mentioned as Iqrab Habis. He saw the Holy Prophet kissing the child Hasan and said: 'I have ten children. I never kiss them'. At this the Holy Prophet said: 'He who does not show mercy is not shown mercy'. Still another Tradition observes: 'He who does not show affection to our juniors and respect to our ancestors is not one of us.

In showing affection, it is necessary to act on the principles of equality, that is no distinction should be made between superior and inferior in this regard—it is not proper to give some gift to one person and to deprive the other person from it on the basis of any distinction. There is the story of No man. Once his father gave him some gift. The Holy Prophet asked the father: 'Have you given such a gift to all your sons?' He said: 'No'. The Holy Prophet said: 'Witdraw the gift you have given'. Another Tradition reports this incident as follows: 'Do you like that all your children should receive equal treatment from you? He said 'Yes'. The Holy Prophet said: 'Then do not do such a thing (do not observe partiality)." Still another Tradition gives the following advice: 'Fear Allah, and mete out equal treatment among your children'.

Special Attention to Bringing up of Daughters : Among Arabs, the daughters had no importance. For this reason, the Holy Prophet has drawn special attention to their character. He said: 'He who gets a daughter and lets her live, does not dishonour her and does not prefer her to the son—Allah will send him to paradise'. *(Abu Daud, Mishkat,* Babul Shafqa Wal Rahma alal Khalq). Another tradition says: 'He who has daughters and who metes out good treatment to them, his daughters will become a block against the fire of hell in his case. *(Bukhari, Muslim, Mishkat)* Still another Tradition says:

> *He who brings up two daughters till they come of age, he and I shall be together like two fingers of the hand on the Day of Judgment.* (Muslim, Mishkat)

Family Planning for the Sake of Proper Bringing up of Children : If poverty comes in the way of the proper bringing u of children, child births should be properly spaced through various methods. Even birth control is permitted if it becomes necessary.

The various methods of birth control that are used in modern times were not there in the days of the revelation of the Quran. So it is not fair to look for some command in the Quran and the Sunnah regarding birh control and to reject birth control on not finding the command there.

The basic consideration in this regard is that the fundamental principles of Islam are not violated. If they are violated birth control should be rejected. But if they are not violated then it is not fair to insist on opposing it. The possibility of both supporting and rejecting it should be kept open, subject to the demands of the circumstances. Just as there may be circumstances which demand the increase of population, in the same way there may be circumstances which demand birth control. Perhaps it is for this reason that the Quran and the Sunnah have not given any definite command regarding this matter.

Birth Control in Islam According to Circumstances : Here, we give some evidences which suggest that Islam is not inimical to the policy of family planning and birth control. The Quran says:

If any of you have not
The means wherewith
To wed free believing women,
They may wed believing
Girls from among those
Whom your right hands possess *(IV - 24)*
Let those who find not
The wherewithal for marriage
Keep themselves chaste, until
God give them means
Out of His grace. *(XXIV - 33)*

In the above Verses, poverty is recognised as undesirable for marriage. It is therefore amenable to reason that if circumstances demand it the size of the family should be restricted through birth control. At the time when the Quran was revealed a birth control method, the *coitus obstructus* (not allowing the semen to go inside the women), was in vogue among Arabs. But it is significant that the Quran did not forbid it. Jabir has taken the silence of the Quran for permission: 'We practised *coitus obstructus* when the Quran was being revealed. Sufian says: 'If *coitus obstructus* was something to be prohibited, the Quran would have prohibited it'. Regarding women the Quran says:

Your wives are
As tilth unto you,
So approach your tilth
When and how ye will; (II - 23)

In connection with interpretation of this Verse, Ibn-i-Abbas, Ibn-i-Umar and Abu Haneefa provide the following comment: 'How ye will mean practising *coitus obstructus* or without it'. Another Verse of the Quran says that only one wife or slave-girl will be more suitable,

To prevent you
From doing injustice *(IV - 3)*

With regard to the interpretation of this Verse, Zaid b. Aslam, Jabir b. Zaid (Successors of the Companions) and Imam Shafai offer the following comment: 'Being contented with one wife or slave-girl implies that you should not have many children'. Sufian b. Ainia has offered the following interpretation: 'To prevent you from doing injustice' (IV - 3) comes close to the suggestions that you should not become insolvent and needy'.

Argument From the Sayings of Saints and Scholars : There are various Traditions regarding the number of children. Some of them encourage big family, others encourage small family. In the same way, there are many Traditions regarding *coitus obstructus*. Some of them imply permission, others imply prohibition of the practice. A study of all these Traditions indicate that in this matter the Holy Prophet had a liberal outlook and was moulding his outlook according to the demands of the circumstances. Otherwise he would have no difficulty in giving a commandment for or against birth control. In the days of Caliph Omar the Conqueror and the ruler of Egypt Amroob. Al-as gave the following lecture to the people. This lecture was moulded according to the Demands of the circumstances and it can be called a declaration of the government policy of that time: O my people! avoid four bad habits, for they cause distress after comfort, misery after prosperity and degradation after honour: (1) Avoid having a great number of children (2) Avoid low standard of life, (3) Avoid wasting your goods through profligacy, and (4) Avoid wasting time in unnecessary and pointless discussion.

This lecture has been quoted by Ibn-i-Hakeem in his history of Egypt
(Futuh-i-Misr wa Akhbaruha, Vol. I, p. 139)

Imam Ghazali and Shah Abdul Aziz have also permitted coitus obstructus *as a method of birth control in view of poverty and destitution.*

After seeking religious sanction for birth control it does not remain important whether the man uses some device or the woman. But the sanction that has been suggested is conditional and applies only to critical cases. If a general sanction for birth control were given its consequence would be dangerous, as western and westernised cultures testify.

Education Regarding Both Man and the Universe Necessary : In addition to bringing up children, education is also the responsibility of the parents. Undoubtedly the West has made great progress in matters of knowledge regarding the Universe, but as regards knowledge about man it is still very much backward. It is successful in understanding the mysteries of the universe but unsuccessful in understanding the mystery of man. David C. Marsh admits that our knowledge of the physical universe has become very wide. We have been able to control and harness the powers of nature to a great extent; but we are ignorant regarding innumerable aspects of man and his affairs to an unfortunately great extent.

A.W. Haslet says that a scientist is not more helpless in other matters of knowledge than he is in the matter of knowledge about man. He can split the atom; can analyse the composition of the farthest star; can harness the power of electricity—but the same scientist is confronted with difficulties when he wants to understand the nature of life and even his own or man's nature. For neither life nor man can yield to any experiment under controlled conditions.

Both Kinds of Education Recommended By the Quran : In the Islamic scheme of cultural reconstruction so much knowledge about man is available that there is no problem in solving human problems. As regards Universe, it has been insisted not only that man should acquire all kinds of useful knowledge but should also maintain progress or evolution of human knowledge, otherwise the survival of the human species will be endangered. Hence, the very beginning of the revelation of the Quran is by the commandment: 'Read' *(Iqra)* the very first Verse of the Quran points to the fact that man is originally a clot of blood. He does not deserve any exaltation on the basis of this origin, but it is only through knowledge that he is exalted to higher and higher stages:

Proclaim! (or Read!)
In the name
Of the Lord and Cherisher,
Who created—
Created man, out of

The (mere) clot
Of congealed blood:
Proclaim! and thy Lord
Is Most Bountiful,—
He Who taught
(The use of) the Pen,—
Taught man that
Which he knew not. *(XCVI—1-5)*

Similary immediately after the creation of man (Adam) this truth was revealed, through a competitive test with the angles, that supremacy is determined by knowledge. The angels themselves have to acknowledge it—

Glory to thee: of knowledge
We have none, save what Thou
Has taught us: in truth it is Thou
Who art perfect in knowledge and wisdom *(II-32)*

The episode of Talut also brings out the truth that supremacy is determined not by wealth, family, or racial or tribal religion, but by knowledge and physical prowess. The Quran relates the episode as follows:

Their Prophet said to them:
'God hath appointed
Talut as king over you.
They said: 'How can he
Exercise authority over us
When we are better fitted
Than he to exercise authority,
And he is not even gifted
With wealth in abundance?'
He said: 'God hath
Chosen him above you,
And hath gifted him
Abundantly with knowledge
And bodily prowess *(II-247)*

Conformity to Contemporary Standards of Prowess and Knowledge : It is not enough to have knowledge and physical prowess. Knowledge and physical prowess should be acquired in conformity with the standards of a particular age. For example, the modern age is an age of science and technology, so in this age the measure of supremacy should be according to modern standards of knowledge and prowess.

The words 'power' (Quwwat) and 'iron' (AlHadid) have been used in the Quran in a manner that indicates that the equipment of power and technological potentialities of man shall go on increasing day by day. Without keeping pace with this progress no community can survive :

Against them make ready
your strength to the utmost
Of your power, *(VIII-60)*
And We send down Iron,
In which is (material for)
Mighty war, as well as
Many benefits for mankind, *(LVII-25)*

Both Kinds of Education Recommended By the Traditions : The Holy Prophet has drawn attention to knowledge in various ways. For example, he says: 'I have been sent as a teacher'. Regarding the Pen (which is a means of knowledge) he says: 'Allah created the Pen first'. The effects of knowledge have been recognised by the Holy Prophet. They are progress and exaltation; undoubtedly 'wisdom' adds to the nobility of the noble person and exalts the low persons to make them sit in the company of the King.

Knowledge has been described by the Holy Prophet as the cause of the leadership of the nations and also of their influence over other people. Knowledge is a weapon against enemy and an embellishment for the sake of friends. Allah raises nations through knowledge and exalts them to the position of leaders. They are followed by other nations and their opinions become decisive for other nations.

God has made knowledge capable of infinite development. He has not confined it to any one (religious or worldly) sphere- 'wisdom or knowledge is the lost property of the knower; he has a right to it wherever he finds it.'

The Holy Prophet has recommended lng journeys for the sake of all useful knowledge:

> *The Holy Prophet has recommended that we should undertake journeys to very remote places for the sake of all kinds of useful knowledge—and without any prejudice too. A Tradition says 'Aquire knowledge even if you have to go to China'. This Tradition has been regarded as 'weak' in terms of the degree of authenticity. But its import is very much in line with the spirit of Islam, and it does not say anything fantastic either. China and Araia are to antipodes. But the ports of Arabia were visited by the merchant ships of China in those days, and Chinese goods were sold in some Arabian towns. Masudi writes that 'Chinese ships visited the ports of Amman, Seraf, Fars and Bahrain'. About the port of Daba in Amman Ibn-i-Habib writes: "There was a port called Daba. On the last day of the month of Rajab, a big market or fair was set up there. In this fair came merchants from Sindh, Hindustan, China and from various places of the east and the west".*

The Holy Prophet Used the Most Important Modern Weapons of His Time : The most important weapons of the days of the Holy Prophet were as follows:

Dabbaba: It was a special kind of armoured car, made for protection against arrows by coating it with layers of thick skin. It was used for the purpose of battering fortresses.

Zabr: It was made in the shape of an umbrella from skin mounted on wood, and was used for protecting the back against arrows'.

Minjaniq: It was a weapon of offence, and was a kind of sling by which heavy stones were thrown at the enemy. *(Lissanul Arab)*

Hasak: It was a kind of thorny shrub which was spread around the fortress and around the enemy army so as to make the way dangerous for the enemy. *(AlQamusul Muhit)*

The Holy Prophet was the First to Use Minjaniq and Hasak : The Holy Prophet imported *Minjaniq* and *Hasak* for deployment in the Battle of Taif. In fact, he himself was the first to use *Minjaniq* and *Hasak*. Ibn-i-Hisham says:

> *A trustworthy person reported to me that in Islam the Holy Prophet himself was the first to use* Minjaniq *against the army of Taif.*
>
> *(Al Siyarul Nabuwiyah, Zikr Ghazwatul Taif)*

Miqraizi says:

> *The Holy Prophet installed the Minjaniq on the fortress of Taif.*

Another report says:

> *The Holy Prophet spread Hasak around the fortress of Taif.*

There are various accounts regarding the *Minjaniq* that the Holy Prophet used. Some reporters say it was imported, while others say it was made by Salman Farsi. After the conquest of Taif, in the year 9 H., Urwabin Masud Thaqafi and Ghailan bin Salma Thaqafi adopted Islam and went to Jarsh and acquired skill in the use of the above-mentioned weapons:

> *Urwa bin Masud Thaqafi and Ghailan bin Salma Thaqafi were not present in the siege of Hunain and Taif. They had gone away to Jarsh to learn the art of using* Dabbaba, Manjaniq *and* Zabr.*(Ibn-i-Hisham,* Al Siyarul Nabuwiya, *Vol. III, Ghazwatul Taif:* A Rauzul' Unuf, *Zikr Talim Ihlil Taif)*

Manufacturing Arms

Jarsh was a town in the suburbs of Damascus. It was under the power of Rome, which was second in greatness in those days. This town had big arms factory. It was conquered by Sharjil bin Husna in the days of Omar's Caliphate. The town was under the suzerainty of Rome, Sharjit conquered it in the days of Omar bin Khattab. *(Imtaul Asma',* Nazala Rasulullah bil' Araj, Hashiya 366)

The Holy Prophet's Command to Develop the Science of Weaponry : When, after the conquest of Jarsh, the arms factory fell to the hands of Muslims, they developed it further. The Holy Prophet incited his people in various ways to learn the arts of warfare. For example he said: 'He who gives up archery after learning it is not one of us'. On another occasion he said: 'By the virtue of one arrow Allah sends three persons to paradise: the maker of it who wants to earn a reward (from God), the archer who shoots it, and the helper who picks the arrow and gives it (to the archer)'. The above argument should make it clear that the Islamic system of education encompasses all spheres of life.

Special Attention to Character-Building : Alongwith the acquiring of knowledge skill special attention is drawn to character-building in the commandments of Islam. The commandments in this regard are addressed to parents and teachers first. In western culture there is a little standard of character. In the Islamic scheme of cultural reconstruction, the standard is there: It is the Attributes of God Himself.

These Attributes are related not only to Beauty but also to Glory (and Power) and Perfection. The qualities of character that emanate from these Attributes have been discussed above. All the qualities are needed,in due proportion, for the development of a balanced character. By innate dispositions, certain qualities may be increased or decreased; but such a thing should not be allowed to happen by human design.

Both the East and the West have Failed Here : Here, in the matter of character-building both the East and the West have failed. About the West, it can be said that it aimed at worldly gain only, and therefore it gave importance only to those qualities of character which are related to the acquisition of worldly gains. But how about the East? The East has not been able to achieve any success in character-building beyond a few moral reforms, and this in spite of its spiritual trumpeting.

The Pattern of Balanced Personality is the Holy Prophet : In the scheme of cultural reconstruction, the pattern of balanced personality is the Holy Prophet. As the Quran puts it:

We have indeed
In the Apostle of God
A beautiful pattern (to conduct) *(XXXIII. 21)*
That the Apostle may be
A witness for you, and ye
Be his witness for mankind! *(XXII. 78)*
Thus have We made of you
An Ummat justly balanced,
That ye might be witnesses
Over the nations,
And the Apostle a witness
Over yourselves *(II-143)*

Those who are perceptive know how perfect and comprehensive the life of the Holy Prophet was.

The Life of the Companions as a Pattern of Character-Building: After the life of the Holy Prophet the life of his companions is a pattern of character-building. These companions performed in every sphere of life such feats as have no equal in human history. If their activities had been confined to any one particular sphere, Islamic civilization would not have come into existence. Nor would it have survived.

Adjacent to Masjid-e-Nabwi, there was an institution called Saffa. This institution trained the companions in character-building. Its activities encompassed all spheres of life in those days. The products of Saffa exemplified a particular way of life. They undertook responsibilities of earning livelihood, education and other responsibilities of citizenship, and along with these the responsibilities of participating in battles voluntarily. Some eminent products of the Saffa institutions were: Abdullah b. Masood, Saad b. Abi Waqqas, Huzaifa b. Yamaan, Abdullah b. Omar, Salman Farsi, Abu Darda, Abu Huraira, Salim, Abu Zar Ghifari, Hanzala, Bilal Habshi and Suheb Roomi. *(Tabaqati Ibni-i-Sad,* Vol. I, II; *Musnad: Ibn-i-Hambal, Vol. I).* Their deeds testify to the education for character-building that the Holy Prophet initiated.

Fundamental Principles of Character-Building : From the Quran the following fundamental principles of character-building can be derived. They are : (1) Gnosis, (2) Utility, (3) Trustworthiness, (4) Responsibility of Caretaking, (5) Justice and (6) Application. We shall discuss them below:

(1) *Gnosis:* It means the realization of the self and the realization of God. On the one hand, it would inculcate virtues like self responsibility, liberal outlook, boldness, contentment and freedom from wants, and on the other, virtues like humility, hope, piety, resignation, discipline and fortitude:

As also in your own

Selves: will ye not

Then see *(LI-21)*

Because God will never change

The Grace which He hath bestowed

On a People until they change

What is in their (own) souls: *(VIII-53)*

Without the realization of the self the realization of God is not possible :

And be ye not like
Those who forget God:
And He made them forget
Their souls *(LIX-19)*

(2) *Utility:* It means that every individual should become useful according to his natural abilities. The individual should be equipped with all kinds of accomplishments, material, moral, spiritual, physical etc. The Quran says:

He sends down water
From the skies, and the channels
Flow, each according to its measure:
But the torrent bears away
The foam that mounts up
To the surface. Even so,
From that (Ore) which they heat
In the fire, to make ornaments
Or utensils therewith,
There is a scum likewise.
Thus doth God (by parables)
Show forth Truth and Vanity.
For the scum disappears
Like froth cast out;
While that which is for the good
Of mankind remains on the earth. *(XIII-17)*

In the above parable, the useful things like silver and gold remain, and the useless things which are the scum disappear like froth. The obvious implication is that in this world only the useful things survive and the useless things gradually perish.

In our Muslim society, the concept of utility has been confined to moral betterment, and thus material power was left to the worldly people. This has resulted in degradation and lowness. Even if moral betterment is accomplished, progress can not be made without physical power. This fallacy has two reasons behind it: (1) The wrong concept of religion led people to think that only by performing certain religious rituals they would achieve all that the worldly people do by tireless effort and striving. This is against God's law of justice. (2) The wrong concept of miracles led to the notion that things, and even the advancement of a nation, can happen without any physical causality. This is against the law of nature. The property of the fire is to burn. He who puts his hand into it, will necessarily get burnt. If the fire was turned into a garden in the case of Abraham, it was a miracle which has no relation to the common laws of nature. But the world is run by the common laws of nature and not by miracles.

(3) *Trustworthiness* : The notion that trustworthiness is the basis of the good life should be promoted. In this world man is like a trustee *(Ameen).* God has endowed him with a Trust and he is to answer for his deeds before God. The Quran syas :

God doth command you
To render back your Trusts
To those whom they are due; *(IV.58)*

In the above verse, the word 'trusts' has a general meaning; it includes all kinds of responsibilities, be they related to one's duty towards God or to one's duty towards fellow human beings. The Holy Prophet has regarded trustworthiness as the basis of faith. He says: 'He who is not capable of trustworthiness, does not have faith'. Another Tradition says: 'The first thing that you will loose from your religion is trustworthiness, and the last thing that you will loose is prayers *(namaz).* Some people will go on saying prayers but religion will not be with them.

(4) *Responsibility of Care-Taking:* Every individual should feel his own responsibility and also the responsibility of others. He should extend whatever kind of help is needed by others, be it moral or material. He should extent this help as a matter of his duty. The Quran says:

O ye who believe!
Save yourself and your
Families from Fire. *(LXVI-6)*

At another place the fulfilment of the needs of God's creature has been described as the giving of a beautiful loan to God Himself :

Who is he
that will loan to God
A beautiful loan, which God
Will double unto his credit
And multiply many times? *(II - 245)*

> *The Holy Prophet once said: 'Listen! everyone of you is the caretaker of others, and everyone will be asked about his responsibility towards those who are under his care.* (Bukhari, *Kitabul Istiqraz) The word* Raai *means: 'Guarding the other person according to his Good'* (Baizawi) *hence Raai is: 'anyone who is the guardian of somebody else'* (AlMunjid). *At another place, it has been said: 'The creatures are the children of Allah. The person who does good to Allah's children is dearer to Allah!* (Mishkat, *Bab fil Shafqa' alal Khalq)*

The care-taking mentioned above should be carried out in a particular spirit. The Holy Prophet has elucidated it through a parable:

> *Think, there is a ship having many people on board. The provisions for their needs (water etc.) are kept in the upper storey of the ship. Those who are in the lower storey keep coming to the upper storey for, say, water. If the people of the upper storey allow them to have water out of a spirit of camaraderie, everything works well, and no untoward incident happens. But if the people in the upper storey deny water to the people of the lower storey just because it causes a little trouble to them, the people of the lower storey will be forced to adopt some other means for getting water. Suppose they decide to make a hole in the bottom of the ship for getting water, and strt making this hole. Now if the people of the upper storey neithe prevent them from making the hole nor allow them to have water, it is evident that the ship will sink. Then, neither the hole-makers will survive, nor those who ignored their responsibility towards them.* (Bukhari, Mishkat: *Bab Amr bil Ma'ruf)*

In the above Tradition, life is compared to the situation of being on board a ship and the needs of life to water. The spirit of co-operation, which should not be violated in spite of some trouble, is emphasized in a beautiful way. The violation of this spirit in the ship leads to the sinking of the ship and the destruction of all its inmates, be they of the upper storey or of the lower storey. All these elements of the parable have a significant bearing on the understanding of the human situation and the truths of social psychology.

5. *Justice*: Justice implies balance in all spheres of life, so that everything may have its course without transgression limits and along the way of temperance. We have already discussed

Justice. Here we shall reinforce the argument by some quotations from the Quran and the Traditions.

The Quran has prohibited intemperance and excess, and has recommended balance and temperance in every sphere of life :

O People of the Book!
Commit no excesses
In your religion: nor say
Of God aught but the truth *(IV-171)*
Say: 'O People of the Book!
Exceed not in your religion
The bounds (of what is proper),
Tresspassing beyond the truth,
Nor follow the vain desires
Of people who went wrong
In times gone by, —
Who misled
Many, and strayed (themselves)
From the even way *(V- 8)*

The Holy Prophet drew attention to temperance, balance and justice. He said:

Do not be harsh on yourselves, otherwise Allah will be harsh on you. For when the people before you were harsh on themselves Allah was harsh on them. Their remnants are now the priests of the worshipping places of the Christians and the Jews.

Once upon a time, three companions visited the house of the Holy Prophet in order to find out the truth about his private worship and prayers. When they were told about it they thought that the worship and prayers were not very much. But they also thought that the Holy Prophet was already among the saved and they themselves were sinners, so perhaps no comparison could be drawn between them. On that occasion, one of the companions took a vow to keep awake all night in prayer. The other said that he would always keep fast. The third one said that he would not marry. When the Holy Prophet came out of his house and when he was told about their vows, he impressed it upon them that they should not be so harsh to thmselves in matters of religion and that they should adopt a moderate or middle cours:

"Remember I have more of piety than you, but I sometimes fast and sometimes eat, sometimes say prayer and sometimes I sleep and cohabit with women. He who deviates from my Way or Sunnah is not one of mine." (Bukhari, Mishkat, Muslim, Abu Daud, *Kitabul Itisam bil Kitab wal Sunna, Fast I)*

6. *Application :* Application means that one's belief and ideals should be translated into one's actions. It means that one's life should be a continuous enactment of these beliefs and ideals. This virtue takes an individual out of the world of self-delusion and brings him into the world of practical life. It puts this Practical life at the very center of his being. The Quran says:

And say: 'work (righteousness):
Soon will God observe your work,
And his Apostle, and the believers: *(IX-105)*
That man can have nothing
But what he strives for: *(LIII-39)*
...to them
We shall pay (the price of)
their deeds therein *(XI. 15)*

The following Tradition brings out the significance of application and the life of action:

'Suppose there are three workers. One of them works from morning till noon; the other from noon till sometime in the afternoon; and the third from sometime in the afternoon till dusk. The first two get one carat each as wages, and the third gets two carats each. Then the Holy Prophet said that the first two are the Jews and the Christians and the third one is my 'Ummat'; this third category worker has such a great efficiency that in comparatively less time he does the same work to earn double wages.

(Mishkat, *Bab Thawabi Hazihil Ummah)*

Punishment for Evil Deeds Postponed In the Case of the Practical : Efficiency is so important that God postpones the punishment of those who are practical. In their case, immediate punishment for evil deeds would cause disturbance in the system of the Universe and in the dialectical process of its functioning. Shah Waliullah says:

Indeed, Divine justice does not let any sinner remain unpunished in this world, except that it may be done on consideration of causing disturbance in the functioning of the world.*(Hujjatullahil Baligha,* Al Jazai alal Amali fil Dunya).

He goes on to add:

> *Many times it happens that the commandment in consideration of the system of the universe becomes more urgent than the commandment in consideration of individual's deeds. It is for this reason that the evil doer is given a long rope and the righteous person has to face hardships. The hardships serve the purpose of breaking down his selfish desires.* (Ibid).

We See Only One Aspect of Reality : In advanced countires, people are not getting punishment for their evil deeds. It is so because their deeds imply dynamism and practical abilities, which make for the dynamic movement of the universe. It is not that evils are not regarded as evils now, in the modern age, or that they have been transformed into virtues. In fact, we human beings have a limited view, and we see only one aspect of reality, whereas Divine Providence sees the total reality. If we were to see all the aspects of reality, we would not raise doubts regarding the functioning of Divine Providence.

In Western Culture Woman is Licentiously Free : In western culture, the supremacy of man has ended, which has resulted in the disintegration of the unity of the family and given licentious freedom to woman. Behind this kind of freedom, the motive is not so much self-reform as of revenge against man. So in every sphere of life woman is pitted against man, so much so that even in the case of immorality of sexual licentiousness, woman claims equal rights with man. In the personal affairs of a woman the husband or somebody else is not entitled to interfere.

Even marriage is regarded as a restraint because it is supposed to restrict personal freedom and frustrate one's enjoyment. Western civilization does make woman 'equal' to man, and even his rival, but it has failed to fill up the "vacuum that woman has left behind her in that particular sphere which was specifically her own. Thus, a vacuum has been created in family life and is increasing day by day and causing all kinds of trouble.

What happened was this that the wrong concept of religion and morality kept woman deprived of her natural right for a long time, and now the licentious freedom and feminine revolt that we see is actually a reaction of the age-old suppression of woman's natural right. Thus, in the present situation both man and woman are uneasy. But things have gone so far that people are helpless to put any check. If somebody dares to do so he is called conservative, which implies the greatest stigma of our time.

Superiority of Man in the Scheme of Cultural Reconstruction : In the scheme of cultural reconstruction, the superiority of man is maintained. Woman has been given her due position and the sphere of her activity has been determined and defined. She can contribute to civilization only by remaining within this natural spheres of hers. In this regard, the following considerations are involved: (1) The nature of sexual relations; (2) The safeguarding of sexual relations; (3) The limits of the activities of woman.

(1) *The Nature of Sexual Relations* : The relation between man and woman is one of pairing and of mutual assimilation. The Quran has pointed this out but has not ascribed it specifically to human beings; it is the general pattern in all living things.

And of everything
We have created pairs;
That ye may receive
Instructions. *(LI-49)*

Glory to God, Who created
In pairs all things that
The earth produces, as well as
their own (human) kind
And (other) things of which
They have no knowledge. *(XXXVI- 36)*

... He has made
For you pairs
From among yourselves,
And pairs among cattle. *(XLII-11)*

The male-female relation is made firm through wedding. The purpose of sexual relation is not the timely appeasement of sexual desire. This relation is made firm so as to form a basis for the whole life. It ensures the well-wedding and survival of both the sexes. The Quran says:

Wed them with the leave
Of their owners, and give them
Their dowers, according to what
Is reasonable: they should be
Chaste, not lustful, nor taking
Paramours *(IV-25)*
They are your garments
And ye are their garments *(II-187)*

The Holy Prophet says: 'The whole world is a means of your benefit, and the best means of benefit is a virtuous wife. Another Tradition says: 'He who has the capability of wedding should wed; for wedding safeguards the eyes (against sinful glances and the private parts). Wedding promotes the spirit of love and sacrifice between the husband and the wife. It provides solace among hardships:

It is He Who created
You from a single person,
And made his mate
Of like nature, in order
That he might dwell with her
(in Love). *(VII-189)*
... He created
For you mates from among
Yourselves, that ye may
Dwell in tranquility with them,
And He has put love
And mercy between your (hearts):
Verily in that our Signs are for those
Who reflect. *(XXX - 21)*

The Holy Prophet said: 'You should not have seen two lovers like those who are joined in wedding lock' *(Mishkat,* Kitabun Nikah, Fast III). At another occasion he said:

> *Next to piety there is nothing more beneficial for a believer than a virtuous wife. If he commands her, she obeys; if he looks at her, she becomes happy; if he swears by her, he has got to fulfil his word; if she is not there, he wishes well for himself and for her goods.* *(Ibid.)*

Marriage and Society

Marriage forms the basis of the institution of the family and acts as a safeguard against promiscuity and the sowing of wild oats. The Quran says:

It is He Who has
Created man from water:
Then has He established
Relationship of lineage
And marriage: *(XXV - 54)*
Your wives are
As a tilth unto you
So approach your tilth
When or how you will;
But do some good act
For your souls beforehand; *(II - 223)*

The point of the comparison of the wife to a tilth is that sexual relation is meant, not merely for the purpose of satisfying sexual desire, but for the purpose of ensuring the survival of the human race. As the cultivator has the responsibility of not merely sowing the seed but also of providing what the land needs and of protecting it, so has the husband similar responsibilities towards his wife.

Role of Man in Family

It is natural for man to be the head of the family. Owing to the natural differences between the two sexes, man is more disposed to being active and tough while woman is more disposed to be passive and soft. Besides, man shoulders the responsibility of earning livelihood for the family. The Quran says:

Men are the protectors
And maintainers of women,
Beacuse God has given
The one more (strength)
Than the other, and because
They support them
From their means. (IV - 34)

The Holy Prophet said:

Man is the care-taker of his wife and children. In this matter he is answerable to God.

(Bukhari, Kitabun Nikah).

Benefits to Women

The recognition of the superiority of man makes no difference to the rights of woman, nor does it make man entitled to greater rewards for good deeds and virtuous behaviour. "Women have rights on men just as men have rights o women', says the Quran. At another place it is said: 'Men will earn their rewards according to their deeds, and women will earn their rewards according to theirs'. (IV - 32)

Purity of Mind and Heart : Islam has confined sexual relations to matrimonial life, and has commanded us to have hearts and minds purified of lustful desires as far as possible. For this purpose, it has emphasized the notion of answerability to God, which is an effective means of maintaining chastity. Thus, the Quran says:

Whether
Ye show what is in your minds
Or conceal it, God
Calleth you to account for it. *(II - 284)*
Say: 'Whether ye hide
What is in your hearts
Or reveal it,
God knows it all. (III - 29)

Seeing the Right

Men are forbidden to stare at women brazenly, for such stares stimulate erotic feelings:

Say to the believing men
That they should lower
Their gaze and guard
Their modesty: that will make
Far greater purity for them:
And God is well-acquainted

With all that they do.
And say to the believing women
That they should lower
Their gaze and guard
Their modesty; (XXIV - 30)

Women have been commanded to exercise control over their speech and voice, for these things too may stimulate erotic feelings.

If ye do fear (God),
Be not too complaisant
Of speech, lest one
In whose heart is
A disease should be moved
With desire: but speak ye
A speech (that is) just. (XXXIII - 32)

Scandal-Mongering and Immodest Talk Prohibited : Indulging in scandals and immodest talk has been prohibited:

Those who love (to see)
Scandal published broadcast
Among the Believers, will have
A grievous Penalty in this life
And in the Hereafter (XXIV - 19)

Exhibition of Beauty and Immodest Dress Prohibited : Exhibition of beauty has been prohibited because it stimulates erotic feelings — 'make not a dazzling display, like that of the former Times of Ignorance (XXXIII - 33). Tight and thin or transparent dress has also been forbidden, for it also involves exhibition of the body. Women 'should draw their veils over their bosoms' (XXIV - 31). The Holy Prophet said:

'The women who exhibit their bodies even after dressing up and thus try to attract others to themselves or to be attracted towards others; and the women who walk mincingly with their neck bent like that of a camel — such women will not enter paradise, nor will they catch even its fragrance'.

(Muslim, Babul Nisa Al Kasiyatul' Aariyat).

Coming out wearing some perfume is also prohibited. The Holy Prophet said:

'The woman who passes by people wearing perfumes so that they may be pleased is in fact a woman who is inviting immorality. *(Nisai, Abu Daud)*

Prohibition Against Meeting of Man and Woman in Privacy : The meeting of man and woman in privacy has been prohibited because it would give an opportunity for Satan to do his work. Do not seek to meet those women in privacy who are not your close relations, for Satan circulates in man like blood *(Muslim,* Kitabul Libas wal Zinah)

Scope of Women's Activities

If woman is allowed licentious freedom and if she is allowed to take part in every kind of activity (lawful or unlawful), it is going to disturb the institution of the family and the proper relations between the sexes. This is why in the scheme of cultural reconstruction the activities of woman are subject to real needs and the permission of her husband. Bertrand Russel gives two reasons for the social evils of western civilization: the emancipation of woman and the device of birth control. But the real reason is the lack of social control, which has created many subsidiary reasons also. Social control is a way of controling the minds and action of the individuals. Various efforts were made to achieve this social control, but these efforts have not met with any success.

The Best Means of Social Control is Religion : The best means of social control is religion, and this is the means used in the Islamic scheme of cultural reconstruction. Religion has the following bearings on human life:

(1) It induces the fear of God and the idea of answerability to God, which controls human actions and thoughts.

(2) Religion helps man to exercise control over his thoughts and feelings, which makes balanced in individual life on the one hand for social stability and solidarity on the other.

(3) It makes for peace of the soul and for the reform of inward and outward life.

(4) It determines the standard for sexual morality and social character and sets up a watch on human relations.

(5) The noble principles of religion make for the control of social evils and protect society against anti-social elements.

The above features of religion have been recognised in every age. All Sociologists affirm the constructive role played by religion in human history. Even Bertrand Russel admits that the fear of hell-fire and of pregnancy were the two factors that guaranteed the preservation of the modesty of woman in the past. Now that the influence of religion has declined and anti-pregnancy devices have emerged both these restricting factors have disappeared and the situation has become what it is.

Possibility of Change in the Sphere of Woman's Activity : The sphere in which woman can play her role and the sphere in which she cannot are matters related to the permission of the husband and the real needs of the community. It is obvious that these determining factors are subject to change in accordance with the change of the circumstances. However, two things must be considered before a particular task is delegated to woman. First, it should be seen that no disturbance is created in the status of woman and in the family institution. Secondly, the laws related to both these subjects should be respected. With these precautionary measures it is not necessary that the woman should cover her face or hands when she comes out to work. The Quran says:

... that they
Should not display their
Beauty and ornaments except
What (must ordinarily) appear
Therein. (XXIV -31)

'Except what (must ordinarily) appear therein' has been interpreted in various ways by exegetes. Here we quote a preferable interpretation. This has been reported by Aisha:

Once the daughter of Abu Bakr, Asma came before the Holy Prophet wearing a thin dress. The Holy Prophet turned away and said: 'when a woman comes of age it is not proper that any part of her body except the hands and the face becomes visible *(Abu Daud)*

Walking out is of less importance as compared to the face and the body. Perhaps for this reason it has not been mentioned separately. But if a society is corrupt and if the modesty of woman is in danger when she comes out, special precaution is needed. This is testified by the following Verse:

O Prophet! tell
Thy wives and daughters,
And the believing women,
That they should cast

Their outer garments over
Their persons (when abroad):
That is most convenient,
That they should be known
(as such) and not molested (XXXIII - 59)

'that they should be known (as such) and not molested' testifies to the consideration of the circumstances and the change in the law accordingly. Certainly Traditions indicate that before the days of the Holy Prophet and even in later times in Arab society there was the custom of covering the face. We need not go into details here. But the reader can refer to the following works for his own benefit: (*Alminar* by Rashid Raza Misri, Vol. X, Chapter 11 and Vol. xiii., Chapters 9-10-11; *Hijabul Maratul Mussallema Fil Kitabe Wal Sunna* by Mohammad Nasiruddin Al Yani (Cairo and Beirut).

Societal Setup

Western Culture could not Provide a Firm Basis for Society *:* The basis of social life is the family. The condition of the family determines the social system. In western culture, the disruption of the family, the invention of new philosophies and the lust for money have precluded the formation of a firm basis for social life. Consequently, life has become mechanical; every person feels himself or herself lonely and uprooted; and even the daughter of a millionaire has to work for her living by doing an ordinary job, for her father abandons the responsibility of supporting her.

Relation of Man with Allah

In the Islamic scheme of cultural reconstruction, the basis of social system is the family. The family is the unit of social system and a miniature society. Just as affection, rights and duties are organizing princiles of the family, in the same way they are organizing principles of the society as a whole, which is conceived as a larger family or the family of God. The members of this larger family are brothers and sisters to one another. Thus, the Holy Prophet said:

> *"All creatures make the family of God. God loves him more who treats His family folks well". Another Tradition says: 'All human beings are brothers (and sisters) to one another'.* (Muslim, Abu Daud).

In order to understand a social system, knowledge of three things is needed. They are: the nature of the family, the nature of human life, and the duties of man in life.

Family Attributes

A. *God has created all human beings from a single pairof common parents:*

O mankind! We created

You from a single (pair)

Of a male and a female, *(XLIX - 13)*

The Holy Prophet aid: 'All human beings are the children of Adam, and Adam was created out of clay'.
(Tabri)

B. *All men are sinless and holy by birth. The Quran speaks of "God's handiwork according to the pattern on which He has made mankind" (XXX - 30). The Holy Prophet says that 'every child is born according to the original pattern of nature'. According to this original pattern, every man is sinless and Holy.*

C. *Human beings are superior to other creatures:*

We have honoured the sons

Of Adam *(XVII - 70)*

We have indeed created man

In the best of moulds, *(XCV - 4)*

There is a Hadith-i-Qudsi which says:

The creature (man) whom I have created with my own Hands and breathed of my Spirit unto him — I shall never put him on a par with those creatures for whom I merely said: 'Be' and they came into being.

(Mishkat, *Bab Badil Khalq)*

D. All human beings have been addressed by the Word of God (revelation)

... and to every people

A guide *(XIII - 7)*

And there never was

A people, without a warner

Having lived among them

(in the past) *(XXXV 24)*

E. *God has provided equal opportunities for all.*

'God has created all that is there on the earth for the benefit of all of you', says the Quran. The Holy Prophet says:

'Except three things man does not have a right on anything else: (1) A house to live in; (2) Garments to cover the body and (3) Water and pieces of bread.'

Life of Man

(A) *The Lord of life is, not man, but God*

God hath purchased all the Believers

Their persons and Their goods (IX-111)

(B) *Life is not a futile activity; it is trust*

Did ye think
That We had created you
In jest, and that ye
Would not be brought back
To Us (for account)? (XXIII - 115)

(C) *Life is not absolutely independent or free; there are certain laws governing it.*

Does Man think
That he will be left
Uncontrolled, (without purpose)? *(LXXV - 36)*

Man has two kinds of duties in life: (1) duties related to the universe and (2) duties related to man.

Duties Related to the Universe

(A) It means making use of human faculties to deploy the things of the universe for man's use:

It is We Who have
Blessed you with authority
On earth, and provided
You therein with means
For the fulfilment of your life *(VII - 10)*

Say: work (righteousness):
Soon will God observe your work,
And His Apostle, and the Believers. *(IX - 105)*

(B) *The means of subsistence should be developed so much that nobody may remain deprived of his living:*

And We have provided therein

Means of subsistence, — for you
And for those for whose subsistence
Ye are not responsible (XV - 20)
It is He Who has
Spread out the earth
For (His creatures). (LV—10)

(C) *Through labour and striving man should develop the things of nature:*

That man can have nothing
But what he strives for (LIII - 39)
... to them
We shall pay (the prize
Of) their deed therein (XI - 15)

The means of human power keep changing according to circumstances. For example, in modern times we have weapons like the rifles, the missiles, the machine gun, the tank etc. and then we have technology, industry, modern trade and commerce, journalism, literature and modern arts and science. All these things go to make up modern civilized life.

The Centrality of God in Matters of Duties : In matters of duties towards the universe and in all affairs of human activity, God should have a central place, and subordination to him should be recognised. Otherwise dreadful consequences may follow and such dreadful consequences can be seen in the materialistic civilization of our times. This is why in those verses of the Quran where attention is drawn towards the order of the Universe and man is encouraged to subject the universe to himself God has been mentioned or suggested in some way. This indicates that for man's activity in the Universe God has a central place and man must subject himself to him. Only then, his reason and experience can guide him properly and further instruction may not be necessary.

Men's Responsibilities

It must be recognised that all human beings are involved with one another, so that if one human being is unjustly killed, it is as if the whole people were killed, and if one human being has been saved from destruction, it is as if the whole human race were saved from destruction. The Quran says that if anyone slew a person:

It would be as if
He slew the whole people:
And if anyone saved a life,
It would be as if he saved
The life of the whole people. *(V - 35)*

Every individual must be deemed responsible for taking care of the other. This care-taking may be material as well as moral and spiritual. The individual will specialise in that sphere of responsibility with which he is more conversant.

Matter in Life

Regarding material responsibility the Quran says:

Serve God and join not
Any partners with Him,
And do good—
To parents, kinsfolk,
Orphans, those in need,
Neighbours who are near,
Neighbours who are strangers,
Companions by your side,
The wayfarer (ye meet),
And what your right hands possess *(IV.36)*
And render to the kindred
Their due rights, as (also)
To those in want,
And to the wayfarer:
But squander not (your wealth)
In the manner of a spendthrift. *(XVII.26)*

As regards subordinates and juniors the Holy Prophet says:

They are your brothers. Allah has made them subordinate or junior to you. He to whom makes his brother subordinate must give him to eat what he himself eats, give him to wear what he himself wears, and must not have assign him any work which he himself cannot do, or if he assigns him such a work he must himself help him, as a co-worker. *(Bukhari, Kitabul Iman).*

Special commandment is given regarding treatment towards women:

On the contrary live with them
On a footing of kindness and equality.
If ye take a dislike to them
It may be that ye dislike
A thing, and God brings about
Through it a great deal of good. *(IV. 19)*
Let the man or means
spend according
To his means:
And the man
Whose resources are restricted,
Let him spend according
To what God has given him. *(LXV - 7)*

In his sermon on the occasion of his last Hajj, the Holy Prophet said:

In your dealings with women fear God. You have made a convenant with them that God has a witnss.
(Muslim; Mishkat, *Bab Hajjatul Wida)*

Regarding treatment with human beings, in general, the Holy Prophet said: 'He who is engaged to fulfil the need of his brother, his need, Allah is engaged to fulfil.' At another place he said: 'The human creature does not become a complete Believer until he chooses for his brother what he chooses for himself.'

Regarding moral and spiritual duties the Quran says:

O ye who believe!
Save yourselves and your
Families from a Fire
Whose fuel is men
And Stone. *(LXVI-6)*
Help ye one another
In righteousness and piety. *(V-3)*

The Holy Prophet said: 'Listen everyone of you is a care-taker or a shephered; and everyone of you will be asked about his care-taking of those who are put under his care'.
(Bukliari, Kitabun Nikah)

Giving Priority to the Needs of Others Over One's Own Needs : One must always give priority to the needs of others over one's own needs. The Quran says:

By no means shall ye
Attain righteousness unless
Ye give (freely) of that
Which ye love. *(III-92)*

What has been recognised as the greatest virtue of the Helpers (Ansars) is the spirit f sacrifice. Attention is drawn to it in the following Verse of the Quran. It is said that the helpers

Give them (refugees) preference
Over themselves, even though
Poverty was their (own lot). *(LIX-9)*

Commandment to Overlook the Defects of Others : One must meet out good treatment of others in spite of their defects, shortcomings and wrongs.

The Quran says:

Let not those among you
Who are endued with grace
And amplitude of means
Resolve by oath against helping
Their kinsmen, those in want,
And those who have left
Their homes in God's cause,
Let them forgive and overlook;
Do you not wish
That God should forgive you?
For God is Oft-Forgiving,
Most merciful. *(XXIV-22)*

The historical context of the revelation of this Verse is as follows.

Some people made a false accusation against Aisha. Among them were some relations of Abu Bakr, whom Abu Bakr supported financially. After the innocence of Aisha had been established Abu Bakr felt bad about the relations whom he supported. He took an oath not to support them. Seeing him do it other companions also did the same regarding their relations. In the context of this situation, the above Verse was revealed. It says that the bad deeds of others are for them. You must not change your good behaviour towards them. The reward is with God; always have hope of getting it from Him and pleasing Him.

Things Necessary for the Maintenance of Social System : The following things are Necessary for the maintenance of the social system:

(1) The standard of honour should be such as to encompass all the people and to be equaly applicable to all of them.

(2) The idols of the distinction of race, family colour and nationality should be broken down.

(3) There should be equality and amity regarding human relations on the level of practical life.

These factors have been given great attention in the Islamic scheme of cultural reconstruction. Some details in this regard would bring them home.

Respect as Prescribed

Instead of the family, wealth, race etc., the standard of honour is character and moral behaviour. This standard can be acquired voluntarily and it is also acceptable to all human beings. The Quran says:

verily ...verily
The most honoured of you
In the sight of God
Is (He who is) the most
Righteous of you. *(XLIX-13)*

The Holy Prophet said: 'One person earns excellence over the other only on the basis of righteousness and piety'. (Mishkat, *fi Shoabil Iman)*

It is very difficult to demolish the idols of race, family etc. Various efforts to do so were made in every age, but without leading to much success. But the Prophet of Islam (peace be upon him) adopted such devices in domestic and social life that people, both of inferior and superior status, began to feel that these man-made distinction of "high" and "low" had no validity. Islam first campaigned for the reform and purification of the minds and then it declared that the distinctions mentioned above were invalid and insignificant.

And made you into
Nations and tribes, that

Ye may know each other

(not that ye may despise each other). *(XLIX-13)*

The Holy prophet said:

No Arab excels over a non-Arab, nor does a non-Arab excel over an Arab.

(Mishkat, *Khutba Hajjatul Wida')*

About colour and language the Quran says: 'And among the signs of God are the creation of the heavens and the earth and the differences of language and colour.

The above distinctions emerge more prominently in matters of marriage, and involve many complexities and subtleties. For this reason, the Holy Prophet and his Companions began the charity at home and broke the idols of these distinctions. The Holy Prophet got his cousin Zainab married to a freed slave, Zaid b. Harisa. Omar got married his son Asim to a milk-seller's widowed daughter. Both these evidences are famous in Islamic history. After reforming his own home Omar gave verdict in favour of marriage without the consent of the guardians, which is called 'marriage without sufficient conditions' *(Ghair Kafu)*. The following incident bears it out. A rich man Mawali, who was one of the freed slaves, sent a proposal for marrying the sister of a Quraish. The Quraish refused saying: 'We are people of a high family. The man does not suffice for my daughter. When Omar came to know of it he sent for the Quraish and said that the man was well to do as well as righteous. If his sister was willing he should wed her to him. The Quraish asked his sister and she expressed her willingness, and the wedding was performed. *(Siyasat—i—Farooq-i-Azam,* Izalatul Khifa, Maqsad II)

Jurists have discussed at length *Kafu* or sufficient conditions for marriage, but in modern times it need not be a subject of discussion. The discussion of the jurists is guided by considerations of compromise with the circumstances. It is not a verdict of the Shariah. The subject came up for discussion after the time of the Holy Prophet and his Companions and stirred up great controversy among the jurists. Among the conditions considered sufficient for marriage are bravery, good family, vocation, financial status, age and religion (moral character). But except religion all the other requisites are subject to controversy. The fact that all the jurists agree on the point of religion and disagree on all other points itself goes to prove that only religion is the condition laid down by the Shariah. The other requisites or conditions are there only for making matrimonial life comfortable. In modern time the other requisite 'sufficiency' obstruction to marriage and become a blot which is an Islamic culture. Hence in our scheme of cultural reconstruction we would consider religion *plus* social status as sufficient conditions for marriage, which were considered so in the era of Prophethood, too. In our scheme education and the ability of earning livelihood should become more important since these are the demands of our time. These factors certainly go to make matrimonial life comfortable.

Quality Relations among Men

The equality and amity in human relations has been emphasised by Islam. This is brought out by an incident in the life of the Holy Prophet. Once the Holy Prophet was talking to the Jews of Mecca on Islam. On that occasion a ragged, blind man (Ibn-i-Umme Maktum) came in and expressed his desire to know something. The Holy Prophet did not like this interruption. At this the following Verse was revealed:

(The Prophet) frowned
and turned away
Because there came to him
The blind man (interrupting).
But what could tell thee
But that purchance he might
Grow (in spiritual understanding)?—
Or that he might receive
Admonition, and the teaching
Might profit him?
As to one who regards
Himself as self-sufficient,
To him dost thou attend;
Though it is no blame
To thee if he grow not
(in spiritual understanding).
But as to him who came
To thee striving earnestly,
And with fear
(In his heart),
Of him wast thou unmindful *(LXXX-1-10)*

Humanity and Equality

When there is slight corruption in society, ordinary reforms will do, but when the corruption is so deep that it seeps into the very fibres of a community strict measures are required and 'high' and 'low' have got to be inverted.

Once Sohail b. Amr, Haris b. Hissham, Abu Sufiah and other dignitaries of the Quraish came to Omar. At the same time Sohaib, Bilal and other freed slaves also came. Omar gave priority to these slaves in giving an audience. At this Abu Sufiah angrily said: 'I never saw such an outrage. These slaves get permission for audience (to the Caliph) and we keep standing at the door, and no attention is paid to us'. Sohail was more, he said: 'it is true; but we should complain, not against Umar, but against ourselves. Islam called equally to all, with one voice. Those of us who lagged behind out of their own negligence deserve to remain behind even today.*(Usudul Ghaba,* Vol. III, Tazkira Sohail b. Amr)

It has been commanded that one should purge in oneself those elements that would cause disturbance in the social order. The Arabic word for purgation or purification is *tazkiya*. Etymologically, it means cleansing something so as to make it capable of growth or development. The *tazkiya* of land means purifying it of weeds, levelling it, manuring, and irrigating it in order to make it capable of growing seeds. In the same way, the *tazkiya* of the self should mean purifying it of evil motives of thought and action in order to make man capable of moral and spiritual growth in accordance with the original, God-made, pattern of his nature. *Tazkiya* of the self has its analogue in medicine. Just as medicine deals with the diseases of the body and their purgation or cure, in the same way *tazkiya* deals with the diseases of the soul and their purgation or cure. *Tazkiya* is needed in all spheres of life, and thus the main mission of the Prophet of Islam (peace be upon him) was *tazkiya*. Many Verses of Quran speak of it and words like *yuzakkikum* or *yuzakkihim* occur at many places. But here we are concerned with the purification of those motives and tendencies which cause disorder in social relations. In the Islamic scheme, there are commandments for their purification. We give some examples below:

Prohibition against Riducule Slander etc. : Riduculing somebody, slandering him, taunting and calling him by bad nicknames, conceiving and propagating evil notions about him, picking up his faults, backbiting him or prying into his secrets—all such things are prohibited in Islam. The Quran says:

O ye who believe!
Let not some men
Among you laugh at others:
It may be that
The (latter) are better
Than the (former):
Nor let some women
Laugh at others:
it may be that
The (latter) are better
Than the (former):
Nor defame nor be
Sarcastic to each other,
Nor call each other
By (offensive) nicknames...
O ye who believe!
Avoid suspicion as much
(As possible): for suspicion
In some cases is a sin:
And spy not on each other,
Nor speak ill of each other
Behind their backs. Would any
Of you like to eat
The flesh of his dead
Brother? Nay, ye would
Abhor it... But fear God: *(XLIX 11-12)*

Prohibition Against Rejoicing at Another's Degradation etc.:

Islam prohibits rejoicing at another person's degradation and debasement. The Holy Prophet says: 'Do not rejoice at the degradation and debasement of your brother. Allah will take mercy on him and make you suffer in his place'.
(Tirmidhi, Mishkat, Hifzullisan, Fasl II)

Making somebody ashamed at his wrong or sin is also prohibited. The Holy Prophet says: 'The man who makes somebody ashamed of the sin he has repented, he will be involved in that sin himself before death comes to him'. *(Ibid)* Behaving as a tell-tale is prohibited. The Quran says:

and heed not...

A slanderar, going about

With calumnies *(LXVIII-2)*

Tradition says:

'Those who behave as tell-tales create mischief among friends'. (Musnad-i-Ahmad, *p. 459)*

Breaking of Engagements, Duplicity and Violation of the Bonds of Kinship Prohibited.

Breaking of engagement is prohibited. The Quran says:

For (every) engagement

Will be enquired into

(On the Day of Reckoning). *(VII-34)*

The Holy Prophet has regarded the breaking of engagement as a sign of hypocrisy. He condemns the man who makes some engagement or promise nd then breaks it and does the opposite. (Bukhari, Muslim)

Duplicity is also prohibited. A Tradition says: 'On the Day of Judgment the Double dealer will be in the worst plight—he is the man who shows one face to some person and another face to other person. (Bukhari, *Kitabul Adab). Another Tradition says: 'He who is a double dealer in this world, his tongue will be of fire on the Day of Judgment.* (Abu Daud, *Kitabul Adab)*

Violating the bond of kinship and showing inconsiderateness to kinsfolk has been prohibited.

The people who do it have been regarded as mischief-makers by the Quran:

Those who break God's covenant

After it is ratified,

And who sunder

What God has ordered to be joined,

And do mischief on earth:

These cause loss (only) to themselves. *(II-27)*

Evil Traits Disallowed

Pride was first manifested by Satan when he said:

... 'I am better

Than he' (Adam) (VII-12)

Pride hardens the heart or seals it up and insulates it

Thus doth God seal up

Every heart— of arrogant

And obstinate transgressors. (XL-35)

Pride deprives man of God's love. The Quran says:

For god loveth not

The arrogant, the vainglorious: *(IV-36)*

Pride or arrogance shuts the doors upon courtesies, which doors are actually the means to enter paradise. The Holy Prophet says: 'He who has a single atom of pride in his heart he will not enter paradise'.

(Abu Daud, *Kitabul Libas)*

Jealousy is the source of all social evils and it is something very dangerous. God has commanded the Holy Prophet and every Muslim to seek refuge with God from jealously—'I seek refuge'

From mischief

Of the envious one

As he practises envy. *(CXIII-5)*

The Holy Prophet says:

Beware of jealousy and avoid it, for jealousy eats the virtues just as fire eats wood. (Abu Daud Kitabul Adab, Bab Fil Hasad)

False accusation, that is, imputing some evil to the other person, which is not there in him, is condemnable (even if the evil is there in him talking about it is backbiting). The Quran says:

And if anyone earns

Sin, he earns it against

His own soul; *(IV-111)*

And those who annoy

Believing men and women

Undeservedly, bear (On themsleves)

A calumny and a glaring sin. *(XXXIII-58)*

Moral Life

Working oneself into anger or getting enraged has been condemned by Islam. Those who overcome their anger are regarded as pious ones by the Quran. Those 'who restrain anger' (III. 134) are the righteous ones according to the Quran. They are those who forgive even 'when they are angry'. (XLII. 37). The Holy Prophet said: 'The heroic warrior is not one who flings down the other person, but one who controls himself in anger'. (Bukhari, *Kitabul Adab, Babul Hazr Minal Ghazab). Another Tradition says: 'Anger is from Satan, and Satan is made of fire. The fire is killed down and extinguished by water, therefore, he who gets anger must perform ablution.'* (Abu Daud, *Kitabul Adab)*

Malice and rancour are condemned because they hamper the fulfilment of one's duties towards God's creatures, just as joining partners with God hampers the fulfilment of one's duties towards God. We are commanded to pray to God for freedom from malice:

And leave not, in our hearts,

Rancour (or sense of injury)

Against those who have believed *(LIX-10)*

The Holy Prophet says: 'Do not have rancour and malice against one another; do not be jealous of one another; live like brothers and sisters'. *(Bukhari, Muslim)*

Regarding showing off and exultation it is said:

And be not like those

Who started from their homes

Insolently and to be seen of men. *(VIII-47)*

And how many populations

We destroyed, which existed

In their life (of ease and plenty); *(XXVIII - 58)*

Use of abusive and obscene language, whether charged with sexuality or rage, has been strictly prohibited.

Let there be no obscenity,
Nor wickedness,
nor wrangling
In the Hajj. *(II-197)*

The Holy Prophet said: 'It is a sacrilege to speak ill against a Muslim, and to murder him is infidelity'. *(Bukhari,* Kitabul Adab). In this regard, another Tradition says: 'A Believer never indulges in taunts and slanders, ill language and obscenity'. *(Tirmidhi Abwabul* Birri wal Sila). In fact any behaviour, gesture, speech or action that creates disturbance in social life has been strictly prohibited.

Some Commandments Regarding Eating and Drinking, Dress etc. : In the Islamic scheme of cultural reconstruction, the social order has been given so much importance that etiquettes have been laid down in respect of eating and drinking, dress and appearance. Obviously, the purpose is to prevent the social evils that arise from bad form. With regard to eating and drinking the following commandments have been given:

1. You must eat with your right hand.
2. You must have an attitude of reverence towards food.
3. You must eat sitting. (If you eat standing, or if you sit on some high place and put your food on some low place, it is against the Islamic way of life.
4. Eat only as much as to cause no indigestion.
5. You must not eat unlawful things or things about which you have doubts as to their lawfulness.

Similarly, there are commandments regarding dress and appearance. For example:

1. You must not imitate or try to resemble any particular community in matters of dress and appearance.
2. It must not be the dress and appearance of those who are proud or indecent.
3. Silken dresses are forbidden for men.
4. The dress must not be such that it does not cover your shame— the parts that decency demands to be covered— or such as is likely to stimulate erotic feelings.
5. Women must be specially careful to maintain modesty in their dress and appearance.

One must take care of two things in matters of spending money and goods:

1. There must be no extravagance, both in terms of appropriateness and quantity of the expenditure.
2. The purpose of the expenditure must not be show-off or impressing the people of poor means with your wealth and position. This is no occasion for going into the details of the subject which has been discussed at length in various books dealing with the Islamic way of life.

Chapter 3

Message of Islam

In order to appreciate the true value of the ethical system of the Arabian Prophet, it must be remembered that, in Islam, the service of man and the good of humanity constitute pre-eminently the service and worship of God Faith without work has no meaning; "this life is but a tillage (mazraa) for the next," and therefore we are told repeatedly, "do good that you may reap there." The mere recognition of a creed or formula does not constitute Islam. It is "a life to be lived in the present." "Dost thou desire to approach thy Lord, a righteously for,-the crooked path never leads to Him." It is pointed out in the language of poetry that man partakes of the nature of the beast as well as of the angel; an he is adjured to leave the nature of the beast, that he may surpass the angel. Striving for the good, the true and the pure is inculcated in the most emphatic terms, "for striving is the ordinance of God, and whatever God has ordained can only be attained by striving."

Moral Values

The ethical code of Islam is thus summarised in the fourth Sura of the Quran:

> *"Come, I will rehearse what your Lord hath enjoined on you,-that ye assign not to Him a partner, that ye be good to your parents; and that ye slay not your children because of poverty: for them and for you will We provide; and that ye come not near to pollution, outward and inward, and that ye slay not a soul whom God hath forbidden, unless by right... and draw not nigh to the wealth of the orphan, save so as to better it... and when ye pronounce judgement then be just, though it be the affair of*

> *a kinsman. And God's compact fulfil ye, that is, what He hath ordained to you. Verily, this is my right way; follow it then."*

And again, "Blessed are they who believe and humbly offer their thanksgiving to their Lord... who are constant in their charity, and who guard their chastity, and who observe their trust and convenants..... Verily, God bids you do justice and good, and give to kindred their due; and He forbids you to sin and to do wrong and oppress."

"Who speaketh better than he who inviteth unto God, and worketh good .... good and evil shall not be held equal. Turn away evil with that which is better."

Again, speaking of Paradise, it says, "it is prepared for the godly, who give alms in prosperity and adversity; who bridle their anger and forgive men; for God loveth the beneficent."

History has preserved, for the admiration of posterity, many examples of patience under suffering exhibited by the followers of other creeds. But the practice of the virtues of patient forgiveness is easier in adversity, when we have no power to punish the evil-doer, than in prosperity.

It is related of Hussain, the grandson of the Prophet, that a slave having once thrown the contents of a scalding dish over him as he sat at dinner, fell on his knees and repeated the verse of the Quran. "Paradise is for those who bridle their anger." "I am not angry," answered Hussain. The slave proceeded, "and for those who forgive men." "I forgive you." The slave, however, finished the verse adding, "for God loveth the beneficent." "I give you your liberty and four hundred pieces of silver," replied Hussain.

The author of the Kashaf thus sums up the Islamic teachings: "Seek again him who drives you away; give to him who takes away from you; pardon him who injures you: for God loveth that you should cast into the depth of your souls the roots of his perfections."

Positive vs Negative

The return of good for evil is preached on all occasions:

> *"Think only of what is good for each, and consider not the wrong that has been done to thee: pardon others readily, and do good unto all. Fair is the dwelling-place of those who have bridled their anger and forgiven their adversaries. Return good for evil."*

To the humble denizen of the earth, "with his mouth in the dust," comes the message from Him to lift up the stricken soul.

"By the noonday brightness, and by the night when it darkeneth, thy Lord hath not forsaken thee, neither hath He been displeased. Surely the future shall be better for thee than the past; and in the end He shall be bounteous to thee, and thou shalt be satisfied Did He not find thee an orphan, and give thee a home; erring and guided thee; goody and enriched thee? As to the orphan, then, wrong him not; and chide not away him that asketh of thee, and tell abroad the favours of thy Lord." "Did ye think we had Made you for sport, and that ye should not be brought back again to us?" .

To the errant sinners, turning with a true penitence to their Creator and crying out to Him,—'O our Lord, punish us not if we forget and fall into sin, blot out our sins, and forgive us,' is conveyed the promise of mercy and forgiveness:—"Come back, come back, whatever thou art, come back; hast thou denied Me or worshipped another for Me, or broken My commandments, come back. This Threshold of Mine is not the threshold of despair. If thou hast forgot thyself, turn with true penitence and come back."

It has been truly said that "the moral idea of the new gospel was set in the common sense of duty and the familiar instances of love."

"Blessed is he who giveth away his substance that he may became pure, and who offereth not favours to any one for the sake of recompense ... but only as seeking to approach the Lord Most High."

"They are the blest who, though longing for it themselves, bestowed their food on the poor and the orphan and the captive (saying), we feed you for the sake of God: we seek from you neither recompense nor thanks."

"Worship God alone; be kind to kindred and servants, orphans and the poor; speak righteously to men, pray, and pay alms."

"Defer humbly to your parents; with humility and tenderness say, 'O Lord, be merciful to them, even as they brought me up when I was helpless.'"

"Abandon the old barbarities, blood-vengeance, and child-murder, and be united as one flesh."

"Do thy alms openly or in secret, for both are well."

"Give of that which hath been given you before the day cometh when there shall be no trafficking, nor friendship, nor interception."

"Wouldst thou be taught the steep path? It is to ransom the captive, to feed the hungry, the kindred, the orphan, and him whose mouth is in the dust. Be of those who enjoin steadfastness and compassion on others."

"Woe to them that make a show of piety, and refuse help to the needy."

"Make not your alms void by reproaches or injury." "Forgiveness and kind speech are better than favours with annoyance." "Abandon usury." "He who spendeth his substance to be seen of men, is like a rock with thin soil over it, whereon the rain falleth and leaveth it hard. But they who expend their substance to please God and establish their souls, are like a garden on a hill, on which the rain falleth and it Yieldeth its fruit twofold; and even if the rain doth not fall, yet is there a dew."

"Judge between men with truth and follow not thy passions, lest they cause thee to err from the way of God." "Covet not another's gifts from God." "There is no piety in turning the face east or west, but in believing in God only and doing good." "Make the best of all things; enjoin justice and avoid the foolish; and if Satan stir thee to evil, take refuge in God." "Touch not the goods of the orphan." "Perform your covenant, and walk not proudly on the earth."

"The birth of a daughter brings dark shadows on a man's face... Kill not your children for fear of want: for them and for you will We provide. Verily, the killing them is a great wickedness." "God hath given you wives that ye may put love and tenderness between you."

"Commit not adultery; for it is a foul thing and an evil way."

"Know ye that this world's life is a cheat; the multiplying of riches and children is like the plants that spring up after rain, rejoicing the husbandmen, then turn yellow and wither away. In the next life is severe chastisement, or else pardon from God and his peace." "Abandon wickedness and the very semblance of it. They, verily whose only acquirement is iniquity, shall be rewarded for what they shall have gained ... .. Those who abstain from vanities and the indulgence of their passions, give alms, offer prayers, and tend well their trusts and their covenants, these shall be the heirs of eternal happiness." "Show kindness to your parents, whether one or both of them attain to old age with thee: and say not to them, 'Fie!' Neither reproach them, but speak to them both with respectful speech and tender affection." "And to him who is of kin render his due, and also to the poor and to die wayfarer, yet waste not wastefully"

"And let not thy hand be tied up to thy neck; nor yet open it with all openness, lest thou set thee down in rebuke in beggary."

"Enjoin my servants to speak in kindly sort." "Turn aside evil with that which is better." "Just balances will We set up for the day of resurrection, neither shall any soul be wronged in ought, though were a work but the weight of a grain of a mustard seed, We would bring it forth to be weighed: and our reckoning will suffice." "Seek pardon of your Lord and beturned unto Him: Verily, my Lord is merciful and loving." "And your Lord saith, 'Call upon Me, I will hearken unto you.'" "Say, 'O my servants who have transgressed to your own injury, despair not of God's mercy, for all sins doth God forgive. Gracious and merciful is He.'" "The good word riseth up to Him, and the righteous deed will He exalt." "Truly my Lord hath forbidden filthy actions, whether open or secret, and iniquity, and unjust violence."

"Call upon your Lord with lowliness and in secret, for He loveth not transgressors, and commit not disorders on the well-ordered earth after it hath been well ordered; and call on Him with fear and longing desire: verily, the mercy of God is nigh unto the righteous."

"Moreover, We have enjoined on man to show kindness to his parents. With pain his mother beareth him; with pain she bringeth him forth: and he saith, 'O my Lord! Stir me up·to be grateful for Thy favours wherewith Thou hast favoured me and my parents, and to do good works which shall please Thee; and prosper me in my offspring: for to Thee am I turned, and am resigned to Thy will." "For them is a dwelling of peace with their Lord; and in recompense for their works shall He be their protector." "Lost are they who, in their ignorance, have foolishly slain their children, and have forbidden what God hath given them for food, devising an untruth against God! Now have they erred; and they were not rightly guided." "The likeness of those who expend their wealth for the cause of God, is that of a grain of corn which produceth seven ears, and in each ear a hundred grains; they who expend their wealth for the cause of God, and never follow what they have laid out with reproaches or harm, shall have their reward with their Lord; nor fear shall come upon them, neither shall they be put to grief; .... a kind speech and forgiveness is better than alms followed by injury."

"God will not burden any soul beyond its power. It shall enjoy the good which it hath acquired, and shall bear the evil for the acquirement of which it laboured.".

"O Lord punish us not if we forget or fall into sin, O our Lord! and lay not on us a load like that which Thou hast laid on those who have been before us, O our Lord! and lay not on us that for which we have not strength: but blot out our sins and forgive us and have pity on us."

"The patient and the truthful the lowly and the charitable, and they who seek pardon at each daybreak:"... "Who give alms, alike in prosperity and in success, and who master their anger, and forgive others! God loveth the doers of good;" [Theirs a goodly home with their Lord]. "O our Lord! forgive us then our sins and hide away from us our evil deeds, and cause us to die with the righteous:" "And their Lord answereth them, 'I will not suffer the work of him among you that worketh, whether of male or female, to be lost, the one of you is the issue of the other.'" "And fear ye God, in whose name ye ask mutual favours, and reverence your mothers-at their feet is paradise."

"Covet not the gifts by which God hath raised some of you above others." "Be good to parents, and to kindred, and to orphans, and to the poor, and to a neighbour, whether kinsman or new-comer, and to a fellow-traveller, and to the wayfarer, and to the slaves whom your right hands hold; verily, God loveth not the proud, the vain boaster."

"He who shall mediate between men for a good purpose shall be the gainer by it. But he who shall mediate with an evil mediation shall reap the fruit of it. And God keepeth watch over everything."

"O ye Muslims! stand fast to justice, when ye bear witness before God, though it be against yourselves, or your parents, or your kindred, whether the party be rich or poor. God is nearer than you to both. Therefore follow not passion, lest ye swerve from truth."

The Brotherhood

Brotherly love and mutual assistance are inculcated in emphatic terms:

> *"Muslims are brothers in religion; and they must not oppress one another, nor abandon assisting each other, nor hold one another in contempt. The seat of righteousness is the heart; therefore, that heart, which is righteous, does not hold a Muslim in contempt; and it is wicked to hold a Muslim in contempt; and all things of one Muslim are unlawful to another, his blood, property and reputation; he must not act or speak that by which the blood of a Muslim might be spilt, and his property destroyed, and his reputation lost." "The people for Paradise are three; the first, a just king, a doer of good to his people, endowed with virtue; the second, an affectionate man, of a tender heart to relations and others; the third, a virtuous man."*

Duties of Musalmans to Each Other

Again, "The duties of Musalmans to each other are six." It was asked: "What are they O Prophet?"

He said, "When you meet a Musalman, salam to him; and when he invites you to dinner, accept it; and when he asks for advice, give it to him; and when he is sick, visit him; and when he dies, follow his bier."

But help to the suffering and the weak is not preached in an exclusive spirit, nor is it confined to Muslims, for it is declared incumbent to assist every oppressed person, whether Muslim or not. "Verily, God will say, at the Day or Resurrection, 'O sons of Adam I was sick, and ye did not visit Me,' and the sons of Adam will say, 'O our Protector how could we visit thee? for thou art Lord of the universe, and art free from sickness.' And God will say, 'O men! Did you not know that such a one of My servants was sick, and ye did not visit him? Did you not know that had you visited that servant, you would have met with favour and pleasure near Me?' And God will say, at the Resurrection, "O sons of Adam, I asked you for food, and Ye gave Me not?' And the sons of Adam will say, 'O our Lord, how could we give thee food, seeing thou art the Cherisher of the universe and art free from hunger and sating?' And God will say, 'Do not ye know that such a one of My servants asked you for bread, and you did not give 'it him? Did you know that had you given him victuals, you would have received its reward from Me.' And God will say at the Resurrection, "O sons of Adam! I asked you for water, and ye gave Me not.' They will say, 'O our Cherisher! How could we give thee water, seeing thou art the Cherisher of the universe, and not subject to thirst!' God will say, 'Such an one of My servants asked you for water, and you did not give it him: did you not know that had you given to him, you would have received its reward from Me?'"

Help of the Poor

"That person who asks, in the name of God, protection from harm by you, or from any one else, then give him protection; and that person who asks a thing from you in the name of God, then give it to him, and that person who invites you to eat, approve of and accept his invitation, and that person who does you a good and benefit, then return it, that is, do a good act to him; but if you have nothing to return him, then pray for him, till you know that you have atoned to him and performed your duty to him."

"Do not say, 'if people do good to us, we will do good to them; and if people oppress us, we will oppress them': say, on the contrary, if they oppress you, you will not oppress them."

Sympathy with Others

"Whoever is kind to His creatures, God is kind to him; therefore be kind to man on the earth, whether he be good or bad; and being kind to the bad, is to withhold them from badness, so that those who are in heaven may be kind to you."

"Strive always to excel in virtue and truth." "Help each other with generosity and piety. He who helps his fellow brethren and tries to do them good, will receive his reward from the Almighty equal to the reward of those who strive to repress wrong-doing."

"All God's creatures are His family; and he is the most beloved of God who tries to do most good God's creatures."

"The best of men is he from whom good accrues to humanity."

"He who tries to remove the wants of his brother, whether he be successful or not, God will forgive his sins."

"He who helps his brother will himself be helped on the Day of Account."

"The Prophet was asked who was the most favoured of God's creatures. He replied, 'He from whom the greatest good comes to His creatures' And then he was asked what actions are most excellent. He answered, "to gladden the heart of a human being, to feed the hungry, to help the afflicted, to lighten the sorrows of the sorrowful, and to remove the wrongs of the injured.' 'He who helps his fellow creature in the hour of need and he who helps the oppressed, God will help him in the Day of Travail.'"

"Thus saith your Lord, 'whilst living, rely on Me for I am all sufficient; do not be avaricious or covet the goods of your brethren; love for them what you love for yourself, guard yourselves from anger, passion and greed, for these are the worst of actions.'"

"He who is subservient to his passions and desires, and forgets in their pursuits his duty to others, is the worst and weakest of God's creatures." "Be persistent in good actions."

"To gladden the heart of the weary, to remove the suffering of the afflicted has its own reward. In the day of trouble, the memory of the action comes like the rush of a torrent and takes away our burden."

"No man is true in the truest sense of the word, but he who is true in word,- in deed and in thought."

"He is true who protects his brother both present and absent."

"Fidelity and truth, purity and gentleness, generosity and sweetness are the best of qualities in man."

A few of the aphorisms of the first Imam, selected at random from the Ghurrar-wad-Durrar, will throw light on the teachings of the Mosque in the days of the Republic.

"He who is most dutiful to those to whom he owes duty In the wisest among you."... "He who is the most learned in the best conducted and behaved in his life. He is the most intelligent is the most virtuous"... "No evil is worse than avarice." "To be kind is one of the best of virtues; to tell falsehood one of the worst of vices. He who fulfils his word is one of the noblest of God's creations." "A bad temper is the worst of afflictions." "To keep free from pollutions is the best of worship. To void evil actions in the best of actions."

"He who sees his own faults is the wisest of men. He who considers himself wiser than others, is the most foolish."

"The worship of God, without gratitude to man, is watering the sand of the desert."

"Fidelity is the beacon which lights the way to heaven."

"Learning is of no value without work; precept of no avail without practice."

"To be forbearing to the faults of your fellow-brethren is an act of charity."

"When you speak, speak the truth; when you attain to power, gently and beneficently with those subordinate to you. When you fall into affliction, be patient; when you have to inflict a punishment, be merciful. When you commit a fault, ask pardon. When you are placed in the seat of justice, be just. When you commit sin, be ashamed. When you see the oppressed, render help."

"Be grateful to those who benefit you. Humility increases your worth. Remembrance of God brings down His mercy."

"He who imparts learning never dies."

"Do not look at the person who speaks, but look at what he speak."

"For the envious, there is no peace. Where there is spite, there can be no true friendship."

"The untruthful knows no modesty."

"No provision [for the next world] is better than piety or doing good actions in this world."

"A man who is the slave of his passions, is the worst of all slaves; and no man has a greater enemy than his own selfishness."

"No action is good unless, the intention is good; nor any word pure unless accompanied by pure action."

"No evil is greater than evil propensities."

"Avarice kills truth."

"Knowledge is the best of blessings."

"Purity of heart is the essence of all virtues."

"Ignorance is the worst of all poverty."

"Kindness and courtesy are better than conferring an obligation."

"To overlook the faults of others is better than alms-giving."

"To forgive when it is in your power to avenge an injury, to love when you are wronged, are the best of virtues."

"Hypocrisy is the destruction of piety; to impose an obligation is destructive of charity; selfishness is destructive of wisdom."

"The good you do alone goes with you into the next world." "Good acts are the steps which take ye to God."

"The peace of the two worlds is a commentary on two words,-love for friends, charity towards enemies."

"On the tablet of my heart I have engraved from the sayings of my father, may his memory be sacred to eternity,—'My child, should you be in the company of one who is fallen, do not be impertinent and do not view him with the eyes of contempt; if, in this world, you cannot make a heart glad, yet act not so as to make the humblest soul sorrowful,'"

"O thou who hast experienced happiness and trouble from good and bad events, and who art in consequence full of thanks, and sometimes of complaints! Do not take high ground, that thy efforts be not vain; be rather like grass, that stands in the way of the wind, or like a bundle of grass, which others carry off on their shoulders."

Tenderness for Children and Respect for Age

Tenderness and affection for children and respect for age are emphatically inculcated. "He is not of us, who is not affectionate to his little ones, and does not respect the reputation of the old; and he is not of us, who does not order that which is lawful, and prohibit that which is unlawful."

"Every young person who honours the old, on account of their age, may God appoint those, in his years, to honour him." "Whoever puts his hand upon the head of an orphan, from kindness, shall have the blessings of God, for every hair his hand shall have covered; and whoever does good to a boy or girl, being orphans, he and I shall be near each other in paradise." "Whoever gives an orphan a dwelling, meat and drink, God will bestow him a place in paradise and forgive his sins."

"He who is not affectionate to God's creation, and to his own children, God will not be affectionate to him."

Sympathy with the Suffering : Sympathy with suffering and tenderness to the woe-stricken and lonely are taught as the highest duties.

"God is merciful to those who are merciful to His creatures."

"Pardon the sins of others that you may be pardoned. If you seek for mercy, be pitiful to the sufferings of mankind."

"He who is kind to an orphan will receive God's blessing on the Day of Account.".

"Verily a man's children are God's gifts."

"He who is merciful to others will himself receive mercy; he who has pity for other's wrongs will himself be pitied by the Lord of the Universe."

"He who does not forgive, will not be forgiven himself."

"'O my servants,' says the Almighty, 'if you seek My mercy, be merciful to My creatures.'"

"They will enter the abode of bliss who have a true, pure and merciful heart."

"The best of alms-giving is that which springs from the heart, and is uttered by the lips to soften the wounds of the injured."

"Modesty and chastity are parts of the Faith."

"He who is modest and chaste, nobody should find fault with him!'

"True modesty is the source of all virtues."

"Humility and courtesy are acts of piety."

"Forgive others, incite all to do good and abstain from wickedness."

"Avoid evil-doers and vain speakers and those who speak falsely."

"God loves those who suppress their anger when angry, and forgive people, and do what is right, and act piously and purely."

"The patient, the forbearing and those who forgive the faults of others, having the power to punish, will receive the reward from their Lord."

"Thus saith your Lord, 'Verily those who are patient in adversity and forgive wrongs are the doers of excellence.'"

"The faithful are those who perform their trust and fail not in their word and keep their pledge."

Last Messenger

"He is not of me but a rebel at heart who, when he speaks, speaks falsely; who, when he promises, breaks his promises; and who, when trust is reposed in him, fails in his trust."

Meanness and slander, hypocrisy and untruthfulness are denounced.

"I heard the Prophet say," says one of the traditionists, "'it is better to sit alone than in company with the bad; and it is better to sit with the good than alone; and it is better to speak words to a seeker of knowledge than to remain silent; and silence is better than bad words. I advise you to be righteous to God, because it will adorn you in every work, withhold yourself from seeing the vices of mankind, and from giving them utterance.'"

Self-abnegation and patience are laid down as supreme duties:

> *"Love is the abnegation of self for another; Divine love is complete self-absorption in the service of God's creatures for His pleasure."*

"Patience is the recognition of God's will in the wrongs of life. Thankfulness is the overflowing of the heart with the fullness of His mercy. Acquiescence (raza) is the acceptance with thankfulness of God's will."

"He that is patient and thankful, loving and gentle to God's creatures, and returns good for evil, and subdues his passion, and forgets his own self for others-will receive a great reward in that he will approach his Lord."

The Persian moralist Saadi speaks of the virtue of patience in these terms:

> *"A great river is not made turbid by a stone; the religious man who takes to heart an injury is as yet but shallow water. If any misfortune be falleth you, bear with it, that, by forgiving, others, you may yourself obtain pardon. O my brother! seeing that we are at last to return to earth, let us humble ourselves in ashes before we are changed into dust."*

Fidelity and truth are most impressively inculcate:

> *"When you speak, speak the truth; perform when you promise; discharge your trust; commit not fornication; be chaste; have no impure desires; withhold your hands from striking, and from taking that which is unlawful*

> *and bad. The best of God's servants are those who when seen, remind of God; and the worst of God's servants are those who carry tales about, to do mischief and separate friends, and seek for the defects of the good."*

Family love and affection are recommended as highly meritorious:

> *"Verily there are some of God's servants, who are neither Prophets nor Martyrs, who will emulate Prophets and Martyrs on the day of Resurrection on account of their high eminence near God. They are a family loving each other, for God's favour, befriending each other to please God and to obtain His love."*

The attainment of God's love is inculcated in the following words which the Almighty addresses to mankind:

> *"Whoever seeks to approach Me by that which I have given as My divine commands, is most loved by Me, and My servant is always seeking to approach Me by holiness; so that I love him: therefore, when I hold him as a friend, I am his hearing by which he hears, and I am his sight by which he sees, and I am his hand by which he holds, and I am his feet by which he walks; if this servant supplicates Me, verily I give unto him; and, if he seeks protection with Me from harm and ills, I give him protection."*

Humanity to Living Creatures : It is laid down repeatedly that not only does God reward good done to human beings, but to all living creatures.

"A woman who had sinned was passing by a dog which was holding out its tongue from thirst, and was near to dying. The woman drew off her boot and tied it to the end of her garment, and drew water for the dog, and gave it to drink; the Lord forgave her sin." The Prophet was asked, "Verily are there rewards for our doing good to quadrupeds, and giving them water to drink?" He said, "there are rewards for benefiting every living creature."

A man once came to him with a bundle and said: "O Prophet, I passed through a wood and heard the voices of the young of birds, and I took them up and put them into my carpet, and their mother came fluttering round my head." And the Prophet said: "put them down;" and when he had put them down, the mother joined the young. And the Prophet said: "Do you wonder at the affection of the mother towards her young? I swear by Him who has sent me, verily, God is more loving to His servants than the mother to these young birds. Return them to the place from which ye took them, and let their mother be with them." "Fear God with regard to animals," used he to say; "ride them when they are fit to be ridden, and get off when they are tired. Verily, there are rewards for our doing good to dumb animals, and giving them water to drink."

Charity : The Prophet's definition of charity embraced the wide circle of kindness: "Every good act," he would say, "is charity. Your smiling in your brother's face is charity; an exhortation addressed to your fellow-men to do virtuous deeds is equal to alms-giving. Putting a wanderer in the right path is charity; assisting the blind is charity; removing stones and thorns and other obstructions from the road is charity; giving water to the thirsty is charity."

"A man's true wealth hereafter is the good he does in this world to his fellow-men. When he dies, people will ask, What property has he left behind him? But the angels who examine him in the grave, will ask, What good deeds hast thou sent before thee?"

He would often tell his disciples, "Do not think any good act done to you contemptible; and I advise you, that you speak to your brother with an open countenance, because that is of the number of good acts and kindnesses. And if a man abuse you, and lay open a vice which he knows in you, then do not disclose one which you know in him, so that there may be no fault but on him."

Charity to Kindred : Charity to one's kindred is placed in the first rank.

"Giving alms to the poor has the reward of one benefaction, but that given to kindred has two rewards; one, the reward of charity, the other the reward for relationship."

The following anecdote will show the value attached to family obligations and the merit of benefactions to one's children-A man came to the Prophet and said, "I have got one dinar." He said, "Expend it upon yourself." The man said, "I have got another dinar." The Prophet said, "Expend that upon your children." The man said, "I have got another dinar." He said, "Expend that upon your wife and your parents and poor relations." He said, "I have got one other dinar." The Prophet said, "Expend that upon your servants." The man said, "I have got another dinar." "You know best the person most worthy of it; and whoever you know to be so, give it to him."

"Whatever we give" says the author of the *Akhlaq-i-Jelali*, "should be given in the fullness of zeal and goodwill, and never be the least regretted either in word or thought. For it would be the height of folly, when God, from the treasure-house of his bounty, has given a fortune to one of his servants, subject to the expenditure in a particular manner of an insignificant fraction, for him to consider the condition as burdensome to discharge. We should spend it simply to please God, and not mix up the act with any meaner motive, lest thereby it be rendered null and void.

We should bestow what we give on such as make a secret of their poverty; we should give in secret: or the ostentation of repute is folly. We find it among the Ahadith:—(the traditions of the Prophet) 'Charity that is concealed appeaseth the wrath of God.' And, again, 'The best of alms is that which the light hand giveth and the left knows not of.' From the Prophet we also have it, that when the just and holy God created the earth, it trembled and could not rest; whereupon He created the mountains to keep it still. At this the angels marvelled and inquired whether any created thing were stronger than a mountain? He told them, yes, fire. Again, they asked whether any thing were stronger than fire? He told them, yes, water. Any thing stronger than water? Yes, wind. Any thing stronger than wind? Yes, alms concealed, which the son of Adam giveth, so that the right band gives, and the left knows it not. Of this the influence is greatest of any; for it averteth the scourge that is ready to fall."

In the battle of life men and women have always felt the need of help from a Power above and beyond themselves whose love is boundless and universal. Is not the human soul better and purer for seeking the help of its Maker in the trials of life? The following prayer shows the value attached in Islam to the outpouring of the human soul to the Giver of all good:

> *"We have reached the night, and so have all other inhabitants of God's empire. Praised be God, one to whom there is no partner; for Him is dominion and praise, and He is powerful over all things. O God ! I supplicate Thee for the good of this night, and for every good that is in it; and I seek protection with Thee, from the evils of this night, and from every evil that may be in it. O Lord ! Verily, I seek protection with Thee from sickness, from age and pride; and from the contentions and calamities of the world and from the punishment of the grave. O Lord ! I have resigned my soul to Thy commands and turned to Thee. I have made over my work to Thee, and relied on Thee, and sought protection in Thee, to show my love to Thee; and for fearing Thee, there is no asylum or redemption from Thy resentment but in Thee."*

"O Lord ! Pardon my faults, and the works which I may have done through ignorance; and forgive my lavishing away, and pardon my sins, which Thou knowest better than me. O Lord I Pardon me my inconsiderate speaking, and blundering; and forgive my wicked labours and intentions and all these are my characteristics. O Lord! Pardon me the faults which I have done before, and shall do after, and those which I have discovered and concealed; and those which Thou knowest better than me. Thou art the first and the last, and powerful over everything."

"O Lord ! Make me a thanks-giver to Thee, and a repeater of Thy name, and a fearer of thee, and a great obeyer of Thee, and a great humbler of myself before Thee, and complainer and repenter to Thee. O Lord! Accept my repentance and wash away my sins and approve my supplications; and strengthen my proofs, and make my tongue true; and show my heart the straight road; and remove away the wicked inclinations of my heart."

A learned critic has called the virtues of Islam, "stoical" The expression was used in an invidious sense, but if patience, forbearance, charity, truth, purity and magnanimity were the distinguishing characteristics of Stoics, I am prepared to admit that the ethical duties of Islam are stoical. In the Akhlak, magnanimity is defined thus:

> *"That the soul take no note of honour or disrepute, pay no regard to affluence or adversity, but remain entirely unaffected by praise or censure, by wealth or want; from the mutations of human affairs admitting neither alteration nor transition, nor impression, nor influence: a spiritual eminence whose heights are only attainable to the most advanced on the paths of research; whose submits are not to be contemplated, but by the choicest of the accomplished."*

"He is a man," says the Allamah Abul Fazl, "of high understanding and noble aspirations, who, without the help of others, recognises a ray of the divine power in the smallest things of the world; who shapes his inward and outward character accordingly, and shows due respect to himself and to others. True greatness, in spiritual and in worldly matters, does not shrink from the minute of business, but regards their performance as an act of divine worship."

"Every man of sense and understanding knows that the best way of worshipping God is in allaying the distress of the times, and in improving the condition of man."

"Have the religions of the worldly tendencies of mankind no common ground? Is there not everywhere the same enrapturing beauty which beams forth from so many thousand hidden places? Broad indeed is the carpet which God has spread, and beautiful the colours which he has given it."

Humility

At the same time men are taught to be humble.

"O men! be humble and lowly. He who guards his tongue from detraction, God will conceal his vices; and he who suppresses his anger, God will withhold His punishments from him; and he who asks pardon of God, God will accept his supplication."

"Whatever jewels thou wearest on thy brow, only humility can give them their lustre. To that talisman paradise opens its gate, and to it opens the heart of man. Dear to all hearts is he whom lowliness exalts; his bending is the graceful droop of the branch laden with fruit."

Dignity of Labour

The dignity of labour preached in emphatic terms.

"There is a tradition from the Prophet," says Tirmidhi, "that a man of the Ansar came to him begging for some help; and the Prophet said,' Have you nothing at home?' He said, Yes, there is a large carpet, with one part of which I cover myself, and spread the other, and there is a wooden cup out of which I drink water.'

The Prophet said,' Bring me the carpet and the cup.' And the man brought them, and the Prophet took them in his hands and said, who will buy them?' A man said, 'I will take them at one dirham.' 'He said, 'Who will give more?' This be repeated twice or thrice. Another man said,' I will take them for two dirhams.' Then the Prophet gave the carpet and cup to that man, and took the two dirhams, which he gave to the Ansar and said, 'Buy food with one of these dirhams and give it to your family, that they make it their sustenance for a few days; and buy a hatchet with the other dirham and bring it to me.' And the man brought it; and the Prophet put a handle to it with his own hands, and then said,' Go, cut wood and sell it; and let me not see you for fifteen days.'

Then the man went cutting wood and selling it: and he came to the Prophet, when verily, he had got ten dirhams; and he bought a garment with part of them, and food with part. Them the Prophet said, "This cutting and selling of wood, and making your livelihood by it, is better for these than begging."

Idleness Reprehended

Idleness is reprehended "God is gracious to him who earns his living by his own labour and not by begging."

"He who is able and fit and does not work for himself or for others, God is not gracious to him.'

"He who works for his own living and does not beg, when he can earn, is one of God's favoured creatures."

"He who neither works for himself nor for others, will not receive the reward of God."

"Pray to God morning and evening and employ the day in your avocations."

The Charge of obscurantism can hardly be laid against Islam, when it is considered how eloquently the Founder recommended the acquisition of knowledge to his followers:

Price of Knowledge

"Acquire knowledge," he used to say, "because he who acquires it in the way of the Lord performs an act of piety; who speaks of it, praises the Lord; who seeks it, adores God; who dispenses instruction in it, bestows alms; and who imparts it to its fitting objects, performs an act of devotion to God.

Knowledge enables its possessor to distinguish what is forbidden from what is not; it lights the way to-Heaven; it is our friend in the desert, our society in solitude, our companion when bereft of friends; it guides us to happiness, it sustains us in misery-, it is our ornament in the company of friends; it serves as an armour against our enemies. With knowledge, the servant of God rises to the heights of goodness and to a noble position, associates with sovereigns in this world, and attains to the perfection of happiness in the next."

"The ink of the scholar is more holy than the blood of the martyr."

"He who leaves his home in search of knowledge, walks in the path of God."

"He who travels in search of knowledge, to him God shows the way to paradise."

"One hour's meditation on the work of the Creator [in a devout spirit] is better than seventy years' prayer."

"To listen to the instruction of science and learning for one hour is more meritorious than attending the funerals of a thousand martyrs,- more meritorious than standing up in prayer for a thousand nights."

"To the student who goes forth in quest of knowledge, God will allot a high place in the mansions of bliss; every step he takes is blessed, and every lesson he receives has its retard. The seeker of knowledge will be greeted in heaven with a welcome from the angels. To listen to the words of the learned, and to instil into the heart the lessons of science, is better than religious exercises .... better than emancipating a hundred slaves. Him, who favours learning and the learned, God will favour in the next world."

"He who honours the learned, honours me."

"Eminence in science is the highest of honours. He dies not who gives life to learning. The greatest ornament of a man is erudition."

"The world is darkness; knowledge is light; but knowledge without truth is a mere shadow."

Man's responsibility was laid down in explicit terms.

"Whosoever gets to himself a sin, gets it solely at his -own responsibility."

"And let alone those who make a sport and mockery of their religion, and whom this present world has deluded, and thereby bring to remembrance that the soul perishes of what it has got to itself, and when they commit a deed of shame they say: 'We have found that our fathers did so, and God obliges us to do it:' say thou: 'Surely, God requireth not shameful doing;... they did injustice to themselves; yonder will every soul experience that which it hath bargained for;'. . . so then, whosoever is directed, it is solely a matter pertaining to himself-, and whosoever goes astray, he himself bears the whole responsibility of his wanderings."

In the purity of its aspirations can anything be more beautiful than the following:

> *"The servants of the Merciful are they that walk upon the earth softly, and when the ignorant speak unto them, they reply 'Peace !' They that spend the light worshipping their Lord prostrate and standing and resting, those that, when they spend are neither profuse nor niggardly, but take a middle course ... those that invoke not with God any other God and slay not a soul that God hath forbidden otherwise than by right, and commit not fornication . . they who bear not witness to that which is false; and when they pass by vain sport, they pass it by with dignity, who say' Oh, our Lord, grant us of our wives and children such as shall be a comfort unto us, and make us examples unto the pious,-these shall be the rewarded, for that they persevered; and they shall, be accosted in paradise with welcome and salutation:-For ever therein,-a fair abode and resting-place !"*

Chapter 4

Islamic Brotherhood

A Conspicuous Period

The Meccan period is conspicuous for persecution of his Companions. The weaker among the Muslims were the main target. Abu Bakr used to purchase the Persecuted slaves and set them free. Bilal the first Muezzin of Islam, a venerated African Muslim, was one of these freed slaves, who used to be spoken of by Umar, as "our master." We are told that one of the usual complaints of the Quraish, against the Prophet (PBUH) was that he "insults our religion and mocks our way of life." They approached his uncle Abu Talib and wanted him, "to stop him or you must let us get at him, for, you yourself are in the same position as we are in opposition to him and we will rid you of him." Things had reached the stage where the Quraish had decided to kill the Prophet (PBUH) and thus save their cherished 'Way of Life'. They were afraid that if he continued propagating the New Way of Life, which Islam offered, then their own religion and their cherished way of life would vanish. They were the established leaders of the existing Way of Life which was followed by the whole of Arabia. It gave them social, economic and religious prerogatives and preferences which would be no more, if their way of life disappeared. As opposed to their way of life, Islam, brought in equality of men and treated the free citizen and a slave on equal footing, in all fields, social, cultural and economic. Their established customs, rules, prerogatives of certain sections and even the philosophy of life on which their way of life was based, were all at stake. They had to do something to save their vested interests.

They made one more effort at conciliation but on their peculiar terms. They took a young man of martial bearing, and offered him for adoption by Abu Talib. In return they wanted Muhammad (PBUH) to be killed at the altar of one of their gods. They argued that they were giving to Abu Talib a young man of excellent physique, who would be an asset to him in all respects. In exchange they were asking Abu Talib for a man who "has severed the unity of your people and mocked our way of life. Either you must stop him or let us get at him."

If the question is examined a little more in detail it becomes clear that the objection of the Meccans was not that a new religion was being introduced in their society or they were afraid of sectarian disturbances. This could not be the reason. They, already, had people who belonged to various religions and they were all living peacefully. The Arabs did not take religion very seriously. They were tolerant of all modes of worship, as long as religion was a matter of personal views and did not disturb the existing social structure. There were in Mecca, at that time, Christians, Jews, Sabians and the Quraish had excellent relations with them. There was a picture of Jesus Christ inside Kaaba itself. It appears that the Quraish were like the Brahmins of India, who were ever-ready to accept under the umbrella of their spiritual leadership any and every mode of worship as long as they were accepted as the supreme religious and spiritual authority.

Their objection to Islam resembled the criticism of Nehru and Gandhi of India, who maintained that the basis of Millah had to be geographical loyalties and not ideological commitments. This objection stemmed from the fundamental belief of Islam in the Sovereignty of Allah. Allah being the sole Sovereign in the universe, He was to be obeyed above all other forces and persons. In practice, it means the supremacy of the Law given by Allah through His Prophets. Those who accepted this Divine Law formed ONE UMMAH to the exclusion of others. This Law included the principle of equality of mankind. Allah has created mankind as equals. Therefore, there should be no difference between an Arab and an Ajami or between a ruler and the ruled. Equality of men and brotherhood within Islam were principles, which had been highly abhorrent to the Jews, the Quraish and the Brahmins alike. Abu Talib, a soft spoken person, was able to postpone the final rift between Quraish and himself.

He called Muhammad (PBUH) one day and having told him what the Quraish had wanted, he said to him, "Do not put a burden on me greater than I can bear."

The Prophet (PBUH) thought that his uncle wanted to aandon hm and he would lose his support and protection completely. He reflected for a moment and replied, "O my uncle, by Allah, if they put the sun in my right hand ad the moon in my left hand, on condition that I abandon this course, until Allah has made me victorious, or I perish therein, I will not abandon it."

The realisatin, that those who were entering the brotherhood of Islam were a people apart, was mutual. He knew that he was creating a new Millah which would follow its own Way of Life known as Islam and, therefore, he and his Millah will be opposed by any and every people that they came in contact with. He realised the intensity of struggle that lay before him. He was, in view of this, prepared to be completely wiped out. He believed in the Sovereignty of Allah, and that His Will was supreme in the Universe and He had said, that he, Muhammad, had been appointed by Him to bring mankind out of darkness of unequality and iniquity into light:

> *"He it is Who sendeth down clear revelations unto His slave, that he may brig you forth from darkness unto light, and lo! for you Allah is Full of Pity, Merciful."*
>
> *(57: 9)*

Allah would not have dlegated such high responsibilities to him if the eventual salvation, through Islam, was not the scheme of things. He was confident of his success with the permission and help of Allah. His whole life was a witness to it. His prayer to his Lord, at the time of Badr was:

> *"O Allah if this little group of Believers is wiped out today there will be none left to obey Your Commands (live according to the Way of Life given by you) until the Day of Judgement."*

His answer to his uncle, Abu Talib, and his prayer to his Lord, Almighty Alla, are symbolic of the Truth that he stood by. He was the Last Prophet. Islam was the final Way of Life based on the Last Revelations. If, therefore, he, and his Companions, the few that were there, were wiped out in the life and death struggle, then there would have been none left to obey and worship Allah as Dictatd by Him in the final Message, He was sendig through Muhammad (PBUH). He was, therefore, confident that Allah would make him victorious. This confidence in the Truth of his Mission and in Him Who had assigned to him.

This Mission is evident troughout the period of the struggle. The other important point uppermost from the beginning wasto organize all those who embraced Islam into a separate Millah, in relation to the rest of the world. These two points, the struggle to the last i.e. the fight unto martyrdom and Believers being an Ummah by themselves, form two most important objectives o the Prophet (PBUH). Islam has held the" uppermost position whenever these two Sunnahs of the Prophet (PBUH), both based on logical explanation of Quranic Verses, have been observed by Muslims".

The Meccans did not give up their opposition because Abu Talib had not withdrawn his support of the Prophet (PBU). "When the Quraish became distressed by the enmity between them and the Prophet (PBUH).. .they stirred up against him folish men who called him a liar, insulted him and accused him of being a poet, a sorcerer, a diviner, and of being possessed...they said that they had never known anything like the trouble they had endured from him, he had declared their mode of life foolish, insulted their forefathers, reviled their religion, divided their community, and cursed their gods." Matters reached the stage when due to the constant persecution of his Companions and persistent opposition to himself, he was forced to say, "Will you listen to me O Quraish? By Him Who holds my life in His hands, I bring to you slaughter." One of them replied, "Depart, O Abul Qasim, for by Allah you are not violent." They often consulted one another in connection with finding of the best way to get rid of him. After one such discussion Utbah bin Rabiyah went, on behalf of the leaders of Quraish, to the Prophet (PBUH) and said to him, "O son of my friend, you belong to us, although by insulting our religion, and traditions of our fathers, you have embroiled us, I have come to you to put an end to this great misfortune. Give an ear to my proposals. May be they find a place of grace in your sight." "Speak, I am listening," said the Prophet.

"O son of my friend! If you hope that your undertaking will make you wealthy, each of us is willing to sacrifice a part of his fortune in order that you should become the richest man among us. If you seek honours, we will set you up lord over us all and come to no decision without consulting you. If you dream of royal privileges, we will make you our king. If o the contrary, the thoughts that inspire you arise from some malady which you are powerless to resist, we will fetch, at any cost, from any country, the most celebrated doctors, so that you may be cured. Choose, therefore."

The Prophet (PBUH) had listened unmoved. "Have you finished?" he answered. He then recited the Surah of the Quran, Haameem Al Sajdah XLI. Muhammad (PBUH) after prostrating himself, rose up and turned to Utbah, saying, "You have heard me, O Utbah? Now it is for you to choose." "Utbah bewildered went back to his companions. He told them, "I have just listened to Words. By our gods, I have never heard anything like it before. It is neither poetry, nor sorcery, nor magic.

O Quraish men assembled! believe me and let this man fulfil his Mission among the Arabs, for his words are full of surprising prophesies. If harm comes to him by the fault of Arabs, you will be freed from anxiety. If on the other hand, he succeeds and conquers the Arabs, his empire will be your empire.. .and thanks to him you will attain the highest pinnacle."

As mentioned earlier, a few points are clear. It was understood by the Meccans that Islam was a complete New Way of Life. As a result it created a new Ummah, which due to its peculiar nature, had to have its own separate communal life. The Prophet (PBUH), from the beginning was convinced, in his own mind of the role Islam had to play and that either Allah will make Islam victorious or he himself will perish in the fulfilment of the duty entrusted to him by Allah. As time passed, this state of affairs became gradually more and more clear. They went so far as to say to him, "By Allah, we will not leave you and our treatment of you, until either we destroy you or you destroy us." They had gone to his uncle and failed to win him over to their side. They had tried to bribe him by offering riches, kingship and chieftainship and he had not accepted either wealth, honour or supreme power over Arabs. They had threatened him and had failed to intimidate him. If he had wanted any of these honours, here was a chance to get it among a society which he knew and understood. He was the grandson of a chief who held the leadership of entire Quraish. He would have inherited it.

The incidence of Utbah bin Rabiyah, leaves no doubt that the desire to achieve power and wealt, never passed through his mind. Riches, power and dominance had been offered to him under the existing mode f life which was not unknown or foreign to him. He had turned away from them in youth. He could not have done so in hazy iagination of power which may or may not have been within a mortal's reach. During his whole life, not even during the period of his success when entire Arabia lay at his feet, did any ambitious thought pass his mind. The idea of his having had "day dreams of power and domination," in his young days, is, to say the least, dishonest scholarship.

The leaders of Quraish widened their plan of persecution and pressurization of those who embraced Islam. Their families were told to put pressure on them to abrogate Islam. The slaves were the worse hit. Abu Bakr purchased a few and set them free, including Bilal the first Muezzin of Islam. "A stage arrived when people were afraid that they may be forced to renounce Islam. When the Prophet (PBUH) saw the affliction of his Companions... and that he could not protect them, he said to them, 'If you were to go to Abyssinia it would be better for you, for the king will not tolerate injustice and it is a friendly country, until such time as Allah shall relieve you from distress."

As a result of this a number of Companions, eighty three in number, according to Ibn-e Ishaq, went to Abyssinia. The Meccans did not like their going away. They were afraid that, if Muslim were able to establish themselves, away from Mecca, they will get strong and become a threat to the Quraish. They sent a party after them to stop them from sailing. When they came to know of the sailing of the boat they organised a delegation which among others was composed of Abdullah bin abu Rabiya and Amr ibn al Aas, and sent them to the king of Abyssinia, loaded with presents for the courtiers, generals and the king himself. The emigration to Abyssinia was successful. The king gave them permission to reside in the capital and they settled there. But soon the delegation from Mecca arrived and requested for their extradition. The king asked for the reason and was told that the refuees had left the religion of their forefathers and thereby committed the sin of weakening the religion so dear to the rest of them.

They also told him that the Muslims held adverse views about Jesus Christ. He sent for the Muslims. Jafar Ibn-e Abi Talib went as head of the delegation. He asked him of his views about Jesus Christ. Jafar recited Verses of Surahn Mairyam. The king was impressed by the passage and refused to hand over the Muslims to the delegation. He promised the Muslims protection and a fair and just treatment. This is the first Hijrah of Islam and can be termed as the first instance of a group of people having been provided political asylum by the government of a neighbouring state. The king and his government stood by their promise and the refugees passed their time peacefully as long as they stayed there.

The failure of the delegation at the court of Negus embittered the Quraish more than ever before. The idea of establishing himself out of Mecca but within Arabia seems to have taken root at this time. The chiefs of Banu Thaqeef, inhabiting Taif and the surrounding hills were powerful. He decided to approach them. He went to Taif, but the chiefs there did not listen and instead employed young men to throw stones at him. He received wounds and returned without any success.

On his return to Mecca he found that the intensity of Quraish opposition had increased further. He realised that the only course open to him and his Companions was to find protection with some tribe at a considerable distance from Mecca. We are told that, "The Prophet (PBUH) offered himself to the tribes of Arabs, telling them that he was a Prophet who had been sent (i.e. had not declared Prophethood on his own accord). He used to ask them to believe in him until Allah should make clear to them the Message with which He had charged the Prophet."

Bohaira bin Firas of Banu Aamir bin Sahsaa understood the Prophet (PBUH) and the likely impact of his Message better than others. He is reported to have said, "By Allah, if I could take this man from Quraish I could eat up the Arabs with him." His conception of Allah, however, was limited and although he had visualised the importance of the New Way of Life preached by the Prophet (PBUH), he was limited in his imagination of the life that could lived, by a people who feared Allah and were prepared to sacrifice every thing on the Path of Allah. He asked the Prophet (PBUH), "If we actually give allegiance to you, and Allah gives you victory over your opponents, shall we have authority after you? The Prophet (PBUH) replied, "Authority is a matter which Allah places where He places." Bayhara in his reply showed his lack of bradth of vision and quickly said, "I suppose you want us to protect you from the Arabs with our breasts and then if Allah gives you victory some one else will reap the benefit. "Thank you. No." They had missed the opportunity and were told so by oe of their elders when they went back to their tribal territory.

A question may be asked, at this sage, as to why did he not go to Habsha, where the ruler had given asylum to a number of Muslims already and who had even refused to hand over these political refugees to the high powered delegation sent by the eldersof Quraish. The answer is that, he could not go to Habsha becaus his object was not that he or his Companions or the Muslim Ummah should remain afe and sound under a society or a government which did not conduct its collective communal life on principles of the Sovereignty of Allh. Habsha may have been acceptable to a few Muslims where they were permitted to live as a minority but Habsha could not be made a centre for him, unless it accepted the Sovereignty of Allh and his Prophethood. Sovereignty of Allah can be established only through the Rule of Law given by Allah.

Sovereignty, in every case, belongs to the power, institution or person whose law is being enforced. If a parliament exercise these functions, then the joint will of the people, through their parliament, possesses Sovereignty. If, on the other hand, Laws Ordained by Allah are Supreme in a land, then it can be said that Sovereignty of Allah is recognised in that land. No land can claim to be a Muslim land, unless it recognises the Sovereignty of Allah, through the implementation of Laws based on the Quran and the Sunnah. When an early historian records, on the authority of contemporary evidence that "He usedto ask them to believe in him and protect him until Allah the Message with which He had charged His Prophet (PBUH)," it means that he is not asking them merely to protect him but he is waring them of the ultimate purpose, the impoition of The Shariah by Allah which would then have to be implmented. It has to be kept in mind that Quranic Law had not yet been Revealed, in full, and, he, therefore, could only refer them to it by saying, "until Allah should make clear the Message with which He had charged His Prophet." The Vahee, Revelation which is referred to inthe Quran'.

> *"And Lo! it is a revelation of the Lord of the Worlds, Wich the True Spirit hath brought down upon thy heart, that thou mayst be (one) of the warners."* *(26: 192-194)*

Thedetails of such Revelations were known to the Prophet (PBUH) and he announced them in his own way, at the appropriate time. Revelations which form the text of the Quran were spoken Words which were later dictated by th Prophet (PBUH); however, he consigned these words to his memory. Allah has referred to these Revelations in these Words:

> *"Stir not thy tongue herewith to hasten it. Lo! upon Us (resteth) the putting togther thereof and the reading thereof and when We Read it, follow thou the reading."* *(75: 16-18)*

To believe in him was to believe in Allah:

> *"Say, (O Muhammad, to mankind) If you love Allah,follow me; Allah will love you and forgive you your sins. Allah is Forgiving, Merciful."* *(3: 31)*

To believe in him meant to believe in him as The Messenger of Allah. As such belief in him could not be complete without first having believed in Allah. He was certain that when they believed in him and Allah as the only Sovereign Power in Universe, then they would be only too ready to lay down their lives to bring about justice through the Rule of Law which was due to be Ordained by Allah.

The Sovereignty of Allah was essential to be established in some piece of land. Unless the Shriah of Islam was practically brought into force, the benefits of Islam to the masses in social, economic, educational and political fields could not be demonstrated. Islam has three levels at which it effects and the effect of its application is visible. At the individua level belief in Allah grants peace of mind, contntment and courageto face the world far better than in other faits.

At the level of society its laws afford justice, fairplay, equal status, freedom of speech and thught a great deal more than humanity has experienced under any organized system of sciety. The third and the last level is the international evel. It is unfortunate to admit that after the era of the guided four Khalifas, even Muslim states have not dealt with other nations in the light of the Quranic Laws on Jihad and Foregn Relations. Space does nt permit of an exhaustive treatment of the subject. Suffice to say that in view of Quranic injunctions Muslims cannot use force unless it is first used against them.

> *"Fight in the way of Allah against those who fight against you, but being not hostilities. Lo! Allah loveth not aggressors."* *(2: 190)*

And

> *"There is no compulsion in religion."* *(2: 256)*

And even whe the aggressor having initiated hostilities and having occupied Muslim territory leans towards cease fire, Muslim must do likewise:

> *"And if they incline to peace, incline thou also to it, and trust in Allah. Lo! He is the Hearer, the Knower. And if they would deceive thee, then lo! Allah is sufficient for thee. He it is Who supporteth thee with His help and with the believers."* *(8: 61-62)*

Certainty of Peace

In view of certainty of peace being attained at individual, society and international levels through the Rule of Law based on the Sovereignty of Allah and His Prophet, the stage has reached that mankind is directed towards the implementation of the Quran and the Sunnah. When the Prophet (PBUH) referred to "Sovereignty being i Allah's hands" he meant to draw their attention to the fact that the soveeignty which he desired and aimed at was the Sovereignty of Allah through the implementation of His Laws.

At the time of Hajj some men from Yathrib visited Mecca. They were members of the tribe of Khazraj. The Prophet (PBUH) spoke to them about Islam and recited to them Verses from Quran. They told him hat they were "allies" of Jews and they had heard from them that according to theirbooks it was clear from certain passages that "a prophet will soon come." His day is at hand. We shall follow him and kill you with his aid." As a result of this meeting they were convinced that he was the prophet about whom the Jews had been telling. These men of the tribeof Khazraj from Yathrib "accepted his teachings and became Muslims." They spoke to him about their tribal affairs, saying that they were a very disunited tribe and expressed their hope that they would be able to live as a united people through him. They said, "Perhaps Allah will unite them through you. So let us go o them (their people) and invite them to this Deen of yours." Having become Muslims, they returned to Yathrib. This was the beginning of an era, which has expanded beyond imagination.

Among them was a man named Asad bin Zurara of Najjar tribe, who returned next year with eleven others and took part in the First Bayah of Al-Aqba. Their Bayah, in the words of Ubada bin al-Samit, of allegiance to the Prophet (PBUH) said: "We will associate nothing with Allah, will not steal, not commit fornication, not kill our offsprings, not slander our neighbour, not disobey him in what is right; if we fulfil this, paradise will be ours; and if we commit any of these sins we will be punished in this world and this will serve as an expiation; if the sins are concealed till the Day of Resurrection, then it will be for Allah to decide. The Prophet (PBUH) sent Musab bin Umayr binHashim with them, to teach them Quran and other thing in Islam. He was to lead Congregational prayers in Yathrib until the arrival of the Prophet (PBUH). Musab lodged with Asad bin Zurara in Yathrib. The spread of Islam, however, was not an easy affair. Opposition soon appeared in the form of the leaders of tribes who were losing their authority, because Musab had started deciding the problems arising among Muslims. Usayd spoke on behalf of the others and wanted Musab to leave Yathrib, saying, "Leae us if you value your life." Musab asked him to sit down for a while and listen to what he had to say. He was won over by Musab as a result of this friendly discourse and he went and recommended Islam to Saad bin Muaz. He also was furious at first, but having listened to the recitation of the Quran he also entered Islam. His conversion opened the door toIslam still wider, as he was not only the chief of his tribe but was effectively influential and universally popular. As a result of these influential persons Islam started spreading quickly in Yathrib, until very soon every household had one or two members, who had embraced Islam. Yathrib, thus became a city of mixed beliefs, as nearly every house contained both Believers and un-believers, living together. This fact had influence on the dictation of some of the Clauses of the Document, which we hope to study in this brief essay. When going into the details of the Charter we may have to refer to this fact of the social life of Yathrib, during that early period, following immediately after Hijrah.

The next event of importance, in the life of the Prophet (PBUH) is the second Bayah of Aqba, which took place during the next Hajj season. On this occasion, the party from Yathrib numbered 73 men and 2 women. Due to Meccan opposition, they had to go, "arriving softly like sandgrouse to our appointment with the Prophet (PBUH), as far as the narrow valley of Aqaba."

At the meeting, Abbas, uncle of the Prophet (PBUH), was also present. Addressing the Believers from Yathrib, he said, "O people of Khazraj you know, what position Muhammad (PBUH) holds among us. We have protected him from our own people, who think, as we do about him, but he will turn to you and join you. If you think that you can be faithful to what you have promised him and protect him from his opponents, then assume the burden you have undertaken. But if you think that you may betray and abandon him after he has gone out with you, then leave him now. For he is safe where he is now."

The reply of the Believers from Yathrib was, "We have heard what you have said." Then addressing the Prophet (PBUH) they said, "O Prophet, chose for yourself and for your Lord what you wish."

It may be realised that the conversation was between forthright outspoken but sincere people. They were honest and were trusted men of honour among their people. Some words and phrases of this conversation need being kept in mind, when studying the Constitutional Charter. For instance, Abbas the uncle of the Prophet (PBUH) had said:

"We have protected him."

In spite of hardships resulting from consistent persecution he was still propagating Islam. Abbas meant that, his family had prevented his enemies from killing him. He was not able, while in Mecca, to establish Sovereignty of Allah. The main object of his Mission had not been achieved. Abbas, however, could not understand the implications of the Mission remaining unfulfilled.

"If you think that you can be faithful to him."

Fear of treachery and unfaithfulness was natural, particularly when an old established Way of Life was being threatened.

"Protect him from his enemies."

Coming events prove that his fears were justified.

The reply of Believers from Yathrib was brief and meaningful. They had said, "Choose for yourself and for your Lord," which shows that Believers from Yathrib had studied Islam carefully and they knew the importance given by the Prophet (PBUH) to the desires and commands of Allah, because of the Revelations he was receiving constantly.

The Prophet (PBUH) had said, "I invite your allegiance on the basis that you will protect me as you would your wives and children." The words, "I invite your allegiance", are to b kept in mind because later on, "allegiance" was expected from all those to whom the Constitutional Charter was given. He is "inviting allegiance for protection," but allegiance to him as The Prophet of Allah is the main point. The protection was to be given to a superior to whom allegiance had been submitted. The 'Bayah' was and is a promise, a word of honour, an undertaking of complete loyalty, as if it was being sworn in the presence of Allah. This fact will have to be kept in mind when studying the Charter.

The Believers from Yathrib had, however, one worry. They said, "O Prophet of Allah! We have ties with other people, and if we sever these, and, later when Allh brings you with victory, perhaps you will return to your own people and abandon us."

He smiled and said:

> *"No! blood is blood. If blood is not to be paid for, then it is not to be paid for. I am of you, you are of me. I will at war against those, at war against you and be at peace with those that are at peace with you."*

This answer of the Prophet (PBUH) is reproduced in the Charter in the form of a Commandment for Believers, for all times tocome. We will be examining it a little more minutely when studying the appropriate Clause.

Before the Believers from Yathrib left Mecca, the Prophet (PBUH) appointed twelve leaders from amongst them "that they may take charge of their peoples affairs." Of those given leadership, nine of them were from Khazraj and the remaining three were from the tribe of Aus. The organization of the Umma, as a socio-political entity, and a full fledged Deen had started. These twele formed the government of Believers, without being called a government. The men appointed were known as Amirs and no more. Even when the Prophet (PBUH) moved to Yathrib and the Constitutional Charter was issued, there was no mention of a government being formed or a state being established. It was Deen of Islam, which was being fully operated and "the affairs of the people were being taken charge of." Even when Abu Bakr took over these responsibilities, he was an Amir over the people in order "to arrange the affairs of the people."

A careful look at this episode makes it evident that every one was certain that the Quraish of Mecca will go to war against the Prophet (PBUH) and those who gave protection to him. The fear of Yathribite was that after Allah will have given him victory, he will return to his people, could mean only that the victory would be against those enemies who forced him to leave his people, and when these enemies— the Quraish—were defeated, he might decide to return to his people in Mecca. A number of post-Hijrah incidents need to be examined in the light of this remark. The man from Banu Aamir bin Sahsaa was also cognisant of this possibility and expressed similar ideas, but not so clearly.

During the conversation prior to the Bayah being taken there was mention of 'fear', 'the need for loyalty' and care taken to guarantee that 'treachery' will not be permitted to occur. All these ideas go to describe the element of uncertainty resulting from the efforts of Quraish, over a number of years, to spread rumours against the Prophet (PBUH) among visiting tribes, at the time of Hajj season.

The enemies of Islam had been constantly outspoke about their future plans of using force to stop the spread of Islam among tribes. If Believers were successful in converting desert Arabs to the Ideology of Sovereignty of Allah, then the superior position held by Quraish would end and they would lose all existing privileges. Quraish, like most rulers of mankind, were advocates of Sovereignty of man and man-made laws. They had no desire to lose their freedom to indulge in worldly pleasure by accepting Sovereignty of Divine Laws which once accepted could not be transgressed without inviting censure and resulting in social imbalances. They realised all these aspects of Islam and were, therefore, determined to fight for perpetual continuity of a secular society.

The mention of force again and again, the stress on loyalty and the mention of certain possibility of fighting in order to defend Believers' right to proclaim the Sovereignty of Allah, leads us to believe that the atmosphere at Mecca, at that time, must have been very tense. The Oath of Allegiance was hardly completed when the news was conveyed to the Quraish and some onewas heard saying:

> *"O people o the station of Mina, do you want this reprobate and the apostates who are with him. They have come together to make war on you."*

This also shows the prevailing trend of general conversation among Quraish, at that time, and their psychological state of war-mania, which had captured their minds. Men in power and desirous of retaining that power at all costs are all the time on the look-out to find every possible excuse for using physical force against those who in spite of being weak dare to challenge their authority. The news that the Prophet (PBUH) had succeeded in getting supporters among the people of Yathrib must have upset the elders of Quraish a great deal. Discussions to counter his development and to use physical force must have commenced among the younger generation of Quraish, even before a proper meeting of the elders could be called.

Believers from Yathrib are certain to have been aware of these developments as is clear from their question and the secrecy maintained by them in arriving at the rendezvous. When they were told to disperse and had returned to their camp, al-Abbas bin Ubada said, "By Allah, if you wish it, we will fall on the people of Mina, tomorrow with our swords." The Prophet (PBUH) did not like any harm to fall on the Believers from Yathrib. He had not yet received any Commandment from Allah to use force even when threatened. He replied, "We have not been Commanded to do that; go back to your caravan."

The Quraish heard about the Bayah and sent some men to find out the exact position. The Mushrikeen from Yathrib, whom these people asked, knew nothing of the Bayah. They, therefore, denied that any such ceremony had taken place. Believers from Yathrib had kept the news limited to Believers only. The Meccan agents went back and the news remained a secret until after the departure of Yathribite caravan from Mina. It shows the extent to which Quraish were prepared to go to stop the spread of Islam. If they had come to know of the details of the meeting at this second Bayah of Aqba, they ould have taken extreme measures immediately even before the Prophet (PBUH) had made preparations for departure to Yathrib. As long as the Prophet (PBUH) could remain physically interned in Mecca, they could preent the spread of Islam. Once he and his Companions of the stature of Abu Bakr, Umar and Hamza succeeded in establishing Islam any where outside Mecca, they felt that they would be handicapped and would have to resort to war against those who gave him protection. Meccan leaders were, therefore very keen to avoid the trouble of going to war by putting a ban on the emigration of any Believer from Mecca. This attitude of Meccans is not in conformity with the behavior of earlier people, who did not accept the teachings of prophets sent to them. In all cases they turned them out or desired that those prophets who insisted on preaching the true religion, should leave their tribal cities and go elsewhere. The attitude and behavior of Meccans, since the beginning, had been to contain Islam, by all possible means, to Mecca alone and then by bribery, cajoling, persecution and all other possible means to see that the movement died out. This difference in the behaviour of Meccans from the behaviour and conduct of earlier people needs further study. In the case of Prophet Lot, may Allah bless him, his people said:

> *"Expel the household of Lot from your township, for they (forsooth) are folk who would keep clean."* (27: 56)

It appears that the reason why the Meccans were bent upon compelling, by force, the Prophet (PBUH) and his Companions to remain as hostages in Mecca so that Islam does not reach a place where its socio-economic organization can be implemented. Later events, after the success of Hijrah confirm this view.

The opposition shown at the time of migration of a few Muslims to Habsha was the result of the same policy decision. Details of the news of Bayah of Believers from Yathrib must have leaked out, particularly because the Prophet (PBUH) gave permission to individuals to migrate as and when an opportunity arose. It was more than permission. As the historian says, "The Prophet (PBUH) commanded his Companions...to emigrate to Medina and to link up with their brethren, th Ansar." Allah will make for you, brethren and houses, in which you may be safe. "So they went out in companies, and the Prophet stayed in Mecca waiting for his Lord's permission to leave Mecca and migrate to Medina."

The first to migrate to Yathrib was Abu Salma bin Abdul Asad of Banu Makhzum, but he had gone before the Second Bayah of Aqba. There were scenes at times when the head of the family wanted to migrate and efforts were made to retain the wife or the children. When houses were found empty the blame of dividing families was put on the Prophet (PBUH): "He has divided our community, disrupted our affairs, and driven a wedge between us." Some of those intending to migrate were caught by their relatives, bound by ropes and forced to apostatize. Most of those migrating to Yathrib did it secretly. Umar ibn al Khattab, went to Kaaba, performed Tawwaf and left openly. He was neither molested nor any effort made to dtain him. People were afraid of him even when he was a young man.

The Great Migration : The Prophet (PBUH) waited for permission from Allah to leave Mecca and move to Yathrib. The Quraish, however, knew that he would leave Mecca, and they got together to chalk out a plan to decide on the best possible way of preventing his migration to Yathrib. They called a meeting of the elders in the conference hall known as *Nadwah*. "The discussion opened with the statement, that as Muhammad (PBUH) had gained adherents outside the tribe, they were no longer safe against a sudden attack and the meeting was to determine the best course to pursue. One advised that they should put him in irons behind bars and then wait until the fate overtook him as befell like the poets Zuhyr and Naabigha, and others.

The Sheikh objected to this on the ground that the news would leak out that he was imprisoned and immediately his followers would attack and snatch him away; then their number will grow to the extent that they would destroy the authority of Quraish altogether They must think of another plan. The alternative suggested was that they should drive him out of the country and did not care where he went or what happened to him. Once he was out of sight, they would get rid of him. They could then restore their social life to its former state. Again the Sheikh objected to the plan saying that his fine speech and beautiful diction and the compelling force of his message were such that if he settled with some Beduin tribe he would win them over so that they would follow him and (he would) come back and attack them in their land and rob them of their position and authority and then could do whatever he iked with them. They must think of a better plan. Thereupon Abu Jehl said that he had a plan which had not been suggested hitherto, namely that each clan should provide a young, powerful, well–born, aristocratic warrior; that each of these should be provided with a sharp sword; then that each of them should strike a blow at him and kill him. Thus they would be relieved of him and responsibility for his blood would lie upon all of the clans."

The Prophet (PBUH) came to know of this plot, but before they could decide on the day and time of attack he received permission from Allah to migrate to Yathrib. He informed Abu Bakr, who had already purchased two camels for the journey and supplies. He took with him all the cash which he possessed. Allah had informed the Prophet (PBUH) through Jibbrail of the plan of the Quraish. He decided to leave on the very night, that had been fixed to kill him. It was an unwritten law in Arabia, which is still honoured in some parts that the privacy of the house of a person is inviolable. If a man is to be murdered he will be killed when getting out of the house. Ali was asked by the Prophet (PBUH) to lie on his bed and return all valuables placed with the Prophet (PBUH) by people as trust, and then migrate to Yathrib. The Prophet (PBUH) then left in the company of Abu Bakr and as arranged reached the cave of Thaur. Next day Ali got up in the morning, and when he emerged from the house the men waiting for the Prophet (PBUH) were surprised but noting could be done.

They searched for him, in the neighbourhood, for three days, while he and his most intimate friend and Companion lay in the cave of Thaur.

Abu Bakr's aughter, Asmaa supplied them with food during these three days. The Meccans had announced a reward of one hundred camels to anyone who would bring him back dead or alive. The stakes were extremely high. If he could not be killed the Meccans would lose their power, prestige, socio-economic superiority over Arabs and the affluence which resulted from their unique position as leaders of socio-religious and economic life simultaneously, which no other class in any nation has ever occupied.

There was a third man with them. He was the guide, Abdullah bin Arqam, who had joined them after they emerged from the cave of Thaur. He guided them along a route not normally used for going north to Syria or even to Yathrib. He reached outside Yathrib on Monday 12th of Rabiul Awwal at about noon. Some say that it was eighth of Rabiul Awwal, which would be 20th of September 622 A.C. After staying in Quba for three days and having constructed a mosque there, he moved to the central part of Yathrib and stayed at the house of Abu Ayub. There was great rejoicing on his arrival in Yathrib by the local Believers, their families, friends and acquaintances. A vacant plot of land was purchased and the construction of mosque taken in hand. Walls were made of stone, the pillars and beams were trunks of date trees and the rest of roof of branches and leaves of this very useful tree. The area then covered by the Mosque of the Prophet (PBUH), as it has been known ever since, is marked by large stone pillars with decorations of flower wreaths upto about two feet from the floor.

On the south and sides were constructed rooms for Ahle-Bait, the family of the Prophet (PBUH). Each room was a few feet in length and breadth and had the barest minimum of household items found even in humblest abodes. A mattress stuffed with leaves of date palm was the only item of luxury.

Until the end of his life he did not change his style of life. In later days, when his share of war booty was considerable and he often presented hundred of camels to visiting embassies he did not use any of it for making his life a little more comfortable even though he needed rest and comfort due to his advancing age. He used to spend a greater part of the night in prayers until the end. Advancement in age and tremendous increase in responsibilities did not make any difference. In Sura Al-Moemenoon, when in Mecca, he had been directed to ask for Allah's forgiveness.

> *And, O (Muhammad) say: My Lord! Forgive and have mercy, for Thou art best of all who show mercy.(23: 118)*

Until the end this remained his favourite Recitation. He had been known in Mecca as a mild, gentle and kind young man. In Median, when he wielded great power and had a great load of administrative and judicial duties to perform; and, for the first nine years, a great deal of defence responsibilities had fallen on him alone, he would stop in the street to shake hands with people and cheer up children. He was not known to have withdrawn his hand first when greeting people and shaking hands with them. He would utilise the first opportunity to go and visit the sick and never missed offering Janaza prayers for the dead. The news of his safe arrival was bound to reach Mecca, and it reached without any loss of time. Traffic between the two cities flowed regularly. Now that he had reached Yathrib where there were already local Muslims in addition to his Companions who had slipped away ahead of him the situation had become grave from Meccan point of view. Though the Muhajirs were hardly forty odd in number, they had started playing an active role in the communal affairs of Believers and were exercising healthy influence over the civic life of the city. It was evident, from Meccan point of view, that the Muhajirs would soon be absorbed into the stream of social and cultural life of Yathrib which meant that when they felt home sick, after some time, they would succeed in persuading their protectors to join them in attacking Mecca. The refugees from Habsha would also join them and with new converts to Islam from neighbouring tribes the force would swell to proportions beyond the defence capacity of Mecca. This was the trend of reasoning in Mecca when news of daily developments started reaching them. The reception given to the Prophet (PBUH) on arrival in Yathrib was unprecedented. No guest in the history of tribal Arabia had ever received such rousing reception. They knew his talents. They had already admitted to themselves that he possessed persuasive powers.

Now that he had settled with, not exactly a Beduin tribe, but all the same a powerful adversary, who, as a result of war among themselves in the recent past had experience of fighting, the Prophet (PBUH) appeared to them a source of serious danger. This fear was not new. During the past few years they were afraid that such an eventuality would develop if they permitted him to leave Mecca. They had failed to keep him under their watchful eye but they decided to take some positive action which was to attack Yathrib, but Arab chivalry demanded that they must warn the Yathribites first. The fact of Yathrib being close to their caravan route to Syria, was to be seriously considered, but if they could win over the people of Yathrib, and persuade them to kill or turn out Muhammad (PBUH) and his Companions, the matter could be ended without any future danger to their trading activities to the North. The Meccans called a meeting of elders in their usual meeting hall, the Nadwah, the house of Qusayy bin Kilab. It was decided to write a letter to Abdullah bin Ubbay, the head of Khazraj, the largest tribe of Yathrib. It so happened that a little earlier the two tribes of Yathrib, Aus and Khazraj, had come to terms and it was under consideration to declare Abdullah bin Ubbay as the king of Yathrib. A crown studded with jewels was being prepared for him. The conversion of a considerable number of his tribe to Islam and the arrival of a batch of disciplined Believers from Mecca had altered the situation. Attention, for the past many months, had been fixed on the expected arrival of the Prophet (PBUH). The news of change in the internal politics of Yathrib and the resulting disappointment of Abdullah bin Ubbay must have reached Meccan leaders as well. This may have prompted them to have addressed the letter to him and not to any one else. They wrote to him:

> *"You have given protection to our men. We swear by Allah that you should either kill them or turn them out of Yathrib. If you do not do that we will attack you and having destroyed you will capture your women folk."*

This was, in a way, an ultimatum of war but in actual fact it amounted to the declaration of war. There was no period or date mentioned by which time the Believers from Mecca had to be turned out of Yathrib. The Quraish knew that this protection had been given as a result of Bayah, which meant in the presence of Almighty Allah and Bayah is not broken, just because, some unreasonable and illegal threat is received.

When the letter reached Yathrib and Abdullah bin Ubbay found an excuse of re-establishing himself as the leader of Yathrib, he gave out that he would use force against the refugees and if they did not leave Yathrib, he would kill them all. He said he was not strong enough to repulse an attack by an adversary as strong as the Quraish. he news reached the Prophet (PBUH). He did not wish that trouble should arise between the Muhajirs and Yathribites, even though the majority of them were those who had not yet accepted Islam. He went to meet Abdullah bin Ubbay personally and told the Khazraj chief that when thinking of using force against the Believers he did not realise that Yathribite Believers will side with Muhajir Believers. The Prophet (PBUH) told him in the end that if he used force against Muhajirin he will ind that "the blood of his people has been shed on both sides." This quietened him.

The realisation that a Believer severs all old connections and every moment of his is offered on the Path of Allah. Believers cannot array themselves in opposite camps. Peace for one is peace for all or none. This philosophy was to be interpreted by him in the Charter under study. He must have explained to Abdullah bin Ubbay that Believers will all be in one camp.

They only fight on the Path of Allah. When fighting is on the Path of Allah, all Believers take part in it, but, on the side of Allah and His Prophet (PBUH). Abdullah understood. History is silent on the issue as to whether he asked the Prophet (PBUH) as to how will Yathrib be defended. We feel that he must have asked thc question and the Prophet (PBUH) must have put him at rest by saying that the Believers were duty bound to fight the invaders. Allah had Commanded while he was still at Mecca:

> *" Sanction is given unto those who fight because they have been wronged; and Allah is indeed able to give them victory.* *(22: 39)*

This was only permission becuse the Muslims had not yet organized themselves into an Ummah and had not yet established a state. War demanded the organization of the Muslim Community and a piece of land to established the Law of the Quran. War can be fought only after proper preparation and organization. This was possile in Yathrib. When the Prophet (PBUH) ad te conversation referred to above it is more than probble that the following two Verses had been Revealed. They are:

> *"Warfare is ordained for you."* *(2: 216)*

and

> *"Fight on the way of Allah against those who fight against you, but being not hostilities. Lo! Allah loveth not the aggressors."* *(2: 190)*

As mentioned earlier the Philosophy of War, Ordained by Allah and demonstraed by the Prophet (PBUH) of Allah, can be summed up in one sentence. Believers cannot be aggressors but they have a duty (Fardha), to repulse any attack against them. If they do not fight back, then they are likely to be punished to the extent that the land occupied by them is given over to some one else.

> *"If ye go not for the He will afflict you with a painful doom, and will choose instead of you a folk other than you. You cannot harm Him at all. Allah is able to do all things."* *(9: 39)*

We feel that when the Prophet (PBUH) answered Abdullah bin Ubbay's question by accepting the responsibility of defending Yathrib through the Believers and "others," who would be prepared to follow the leadership of Believers and fght alongside with, then Abdullah bin Ubbay could not object. He could alays play the role of remaining neutral. If the Believers succeeded, he and those who followed him, ould reap the fruits of the efforts of Believers

If, on the other hand, Believers were likely to be defeated he would not join in the battle. As a result he would not be punished by the Meccans. His conduct, throughout the period of war with Mecca supports this view. There must have been a certain amount of further discussion with him and the Prophet (PBUH) who had a very disciplined mind and who believed in straight dealings, must have told him that he would like to ssue a Document giving details of the manner of defending Yathrib and legal basis of affairs of the people of Yathrib. If he was to defend Yathrib, he must have the last word in the Land, which was being defended. This meant that a state and a country had to be established in which Sovereignty would rest with Allah, because it was the Believers who had accepted the responsibility of creating the state, and running it, including the Internal Security and the Defence of the state. Abdullah bin Ubbay had no grounds to oppose this decision of the Prophet (PBUH).

This was the background and the basis of the Constitutional Charter of Yathrib, the town which had given him and his Companions asylum and which had now no option but to accept to be defended by him and his Companions, as a result of the Command of Allah.

> *"He is Allah, than whom there is no other God, the Sovereign Lord, The Holy One, Peace, The Keeper of Faith, The Guardian, The Majestic, The Compeller, The Superb. Glorified be Allah from all that they ascribe as partners (unto Him). He is Allah, The Creator, The Shaper out of naught. The Fashioner. His are the most beautiful names. All that is in the heavens and the earth glorifies Him, and He is Mighty the Wise." (59: 23-24)*
>
> *"Glorified be Allah, the Lord of the Throne." (21: 22)*

The Guidelines

The following clauses deal with the general issues.

Clause 6: "All parties will redeem their prisoners with kindness and justice according to practice among Believers".

We have already looked at this Clause under Laws pertaining to defence matters. It would not be out of place to examine it under Laws or Directions of general nature. The matter deals with humane treatment of members of the Armed Forces. Itwould, therefoe, clarify matters, if it was examined from the point of view of the individual in a Muslim society.

Islam, complete submission to the Will of Most Kind and Benevolent Alah, enjoins kindness amongst its members and expects mutual hep and consideration between groups, which comprise the Ummah. When war takes place through the invasion of any part of the Ummah, Jihad becomes a Duty of all groups:

> *"Warfare is ordained for you, though it s hateful unto you".* *(2: 216)*

Even when the persecuted happen to be un-Believers Allah expects, that Believers in His Benevolent Sovereignty, must go to their help:

> *"How should ye not fight for the cause of Allah and of the feeble among men and of women and the children who are crying: Our Lord! Bring us forth from out this town of which the people are oppressors! Oh give us from Thy presence some protecting friend".* *(4: 75)*

When war takes place, some achieve the highest honour of becoming martyrs, some get wounded and there is a possibility that some may be taken prisoners by the enemy. They had gone to war for the common cause of the Ummh. Therefore, it is the collective duty of the Ummah that these prisoners are redeemed with Islamic kindness, which means, as early s possible and without any thought of how high the cost may be. Until the advent of Islam, and particularly until this Constitutional Charter was dictated by the Prophet (PBUH) of Islam, the redeeming of prisoners was nota statuary obligation in any known law of either any civilised society or of barbarians. In it the Believers were ordered to rdeem their prisoners with kindness and justice, which is the hallmark of Believers. The others, which meant the Jews and idolaters were given a chance to live under the guidance of Believers and to fight alongside them, on the Path of Allah. If they availed of this option, they were expected to show the same kindness to their brothers and to come up to the same standard of justice, which was common among the Believers. They were, therefore, bound by law to redeem their prisoners, under this Clause, Clause 6. If this is the standard expected of allies of a Muslim state, it would be correct to assume, that a, "Muslim state has of necessity to be a welfare state.... particularly with reference to economic justice."

Man seems to have had a rebellious trait, developed in him, as a result of the persuations of Satan, which he, at times, is unable to control. Prophets sent by Allah have tried and have achieved varying results but those who are disposed to rebellion, have reverted to the path of selfish and shortsighted policies. These rebellious elements, who on most occasions are only a small minority, create enough mischief to upset the genera peace of society. Men of influence in all denominations have warned mankind of the dangers hidden in following the path of mishchief with different results. A modern writer has sounded warning of the same nature by saying, "I feel sure that man faces the worst half millennium in his terrifying history. For man, today, must quickly learn who and what he is and how he is governed in nature, or else...bring upon himself.... wars....rebellions....." Another writer has warned that science has, so far, failed to give directions, leading to peaceful communal life, "The tragedy of our times is that the science of destruction has run amock. And th problem is how to synchronize the science of life with the science of death."

A Peaceful Life : The Prophet (PBUH) was teaching mankind the way to a communal life of peace, love and justice. He knew that mankind would not give up war unless and until Islam had become the Universal Way of Life. Until then war had to be discouraged but steps had to be taken that the miseries of war were minimised as much as possible. He was leading mankind to that Way of Life which would eventually lead to the synchronization of the science of life and science of death.

Clause 18: "The enemies of Jews will not be helped."

We have touched on this question, under Laws governing Jews only. We would like to add a few words here that this neutrality between the enemies of Jews and the state of Yathrib was to be resorted to in case the Jews did not accept the leadership of Believers and did not take part in war alongside with them. If, however the Jews followed the Believers and fought alongside with them, then, they were to become a part of the Ummah and enemies of Jews were to be enemies of Believers. In case the Jews did not desire to become a part of the Ummah then a neutral position was to be maintained with the enemies of Jews. This appears to be the beginning of Laws of Neutrality. Modern writers call it the theory of "Neutral Law." It has been said that, "Modern theory has paid tribute to the doctrine of neutral law for their contribution to the so-called "modern system of International Law."

First in Legal History : This Clause and a few others, establish the fact that this was the first Document in the legal history of human efforts in the international field. It must be remembered that the directions contained in this Charter, under general rules, are meant for the guidance of entire mankind. Minorities will exist, among all nations, for a long time to come. There must, therefore, by some universal understanding with regard to the treatment to be meted out to minorities. This Charter shows a way towards those basic concessions to be provided to minorities.

Today, fourteen centuries after the dictation of this Charter by an unlettered Prophet of Allah (PBUH), we notice that there are still people in this world who refuse to their minorities the right to exist. This only happens in those countries, where the Sovereignty of Allah is being denied.

Clause 27: "If any un-Believer, kills a Believer, without good cause, he shall be killed in return, unless the next of kin are satisfied. All Believers shall be against such a wrong-doer. No Believer, if he believes in Allah and the Last Day will be allowed to shelter such a man. Whoever shelters such a man, on him will be punishment of Allah on the Day of Judgement."

Law and order had to be maintained in this newly established state. Severest punishment was being declared for breaking a fundamental law of the land. Believers were the party, which was running the state as the Government Party, which had accepted the responsibility of the defence of the teritories of the state of Yathrib. If a member of theruling party was murdered without good cause it was important that the culprit should be punished. It was, however, laid down that if the next of kin desire to pardon the culprit n punishment will be meted out to him. The society being a mixed society, it was possible that the culprit was a close relative or a friend of one of the Believers.

The state was new and young. It did not have time to lay down procedures of liigation. In any case this Charter was the fundamental law and procedural rules are not included in such documents. Henceno punishment was specified for this crime.

Clause 28: "When you differ on anything the matter shall e referred to Allah and Muhammad (PBUH)".

The point to note is that in multi- Ummah society the highest authority to arbitrate is being named Allah and His Prophet Muhammad (PBUH). The Jews were to remain as Jews and the Mushrikeen, though not specifically mentioned, were to continue in their belief as before. In spite of it Allah was being accepted the final authority, which meant that His Laws as conveyed to them by Muhammad (PBUH) was being accepted as the Law of the Land. It speaks volumes about the manner in which the Prophet (PBUH) and his few Companions must have conducted themselves during the very short time that they had been living among Yathribites since Hijrah.

The conduct of Ansar Muslims, who had invited the Prophet (PBUH) and the change brought in their conduct and character since becoming Muslims, must have had a tremendous influence on the others. The spread of Islam in Indonesia and various parts of Afica has been the result of similar influence of Muslims penetrating into the interior.

This Clause leads to the conclusion that he Prophet (PBUH) was able to impress on Yathribite non-Muslims that what was being Revealed to him was from Allah and in exactly the same manner as had been revealed before him to othr Prophets like Ibrahim and Moosa. In other words, they had accepted Sovereignty of Allah to be exercised through him.

This meant that Laws of Islam were to be the Law of the state of Yathrib, and all customs and traditions in operation were to become ineffective and illegal, if they contravened any Laws Revealed to Muhammad (PBUH). The final authority in a state, whether it is a monarch or a house of representatives is the authority which has the right and prerogative to make law. Hence it is called the sovereign authority. Acceptance of Laws Revealed to the Prophet (PBUH) by Allah, amounted to the acceptance of Sovereignty of Allah in practice, but without acknowledging in verbally.

Clause 32: "Loyalty gives protection against treachery."

The declaration of war by the Quraish of Mecca had made it essential that every body should e warned against treachery at this time of grave danger to the entire population of Yathrib. We have dealt with this Clause under Laws pertaining to Defence, bu being a Law of general nature affecting the very existence of the realm and of such a nature that it will affect Muslim countries for ever it must be studied in greater detail keeping in view conditions faced by Muslim Ummah today and are likely to continue to affect for a considerable period in the near future.

Greatest Danger : The greatest danger to Muslim lands from treacherous activities is from the followers of pseudo-prophets, produced by European influence, during the nineteenth centur. The followers of these new religions claim to be Mslims, while holding beliefs contrary to Islam. These non-Muslims going about with Muslim names and observing some of the practices of Islam will act as secret agents on behalf of foreign powers. They will play the part of Kaab bin Ashraf and Abdullah bin Ubbay without a moments, hesitation.

It so happens that these non-Muslims, happen to be nationals of a number of Muslim countries, which, until some years ago, happened to be British colonies. The governments of these countries have to be vigilant. They must pay special attention to the security of their plans particularly in matters of defence. They have been directed not to employ such people in appointments of trust. Allah has Ordained:

"Do not take in trust accept yourselves." *(3: 118)*

The military position of Yathrib, as compared to Mecca was even worse than a small Muslim country of today, when compared to one of the super powers. The effort to defend against Mecca could not be given up. The consequences of defeat could not be imagined. It meant complete annihilation. Consideration of terms for existence at the end of an unsuccessful battle was out of question. It is an old axiom that, "Similarity between opponents creates laws of warfare, while dissimilarity leads to unlimited or absolute warfare," which in the sixth century meant complete annihilation. Normal rules of warfare are not observed, where the weaker side is so weak that it cannot proclaim its opposition openly. The Prophet (PBUH) had decided that Yathrib should have no weak spot on the home front. Only then could he hope to face the enemy with all availabl strength.

Loyalty, a Quality : Loyalty is a quality which has in itself the quality to furnish defence against treachery. None dare accuse a loyal person of a crime connected with or the result of treachery. The loyalty of Companions of the Prophet (PBUH) was above suspicion. It was this loyalty of theirs, which kept the internal cohesion of Yathrib intact. The first successor of the Prophet (PBUH), Abu Bakr was known for his loyalty to the Prophet. It has been said that, "The secret of Abu Bakr's strength was his faith in Muhammad (PBUH)..... Abu Bakr had no thought of self aggrandisement. Endowed with sovereign and absolute power, he used it simply for the interest of Islam and the people's good. He was too shrewd to be himself deceived, and too honest to himself to act the part of a deceiver. To the last moment of his life he had the good and freedom of the population, uppermost in his mind, who had entrusted themselves into his hands. His will was symbolic of the manner be looked at his responsibilities. "To him who shall succeed, give it as my dying request that he be kind to the men of this city, which gave a house to us and to the faith.... And the Jews and Christians, let him faithfully fulfil the covenant of the Prophet (PBUH) with them." Muir, like other writers, refers to the Charter a covenant. With Companions like Abu Bakr and Umar there could not flourish many disloyal men around.

Clause 33: "The freedmen of Thaalba will be afforded the same status as Thaalba themselves."

This decision was in conformity with the spirit of Islam. Islam encourages people to set free their slaves, so that a free society comes into existence. A slave, is no better than an animal. He has no stakes in the preservation of the society in which he lives. A free citizen of a society of equals does not surrender, because, surrender makes him slave of the victor. Nations who lost their battles two hundred years ago remained slaves for two centuries. Even when they gained political freedom they continued to be economic slaves of the erstwhile masters. They have suffered because their grand parents surrendered to foreigners. This Clause shows the path to equality and freedom of man and was dictated to make certain that those who were freed and were slaves no more should be really free and prove themselves as honourable asset to the society in which they lived.

Clause 36: "Anyone who kills another without warnin amounts to his slaying himself and his household, unless the killing was done due to a wrong, being done to him."

Murders and killings upset and unbalance the smooth running of a society. Killings without warning possess an element of deceit and treachery, particularly when the killing is not to avenge a wrong already done by the culprit.

The warning, that such a killing amounts on the part of the murderer make to himself liable to killing and other members of his household was appropriate to the times. To avenge one murder, people of that age were apt to kill entire family of the culprit. Murders are the worst of crimes in any society, and when their numbers increase the sense of security, and living among reliable human beings disappears.

Clause 41: "A man will not be made liable for the misdeeds of his ally."

It had been said in Clause 3 and 5 that prisoners will be redeemed with kindness and justice common among Believers. This was a clause which proved that justice was kept uppermost in the Laws promulgated in a society, led by Believers. Clause 34 had referred to alliances but no could be made responsible for the misdeeds of his ally. This Law appears to be the forerunner of the following Ayah of Quran:

"And no burdened soul can bear another's burden".(35: 18)

The allies of Jews had been given the same status as the Jews themselves, but this could not make them liable for the misdeeds of their allies.

Clause 42: "Anyone, who is wronged must be helped."

Kindness and justice had been declared as the common practice among Believers. The Basic Law being given to Believers had to come upto the standard of justice expected of Believers. If a wronged person was not aided by the Law itself and law enforcing authorities in a society composed of Believers, then it could be said that justice was a common practice among Believers.

Clause 45: "A stranger, who has been given protection will be treated as his host, while doing no harm and is not committing any crime."

Protection could be given by any one of the nationals of Yathrib. It was, however, being assured, that the protected will be treated at par with his host. He could not expect a higher reward than the person who gave him protection. It was the right of the host that his guest received the same treatment, which he was entitled to.

This protection, however, became null and void if he committed a crime. The case of Kaab bin Ashraf should be examined keeping this Clause, as well, in view.

Clause 46: "Woman will be given protection only with the consent other family." This was a social matter, but if handled carelessly it could develop in a long drawn war. Women are considered a protected trust to be honoured by men of that family or tribe. If a woman is forcibly carried away or given protection against the permission of her family, the act will amount to destroying honour, prestige and respectability of that family and tribe. To avoid any such trouble with the neighbouring tribes, a law was enacted that no one will give protection to a woman, unless the family of that woman had given permission to her to seek protection in Yathrib. Women of all tribes, inside and outside the state of Yathrib, were being given the honour they deserved.

Clause 47: "In case of any dispute or controversy, which may result in trouble the matter must be referred to Allah and Muhammad (PBUH). Allah will accept any thing in this Document, which is for bringing piety and goodness."

This Clause declares in no uncertain terms, the place where power rested in this newly established state of Yathrib. It means that the fundamental law of the land revolved around the belief in the Sovereignty of Allah. This Clause further reiterates this belief. It means that differences and disputes must be resolved in the light of Shariah. As Shariah is the result of interpretation of Revelations from Allah, the decision, therefore, rested with the Prophet (PBUH).

All those present in the assembly were recognizing the Sovereignty of Allah and His Prophet (PBUH) even though they may not have accepted Islam in total. They were thus, Constitutional Muslims for having accepted the Constitution based on Shariah—which gave the last Way of Life—Islam.

Clause 51: "Every one, will have his share, n accordance with which pary he belongs to."

As it happens in the case of political parties, the individual member, in case he differs with the official views of the party, cannot evade responsibility for the decision of the party. It was the same in tribal system. The views of the individual carried weight until such time as te decision was made. Once the decision had been taken by the tribe or the sub-tribe, all individuals had to abide by it. Their rewards or responsibilities had to be decided in relation to the pary, to which the individual belonged.

It was only fair that individual's responsibility should be in accordance with that of his tribe.To avoid future complications, it was best to have the principle accepted and announced through the Charter.

Clause 53: "Anyone who acts loyally or otherwise does it for his own good."

People knew of the impending war. They knew that it would be a fight to the end. If the invasion came all were likely to suffer equally. The Meccans were not likely to show compassion to those, who did not take part in fighting. When a place is destroyed or looted the invader does not look round for those, whom he would like to spare or those who would like to be spared. The decision to follow the leadership of Believers was being taken up voluntarily and after consideration of the result of accepting the responsibility or evading it. It was neither a favour nor act of grace towards the Believers. Loyalty to this cause, in future, was also to be for their own good.

Clause 54: "Allah approves this Document."

This Clause has to be viewed keeping the occasion of the dictation of the Document in view. The Hijrah, the construction of the mosque, the declaration of war by Mecca, the decision to defend Yathrib, were all incidents connected with the purpose of the dictation of this Constitutional Charter.

The contents of the Charter studied so far have also to be borne in mind. The Document opened with the words "From Muhammad, Prophet of Allah (PBUH)" This was accepted by all those present including the Jews and un-Believers. The superior status of Believers had been established. The Sovereignty of Allah and His Prophet had been categorically explained and accepted. In matters of dispute the final arbitrator was to be the Prophet himself. Now finally the seal of

Allah's approval was being put on to the Document. It was not a part of the Quran — not a clear Revelation — but a Document isued by Muhammad (PBUH) His Messenger — to which His consent had been obtained, and this Consent of the Almighty was being announced in open Court.

From Hijrah to the dictation of the Charter, the Prophet (PBUH) had given guidance and conveyed his decisions in the light of the Training and Guidance received by him from Allah. He does not appear to have received any clear cut Ordinance from Allah as to the nature of the State and Government of Yathrib. He hadto establish the Deen — Way of Life — of Islam, which was based on the full, complete and unadulterated Sovereignty of Allah, but the details of his ConstitutionalCharter were to be filled in by Muhammad himself. As Hafiz Ghulam Sarwar has said, "Although Muhammad (PBUH) was inspired, as to what Allah wished him to do, the ways and means of carrying out His Message were left to Muhammad (PBUH). This was his part of the work. Allah would show him the path, but Muhammad (PBUH) himself had to walk it."

His was a great responsibility. There was a time, when he did not know, what were the responsibilities of a prophet of Allah. He had been "Quite unaware of the fact that he was to be Commissioned by Allah as the Last of the Prophets. We do not find any hint direct or ndirect, that his mind was preparing blueprints of any religious adventue." We have, therefore, to be content with the exact situation. The Document was from him and not a Revelation from Allah, but it had His Approval.

Allah's Approval : Allah's approval was iven, because it was for the good of humanity. It laid down, that matters were to be conducted in accordance with kindness and justice of the highest standard — the standard whichhad been placed before the best Ummah so far created amongst mankind (3: 110). It has been unfortunate, in fact a tragedy that this ocument has been overlooked by statesmen, both Muslim and non-Muslims of the past centuries. As a result the world has drifted towards man made totalitarianism, which is the product of human mindin its totality. Its authors have also realised the dangers to which it is leadig humanity. "It is only now, when Western humanity is faced with the appalling result of its work of destruction that it is beginning to realise, what has happened and to look back on the road it has travelled......Yet it has not reached the point of admittin that this totalitarian state is not the invention of a handful of criminals in the grand style, but its own product, the incalculable consequence of its own positivism, a position void of faith and inimical to metaphysics and religion. It will not yet believe that it is the incontrolable result of man's loss of faith in the Divine Law, in an Eternal justice," "justice which is the main theme of Islam, justice which alone can keep society free from internal intransigencies."

Clause 55: "This Document will not protect anyone, who is unjust or commits a crime."

Defence of the realm is a commendable action. To have joined the defenders of Yathrib and agreed to abide by the contents of this Constitutional Document was an honourable undertaking, but it did not give a license to commit injustice or any act contrary to Law. On the contrary it demanded greater care to behave in an honourable manner and administer justice of the standard Commanded by Allah.

The king can commit no crime. It may be justifiable in societies, where the king is the source of Law. In Islam the source and fountain of law is Allah himself. No man, therefore, can be above law and as such membership of this document also carried added responsibilities but no immunity.

Clause 57: "Allah is the protector of the good people and those who fear Allah; and Muhammad (PBUH) is the messenger of Allah."

This is a statement of fact, an annunciation of the after tried and experienced Omnipotent Protection of the Most Merciful Allah. Allah is Good and protects His good servants, who fear Him and abide by His Laws. These Laws have been Revealed by Him to His Prophet and Messenger Muhammad (PBUH).

This Document laid the foundations of Revealed Law of Allah. This Document at the same time Commissions Muhammad (PBUH) to interpret, explain, promulgate, administer and live according to the Lawof Allah, so that his action can serve as the practical demonstrations of His Law until time comes to an end.

> *"And in the day when the Hour riseth the urighteous will despair".* *(30: 12)*

The Charm of the Desert

According to the prevailing custom, among the Quraish, the child was handed over to Halima Saadia, of a branch of the tribe of Huwaizan, after a few days, tobe brought up, in the desert. Although the Qurash were a city people and tradesmen who were acquainted with international markets from Aden to Istanbul yet they liked their male hildrento grow up in the free atmosphere and clean air of the desert, so that they grew up as bold and upright men who could defend their honour.

The desert of Arabia seems to have a charm of its own. An English poet has paid ribute to Arabia in touching words. He sings thus:

Far are the shades of Arabia
Where the princes ride at noon.
Sweet is the music of Arabia
In m heart when out of dreams
Descry her gliding streams
Hear her strange lutes on the green banks
Ring loud with the grief and delight.
They haunt me—her lutes and her forests
Still eyes look upon me
Cold voices whisper and say—
He is crazed with the spell of Arabia
Walter De La Mare
Such is the charm of the Arabian desert

The period of Muhammad (PBUH) with the Huwaizan turned out to be longer than usual. At the end of the stipulated period he was brought back but due to some epidemic in Mecca, Amina, the mother asked Halima Saadiya to look after him a little longer. This allowed him to live close to nature a little longer and develop a liking for the desert so dear to an Arab. He was five years old when he started living with his mother. Some sources place this event when he was six years of age. We are not told how relations developed, between mother and son, but the affection with which Muhammad (PBUH) remembered his mother in after life shows that relations must have developed fairly quickly between the two. The mother decided to visit Yathrib and show her young son the grave of his father. While journey to Yathrib and the period of stay there must have further developed the much needed affection between the two but maternal love was not destined to shape the character of "Mercy to Mankind." The mother died during the return journey at Abwaa, a small halting place, which he visited specially after Hijrah. This journey must have further brought him closer to nature but the loss of mother to an orphan child of a little over six years of age, alone in a caravan, developed in him the fortitude and patience so needed to face the turbulence of the world at large.

Chain of Thoughts : None can tell the chain of thought which was generated by the loss of the only person so close to him in this vast world. The caravan marching towards Mecca, the desert on all sides, the maid servant Umm Aiman, sitting in the litter on the other side of camel, were all that could distract from the acute sense of loss suffered by him. He never spoke of those days in his later years. In what manner Umm Aiman, herself a young girl conveyed the news and meaning of death to her ward, is not known. How she consoled him is a secret and will remain so for ever. What was his reaction and how patiently he bore the loss has not been narrated by Umm Aiman.

He had been deprived of a "father figure" from birth. A normal man looks to his early days and takes guidance from the memories of his father, and the manner in which his father used to meet various situations. An average person considers his father as the wisest human being. Muhammad (PBUH) had been denied this most valuable source of inspiration because Allah desired that he should not be guided by the behaviour of any human source. Allah had shaped events in a manner that Muhammad (PBUH) had to remain in the desert for a much longer period than was the usual custom. If he had come back to the city at the age of three years, it was possible that he might have been sent to a learned person to learn how to read and write, but Allah had wished that he should remain Ummi—illiterate, and thus avoid all sources of human learning and wisdom prevailing at that time and in that age.

At Abwaa he was denied the benefit of the guidance which a cultured lady of that period could provide for him. His mother a kind lady could have, in a practical way, demonstrated to him, even though, in an imperceptable manner, what love, compassion, mercy and kindness mean. "Mercy to Mankind" was to learn these lessons from Almighty Allah Himself. On return to Mecca Umm Aiman delivere the trust to the venerable old man, Abdul Muttalib, a chief of the Quraish, the randfather of the child. He was respected and could have taught his beloved intelligent grandson the secrets of leadership of men. This was not to be. Allah had decreed that He had his own plans to teach him Wisdom, Leadership and all that would be needed to guide mankind for all times to come, n His Own Way, and remove from him all those influences and practices learnt from wisdom resulting from human endeavours. Very soon the grandfather also died and young Muhammad (PBUH) hardly eight years of age, went to the household of his uncle Abu Talib, who loved him greatly but was not very well off as far as worldly means were concerned. Muhammad (PBUH), as a result had to become a shepherd very early in life. The herd included goats of neighbours also and what they paid helped i defraying expenses of Abu Talib's household.

Journey outside Arabia : Abu Talib, like other members of the tribe, went out with caravans for purposes of trade. Muhammad (PBUH) was twelve when, on his insistence, he was taken out on a trade journey to Syria. There are hints by Orientalsts that during this journey, his meeting a Christian hermit taught him the stories in Bible and he repeated these stories after declaring his Prophethood. This suggestion is so illogical that it need not even be discussed. A boy of twelve does not become a learned man after meeting a philosopher, during his short stay at a caravan serai.

There must have been other journeys. He started trading on his own account very early in life. It was the prevailing custom that those members of the tribe who did not wish to undertake long journeys would entrust their goods to other members of the tribe. Muhammad, very soon, became popular among such members of the tribe, for his honest dealings, and giving better dividends to people, he earned the rare title of Al-Ameen — The Trustworthy.

It was a time when boundaries of states and areas of tribal sovereignty were not very clearly demarcated and merchants ran the risk of having their goods confiscated if they ventured into areas where disputes between rival claimants had not been settled. Knowledge of geography, alternative routes, political affiliations of tribes, social customs, cultural differences and religious practices along various trade routes were to be learnt by merchants regularly visiting these trade routes and markets. It was also necessary to know a great deal about lands from where the items of trade in these markets commenced their journeys. Knowledge of the details of supply and demand of particular commodities in various countries had to be gathered by these merchants. The knowledge of the habis of the merchants of Middle East and Europe who were dependent on trade through Arabia were no less important. Goods to be carried to Syria had tobe those which would find ready market in the Middle East, for onward despatch to Turkey, Greece and farther west in Europe. International markets are not easy to understand. Supply and demand graphs keep changing overnight and not all those involved in supply or purchase of goods from abroad can forecast the trends of market correctly. Wires, cables, telephone calls and air journeys have made a great difference to international trade and commerce. How much more intricate it must have been in his time can be imagined correctly with difficulty. Goods exchanged at these trading centres had travelled thousands of miles over land and sea, and at times making use of both means of transport. Their sources were too distant to know of the vagaries of weather and other natural calamities. A merchat purchasing silk of a particular pattern in China, or spices in Jakarta and selling them in the market at Aden or Yenbo could never be sure that, if, after many hazards, he reached safely at these sea-ports, there would be merchants to lift his goods and there would be enough load of goods available there which would be in demand in his home market.

Study of Minds

Muhammad (PBUH), as was natural must have studied the minds of men from distant lands of east and west, and, as was natural for a young man of reserved and contemplating nature to have thought of the secrets of nature and the power behind the sun, the moon, the stars and how these celestial bodies have influence over the rising and falling of the vast expanses of water of numerous oceans.

This period of his life, however, has not been reported upon as fully as later part of his life. It may be so, because, as a young man he was quiet, did not drink or join other young men in their social and cultural activities and pursuits of pleasure. His search for the ultimate Reality, the Truth could have been the result of his deliberations during these journeys. Allah has referred to his search for Truth in the following Words:"

> *"Did He not find thee wandering and direct (thee)"?*
> *(93: 7)*
>
> *"And may perfect His favour unto thee, and may guide thee on a right path."* *(48: 2)*

We are told that after the war of Fajjar, a number of young men joined together and formed a society which swore that they would try their best to get the rights of weaker members of society, restored to them. The group was called, "members of Half-al-Fudhool— "People of Pact of Justice." When relating how much he was impressed by the idea of helping the weak to get his rights he is reported to have said, "If there was a group of this nature today I would join it." When he said this he was the head of the State of Medina. It probably meant that he would join a similar group formed of other heads of neighbouring states, because, within the State of Medina he had already succeeded in creating a sociey in which fullest possible justice was being administered. The world at large was being denied justice at that time. A group of states, of the nature of Half-al-Fudhool, would see that justice was done in problems connected with the rights of small nations. If a council of the heads of rulers of Middle East had been possible, how different would the world have been today. His letters, as the head of State of Medina and the Last Prophet of Allah to the rulers of neighbouring states need to be studied from this point of view.

He had travelled in these lands as a merchant and he must have known the conditions under which a common man lived and toiled to look after his needs and those of his family. When writing letters, inviting these rulers to embrace Islam, he had kept their people in mind. He had said in his letter to the Roman Emperor, "If you do not accept, then the responsibility of the sins of people of the land will be on you."

The rulers of these states would have earned double reward if their people had led a freer and a happier life as a result of their rulers embracing Islam. International markets of those days, when there were no visas and no restrictions on entry into foreign lands, except the hazards of journey, gave a greater international look, than at present although travel facilities have increased many times.

A mind which hadbeen introduced to life under the vast expanse of desert sky and the limited approach to life on the other hand must have reacted in a mixed manner to the varied scenes and strange ideas of men from different lands. We have very little evidence to fall back upon, to guide us to the shaping of his ideas during this period. We, however, know, as we are told, that he was respected by all as a result of his honesty, sincerity and readiness to help the needy. When rebuilding of Kaaba was taken in hand, and the question of placing in its proper place the sacred "Black Stone" came up every branch of the Quraish desired that this honour should be bestowed on its members alone. "Matters reached the stage where bloodshed appeared imminent and the work stopped for a few days, Umayyah bin Mugheera, an elderly person advised of leaving the matter to Allah. Whoever entered the precincts of Kaaba, through Bani Shaiba gate, should be appointed as the arbitrator." The elders of various branches assembled at the appointed time to see who would enter first from Bani Shaiba gate. It happened that Muhammad (PBUH) was the first to emerge from behind the hill of Safa and enter the Haram. Someone shouted, "It is the Ameen, The Trustworthy." The problem was at once placed before him. His decision was prompt and such that none would be offended. He proposed that the four large branches of Quraish must nominate a representative. When this was done, he spread his mantle on the ground, placed the Sacred Black Stone on the mantle and asked the four representatives to lift the mantle from its four corners and take it gently to the corner of the Kaaba, where it was to be fixed. When they arrived with the stone at the spot, he lifted it up and with the help of all four reprsentatives fixed it in its proper place. This issue was thus solved amicably and bloodshed was avoided.

His reputation for honesty was so well founded and well known that it reached the ears of Khadija, a rich widow, who had substantial business abroad. She entrusted her merchandise to him during one of the trading seasons. The profits that he brought were far more than used to be, in the case of earlier trading activities. This business partnership only ended when, after usual enquiries, Khadija sent word that if marriage was acceptable to him, he should arrange through his uncle, Abu Talib, and ask for her hand. Apart from being a widow her father was dead and one of her uncles acted as her guardian during the Nikah ceremonies.

It was an ideal of a happy life. Her age at the time of marriage with the Prophet (PBUH) is said to be forty years. Dr. Hamidullah, however, on the strength of Muhammad bin Habib Baghdadi's book Kitab-ul-Muhabbar says that it was 28 years. The fact that they had eight children, four sons and four daughters, of whom three have left children behind, appears to support this view. It, however, needs further study. After forty years of age the remaining span of middle age is too short to have more than three or four children.

Contemplation and Meditation : Some time after marriage he is known to have turned towards contemplation and meditation. His journeys to various international markets, travelling through hundreds of miles of sandy deserts, barren hills and thick forests must have inclined his thoughts to the Creator of all those. He must have met thousands of people both good and bad, pious and inclined towards evil, powerful and weak and must have thought of finding out the truth for himself. It is only natural for a man of his reserved and sober nature to turn towards the Creator. It is not that the Arabs did not believe in a Supreme Being. They had the concept of Allah but He had been relegated to an inactive position. The three hundred and sixty odd gods with names like Lat, Uzza and Manat according to their belief, had all the power, which helped human beings. Allah was there, but did not interfere or direct the affairs of mankind. He was to them just a Name and no more. These and other thoughts, not possible of being defined by a layman, like the present writer, must have appeared to him and he would have started searching for the Turth in right earnest. He chose the cave of Hera on Jabal-e-Noor, as his usual venue for contemplation. The word Hera means 'one that is found after searching'. He used to spend days there. He would take water and some provision for three or four days. If he did not return on the stipulated day, we are told, that, Khadija would take food and water for him and thus enable him to prolong his stay in Hera. We know nothing of the subjects tat he addressed to himself during this entire period. He was alone with nature nd that was enough for him. If the mind of man, the most balanced Creation of Allah can be turned to the Supreme Will, coud any mundane thought remain in the tiny mind of man which is supported by His Spirit.

llah Himself was preparing him, though not known to him, in a manner that his mind should be ready to receive The Final Divine Message for the guidance of mankind. This Last and Final Message to mankind was to terminate and end for all time the system of Divine Revelation which had been in vogue from the days o Adam and Nuh. There was a purpose in this ending of Allah's Message, which had always been a Blessing of Allah but it had, thrughout the ages, tied the mind of man to get directions from Him, through His chosen Messengers. This had resulted in numerous schisms and innumerable denominations under the umbrella of a number of so-called religions. This was hindering the physical and spiritual progress of man, which in itself was a barrier to the ultimate achievements ofmankind—The conquest of elements and of nature itself.

Inherent Powers of Innovation : Man has been bestowed with a mind which has inerent powers of innovation the heights of which have not yet been scaled and which is still in the process of developing. Allah's Messages through the ages have been commensurate with the progress made by the mind of man.

The Final Message which was to be beyond Time and Space, was not sent until such time that mind of man had not reached the requisite maturit. His mind — the mind of Muhammad (PBUH) was being prepard in the cave of Hera to develop to a standard which will be needed by the mass of humanity near the Dooms Day, to unravel all the secrets of nature. Mankind by then would have practically "put to service whatsoever is in the heavens and whatsoever is in the earth," and the Sun, the Moon, the countless heavenly bodies and their constellations would have floated through the Cosmos, and arrived at the final destination.'

To reach that stage of mentaldevelopment, where man will be able to master and benefit from all that is in nature, he needs knowledge far in excess of what his mind can imagine today. As long as man is divided in ethical, linguistic, and geographical groups and on the basis of faith and religion, he will never be able to conquer that limit of knowledge. He needs peace for such great heights of mental excellence and gain scientific and philosophical knowledge and truth. To overcome all these differences man had to be given an ideology which would surpass all such minor differences and prejudices that keep mankind divided.

Allah in His Mercy and Benevolence, closed the door of all religions an gave to mankind One Last and Final Way of Life, and did not even call it a religion. This Way of Life, which can contain all modes of thought was named by Allah Himself as The Way of Life of Peace.

> *"This day have I prfected your religion for you, and completed My favour unto you, and have chosen for you as religion Al-Islam."* (5: 3)

Mankind was invited, for this very reason, to forget all minor differences and join to work together to give Peace to humanity through cooperation on those parts of Belief which were common to all schools of thought or whatever denomination people wished to be given to themselves. Muhammad was Ordered by Allah to:

> *"Say O People of the Scripture! Come to an agreement between us and you that we shall worship none but Allah, and that we shall ascribe no partner unto Him, and that none of us shall take othersfor lords beside Allah."* (3: 64)

We shall come to that part later on, as to how Muhammad (PBUH) the last Prophet of Allah whose Mission was to live and demonstrate the manner in which mankind had to be brought on to the same patform, acted on this Verse, and invited People of The Book to join with him and more towards the ultimate objective of unity and peace of mankind. He did this through this Document which we have undertaken to study.

Mankind which had been bestowed with knowledge at the time of his Creation, and Commanded to read, recite, study and absorb all possible knowledge through the pen will, one day, climb the platform of Islam and will seek knowledge even when available in far off China.

Te Last Message, for unity and peace of mankind, in the very Words of Allah, was conveyed to mankind as a Trust fom Him. Every word that was Revealed was dictated to scribes and was written down on paper, wood, bone, skin,stone or whatever material was available. Men were encouraged to remember it word for word, a practce which is even today being carried on all over the world.

A message through wordsis like the theory of a problem. For mankind, particularly those generations which were not in existence at the time, the words were like a written desire, to be translated into action at a later stage. The Prohet (PBUH) lived his life in accordance with the Words of the Quran. Every action of his has been recorded meticulously. No life whether ancient or modern has been passed down containing so accurate details of it as his life has been recorded. The wonder is, that from the space of one life time, particularly the period at Medina, all aspects of life of an average human eing can receive guidance from it.

Whether a man lived during the first century after his death or the fourteenth century after him, and whether he was in Arabia then or is in Japan or United States of America today, whether it be a merchant, a husband, a neighbour, a politician, a statesman, a ruler of state or the supreme commander of a victorious army, he can receive the most moral, the most ethical and the most profitable guidance from the Sunnah of the Prophet (PBUH).

Allah's Promise : Allah had promised, that he will protect the Quran from all kinds of adulterations and will retain it in its original form for ever. He has been Most Kind. Not only that. He has looked after the details of His Messenger's Sunnah as well. raise be to Allah, the Mighty, the Kind, to The Most Compassionate.

An unseen hand, unknown to him, had been guiding him to fulfil the destiny of mankind. At the appropriate time when the heart and mind were well tuned and all senses were awake and in harmony with the All Pervading, Mighty, All Knowing, Allah's Mercy, the man, Muhammad son of Abdullah, an orphan child of Amina, was elevated to the highest pedestal that mortal man could conceive of occupying — the pedestal of Mercy to Mankind.

It was mercy to entire mankind because the life he led, the laws which were promulgated by him, and the collective communal life, of which he was to give practical demonstration, wasto benefit millions after millions in every age. They were to copy his laws, make slogans of his actions, like liberty, freedom, equality, fraternity, justice for all, education, social service and untold number of minor and major acts, which, he initated and mankind was to emulate, even though denying him the credit and the status of a guide from Allah.

Liberty, equality, and fraternity have been practiced by Muslim societies all the world over. The West copied these phrases during the closing years of eighteenth century. It was first in France that "equality" became a slogan. The impressions of these slogans created on Englishmen are vividly described by an Englishman while he was travelling in the East where he had come across Muslims who really practiced equality. He writes:

> *"Our demagogues have translated the French words 'liberate, egalite, fraternite,.... by the English words, liberty, equality, fraternity, and because there is much resemblance in the sounds, they would persuade the people that there is also a resemblance in the ideas. Facts teach us that liberty signifies the most horrible tyranny, silencing all low, and violating all property; that egalite*

(equality) signifies murdering foreigners and the higher classes, and pulling over the pople men of the most low, ignorant, and wicked.... Fraternite, in France, signifies being a Frenchman; applied to other nations, it signifies, forcing on them a government, plundering their property, and taking their wives and daughters."

Allah, The Most Powerful, has powerful means at His disposal to speak to mortal man. When He sends His Angels (if we may call his messengers by this name) which convey His Commands to mankind are powerful beings, even though they may be ethereal, and they have spoken Allah's Words to His Prophets.Adam, Nuh, Ibrahim, Moses, Jesus, to name a few, they all received Allah's Commands through Angel Jibbrail — Jibbrail — the most powerful source of conveying Messages to His Servants.

"That this is in truth the word of an honoured messenger. Mighty, established in the Presence of the Lord of the Throne, (One) to be obeyed, and trustworthy."(81: 19-21)

He had to be obeyed.

He appeared before Muhammad and passed on the Command of Allah. "Read."

The Ameen, who had been the trustworthy, the truthful, throughout his life replied, "I cannot read."

The mighty messenger of Mighty Allah pressed him in an embrace which hecould hardly bear and Allah's Command was repeated again "Read."

Muhammad son of Abdullah gave the same answer. "I cannot read."

The pressure was felt and borne again and the Command from Almighty Allah was repeated third time.

"Read."

The unlettered became learned, wise and knowledgeable with the Grace of Allah, and from this moment onward Muhammad son of Abdullah became Muhammad The Prophet of Allah (PBUH).

"O ye who believe. Ask blessings on him and salute him with a worthy salutation." (33: 56)

Because "Allah and His Angels shower blessings on the Prophet."

The experience had exhausted him. All spiritual experiences are trying, tiring and exhausting in the extreme— so say the - knowledgeable. Man is the sum totalof the spiritual and the material. Allah, having made him out of clay, granted life to him through the action of water and when He had given him hs beautiful shape He infused a little of His Spirit into Him and then granted a little of His Own Knowledge, because He had destined him to be His Vicegerent on earth.

Muhammad was a man in his feelings and reactions to unusual incidents lke all other men. He had long been in search of Truth but not having had a single lesson or guidance from any oher man or woman, he got worried to the extreme. The experience of being face to face with Jbbrail and being embraced by him, infused into his heart mighty feelings, he was un-nerved. He could not help it.

> *"nd lo! thy Lord! He is indeed the Mighty, the Merciful. And lo! it is a Revelation of the Lord of the Worlds, Which the True Spirit has brought down Upon thy heart, that thou mayest be (one) of the warners. In plain Arabic Speech."* *(26: 191-195)*

We re told that he was very worried. Allah brought him to normal mental and spiritual condition. His prayers, his meditations and his search of The Truth was for the sake of Truth and not for material or other gain. He had not been a pupil to any learned or to any other-worldly person. If he had known what Revelation is, he would have, at once, realised that his efforts of years of meditation had borne fruit and there would have been no cause, in his mind, to have worried about his unusual experience. He went home and took solace from Khadija, the "Pure," a great lady from all standards. He told her to cover him with a blanket. She obeyed and when he had calmed down he told her of the whole incident and said, "I am afraid of my life."

She had known him for years. She replied,

> *"Allah will not treat you thus because he knows your truthfulness, your great trustworthiness, your fine character, and your kindness."*

Khadija's words were good and comfoting and must have reassured him a great deal but the matter was not such that it could be disposed off in a little while or even in a day or two. The experience was unique, in that, the Voice had originated from the Conscious Will of the Creator of man and universe. He knew or must have known, that He had spoken to Prophets before but he had never desired, imagined or dreamed that he will be called upon to join the company of the chosen ones. If he had desired any such thing it would have been shown in his words or deeds. It never did and Allah was later on to remind him to tell people, and

> *"Say, If Allah had so willed I should not have recited it to you nor would He have made it known to you. I dwelt among you a whole lifetime before it came to me). Have ye then no sense"?* *(10: 17)*

If he had ever desired to become a saintly person, those around or near him and particularly those who had remained in close contact with him during trade journeys would have known of his inclinations and would have said so.

Khadija had a cousin, Warqah bin Noufal, who was a man well versed in Scriptures but had become blind due to old age. She visited him and told him the story. He reassured her and told her that there had come unto Muhammad the greatest Namus, the same that came to Moses. He assured her that Muhammad was a Prophet of Allah. He asked her to tell her husband that he should rest assured of Allah's help. She returned home and repeated the words ofWarqah to Muhammad (PBUH) but he could not believe it just becuse a wise old man had said so. Belief in Allah and belief in himself as the Prophet of Allah had to be bestowed and repeatedly drawn attention to the extent of duties and responsibilities attached with such a high office. As said earlier, he had laboured for years to know The Truth, but he had never aspired for any personal elevation. Warqah may be right but he had to await and see what Allah had decreed and what exactly was expected of him. It is difficult, and in point of fact, impossible to mark out the stages through which Muhammad (PBUH) may have passed to Believe that he really was the Prophet of Almighty Allah, to whom he had been praying for Guidance for years.

To be His prophet was the greatest honour. He hd never dreamed of it and yet the Verses Revealed on Jabal al-Noor, in the cave of Hera, were meaningful and of great significance. A man who had travelled abroad, met and had done business with people of many nationalities and lands,had been respected in society and had been speding days contemplating on the sun, the moon, the stars, the way they moved, through different seasons, but yet according to a fixed plan and at a fixed speed, cutting across each others path and yet not colliding. These and other tokens of the Master Mind of all Powerful Allah were not for nothing.

ll these must fit into some plan, a plan which would also have a special place for man, the only rational creature he had come across in his numerous journeys. His mind must have gone to the Words Revealed during the first encouner with the Angel Jibbrail. These Words were to be repeated, nay read, recited and deliberated upon by him again and again.

"Read:"

"In the Name of the Lord Who Createth."

He would have stopped to think. That henceforth he had to read and contemplate, in the Name of the Lord of all these floating constellations, the earth, the moon and all there is in them all, and to Read. Yes, to read and to think and deliberate on the greatness of his Lord. He is Great. There is no doubt. His Creation, which the eye can see is vast beyond imagination. To prove that man is His slave and servant he must study His creation. Yes! man must see things logically, rationally nd systematically.

And then his mind would go towards his responsibility. He had been told to read, recite and ... Could it not be that he had to tell men and women to read and study His Creations. And his mind would go to strange things and to man himself as a Creation of Allah. And the following Words of the Revelation must have boomed large before his mind:

"Createth man from a clot."

Man, the beautiful, the knowledgeable, the learned, the scientist, the preacher of religion, the wealthy merchant, the ministers, courtiers and rulers of other men; they all were created from a clot. They must be told this, so that they humble themselves and prostrate themselves before their Lord. What secrets could be unveiled and steps taken to improve conditions for man if he was to know exactly what processes his life went through from the stage of a clot to a healthy human child. He would not have guessed it then but history records that his insistence on learning and acquiring knowledge would take man out of the orbit of earth and not only land him on to a distant planet but this knowledge would bring him back safely to his present abode, the earth, which itself needs further probing intoit. And He has repeated the Command, "Read." It is no doubt to emphasis but also because "It" goes on to say: And thy Lord is the Most Bountiful, because He had placed His entire Universe at the service of man — His Viceroy on earth.

And these bounties of Allah, The Most Merciful can be made use of only through knowledge, the result of "reading, reciting, deliberating and examining." Allah's bounties pile up when the 'pen' is used. Man's memory is limited. If knowledge was to be passed on from memory to memory it would remain limited and eventually stagnate. It has been through the use of pen that the knowledge acquired by numerous generations has been preserved. It goes on accumulating generation after generation.

Acquisitin and then preservation of the wealth acquired through pen has made human life more pleasant after every generation and has brought mankind to the doorstep of the unchartered expanse of this universe. Allah gave to man the use of pen. Pen has recorded knowledge of hundreds of generations and Allah has to be praised for teaching man the use of pen. Through "Pen," Allah :

> *"Teacheth man what he knew not."* *(96: 5.)*

How long he must have thught on the Words Revealed to him in the very first Revelation cannot be known. It must have, however, brought him nearer to his "Belief in himself as the Messenger of Allah..." He had always believed in Allah and Allah had now commanded him to read, recite and think so that he should, from then onwards, believe in himself as the Messenger of Allah. Without, his own belief in himself as the Prophet, Allah's Command could not be communicated to mankind. He was given Revelations on subsequent occasions in which reference was drawn to himself, because it was essential that his belief in himself must be firm and without any flaw. Some of the opening Verses of Makki Suras ae of interest in this respect.

> *"Alif. Lam. Ra.*
>
> *These are verses of the wise Scripture. Is ita wonder for mankind that We have Inspired a man among them."*
> *(10: 1-3)*

This Wisdom of the New Philosophy of Life based on the unshared Sovereignty of Allah is destined to lead mankind to Eternal Bliss. This Book is not only full of Wisdom, it is also "Plain" and easy to understand.

> *"These are Verses of the Scrpture that maketh plain. Lo! We haverevealed i, a Lecture in Arabic, that ye may understand."* *(12: 1-2)*

This fact, that this Book of Wisdom has been Revealed to Muhammad (PBUH) as to be kept in mind all the time. Initially it had to be kept in mind by Muhammad (PBUH) himself, for instance, the following Verse:

> *"These are Verses of the Scripture. That which is Revealed unto thee from thy Lord is the TRUTH (and*

you were, for years searching TRUTH) but most of mankind believe not. Allah it is who raised the heavens without visible support, then mounted the THRONE, and compelled the sun and the moon to be of service."

(13: 1-2)

Truth had been revealed to His chosen men in all ages:

"There is no God save Him, the Alive, the Eternal. He hath revealedunto thee (O Muhammad) the Scripture with truth. Confirming that which was (revealed) before it, even as He Revealed the Torah and the Gospel." *(3: 2-3)*

The object of the Book being revealed to him was also being explained to him.

"(This is) a Scripture which We have Revealed unto thee (O Muhammad) that thereby you mayest bring forth mankind from darkness to light, by the permission of your Lord." *(14: 1)*

The treatment of this subject in this forthright manner is not confined to opening Verses of Surahs only. It has been emphasized elsewhere as well. For instance:

"Lo! We, even We, have revealed unto thee the Quran, a revelation; So submitpatiently to thy Lord's command, and obey not of them any guilty one or disbeliever."

(76: 23-24)

When studying any incident of Muhammad's life it must be borne in mind all the time that previous to his enlightenment in the cave named Hera, he had no knowledge of those Divine subjects, which were being Revealed to him. When Prophethood was conferred on him the dis-believers were all the time using all means at their disposal to dissuade him from embarking on this great Mission from Allah. He was, therefore, every moment in danger of exposure to the misleading of others. Allah warned him of such moments:

"But for the grace of Allah upon thee (O Muhammad), and His Mercy, a party of them had resolved to mislead thee but they will mislead only themselves and they will hurt thee not at all. Allah Revealeth unto the Scripture and Wisdom, and teacheth thee that which thou knewest not. The grace of Allah toward thee hath been infinite."

(4: 113)

Revelation of the Eternal Message, a message which will be applicable for all lands, for all people and until the end of Time, is a

Miracle from Allah, which needs to be studied with great care and sincerity.

A message surpassing Time and Space is being put before humanity of all ages by a man who never sat at the feet of any teacher, any sage, or philosopher is a phenomenon demanding attention from all those who have regard for truth. The wonde and the miracle, on his part, is that from the time he was given this Mission of conveyin Allah's Message to mankind, he translated the theory ino practice, and demonstrated to his generation, and the coming generations of mankind, the leadership of an Ideal Society, who believe in the New Way of Life.

> *"Blesed is He Who hath revealed Unto His slave the Criterion (of right and wrong), that he may be a warner to th people."* (25: 1)

But there is, in reality, nothing to be surprised at, because the Revelation is from Allah. He says:

> *"The revelation of the Scripture is from Allah, the Mighty, The Wise. Lo! n the heavens and the earth are portents for believers."* (45: 2-3)

Man's mind must be satisfied. Satan was there and is still there to whisper doubts. Allah has, therefore, brought home to mankind that there should remain no doubt regarding the issue of a man rising to hitherto such unsealed heights of Wisdom, as Muhammad demonstrated. He says:

> *"The Revelation of the Scripture is from Allah the Mighty, the Knower, The Forgiver of sins, the Accepter of repentance, the Stern in punishment, the Bountiful. There is no God save Him, Unto Him is the journeying."* (40: 2-3)

Because the conveying of good tidings to the righteous and warning of punishment to the evil doers are tasks both equally necessary, the Prophet (PBUH) has been adjudged as the final witness on the Day of Judgement. Allah has said :

> *"O Prophet! Lo! We hae sent thee as a witness and a bringer of good tidings an a warner. And as a summoner Unto Allah by His Permission, and as a lamp that giveth light."* (33: 45-46)

And

> *"Lo! (O Muhammad) We have sent thee with the truth, a bringer of glad tidins and a warner. And thou wilt not be asked about the owners of hell fire."* (2: 119)

Muhammad (PBUH) was the first and the direct recipient of Allah's Commands contained in the Quran. He had to be the first Believer and he became the firt Believer. Allah in His Wisdom has confirmed the superb belief of Muhammad (PBUH).

> *"The messenger believeth in that which hath been revealed unto him from his Lord And (so do) the believers."* *(2: 285)*

It was this unflinching Belief in Allah and His Words that carried him through the hard days of persecution, by his own people, against him and his Companions, the Believers, about whose Belief Alah has testified in the Verse given above. It was this rock like belief in Allah and His promise, at a time, when he and his Compaions were being attacked by Meccan superior forces and Allah had said:

> *"Faint not, nor grieve, for ye will overcome them if ye are (indeed) believers."* *(3: 139)*

They proved that they were true Believers and Allah kept His promise to the minutest detail.

> *"It is a promise of Allah. Allah faileth not His Promise, but most of mankind know not."* *(30: 6)*

Muhammad (PBUH) and his Companions knew this ad believed in it. His proclamation of his being Allah's Messenger was to be conveyed to all mankind. The emphasis which was being laid on this fact, of addressing entire humanity, was to remind that both the Quran and the Sunah had to be kept alive for all times:

> *"Say (O Muhammad) O mankind! Lo! I am the messenger of Allah to you all — (the messenger of) Him unto whom belongeth th Sovereignty of the heavens and the earth. There is no God save Him. He quickeeth and He giveth death. So Believe in Allah's messenger, the Prophet who can neither read nor write, who belieeth in Allah and in His Words, And follow him, that hoply ye may be led aright."* *(7: 158)*

The Mission progressed slowly. He announced it to the membersof his family and then to the people of Mecca.

Khadija was the firs to accpt his Prophethood. Zaid must have been next but, somehow, history books relegate him to the third or fourth position. Ali is said to be the second but the occasion when he announced it was at a feast which took place sometimes after the original announcement. He is said to be twelve years of age. According to the version given about Abu Bakr's embracing Islam, it appears that he was the first person outside the family to have entere the fold of Islam.

He may have felt that the progress of Islam was not as it could have been. This thought may have depressed him. Allah who knows the innermost thoughts of man, at once, consoled him by saying:

> *"Ta Ha. We have not revealed unto thee (O Muhammad this Quran, that you should be distressed, but as a reminder unto him who fearth, A revelation from Him Who created the earth and the high heavens." (20: 1-4)*

His task was confined to conveying the Message but the acceptance by people depended on their decision whether they desired to remain in darkness or wished to see light.

> *"(This is) a Scripture Which We have revealed unto thee (O Muhammad) that thereby thou mayest bring forth mankind from darkness unto light, by the Permission of their Lord unto the Path of the Mighty, the Owner of Praise." (14: 1)*
>
> *"O Messenger! Make known that which hath been revealed unto thee from thy Lord for if thou do it not, thou will not have conveyed His Message. Allah will protect thee from mankind Lo! Allah guideth not the disbelieving folk." (5 67)*

After this Verse was Revealed, the guarding of his residence, at night, was discarded. This is a Surah of Medina, and, belongs, to the early days after Hijrah, when the Meccans had started invading the territories of Medina.

Chapter 5

The Ideal Way of Life

Divine Law

Process of Revelation : What is the consequence of abstracting the text and treating it symbolically? Our impression is that such an interpretative approach either becomes trivializing or fascist. The trivializing aspect comes about because truths are abstracted from their context and end up being recorded as bland statements, like 'Islam is peace', or 'Islam teaches us to be just', or 'Jihad means to struggle for peace'. In such a context, how important could careful adherence to the *ahkam* (legal properties) be? The fascist part comes about because the ke interpreter gets to play games with symbls that are manipulated exclusively by him and his cohorts. In that context, external or outward or literal Islam, with its laws and regulations, is so much drivel for people not sufficiently elevated. (One could call the first approach *ibahiyyah* and the second *batiniyyah).*

Holy Quran First : In contrast, the consequence of closer readings of the revelation, of more grammatically aware and precise readings, of increased attention to the tiniest details of the revelation in its original language is, ironically, a discovery of a polysemantic and multifaceted text. The broadest, most varied and dynamic, vibrant and living understanding of the revelation comes from the closest, most careful, detailed, linguistic, and literally based reading. It happens too that the closest fidelity to the *ahkam* (such as those related to placing one's hands while standing during the *salah,* for example) opens up a range of authentic and true positions. Instead of denigrating the truth of following normative practices by trivializing them, this interpretation invests great significance and relevance to multiple true positions;

instead of in-group fascism, this interpretation affirms other true positions, without denying any one of them.

In one passage we saw Ibn al-Arabi incorporating the peculiar linguistic fact that in the Arab language the word *khafiya is* its own antonym, such that, for those of the perception, the Hidden is the Manifest, the exposed is the concealed. When I mentioned this to a colleague of mine, she said that the secrets of the Quran are safely hidden away—in the outside, literal text! As with Poe's purloined letter, the best place to hide something is in the most exposed place. The *haqqiqah* is the *Shariah*.

Let us examine the depths, details, and particularities of one portion of a verse to show what kind of polysemanticism comes about with a close; literal reading of the revelation. This portion of a verse in the chapter *al-Maidah* sets down the description of *wudu*. The portion reads, *O you who believe. When you go to the salah, wash your faces and your hands to the elbows and wipe your heads and your feet to the ankles [5:6].* The two operative imperatives are wash (ghusl) and wipe (m.s.h.). The question is which imperative governs the phrase 'your feet'. Wiping is where wet hands brush over the bodily part in question, whether head or foot. Wiping the feet entails a brisk movement similar to the wiping over the shoes, and Sunni scholars have generally believed this movement of wiping over the bare feet to be negated by the *Hadith* evidence in which the Prophet Muhammad admonished a group of Muslims to pay attention to their heels in *wudu,* saying, 'Woe to the heels in hell-fire'.'

This particular line of argument unfolds as follows. The obvious and literal meaning of the verse in the Quranic Arabic indicates the feet, much as in English 'wipe your heads, and your feet', means 'wipe your heads, and wipe your feet'. But the *Hadith* seems to indicate 'washing' the feet, so as to make sure the heels are covered in *wudu.* How should these two different indications be reconciled? We examine some of the major arguments which seek to do just that below, and then we examine Ibn al-Arabi's treatment of this issue.

Let us look first at three areas essential to this *fiqh* debate. First, the recitations involved for the verse; that is, the authentic, correct *(sahih)* recitations of the word 'your feet'. Second, the list of authorities and what method of *wudu* of the feet they practised, and why. Third, the arguments proffered by scholars over the ages to address this issue. The raw citations and data are to give the reader a glimpse of the intricacies and fine points of the classical scholarly discourse, where the direction one moves toward truth is not out towards abstraction and generalization, but in towards detail and specificity. As with fractal geometries, Escher's drawings, Borges and Eco's writings, the 'truth' of things lies in the patterns one perceives as one peers closely and with a narrower field of view. The weight of this massive debate should demonstrate the futility of the desire for conclusion and answers, and should begin to show us instead the value of searching for polysemanticism in randomness, complexities, and ambiguities.

Good Recitations : There are three recitations of 'your feet', namely *arjulakum* (with *nasb), arjulikum* (with *khafd),* and *arjulukum* (with *raft*) :

1. The first recitation is recited by Nafi ibn Abu Nuaym (169/785), Asim ibn Abu al-Nujud (127/744), and Ali ibn Hamzah al-Kasai (189/801).
2. The second recitation of *arjulikum* with *khafd* is that of Abd-Allah Ibn Kathir (120/737), Abu Amr ibn al-Ala (1455/771), and Hamzah ibn Habib (156/772).
3. For the third recitation, Nafi is reported, by Walid ibn Muslim, to have also recited *arjulukum* with *raft*, and it is the recitation of Hassan and al-Amash Sulayman?

Generally, but not necessarily, as we shall see, the recitation of *arjulakum* supports a reading that implies that the operative imperative here is 'wash'; the recitation of *arjulikum* supports a reading that implies that the operative imperative is the proximate verb 'wipe'; and the rare recitation *arjulukum* supports a reading that implies that either of the two imperatives are operative—wipe *and wash* your feet.

Effective Authorities : The following are authoritative positions of early Muslims.

Arjulakum : Washing

Urwah ibn Zubayr *(nasb):* recorded in Ibn Mundhir.

Mujahid ibn Jabr *(nasb):* in Ibn Mundhir.

Nafi ibn Abd al-Rahman *(nasb):* reported from Abu Ubyd, in Ibn Mundhir.

Qusai *(nasb):* in Ibn Mundhir.

Abu Ubayd al-Qasim ibn Salam *(nasb):* in Ibn Mundhir.

Al-Shafii *(nasb):* in Ibn Mundhir.

Ali *(nasb):* al-Qurtubi records, 'Asim ibn Kalib reported from Abd al-Rahman that he said, Hassan and Hussain, Allah's mercy on them, recited *wa arjulakum,* and Ali heard that, and was adjudicating between the people, and said *arjulakum.'* Ibn Mundhir confirms that Ali recited with *nasb.*

Arjulakum : Wiping

Ibn Masud : *(nasb :* wiping);

Ibn Abbas *(nasb :* wiping): al-Qurtubi records, 'It was reported from Ibn Abbas that he said *wudu* is two washings [arms and face] and two wipings [head and feet]'.

Ibn Qudamah records, 'It is related from Ibn Abbas that he said, I do not find in the Book of Allah anything but two washings and two wipings."

Ibn Kathir records that Ibn Abbas wiped the feet. He says, 'Ibn Abu Hatim said, *haddathana* my father *haddathana* Abu Mamar al-Mungari *haddathana* Abd al-Wahhab *Haddathana* Ali ibn Zayd from Yusuf ibn Mohrin from Ibn Abbas about this verse that it is a wiping.'

Ibn Majah records in his *Sunan, 'haddathana* Abu Bakr ibn Abi Shaybah *haddathana* Ibn Ulayyah, from Ruhi ibn al-Qasim from Abd-Allah ibn Muhammad ibn Aqil from Rubayya, who said, Ibn Abbas came to me and he asked me about this *Hadith,* that is, the *Hadith* in which it was mentioned that the messenger of Allah *(sallallahu alayhi wa sallam)* did *wudu* and washed his feet. Ibn Abbas said, "The people insist on nothing but washing, but I do not find in the Book of Allah anything but wiping"."

Arjulikum : Wiping

Al-Hassan al-Basri : in Ibn Mundhir.

Sulayman ibn Mohrin al-Amash : in Ibn Mundhir.

Abu Jafar : al-Razirecords, 'The people disagree about wiping the feet and washing them', and Ibn Abbas, Anas ibn Malik, Ikrimah, Shubi, and Abu Jafar Muhammad ibn Ali obligate wiping, and it is the position of the Imamiyyah among the Shiah.'

Ikrimah ibn Abd-Allah: al-Qurtubi records, 'Ikrimah used to wipe his feet. He said there is no washing for the feet: The Quran was sent down with wiping them.' He also records that Ibn Jarar said, *'haddathana* aqub *haddathana* Ibn Uliyah *haddathana* Ayub who said, "I saw Ikrimah wiping his feet, and he argued for it".'

Abu Dharr: Ibn Hajar (852) in *Fath al-Bari* records that to the *Hadih* 'woe to the heels in hell-fire', Abu Dharr added, 'And he did not wipe his feet."

Al-Qatadah : al-Qurtubi records that al-Qatadah ibn Daamah (117/735) said 'Allah made required two washings and two wipings.'

Arjulikum : Washing

Amr ibn Sharhbil al-Shubah : in Ibn Mundhir. He is recorded as saying, 'The Quran came down with wiping but the Sunna is for washing.'

Al-Thalab : Ibn Manzur in *Lisan al-Arab* cites Abu al-Abbas al-Thalab (291/903) as saying, 'The Quran came down revealing wiping but the Sunna is for washing."

Anas : al-Qurtubi recors that Al-Hajjaj ibn Yusuf al-Thaqafi (95/714), governor of the eastern provinces, 'gave a *Khutba* in Ahwaz and mentioned *wudu.* He said, "Wash your faces and hands and wipe your heads and feet because there is nothing of the sons ofAdam closer to filth than his feet, so wash them, their bottoms and their tops, and their tendons." Anas ibn Malik heard that and said, "Allah spoke the truth and Hajjaj spoke a lie, because Allah said, Wipe your heads *wa arjulikum.* When he wiped his feet, he (simply) moistened them".' Al-Qurtub also records, 'It is also reported from Anas that he said the Quran was sent down with wiping but the Sunna is with washing.' Ibn Mundhir records the above from Ibn Umar and also records, '*haddathana* Ismail *haddathana* Abu Bakr *haddathana* Muhammad ibn Abi Adwi from his father that Anas used to wash his hands and feet until they dripped.'

Ibn Kathir records the same story about Hajjaj: 'Ibn Jarar said *haddathani* Yaqub ibn Ibrahim *haddathana* Ibn Uliyah *haddathana* Hamid who said Musa ibn Anas said to Anas, when we were with him, O Abu Hamzah, Hajjaj gave us a *Khutba* in Ahwaz, while we were with him and he mentioned purification. He said, "Wash your faces and wipe your heads and feet because there is nothing of the sons o Adam closer to filth than his eet, so wash them, their bottoms and their tops, and teir tendons." Anas heard that and said, Hajjaj spoke a lie: Allah said, *Wipe your heads wa arjulikum.* When Anas wiped the feet, he moistened them. The chain is authentic.' Ibn Kathir also confirms: 'Ibn Jarar said *haddathana* Ali ibn Sahl *haddathana* Mumal *haddathana* Hammad *haddathana* Asim about the case of Anas, and he said. The Quran came down with wiping but the Sunna is for washing. This too has an authentic chain.'

Arjulukum : Wash and Wipe

Hassan (combine): al-Zamakhshari records that Hassan said, 'It is a combining of two matters.' He also records, 'Hassan recited *arjulukum* with *raf,* with the meaning *wa arjulukum,* washed or wiped to the ankles'.

Daud (combinc): al-Razi records that Daud al-Isfahani al-Zahiri obligates combining the two; it is also the position of al-Nasir of the Zaydis.

Al-Nuhhas (combine): al-Qurtubi records, 'al-Nahhas said one of the best things said about the issue is that wiping and the washing are both obligatory together, so the wiping i obligatory because of the recitation of one who recites *nasb,* and the two recitations have the status of two verses.'

Arjulikum or Arjulakum : Wash or Wipe

Al-Tabari (choice): al-Qurtubi records that 'Ibn Jarar al-Tabari (310/ 922) judged that required for the feet is to choose between the washing and the wiping.' Al-Razi adds that this was Hassan al-Basri's position too, recording, "The position of Hassan al-Basri and Muhammad ibn Jarar al-Tabari is that the one responsible [for *wudu]* chooses between wiping and washing."'

Ibn al-Arabi al-Maliki records that Muhammad ibn Jarar al-Tabari ,reasoned that the recitation *is arjulikum* with *khafd* in conjunction with the head, so the head and feet are wiped, and the recitation with *nasb is* in conjunction with the face and arms, so they are washed; so in that way it functions in accordance with both recitations."

Al-Nawawi adds, 'Jubbai, the head of the Mutazilahs, chose between wiping and washing."'

Arguments from Sunna : The conclusive argument for the classical Sunni scholars for washing is based on Sunna. A terse argument for washing is that given by Ibn al-Arabi al-Maliki, who says, 'Our proof is the continuous practice *[amal al-mutassil,* that is, from the time of the Prophet (PBUH) to today, of washing the feet] and the multiple unbroken chains of transmitted text *[naql al-mutawatir]'.* Related to this argument for washing is the consensus of the scholars, described by Al-Qurtubi as his last proof, namely,

Consensus *[ujma].* They agree that the one who washed his feet has in fact fulfilled his obligation, but they disagree about one who has wiped his feet. Certainty is with what they have agreed about and not with what they have disagreed about. The transmitted tradition of all the vast majority *[jamhur]* is from their Prophet (PBUH) that he washed his feet in his *wudu,* once, twice, and thrice, until he had cleaned them. But while the Sunna is to wash, this was not always the case. Ibn Qudamah reports, 'Said *haddathana* Hashim that *akhbarana* [it was told us in the form of a report] Ibn Ata from his father that he said *akhbarani* [it was told me in a report] Aws ibn Aws Abi al-Thaqafi that he saw the Prophet come to a *kizamah* of the people of Taif, and he did *wudu* and wiped his feet. Hashim said this was in the initial period of Islam.' Interestingly, the Sunna of washing is so established that when

Ibn Manzur cites this *Hadith* in order to explain *kizamah* in his dictionary, he says this: 'The *kizamah* is a pipe under the ground and water flows through it. It is mentioned in the *Hadith* that the Prophet came to a *kizamah* of the people and did *wudu* with its water and wiped over his *shoes."'*

But besides the argument from Sunna, the classical Sunni scholars also provide numerous arguments for washing based on the Quran. Most of these arguments are linguistic, but some fall into other categories. Let us look at the other categories first.

Symbolic Arguments : Al-Zamakhshari (d.538) in his commentary *Kashshaf* records *wa arjulikum* and says, 'The majority recite *arjulakum* with *nasb,* thereby indicating that the feet are to be washed. If someone asked me why did you [O Zamakhshari] make it recite with *jarr* [that is, *khadf arjulikum]* and make the admission of a property of wiping [when you actually argue for washing the feet], I would say that the feet are among the three bodily parts washed with a pouring of water on them, so they are places of anticipated wastefulness—that is blameworthy, and actual wastefulness is forbidden—so the feet are placed in conjunction with the third part, which is wiped (i.e., the head), not so as to wipe them, but in order to remind one of the obligation of frugality in pouring water over them.'

So avoiding waste is a consideration which explains away the linguistic inclination toward wiping. This argument relies neither on the Sunna of *wudu* nor on other linguistic possibilities. This is al-Zamakhshari's major argument, and it is repeated by many of the great classical scholars.

Another argument which does not rely on the Sunna nor on linguistic evidence appeals to a sense of symmetry in *taharah.* The argument is recorded by Al-Qurtubi in this way:

Amr al-Shabi said Jibbrail sent down wiping: Do you not see that *tayammum* has wiping for what was washed [in *wudu*—hands and face] and eliminates what was wiped [in *wudu*—head and feet]?

Ibn Kathir uses this argument too, recording that :

Ibn Jarar said *haddathana* Abu al-Sayb *haddathana* Ibn Idris

from Daud ibn Abu Hind from Shaabi that he said, Jibbrail came down with wiping, then Shaabi said, Do you not see that *tayammum* is wiping what was washed and it eliminates what was wiped?

Ibn Qudamah uses this argument as well.

Linguistic Arguments : Now let us turn to the linguistic arguments. I have collated six different linguistic arguments. These include attempts to show that it is possible in the Arab language (meaning the Arabs have used such a linguistic configuration in the period before and during the descent of the Quran) to have 'your feet' be governed by the initial verb 'wash'.

The first linguistic argument we consider is lexigraphic. Al-Qurtubi records, 'Abu Zayd al-Ansari [215 A. H./830 C. E.] said, wiping in the Arab language is washing and wiping. An example is that the Arab says about someone after *wudu* who has washed the limbs that *tamassaha* [he has wiped].' This argument accepts that 'your feet' is governed by the proximate verb 'wipe', but goes on to posit that `wipe' in effect means a light washing.

Al-Qurtubi also argues that the word 'wipe' may also apply to 'wash'. However, wipe is usually seen as a subset of wash. The argument of al-Qurtubi is that 'Abd al-Haqq ibn Atiyah (546 A. H./1151 C. E.) said, "There are people among those who recite with a *qisrah [khadf]* who judged that the wiping of the two feet is a washing. It is correct that the word wiping shares multiple meanings, applying to wiping and to washing".'

A second argument takes the instances of imperative verb plus a delineated or non-delineated object, as they occur in the verse for wudu and for *tayammum.* We have for *wudu* a clear 'wash the hands to the elbows'. When it comes to *tayammum,* we have a clear 'wipe your face and hands'. Based on these instances, the arguments goes, we see that objects governed by the imperative 'wipe' are not given delineations, and the object that is definitely governed by the imperative 'wash' is given delineation, that is, up to something. Therefore, when we come to 'your feet', and we note that they are delineated with 'up to the ankles', we can conclude that the governing verb must be 'wash'. Al-Qurtubi says, 'Allah bounded the area and said *to the ankles* as He said about the arms *to the elbows.* This proves the obligation of washing the feet, but Allah knows best.'

Ibn Hisham in his *Mughni al-Labib* and al-Zamakhshari in his commentary on 5:6 say, 'It was said *to the ankles,* so He mentioned the end-point, and that dismisses the supposition that the feet are wiped, because wiping is not given an end-point in the *Shariah.*'

A third argument is based on the idea that the sequence of bodily parts purified in wudu-face, hands, head, feet-is given precedence over syntactical considerations. To illustrate this argument, suppose that the imperatives were given precedence. We would then have, 'Wash your face, hands, and feet, and wipe your head'. But because the head should be washed before the feet, we have, 'Wash face, hands, (but wipe) head, and feet', meaning 'and wash too your feet'.

Al-Qurtubi with this argument, juxtaoses the strong case for wiping based on the Quran and the strong case for washing based on the Surma. Given this tension he argues that thre must be an overriding concern which motivates the inclination of the Quranic phrase towards wiping. That concern, he says, is the sequence.

Al-Qurtubi says :

> *And it is said, Allah has* wiped *what you have when He has* washed *and purified you from your sins.* So *if it* is *from Arab tradition that the wiping may mean washing, then the statement which preponderates is this statement:* if *the consequences of the recitation with* khadf is *washing... and the many* Hadiths *fix washing, and there is the warning not to neglect the washing* of *the feet in the numerous reports published by the Imams, then the wiping for the head is rather inserted between the things which are washed [arms and feet] for the sake of sequence, that the head should be wiped before the feet are washed, according to this syntax: so wash your faces and your arms to the elbows, and your feet to the ankles, and wipe your heads. But as the head is done before the feet, it precedes them in the recitation—Allah knows best—not because they share with the head in being wiped, but because the head precedes the feet in the procss of purification.*

Abu Thawr (d. 240) also explains that there must be some overriding concern which interrupts the list of bodily parts and their imperative verbs. He says that the reason your 'feet is placed' after 'your head' is not because it should take the imperative 'wipe', but because the verse is rather establishing the sequence of *wudu*. He says, 'The munificent verse mentioned something wiped [the head] among the things washed. The custom of the Arab when he mentioned like things and unlike things [e.g., wiped and washed bodily parts] is to gather the like things and then to put the other thing in conjunction to them [last], and that custom is not opposed except for a bounty, and the bounty, here, is the [teaching of the] sequence [of *wudu].*" Ramli [d. 1004] uses this argument to in his commentary to the *Minhaj* called *Nahayat al-Muhtaj*.

A fourth argument is that in the Arab language before the descent of the Quran, there is a kind of poetic sentence which puts two objects into conjunction, but where the second object is not governed by the same verb as the first object. This would explain how the Quranic phrase puts 'your heads' into conjunction with 'your feet', while the first object is governed by 'wipe' and the second is governed by something else, in this case 'wash'.

Ibn Manzur argues this way in *Lisan al-Arab*. He says, 'So one who recites it *arjulakum* does so for two reasons. First, in this there are things anterior and things posterior, as if He said, 'Then wash your faces and arms to the elbows, and your feet to the ankles, and wipe your heads', thereby putting things first and putting things last so that *wudu* would be a succession of things one after another.

Then, it is as if He meant, 'Wash your feet to the ankles' because His statement *to the ankles* has already proven that is just as we described it [that is, the argument of delineation], so 'your feet' is arranged with washing, as the poet said:

If only your husband had come tomorrow!

Armed with sword, and lance meaning 'armed with sword, and carrying a lance', where the verb `carrying' is supplied, as 'armed' is an inappropriate verb for 'lance'. Ibn al-Arabi al-Maliki uses the same verse to show that the noun of `feet' may be in conjunction with the word 'head' but not in conjunction with its meaning (that is, 'wipe'), like the poet's verse:

I saw your husband, clamoring

Armed with sword, and lance.

Al-Qurtubi multiplies the examples of this use of language. He says, 'The Arab puts something in conjunction with something with an act which applies to only one of them.

The Arab says, "I ate bread, and milk", meaning, "I ate bread and I drank milk".' Another example is the statement of the poet:

I fed them straw, and cold water.

Another example is [from Labid ibn Rabiah]:

The two used the leaves of the cabbage plant, Giving birth

On the banks to her gazelle, and her brood.

Another example is:

I drank milk, and dates and cheese.

'The *taqdir* [the meaning of sentences with ambiguous syntactical elements] is as follows: I fed them straw, and gave them water to drink; the one giving birth on the banks to her gazelle; and the other brooding her ostrich (the ostrich does not 'give birth to' but rather 'broods' the egg); and finally, I'drank the milk, and I ate the dates. So, His phrase *Wipe your heads, and your feet* could be in conjunction with washing in spite of the conjunction with wiping, carrying the meaning and purport of washing. But Allah knows best.'

Al-Jurjani (d. *816),* al-Zamakhshari's commentator, also uses the poet's verses:

Armed with sword, and lance

And feeding the animal straw, and cold water.

A fifth argument is based on the different instances of *jarr,* which means the vowel 'i' *(khafd)* given to a word because of proximity. Al-Qurtubi finds this in the Quran, where we have, *Sent down to you will be a flame of fire, and smoke (55:35),* where 'and smoke' *is muhasin* (in some recitations), which *is khafd* because of *jarr,* because 'the smoke' means 'fumes', so the meaning is 'sent down to you will be *smoke,* and a *flame* of fire', where *smoke* and *flame* are the direct objects of the sentence, even though *smoke* is in *khafd.*

Also, al-Qurtubi adds, 'He said, *No, it is a glorious Quran, in a tablet preserved' (85:21-2).* Here *preserved is mahfuz-in,* which *is khafd* because of *jarr.* In this sentence, *Quran-un, majid-un,* and preserved are all nminatives (raft so that one would say, 'It is a Quran, it is glorious, and it is preserved, in a tablet', but instead of *mahfuz-un,* we have *mahfuz-in,* which is explained as being from proximity to *fi lawh-in* (in a tablet).'

Al-Qurtubi also cites Imru al-Qays, who said: *kabir-u unas-in* fi *bijad-in muzammal-i* meaning, 'He is great among the people, in his striped garment, wrapped up.' AI-Qurtubi remarks, `*muzammal-i is* made *khafd* by proximity, because "wrapped up" refers to the man, not to the striped garment, so that its inflected termination would otherwise be *raf".'*

He also says, 'It is like the Arabs say, *hadha juhr-u dabb-in kharib-in* [this hole of a lizard, deserted]. The word *kharib-in* [deserted] is made *jarr* even though it would be raf.' That is, the sentence reads, 'this deserted hole of a lizard.' He says, 'This is the position of Akhfash and Abu Abidah, but al-Nahhas rejected it and said this statement is a great error, because it cannot be that the proximate be brought into relationship with something in such a sentence, but it is really an error, like changing the vowel to achieve a rhyme.'

Ibn Kathir remarks that the recitation with *khafd is* 'produced because of proximity and the relationship [to wipe your heads] in the sentence, as in the Arab's sentence *juhr-u dabb-in kharib-in,* and as in His statement, *They will have on them clothes of silk, green, and brocade [76:21].* This is common in the language of the Arab.'

The grammarian Ibn Hisham says, 'A word gives governance to another word when it is in proximity to it, like the statement of some of them: *hadha juhr-u dabb-in kharib-in* with *jarr* but most of them make it *raf.*' That *is, kharib-un;* this is a hole *(juhr-u),* deserted *(kharib-un),* of a lizard *(dabb-in).* He also cites Imru al-Qays's verse:

ka-anna abanan *fi* afanini wadqihi

kabir-u unas-in *fi* bijad-in muzammali.

Ibn Hisham al-Ansari also argues from a passage in 56:11-22, which reads in part, 'These will be nearest to Allah, in gardens of bliss .... Circling them will be ever fresh youth, with goblets, glasses, and cups ... and fruits ... and flesh of fowl ... and black/white eye'." One question in this passage is what governs the phrases. Ibn Hisham notes that some take 'black/white eye' as *jarr,* that *is, hur-in,* so that 'black/white eye' is governed by 'ever fresh youth'. The meaning is then 'ever fresh youth ... with black/white eye'. But the conjunction could go all the way back to 'gardens of bliss'. Then, we would have 'gardens of bliss', with 'many fruits', and 'flesh of fowl', and *hur-in ayn-in,* which is then read as a synecdoche, as in 'companions with *hur-in ayn-in'. 'Cups'* would be in conjunction with 'ever fresh youth', so that it would be 'ever fresh youth, circling them with cups'. But Ibn Hisham ends his discussion with the comment, 'Actually, the *khafd* of proximity is rare.'

Ibn Qudamah quotes Imru al-Qays' verse which we saw and also:

fa-zalla tuhatu al-lahm min bayni mundij-in

safifa shiwa-in aw qidir-in mu ajjabi

The meat cooks erred between a well-cooked

grilled row and quick boil

where *qidir-an* (cooked in a pot) is made *jarr—qidir—in—by* being in conjunction with what is proximate, but referring back to *al-lahm* (the meat). Ibn Qudamah also cites the Quran, where we have *inni akhafu alaykum adhaba yawm-in alim-in (I* fear for you the punishment of a grievous day) (11:26), saying that *alim-in is jarr* because of the proximity of 'day', while it is a description of the punishment, which is *nasb* (the direct object), because of its proximity to the proximate *yawm-in.*

But Ibn Manzur questions the occurrence of the *khafd* of proximity as proving 'washing' in this verse by citing Abu Ishaq, the grammarian, who said, 'Making a noun *khafd* because of proximity is not permitted in the Book of Allah, while it is permissible for poetical imagery.'

Al-Razi too, is doubtful about this argument. He says that the *jarr* of proximity means that the 'feet' are the conjunction with 'wipe your heads', and are governed by 'wipe'. He cites the arguments that this *jarr* is not conclusive, saying 'If it is said no, it is not possible to say that this vowel "i" is there just because of proximity [while "feet" is still in conjunction with "wash your faces"], as it is in the statement:

juhr-u dabb-in kharib-in

and the poet's verse:

kabir anas *fi* bijad-in mazmal-i

we say that is false.' Al-Razi says the above examples may be explained by poetical exigency.

Second, in the above examples, there is no question of ambiguity. In the statement *juhr-u dabb-in kharib-in* the word, 'desrted' cannot be describing the lizard but must be describing the hole. So, he concludes, 'in this verse certainty in the face of ambiguity is nt produced.' For al-Razi, the linguistic argument of *jarr* is ultimately inconclusive.

Al-Shawqani cites the possibilities of an argument of *jarr,* but then acknowledges its weakness and sustains an argument from Sunna. He says, The ones who argue that washing the feet is not obligatory, argue from a recitation of *jarr* in His statement *arjulikum* being in conjunction with His statement *your heads.* They say *arjulikum is* one of the [three of the] seven recitations which are authentic. There is an argument for the conjunction being with washing the faces, even though it is recited with the *jarr* of the proximate; this has been related by the majority of the Arab 21 Imams, like Sibawayh and Akhfash, but it certainly *is* very rare; it differs from the obvious meaning ad it cannot sustain the contested position. We argue instead that obligatory is carrying the argument with *his (sallallahu alayhi wa sallam)* consistent practice of washing the feet.

Finally, there is an argument that there is an ambiguity in washing or wiping the feet precisely so that the verse can bear two contexts: wash the feet in one context, and wipe the feet when they are shod.

Al-Qurtubi says, 'It has been said that if the *khafd* of the feet rather mentions restrictively wiping them, it could be for when the feet have shoes on. We learn this restriction from the messenger of Allah, as it is not correct about him that he wiped his feet, except when they were shod. So thereby the messenger of Allah explained with his action the context for washing the feet and the context for wiping them. This is a fine argument.'

Ibn al-Arabi al-Maliki also gives this argument, saying 'Or, the meaning of "wiping" could be for the context of wearing shoes, so the two recitations could be for both contexts [bare feet and shod feet], once *nasb* for the bared feet and once *khafd* for the covered feet.'

Ibn al-Arabi's Position

Ibn al-Arabi alludes to this argument when he discusses the *fiqh* disagreement about what to do when wiping over the shoe when there is a tear in the shoe. He says, 'We argue for wiping what emerges, because we were commanded in the Book of Allah to wipe the feet, so when something of the foot emerges, we wipe it. Thus, there should be no obstacle in wiping the torn shoe where som of the foot sticks out, because the verse's imperative of 'wipe' fits both cases of shod/bare foot. Ibn al-Arabi reviws the various positions of the Ulama, saying, 'The Ulama concurred that the feet belong to the bodily parts of *wudu*, but they disagreed about a format of their *taharah,* whether that is through washing, wiping, or choosing between the two.' As we saw, the position of washing is the position of the majorityof the classical Sunni scholars; the position of wiping is the position of many companions and successors, including Ibn Abbas, Anas, and Ikrimah; the position of choosing between the two is that of al-Tabari, Hassan al-Basri, Jubbai, Nasir, and Daud. It is appropriate here to mphasize that Ibn al-Arabi is neither part of the Zahiri school of jurispudence associated with Daud and Ibn Hazm, nor is he a part of the Shiite school.

Ibn al-Arabi says, 'Our position is choice' and goes on to say 'the combination is best'. This last phrase probably refers to al-Nahhas own position which is characterized by al-Nahhas as `one of the best things said about the issue'. We saw above that al-Qurtubi recorded, `al-Nahhas said one of the best things said about the issue is that the wiping and the washing are both obligatory together, so the wiping is obligatory because of the recitation of one who recites with *khafd* and the washing is obligatory because of the recitation of one who recites with *nasb,* and the two recitations have the status of two verses.'

There is an argument of Ibn Hisham found in his classical grammar *Mughni* which holds that the *wa* (and) could have the meaning of *aw (or).* In this case there is a linguistic argument for choice. The argument goes as follows.

The meaning of the *wa* here could be 'choice'. One of (the poets) said,

They said, Go far away, choosing for her
patience 'wa' crying
She said, Crying is healthier if I want revenge.

The meaning then is patience *or* crying if patience is not joined to crying (that is, patience *and* crying).

Ibn al-Arabi's position embraces two themes, ease and relief of difficulty, based on the verse *We did not make for you in the religion any constriction (22:78),* a verse which begins with *jahidu fi Allahi* (exert for Allah) and suggests the *Ijtihad* of effortful exertion to understand the determined properties *(ahkam)* and the many consequences of a polysemantic text.

Wiping and washing are related as two forms of purification, the one being subsumed' in the other. Ibn al-Arabi says, 'Know that washing contains wiping from one perspective, so the one who washed has already subsumed wiping in it, just as star light is subsumed in the sun's light.' He acknowledges too that it is possible to see wiping simply as a synonym for washing, as we saw above, saying, 'The one who has wiped did not wash, except in a position of the one who believes, and quotes the Arabs, that "wiping" is a word for "washing", so they are synonymous.'

In Ibn al-Arabi's *fiqh,* each command which is operative in the outwardness is also operative in the inwardness. The command of this verse, therefore, has an inward dimension. He says,

The correct meaning f the *hukm* for the inwardness is that wiping is used for whatever specific practices are necessitated and washing for whatever general practices are necessitated.

Because of this, we propounded choice commensurate with the moment, because perhaps you run to a philanthropist for a designated need, on behalf of an individual himself, then that is in a way station of wiping. And perhaps you run to the king for a need diffused over the entire population, or needs, so that that individual would be included in this general public, so this is in a way station of washing in which is subsumed wiping.

Now Ibn al-Arabi investigates the linguistic evidence of the verse. He notes, 'As for the reciting of His statement [Wash *your faces,* and *your hands to the elbows, wipe your head] wa arjulukum* [your feet] [5:6], with either *arjula,* or *arjuli*—on account of the letter *wa*—according to whether the *wa* is in conjunction with "wipe", through *khafd,* or in conjunction with "wash", with the vocalization *arjula.* Our position is that even the recitation *arjula* does not actually contraindicate wiping, because this wa may be the 'and of simultaneity', and the 'and of simultaneity' makes the word *arjula.*'

Even though the recitation of *arjulakum* which we noted above, was generally associated with the argument for taking the initial verb 'wash' as the operative imperative, the argument for wiping is still linguistically strong. Ibn al-Arabi then gives examples of the 'and of simultaneity'. He says:

> *You say,* qama Zayd wa Umar-an*; and* wa stiwa-al-mau *was* l-khashabatan*; and* wa ma anta wa qasat-an min tharid; *and* wa marrartu bi-Zayd wa Umar-an. *You mean, (I passed Zayd) with Umar. And likewise for the one who recites [with* nasb*]* Wipe your heads and your arjula, with a.

So,

The argumentation of the one who argues for wiping, in this verse, is stronger, because his argumentation shares with the proponent for washing in giving expression to the recitation arjula. But one who argues for washing does not share with the proponent for wiping in giving expression to the recitation *arjuli.*

From the verse 'wiping' is stronger, and the proponent for 'wiping' can point to either vocalization for proof.

Among 'our colleagues', Ibn al-Arabi says, there are those who 'preponderate the specific over the general, and among them there are those who would preponderate the general over the specific: all of that absolutely.' Using the metaphor developed above, some of our colleagues always go to a specific philanthropist, and others always go to the king. They are not sensitive to the context, but instead go fixedly and rigidly to one place.

Ibn al-Arabi then says,

> *But our position is other than that. We walk with the Real according to a determined property* [hukm] *of the circumstance, so we generalize where He generalized, and we make specific where He makes specific.*

We do not initiate a property, because one who initiated a property has already initiated in his self Lordship, and the one who has initiated in himself Lordship has already diminished his servanthood, to the extent of this issue. And if he has diminished his servanthood, to that extent, he shall diminish the divine self-disclosure of the Real in him. And if he has diminished the divine self-disclosure of the Real in him, he has diminished his knowledge through his Lord. And if he has diminished his knowledge through his Lord, he is ignorant about Him to the context he diminished it, because if there should appear to that one, the one who diminished it, a property in the world [the macrocosm] or in his world [the microcosm], he would not recognize it. Because of this, our position is that we do not initiate a property in one fell swoop.

Ibn al-Arabi is completely familiar with the range of arguments produced by the legal scholars of his time. Their arguments generally seek closure and finality—although without exception, the final theme among all the classical scholars is 'But Allah knows best.' That is, even though they desire closure and finality, the classical scholars leave the door open to continuing divine guidance.

The desire to achieve a single and monolithic understanding of Islam is a perennial problem. Every *Qadi* who ever insisted on having the right to use *ijtihad* to settle cases, using any of the schools of jurisprudence which best applied for that particular case, was also fighting against the desire of the sultan and state to codify and impose a Procrustean vision of Islam.

So the sum consequence of the polysemantic text of washing/wiping the feet is 'that or perhaps that', or 'this and that'. The more one knows about this verse, the more one is aware of not knowing. For Ibn al-Arabi, the response to 'not knowing' is not *qiyas* or *ray* but *taqwa,* becoming protected by Allah through doing acts which will protect oneself from His punishment (which is its Arabic definitin).

Interestingly enough, the conclusion or last word of Ibn al-Arabi for every issue, then, *is taqwa,* and this is a conclusion which is valid for every level of knowledge. Ibn al-Arabi's treatment of this particular issue is to multiply its polysemantic nature, to increase the possibilities, to deconstruct false closures and *taqayyid,* and the smugness of 'knowing'. He seeks to convince his audience that for this and every issue we must void ourselves of Lordship and exaltedness, becoming instead humbly receptive and alert to divine command.

In the mater of purity *(taharah)* in the same verse we have been considering (5:6), Allah says that He does not wish for us any constriction *ma yuridu Allahu li-ajala alaykum min haraj,* but instead, *He wishes to make you pure.* Then, following this verse He tells us to remmber our covenant with Him, when we said, 'We hear and obey'. One might gloss here we listen, we hear, and we obey. For Ibn al-Arabi, assumption of lordship on our part, whether openly or not, precludes our listening, hearing, and ultimately, obeying. And right after that, Allah says, *And have taqwa [fear] before Allah; Allah is aware of the bottom of the hearts! (5:8).*

God's Injections

There is a great thirst for the direct word of Allah. Knowledge in the Quran is linked with water; rain comes down from the heavens, the parched earth drinks it, and vegetation is produced. Muhammad received the rain, which comes 'freshly from its Lord'. Rain is the direct knowledge which Allah gives to make us whole. River water is indrect knowledge—knowledge from our intellects—which gets mixed up with impurities and is subject to pollution. I used to joke that now we have acid rain: but, now I think that is our situation indeed. We no longer have the direct, clean, pure rainwater which Allah provides because the medium above us is itself polluted.

Clearing the Air : We have tried here to clear the air of the irritants and obstacles which come in the way of hearing the word directly. Wat Ibn al-Arabi does, above all, is to prpare hi audience for the encounter and then to become transparent before the encounter. His intellect, his genius, and hisskill pale in comparison with this gift: a way to hear in clear and clarifying language, the divine word.

And as therefore neither conclusions nor resolutions are appropriate, we take up three passages from Ibn al-Arabi's *fiqh*.

Three Passagesfrom Al-Arabi

The First Passage : In the first passage, we hear Ibn al-Arabi's discussion on *awrah*. This word is not translatable, but it is describable. Classically, *awrah* meant the part of the body, men's and women's, which had to be covered. The classical *fiqh* books spent most of their time discussing he man's *awrah* and the man's clothing. Today of course, *awrah* means the shameful part of women, including their voices, smell, and very presence. In fact, in Urdu, woman herself is called shameful—aurat. In order to recover the direct knowledge of the Quran, let us take up Ibn al-Arabi's discussion here; I have first translated Ibn Manzur's descriptions of key words needed for this passage from Ibn al-Arabi's *Futuhat al-Makkivvah.*

Awrah ('w.r.): Ibn Manzur says, 'The *awrah* of the man and the woman is their private parts.' And 'the *awrah* is everything that causes embarrassment if it is exposed.' Also, 'The *awar* ['w.r.] has only one eye'. He also says, 'Covering the *awrah* during the *salah* and other than the *salah* is obligatory; about covering it when secluded there is a disagreement'. And 'in the Quran we have, Our *houses* are *awrah* (33:13), that is, they are open to the thief because the houses have been cleared of the men, but Allah caught them in their lie, saying, *But they* were *not awrah, they only, wanted to desert* [33:13]. It is said its meaning is. Our houses are *awrah,* that is, our houses are near the enemy and we were stolen from them. But Allah knew that their intent was deserting the battle.'

Ibn al-Arabi says, 'The Ulama agree that covering the awrah is obligatory, with no disagreement, and absolutely, that is, during the salah I shall mention its boundary of the man and the woman.'

Mayl (m.y.l.): Ibn Manzur says, '*Mayl* is inclining toward something.'

Ibn al-Arabi says, 'The crossover for that in the inwardness. It is obligatory on every intelligent person to cover the divine secret which, if it were disclosed, would lead someone, who was neither knowledgeable nor intelligent, to a lack of a sense of taboo toward the Side of the divine, Exalted, Forbidden, because the reality of *awrah* is *mayl*. Because of this that personsaid *Our houses are awrah* [33:13], that is, inclined, bent on destruction, when they sought to desert; then Allah caught them in their lie, before His Prophet, with His word, *But they were not awrah*; *they* only *meant* to deset [33:13], that is, to desert what you [Muhammad] called them to. There is also the *awar* [one-eyed man], because his view inclines [m.y.l.] to a single perspective.

'Like that it is appropriate that the knowledgeable one cover from the ignorant one the secrets of the Real; secrets like His word, *There* are *no whisperings of three except He is the fourth [58:7];* His word, *We are closer to one than the jugular vein [50:16];* and His word, *I become his ear, and his eye, and his tongue,* because when the ignorant one hears that, it leads him to forbidden conceptualizations like divine incarnation or bounded divinity. Therefore, it is appropriate that with which the Real turns and inclines to the hearts of the knowledgeable ones—Exalted is He and Holy—with His address, be covered up with whatever His Maesty necessitates of Independence absolutely from the worlds; in addition to His word on the tongue of His messenger, *I was hungry and you fed me not, I was sick and you visited me not, I was thirsty and you did not give me to drink.*

'So he covers up the knowledge of this secret from the ignorant one and he does not add to what He said as a commentary to it [that is, I *was hungry]* at all. He covers up as the Real does with His word, *So and so was sick, and if you had visited him, you would have found Me with him.* This is more ambiguous than the first statement, but He gives in this commentary to the ones who know Allah, another knowledge about Him which they did not have. That is that in the first He made Himself the very same sick and hungry one but in His commentary He made Himself the Helper of the sick one, as He is *with him,* because whoever helps the sick one is with him. How far away is this from the One who made Himself the sick one himself! Each statement in that way is real, and to every real *[Haqq]* is a Reality *[Haqqiqah].'*

Ammi (' m.m.): (This is one of the most loaded classical words, usually full of the absolute class distinctions of the elite and the mass.

Ibn al-Arabi's use of the word is, however, quite different and is tied into one of the descriptions used by Ibn Manzur). Ibn Manzur says, 'A *ummayy ['m.m.]* man and a *qusriyy [q.s.r.,* utmost] man. The *ummayy* is the *amm* and the *qusriyy* is the *khass.* In the *Hadith:* When he used to go home, he gave upon entrance three *juz*': a *juz* to Allah, a *juz* for hisfamily, and a *juz* for himself. Then he apportioned *juz* for him and the people and he correlated that portion to the *ammah* through the *khassah,* meaning that the *ammah* were not with him at that moment, so the *khassah* communicated to the *ammah* what they heard from him; it is as if the benefits were transferred to the *ammah* from the *khassah.'*

According to Ibn al-Arabi, 'As for the covering up of that before the *ammi,* it is that one say to him about His statement, You *would have found Me with him* that the condition of the sick one is certainly that of dependency and need of the one in whose hand is the cure—and that is no one but Allah, so mostly what we need is to remember *[dhikr]* Allah with each instant to repel what befell him, which is different from the healthy one: He said, I *Myself am seated with the one who remembers [dhikr] Me.* This is the healthy condition. The *ammi* is satisfied wth it and the knowledgeable one stays with what He taught him about that upon his knowledge; this is the cover up of the divine *mayl* from the gaze of the *ammi.*

'The Ulama then disagree about whether covering the *awrah* during the *salah* is a precondition for the validity of the *salah* or not. There is one who saysthat covering the *awrah* is one of the Sunnas [voluntary but customary practices] of the *salah,* and there is one who says that it is one of the obligations of the *salah.*

'As for the crossover for that spiritually, we have already taught you the concept of *awrah* above. About this issue, as it is established [by an authentic *Hadith]* that the on praying is in intimate conversation with his Lord an that the *salah* has been divided in two between Allah and His worshipper, so the one who sees predominate [in this issue] that the Real s the One praying through theacts of His worshipper, that is, the outward practices of the worshipper in the *salah,* as it is established that *Verily Allah said on the tongue of His worshipper during the salah, Allah hears the one who praises Him [sami Allahu li-man hamidah]* when one rises after *ruku,* and the worshipper is the speaker, certainly; and He said, *Give him [asylum] so that he may hear the Word of Allah [9:6],* while it is the messenger (PBUH) of Allah, who is reciting, certainly; [that one who takes this position says] the covering of the *awrah* is one of the obligations of the *salah,* that is, the likes of this should not be made manifest before the *ammi,* meaning its supra-sensory meaning and its secret, which is knon by the knowledgeableone; rather, the *ammi* should believe in it [without understanding it], asis mentioned, *Only the knowledgeable ones will understand it [29:43].*

'And the one who sees that there is no gradation in this issue between the knowledgeable one and the *ammi,* and that there is nothing but what the text relates, and if t causes to lead, before the hearer, towards what it leads toif he does not go outside of what the language requires for that—even though their degrees are granted preference [one over another], then the covering of the *awrah* in his view is one of the Sunnas of he *salah,* not one of its obligations. *Allah sayswhat is real, and He is the guide of the way [33:4].*

'About the boundary of the *awrah,* there is one who says that the *awrah,* for the man, is the two private parts and there is one who says that it is, for the man, from the navel to the knee. It is, according to us, only the private parts. 'The crossover for that spiritually: whatever is blameworthy, hated, and filthy of humankind is the *awrah* according to Reality. The two private parts are a place for what we mentioned. It is at the location of the unlawful; and in addition to the private parts is what encroaches on the private parts, the navel on the upper and the knee on the lower; the encroaching area is at the location of the Doubtful, and it is appropriate that one protect oneself [w.q.y., cf. *taqwa]* [from the Doubtful], because *The herder going around the enclosed precinct may almost get into it* [and so should stay well away from the boundaryof the Unlawful].

'About the boundary of the *awrah* for the woman, there is one who says that all of her *is awrah* except the face and palms and there is one who argues for that and adds that her feet are not *awrah.* And there is one who says that all of her is *awrah.* As for our position, there is nothing *awrah* of the woman, in fact, except the private parts, just as He said, (*their sawah (two private parts) became visible to them, and they [Adam and Eve] started weaving for themselves the leaves of the Garden [7:22],* so He treated Adam and Eve the same in the covering of the private parts; they are the two *awrahs.*

Even though the woman is commanded [in the last Shariah, of Muhammad] to cover [more], and that is our position, yet this is not because of it being *awrah.* That [covering of the leaves of the private parts] is a legal property set down by Shariah mentioning covering; but it is not necessary that anything else be covered as *awrah.'*

The Second Passage : To understand this second passage, we need to understand Ibn al-Arabi's Arabic conception of *sawm.* It will become immediately clear why this word can not be translated, either by 'fasting' or by any conventional Arabic phrase.

Ibn al-Arabi begins his large chapter on the *sawm* with its definition. He says, 'You should know—may Allah strengthen you!—that the *sawm is imsak* [abstention] and *rifah* [elevation].' As usual, we turn to the description of the word in *Lisan al-Arrab* and find the same: Ibn Manzur says, 'The word *sawm* in the language is *imsak* [abstention] from something and *tark* [leaving] it.'

This is the first description. For the second, Ibn Manzur says, 'There is *sama* [from the same three letter root s.w.m. from which the word *sawm* is derived] the day when it draws up and rises to the zenith of mid-way. Imru al-Qays (one of the pre-Islamic poets whose Arabic usage is authoritative) said, *idha sama an-nahar wa hajjara* (the day rose up and became mid-way).'

To demonstrate the second description, lbn al-Arabi says, 'One says, *sama an-nahar* when the day elevates. Imru al-Qays said, *idha sama annahar wa hajjra,* that is, became elevated. Because the *sawm* has been elevated above the rest of the worships [the pillars of Islam, suh as *salah* and *zakah]* by a degree, it is called *sawm.* He—Exalted beyond—elevated the *sawm by* refusing any similarity with it to the worships, as we shall explain. He takes the *sawm* away from His worshippers even though they are doing it as a worship and attaches it to *Himself-subhana-hu* [He is exalted beyond]-and gives with His hand the reward to the one with the attribute of *sawm* who does it. He links the *sawm* to Himself by refusing any similarity [of it to the other worships].'

Ibn al-Arabi will explain below why the *sawm* is elevated above the other worships using the same evidence which Ibn Manzur uses. Ibn Manzur says, 'There is a *Hadith* where the Prophet (PBUH) said, Allah said, *Every act of the offspring ofAdam is theirs, except the sawm, because it is for Me.* Abu Ubayd said, Allah has made the *sawm* special with it being His and as being something which He rewards.'

In fact, the conception of elevation *(rifah)* and abstention *(tark)* both point to the particular description of *sawm.* Ibn al-Arabi says, 'The *sawm* is in reality a *tark,* not a practice, and the refusing of similarity is a negative attribute which intensifies the relationship of the *sawm* to Allah. He said about Himself, *Laysa ka mithlihi shayun* [There is nothing like Me] [42:11], so He refused that there should be to Him a *mithl* [similar], because *He—subhana-hu—has* no *mithl,* according to intellectual and *Shariah* proofs. And al-Nasai [one of the authoritative collectors of *Hadith]* published from Abu Umamah that he said, "I came to the messenger of Allah and I asked him, Command me with a command which I can ake from you. He said, On you is the *sawm,* because it has no *mithl* [there is nothing like it]." Thus, he refused tat any of the worships which are made *Shariah* for the worshippers be made similar to it.'

In order to pursue this particular conception, Ibn al-Arabi continues with the usual evidence for this worship. He says, 'And Muslim published in his authentic collection from Abu Hurrayrah that he said, The messenger of Allah said, *Every act of this offspring f Adam is theirs, except th sawm; I reward it.* And *siyam (sawm) is* a shield; when there is a *sawm* day for one of you, do, not be loud and noisy on that day. If someone insults you or fights you, say, I am one with the matter of *sawm [saim], I am a saim* [one fasting]. And by the one in whose Hand the soul of Muhammad is, the breath of the one with *sawm is* better, according to Allah, on te day of judgement, than the scent of musk. And the one with *sawm* has two joys which he enjoys: when he breaks [fast] with his *iftar* there is a joy and when he meets his Lord there is a joy in his *sawm.'*

The last phrase is awkward and not an expected turn of phrase. This should be a signal to us that something quite particular is happening. Indeed, taking the conception of *sawm* which Ibn al-Arabi has developed gives an explanation why we have this strange turn of phrase. He says, 'Knw that as he refused any similarity with the *sawm,* as was established in what preceded with the *Hadith* of al-Nasai and the reality that *Laysa ka mithlihi shayun* [there is nothing like h/Him, 42:11], the *saim* meets with his Lord by the attribute of *Laysa ka mithlihi shayun* and sees Him by it, so He is the Seer who is Seen. Because of this, he said, There is a joy in his *sawm,* and he did not say, There is a joy in meetig his Lord, because the joy is not a joy enjoyed by himself but is a joy enjoyed in *it.* And the one about whom the Real is his eyes with which he sees and witnesses, he himself does not see except by His seeing.'

This last phrase is the thematic *Hadith qudsi* which is as follows: 'My *abd* draws near to Me by means of nothing dearer to Me than that which I have established as a duty for him. And My *abd* continues drawing nearer to Me through supererogatory acts until I love him; and when I love him, I become his ear with which he hears, his eye with which he sees, his hand with which he grasps, and his foot with which he walks.'

Concluding, he says, 'So the joy of the *saim* is his meeting at the degree of refusal of similarity. His joy in the *iftar* [breaking of the fast] is in the world, in respect to giving due to the physical self which needs nourishment for itself. As the *abd* is described in this *Hadith* as having *sawm,* and deserving the name *saim* because of this description, so after the affirmation of his *sawm* the Real negates it and attaches it to Himself, saying, [Every act of the offspring of Adam is theirs] except the *sawm;* it is Mine [or, it is for Me], that is, an attribute of *samadani* [cf. *Allah ussamad] [* 112:2], which is being beyond needing nourishment. "It is Mine only; even though I may describe you with *sawm, I* so describe you by some delimiting metaphor of *tanzih* [being beyond an attribute], not by the absolute *tanzih* which is appropriate to My Majesty. So I say, And I reward it." So the Real rewards the *sawm* for the *saim* when he turns to his Lord and he is cast to his Lord by the attribute of "He has no *mithl"*—which is the *sawm,* as the one to Whom "There is nothing like unto" cannot see anything but one whom "There is nothing like unto." Abu Talib al-Makki-he was one of the masters of the folk of tasing determined the text *jaza-u-hu man wujida fi rahl-ihi fa-huwa jaza-u-hu* [12:75]—for what this verse requires for this circumstance.'

Now we can turn to the passage in question. 'The most surplusing and balanced *sawm is* "fasting" one day for yourself and fasting one day for your Lord an between them a day breaking fast .... But when some of them saw that the right-claim of Allah is more right, they did not see treating equally the right of Allah and the right of the worshipper, so they fasted for two days and broke fast for one day. This was the fasting of Mary, because she saw that *men have a degree over women* [2:228], so she said, Perhaps I shall make this second day of fasting one to counter this degree. And that was how it was, because the Prophet *testified* that *she* was complete [perfect], just as he testified to the completion of the Men.' And when she saw that the testimony of two women was balanced with the testimony of one man, she said, "Two days fasting for me is at the level of one day fasting of the Man." Thus, she got the station of the Man for that, and she equalled David in surplus in the fast. So because of this, the one who overcomes in himself his *nafs* has overcome in himself his [tendency to] divinization; then it is appropriate that he treats his *nafs* as May treated her *nafs* in this context, lest her *nafs* overtake her *aql*; his is a fine allusion for the one who understands it.'

Dahr: Ibn Manzur says, *'dahr is* an extremely long time'. And 'there is the *Hadith,* Do not revile *the dahr because Allah is dahr.'*

Qayyum (q.w.m.): Ibn Manzur says, 'The *Qayyum,* one of Allah's names; Allah is Standing up by Himself absolutely, not by [the help of] anyone.'

Ibn al-Arabi continues, 'When completion became hers, she caught up to the Men, and the most completion was hers in her catching up to her Lord. It was like Jesus son of Mary, her son,·because he used to fast *dahr* and not break the fast, and he used to stay up (q.w.m.) at night and not sleep. Outwardly, in the world he was with the name *dahr* in the day and with the name Qayyum—the one whom *sleep does* not *seize,* nor *slumber* (2:225) at night. So divinity was claimed for him, and it was said, Allah is the Christ, son of Mary (5:72), and that was not said about any prophet before him, because the most that was said about Uzayr was that he was the son *of Allah* (9:30). It was not said, He is Allah.'

Kufr: Ibn Manzur says the word *kufr* is derived from *satr*(veil, cover). *Kanaf:* Ibn Manzur says, In the *Hadith* of Ibn Umar, we have about salvaion, The believer draws closer to his Lord on the day of judgement until He places over him His *kanaf.* Ibn Mubarak said, He meant, He covers (s.t.r.) him.

'So look at what effect this [divine] attribute had,' Ibn al-Arabi says, `from behind the veil of the unseen, on the hearts of the veiled ones of the folk of disclosure such that they said, *Allah is the Christ, son of Mary* [5:72]; *kufr* is related to them for that, set up as an excuse for them, because they did not commit *shirk;* rather they said, He is Allah, and the one who commits *shirk* is the one who makes ith Allah another god. So this is one doing *kufr,* not *shirk.* Therefore, He said, They have done *kufr* who say, Allah is the *Christ, son of Mary*, thereby attributig to them a sitr [a cover, that is, *kfr*]*;* they took the humanity of Jesus to be a locus of divine manifestation [*majalla*]. Jesus warned him [self] about this station, in what Allah reported, as a confirmation for them concerning what they said. Christ said, O *Bani Israil, worship Allah, my Lord and Your Lord.* They said, That is what we are doing! So they worshipped Allah through him. Then He said to them, *The one who commits shirk with Allah, Allah has made forbidden to him the Garden [5:72],* that is, Allah has made forbiden His *kanaf* with which He covers [s.t.r.] him; but Allah already described them with being covered [s.t.r.] in that He described them with *kufr.* This is a verse hose literal meaning gives exactly that which the matter itselfgives of that. The *tawil* [allegorical interpretation] of the verse is caught up in blameworthiness; if youcomprehend what we have mentioned about it, you will fall into the great ocean and you will not be saved from drowning in it at all, because it is the endless ocean. There is no deeper' word of Allah for the one who sees it andhas eyes to see it and is from Allah concerning it *upon insight [12:108].'*

The Third Passage : Ibn al-Arai says, 'Abu Ahmad mentioned in a *Hadith* of Abd-Allah ibn Buayl ibn Waraqa al-Makki frm Amr ibn Dinar from Ibn Umar from Umar that he vowed to sit ('k.f.) in he sacrd mosque, and the messenger of Allah (PBUH) said to him, Si in *itikaf* and do *sawm.'*

Awliya: Ibn Manzur says, 'The *waliy [* singular of*awliya]* of the right hand is the one who is in charge of one's command and executes his tasks.'

'Its connecting crossover: Rasululah, the messenger of Allah commanded the one desiring to stand [q.w.m.] with Allah that they should stand with him by the attribute which is Allah's, and that attribute is the *sawm,* so that one should be with Allah, by Allah, for Allah, so nothing of them would be seen except Allah. This is the circumstance of the folk of Allah. It was aked of the Rasululah, Who are the *awliya* of Allah? He said, *Thos who, when they are seen, Allah is remembered [dh.k.r,* cf. *dhikr],* that is, in order to be made real by Allah they disappar in him from them and from the eyes of creation, so when the people see them, they see nothing but Allah, so their remembering of Allah is their seing the *awliya.* It is like the above-mentioned verses. This is the station which the Rasululah asked for in his prayer, *And make me nur [n.w.r.],* and Allah answered his prayer, as we were told that he was sent to people *as one of good tidings, warning, clling to Allah by His leave, and an illumined lamp [sirj munir, n.w.r.]* 33-45-6; so He made him *nur* as he asked.

'His word to his Lord, *And make me nur,* was, So that I would be in my essece the ver divine nam itself *al-nur,* and the one whom the Real is *hi ear, his eye, his tongue, his hand, and his fot;* and one who *would not speak from caprice [53:3].* So he isnot he, and nothing remains for the one who see him, who sees him, except Allah, that being known by the one who sees or not this is the way the folk of knowledge of Allah witness him.

'Among the believers there are the *khulafa [kh.l.f.,* onesrepresenting someone behind the, singular *Khalifa]* who manifest in the world and among the masses with the attributes of the one who is behind [kh.l.f.] them. Bilqis [the queen of Sheba] said about hr throne, *ka'anna-hu huwa,"* but it was nothing but *huwa [it/Him]!* But her veil was the extreme distance [between hr palace and Solomon's] and the force of convention [which says thrones do not transport themselves across large distances instantly], and she was unaware of Solomon's power with his Lord, so this veiled her from saying, *huwa huwa* [it is It; he is He; etc.]. So she said, *ka'anna-hu huwa.* And what distance could be greater than one to whom *there is no mithl* [like] compared to one whose *mithl is* things? The complete one [Muhammad] sad, *Indeed I myself am a human being who is your mithl* [like yourselves]-this based on a commad of Allah. It was said to him, *Say,* and he said, *Say: indeed I myself am a human being who is your mithl [41:7],* and by this we know that it is based on a command of Allah, because he conveyed the command to us just as he conveyed what was commanded.

'This statement is a remedy for the sickness which arose in the one who worshipped Jesus in his commentary; they said, *Indeed Allah is the Christ, son of Mary [5:72],* missing a great knowledge in that they said *son of Mary* and they did not realize. Because of this, Allah said in raising proof against the one with this description [the *mushrik*], *Say: Name them* [thạt is, name the partners of Allah, 13:33], but they could not name him [e.g., *Allah, the Christ, son of Mary*] except by one of the names they knew him by, in order that he understand from them what they meant, because when they gave them [the partners] names, it became clear, in the name itself *[Allah, he Christ, son of Mary],* that he was not one of the messengers who were sent demanded that they worship.

'But we rather said, *huwa huwa* [h/He is He] based on whatsound disclosure gives the *khass* and what clẹar faith gives the *amm,* just as the prophetic report from the divine relates, that Allah, when He loves His worshipper, He becomes his ear, his eye; and He mentions is faculties and limbs. And humankind is nothing but these faculties and limbs which the Real makes his he-ness itself.' So if you are a belever, do you know what you believe in? And even if you are one with a sound vision, do you know what you saw? Most of this propetic explanation about Allah is concerned with th human faculty so that the believer would be one with a state of seeing, so that one would know by that the One who is the entity itself of the things and the entities.' Muhammad (PBUH) son of Abdullah and grandson of bdul Muttalib of the well-known tribe of Quraish was born at Mecca, on Monday the 12th of Rabiul Awwal, during the Year of Elephant, corresponding to 22nd of April 571 A.C., 53 years before Hijrah.' It was an event of great rejoicing in the house of Abdul Muttalib, a venerated old chief amongst theQuraish. Abdullah, father of the child, had died, a few months earlier, during a visit to Yathrib. The child was named Muhammad, 'The Praised one,' by the grandfather. It was a name unusual in Arabia, but the old chief liked to have his grandson grow up as a person worthy of praise and honour. The mother Amina, also gave the child a name.

It was Ahmad, 'worthy of praise.'

Chapter 6

Moral Culutre in Islam

Hajj (Pilgrimage)

The pilgrimage to Mecca in Saudi Arabia constitutes the fifth and last of the acts of worship prescribed by Islam. The Quran says:

> *"Pilgrimage thereto is a duty men owe to Allah - those who can afford the journey."* (3: 97)

To make the meaning of this verse clear, it is necessary to read the previous verse also:

> *"The first house of worship appointed for men was that at Mecca; full of blessing and of guidance, For all kinds of beings: In it are signs evident whoever enters it attains security; pilgrimage thereto is a duty men owe to Allah- those who can afford the journey."* (3: 96-97)

The literal meaning of the word Hajj is the will and desire to visit, but in the terminology of the Shariah, it means the will to visit the Holy Kaaba which was the first structure built by Hadrat Adam for the worship of Allah. Then, about 4,500 years ago, Hadrat Ibrahim and Hadrat Ismail rebuilt it at the command of Allah. The story of the rebuilding of the Kaaba is thus related in the Holy Quran:

> *"And remember, Ibrahim and Ismail raised the foundations of the House (with this prayer):*
>
> *"Our ord, Accept (this service) from us:*
>
> *Our Lord! make of us Muslims, bowing to thy (will) and of our progeny a people Muslim, bowing to thy (will); And show us our places for the celebration of (due) rites."*
>
> *(2: 127-128)*

From the words of this prayer, the purpose for which the Kaaba was built, becomes clear and we come to know that its completion was ordained at the ands of the children of Hadrat Ismail who settled at this spot nd from them, the Holy Prophet (PBUH) was raised for the perfection of this purpose.

Pilgrimage to the Sacred House is not an obligation. It is compulsory only on those who are sound of mind, adults and have theprovisions of travel. All those persons who fulfil these obligations and yet abstain from performig Hajj once in their lifetime give a lie to their being Muslims. A *Hadith* of the Holy Prophet (PBUH) states:

> *"If a person is not hampered by any disease, real necessities or a tyrannical ruler and yet does not perform Hajj, his death and the death of a Jew or a Christian are the same."*

Hajj constitutes a form of worship with the entire being of a Muslim, with his mind, body and soul, with his time, money and the sacrifice of all comforts of life to assume for a few days, the condition of a pilgrim totally at Allah's disposal.

Hajj is the only pillar among the fundamental pillars of Islam which requires both physical and financial sacrifices. Prayer and fasting are only physical worships and nothing is spent in their performance. *Zakat* is only financial worship, it does not require any physical labour. But in performing *Hajj* both physical and financial sacrifices are required.

The rites of Hajj centre on complete submission and devotion to Allah. At the same time, they serve as an example of total submission and obedience of Prophet Ibrahim, especially his willingness to sacrifice what he loved most in the world, his son Ismail, at Allah's Command.

Pilgrims come for Hajj from all parts of the globe. As they approach Mecca, they enter into the state of *Ihram,* which means divesting oneself of all marks of status to assume the humble dress and conditions of a pilgrim devoted wholly to Allah. The pilgrims are to abstain from marital relations, quarrelling or from using bad language. They are also prohibited to harm any living thing in the boundary of Mecca.

Hajj is one of the fundamental religious institutions of Islam. It is the greatest of all acts of worship; it is in fact, the culmination of worship. It is an exhibition of brotherhood, equality, punctuality and discipline. It affords an opportunity to Muslims from various countries of the word to become acquainted with one another and of discussing common problems facing the Muslim community.

According to Abu Hurrayrah, the Holy Prophet (PBUH) said that anyone who visits the House of Allah, does not indulge in foul language and avoids the disobedience of Allah, will become as pure and free from sins as a child.

At another place, the Holy Prophet (PBUH) said:

> *"Hajj which is free from sins and defects is rewarded with Paradise. "*

The mportance of *Hajj* has been well described by Imam Abu Hanifa who said that *Hajj* is the greatest of all worship, Ibadat, enjoined in Islam. Its chief importance lies in the fact that it strengthens one's faith in Islam.

Method : Hajj is an annual congregational worship which is performed in the twelfth month of the Muslim calendar, that is Zil-Hajja. The main stages of *Hajj* are as follows:

Ihram : The pilgrim puts on the Ihram, two white sheets of unsewn cloth. One sheet is used for covering the lower portion of the body (from the navel downwards) and the other is to be used for covering the upper portion of the body. The head remains uncovered.

The *Ihram* fo women is their everyday ordinary clothes. It is compulsory for women tocover their heads, but no cloth should touch their faces. Before putting on the *Ihram,* the intending pilgrim should first take a full bath, and clean the body thoroughly. He may now put on the *Ihram,* and cover his head with some unsewn piece of cloth and offer two Rakats of *Nafal* prayers.

Immediately afterwards, he should remove the cloth from his head and with his face towards the Kaaba, make the *Niyyat* of offering the *Hajj.* After this, he should recite the Talbiah in a loud voice:

> *"Here I am at Thy service, O Allah! Here I am at Thy service. There is no partner with Thee. Here I am at Thy Service. All praise and all blessings and favours belong to Thee, and all sovereignty is Thine. Thou hast no partner."*

The pilgrim has now formally entered the state or condition of *Ihram* and is subject to all the prohibitions and restrictions *of Ihram* which are as follows:

1. Wearing sewn clothes (by males).
2. Wearing of shoes which cover the raised bone of the feet.
3. Putting on a bandage on the head or face.
4. Covering the head or face. Women are required to cover their heads only.

5. Shaving, cutting or trimming of hair.
6. Cutting of nails.
7. Using perfumed hair oil, or any kind of perfume.
8. Using abusive or foul language, or quarrelling.

The following are the undesirable acts *of Ihram:*

1. Rubbing the body for removing dirt or dust.
2. Using perfumed soap for washing the body or face. Bathing with water is prmitted.
3. Combing the hair, or passing the fingers through the hair or scratching the head, as these acts may cause the hair to fall, or may kill the lice in the hair.
4. Smelling perfume or some sweet-smelling grass.
5. Using a pin or needle for holding the sheets of the *Ihram.*
6. Using spices in food such as cardamom, clove or cinnamon or using perfumed tobacco.

The following are the permitted acts of *Ihram:*

1. Use of tooth brush or miswak.
2. Harmful insects may be killed.
3. Halal animals, but not hunted, may be eaten.
4. The use of blanket for covering the body, but not the head or face is allowed.

Ihram is the first and foremost *Farz* of *Hajj* and *Umrah.* It is a declaration of one's intention *or Niyyat to* perform *Hajj* or *Umrah. Ihram* is the visible indication or symbol of the pilgrim's renouncing all the vanities of the world to devote himself to the worship of Allah. *Ihram* is a time of forbearance and patience. It symbolises purity, renunciation and the equality and brotherhood of all believers.

After completing Ihram the pilgrim enters Haram, the sacred area around Mecca. Kaaba, the holiest and most sacred place for Muslims is in Mecca and there are strict rules for the preservation of its sanctity. For this purpose, several circles have been drawn around the Kaaba. The first and innermost circle is called Masjid-e-Haram. The second circle is called Mecca Mukaramma, the city of Mecca, forbidden to non-Muslims, within which living things are protected from violence. It is a place of peace and security. If anyone seeks an asylum in Mecca, he cannot be captured or killed; the hunting or killing of any bird or animal is prohibited, even the cutting of its trees is forbidden.

Haram : The third circle is called *Haram,* the boundaries of which were fixed by Allah's comman first by Adam and then by Ibrahim. The Holy Prophet (PBUH) got pillars erected to indicate the boundaries *of Haram.*

Mawaqit : The fourth circle is called Mawaqit. These are the places beyond which no one proceeding to Mecca for *Hajj* and *Umra* can advance without putting on the *Ihram,* otherwise he shall have to offer a sacrifice as penalty.

Kaaba or the House of Allah, according to old tradition, was constructed on the earth by angels nearly two thousand years before the creation of Adam. When Adam was sent down on earth, the angels indicated to him the exact location where this House had been constructed by them and Adam built the Kaaba. The House of Allah disappeared on account of the Flood during Hadrat Nuh's time. It was then r-constructed by Ibrahim and his son Ismail. At one place in the Holy Quran, Allah has called it 'My House' and at another place He has called himself Rabb of this House. There are twenty-four gates through which this House may be entered, but it is best for the pilgrim to enter through the Bab-as-Salam.

Mounted in silver and set in the south-eastern corner of the Kaaba is the sacred Black Stone, Hajr-e-Aswad received by Hadrat Ismail from the angel Jibbrail during the rebuilding ofthe Ancient House. According to tradition, this stoe was milky white; it has become black because of the sins of people. This oly stone was touched or kissed by Hadrat Ibrahim and by the Holy Prophet (PBUH). Its kissing is symbolic of pure love of Allah and our resolve to obey Him in all matters.

Standing apart from the Kaaba but within the areawhich encompasses the ancient House are:

a. *Well of Zam Zam:* This well is in the south-eastern side of Masjid-e-Haram. The spring that feeds this well sprangup from under the feet of Ismail, when his mother Hajra, was searching for water for her infant son between the Safa and Marwa hills. From that time till the present day, millions of people have drunk the water of this well.

b. *Maqam-e-Ibrahim:* The place of Ibrahim. This is a stone on which Hadrat Ibrahim stood while constructing the Kaaba.

c. *Hatim:* This is a small area, between Rukn-e-Shami, the corner facing Syria and Rukn-e-Yamani, the south-western corner of the Kaaba but was not included in the covered enclosure. The offering of prayers in the *Hatim* is held to be like offering prayers inside the Kaaba.

Tawaf: The pilgrim enters the Great Mosque an walks seven times around the Kaaba. This is called Tawaf. Each of the seven circuits is called Shaut. Traditionally, *Tawaf is* begun by touching or kissing the Black Stone.

There are several kinds of *Tawaf:*

a. *Tawaf-e-Ziyrat also called Tawaf-e-Ifadah or Tawaf-e-Rukn:* It is a Rukn or obligatory component of Hajj and must be performed between the dawn of 10th and 12th of Zil-Hajj.

b. *Tawaf-e-Qudum:* It is *Sunnat* and is performed on entering Masjid-e-Haram.

c. *Tawaf-e-Sadr or Tawaf-e-Wida:* This is performed at the time of departure and is Wajib for all those living outside the Mawaqit.

d. *Tawaf-e-Umra:* It is obligatory or *Farz* for those performing *Umra.*

c. *Tawaf-c-Nafal:* Any *Tawaf* other than the preceding four categories is called Tawaf-e-Nafal. There is no restriction as to the time or number of such Tawaf, but they must be performed after wudu and Niyyat and in the prescribed manner.

After completing the seven circuits, the pilgrim goes to the Al-Multazim or the place of Holding and prays to Allah for forgiveness. This is a portion of the wall of the Kaaba between its door and the Hajr-e-Aswad.

Sayi : The pilgrim then performs the Sayi which is running seven times between the Safa and Marwah hills. These two hills are close to the well of Zam Zam. Safa is to the south-east, from which the *Sayi* is commenced and Marwa is to the north-east where the *Sayi* ends.

It was between these two hills that Hadrat Hajra, wife of Hadrat Ibrahim, ran several times in search of water for her infant son, Ismail.

It is in memory of this that *Sayi* is performed. This ritual expresses respect for maternal love and gratitude to Allah, who made the sacred spring of Zam Zam appear for Hadrat Hajra's relief.

The commandment about *Sayi* is contained in the Quran:

> *"Behold! Safa and Marwa are among the symbols of Allah. So if those who visit the House in the season or at other times, should compass them round."(2: 158)*

The pilgrim should first climb on the Safa hill. It is not necessary to climb the hill fully. He should climb to such a height only as would afford a view of the Kaaba. After descending from Safa, the pilgrim should move towards Marwa and thereafter; walk briskly between the two hills.

Journey to Mina: After the *Sayi,* on the morning of 8th Zil-Hajja, the pilgrim journeys to Mina, a plain which lies between Arafat and Mecca, about four miles east of Mecca. The pathway into this plain passes through a hill called Aqaba which is famous in the history of Islam as the place where the Holy Prophet (PBUH) took the two pledges fom the Ansars of Medina. The pilgrims must reach this place before noon, so that the Zuhr prayers may be performed there. On the way to Mina and in Mina, the pilgrim should continue o recite Talbiah, Darood and Kalma Tauhid.

It is desirable to offer the *Zuhr, Asr, Maghrib,* and *Isha* prayers of the 8th Zil-Hajja and the *Fajr* prayers of the 9th Zil-Hajja in Mina.

Wuquf-e-Arafat: On the next day, that is, on the 9th of Zil-Hajja which is called Yaum-e-Arafat, the pilgrim should leave Mina after the *Fajr prayers* and move on to the plain of Arafat.

This plain is situated at a distance of nine miles from Mecca and about six miles from Mina. According to tradition, it was in this plain that Adam and his wife were reunited after years of wanderings. It was in this plain that the Holy Prophet (PBUH) delivered his Khutba Hajjat-ul-Wida and where he received the final revelation about the completion of Islam:

> *"This day have I perfected your religion for you, completed My favour upon you and have chosen for you Islam as your religion."* (5: 3)

The stay in the plain of Arafat is called Wuquf-e-Arafat. The best form of Wuquf, deserving the highest spiritual reward is to remain standing, facing the Qibla, while reciting *Talbiah, Istighfar, Kalma Tauhid* and praying to Allah. The assembly at Arafat is the most important part of the *Hajj,* without which *Hajj* would be incomplete. The stay at Arafat is the supreme experienc of *Hajj.*

The Zuhr and Asr prayers on the 9th of Zil-Hajja are to be offered together in this plain.

Journey to Muzdalifah: Immediately after sunset, without offering Maghrib prayers, the pilgrim should leave Arafat for Muzdalifah, a plain between Mina and Arafat about six miles from Mecca and three miles from Mina. In the Holy Quran, this place is called the Sacred Monument and the Muslims are especially asked to remember Allah at this place:

> *"Then when you hasten from. Arafat remember Allah near the Holy Monument."* (2: 198)

At *Muzdalifah* the Maghrib and Isha prayers are offered together at one time. The whole night at *Muzdalifah* is to be spent in prayer and remembrance of Allah. After saying the Fajr prayer on the 10th of Zil-Hajja before sunrise, thepilgrim should leave for Mina. Pebbles for throwing at the devil (shaitan) are picked up from here.

Rami of Jamarat-ul-Uqba: The pilgrim now proceeds to Mina just before daybreak. Here he spends three nights stoning the three stone pillars called Jamarat, That which is nearest to Mecca is called Jamarat al-Uqba, the second which is near the mosque of Mina is called Jamarat-ul-Wusta. At a little distance from this place is the Jamarat-al-Sughra or the smallest Jamarat.

It is reported that Satan (shaitan) tried to deceive and mislead Hadrat Ibrahim at these three places and Hadat Ibrahim stoned the devil. It is in memory of this, that Rami te symbolic ceremony of stoning the devil (shaitan) is held at Mina. It is to show that we reject the devil and obey no one but Allah.

On the 10th of Zil-Hajja, the pilgrim must cast seven of he forty-nine pebbles collected at Muzdalifah at *Jamarat-al-Uqba* only. The approved method of doing Rami is to stand about five or six feet from the stone pillar, hold the pebble with the thumb and forefinger of the right hand and throw each pebble, one after the other and while doing so, the following is to be recited:

> *The pebbles should fall as close to the pillar as possible. Immediately after the Rami on the 10th, the Talbiah is to be stopped.*

Sacrifice: Returning from the site of Jamarat-al-Uqba, the pilgrims offer a sacrifice in memory of Hadrat Ibrahim who was willing to sacrifice his son Hadrat Ismail at the Command of Allah. This sacrifice is also part of world wide celebration which unites Muslims everywhere in the common rite of Eid-ul-Adha. Both the sacrifice and the throwing of stones are only outward acts. The real thing is the sirit of piety and submission to Allah which these acts express.

After the sacrifice, the male pilgrim should shave his head. The female pilgrim may clip a lock of hair only. Now the pilgrim is no longer in *Ihram* and the robes can be put off. The pilgrim may now cut nails, take a bath and wear ordinary clothes. However the prohibitions of *Tawaf* are not yet lifted.

Tawaf-e-Ziyarat: The pilgrim should now try to reach Mecca as quickly as possible for the *Tawaf-e-Ziyarat* which is the second most important item of Hajj, the first being Wuquf-e-Arafat. If *Tawaf-e-Ziyarat* is not performed, the Hajj shall be void. If *Tawaf-e-Ziyarat* is performed after the 12th of Zil-Hajja of the year in which the ajj is performed, sacrifice shall have to be offered as penalty.

After *Tawaf-e-Ziyarat,* the pilgrim should return to Mina to pass the night there.

Rami on 11th and 12th: On 11th and 12th of Zil-Hajja the prescribed time for Rami is after declining of thesun before the *Maghrib.* On both these days, the seven pebbles shall have to be thrown, one after the other, in the prescribed manner, at each of the three stone pillars in this order:

1. Jamarat-ul-Sughra, which is the first of the three pillars while proceeding from Mina to Mecca;
2. Jamrat-ul-Wusta, which comes next; and
3. Jamarat-ul-Uqba which comes last.

Tawaf-e-Wida: On his return to Mecca from Mina, the pilgrim should per form the *Tawaf-e-wida.* This *Tawaf* should be performed before leaving Mecca.

Before departure from Mecca, the pilgrim should go to Al-Multazim, offer two Rakat prayers at Maqam-e-Ibrahim, kiss the *Black Stone* and drink water from the *Zam Zam.*

Faraiz or Obligatory Acts of Hajj

1. Putting on the *Ihram* and making the *Niyyat* of *Hajj* and reciting the Talbiah.
2. Wuquf-e-Arafat i.e. staying in the plain of Arafat between the declining of the sun on the 9th of Zil-Hajja upto the dawn of the 10th Zil-Hajja.
3. Tawaf-e-Ziyarat on the 10th, 11th or 12th of Zil-Hajja after the shaving of the head or the shortening of the hair.

These three obligatory duties are to be performed in the prescribed order and in the prescribed manner. If any of these three *faraiz* is left out, there can be no *Hajj* and the mistake cannot be set right by sacrifice.

Secondary Imperatives or Wajibat of Hajj:

1. Stay at Muzdalifah,
2. Sayi between Safa and Marwah,
3. Stoning the devil,
4. Sacrifice,

5. Shaving the head (males) or shortening the hair (females),
6. Tawaf-e-Wida.

If any of these items is left out, the *Hajj* shall not become void; but the pilgrim shall have to pay the penalty either in the form of sacrifice or sadaqah.

Sunnats of Hajj:

1. Tawaf-e-Qudum;
2. Spending the night of the 9th Zil-Hajja in Mina;
3. Leaving Mina after sunrise on the 9th for Arafat;
4. Leaving Arafat after the departure of Imam;
5. Staying the night at *Muzdalifah* on the return from Arafat;
6. Taking a bath in Arafat.

If any of these *sunnats* cannot be performed, there is no penalty.

Umra : The word *Umra is* usually translated as minor pilgrimage and it is commonly translated as *Hajj-e-Asghar*. Although many acts of worship performed in *Umra* are the same as those performed during *Hajj*, there are certain fundamental differences between the two. While *Hajj* is obligatory, *Umra* is not. *Hajj* can only be performed on the prescribed dates, but no date or time has been fixed for *Umra.* There is no *Wuquf-e-Arafat,* no *Wuquf-e-Muzdalifah,* no stoning of the devil, no combining of prayers, no *Tawaf-e-Qudum,* no *Tawaf-e-Wida* and no sacrifice of animals in *Umra.* The *Ihram* is an essential condition for *Umra. Tawaf, Sayi,* shaving of the head or shortening of the hair are components or *Arkan of Umra.* In *Umra,* the *Talbiah* is stopped at the beginning of the *Tawaf.* It is undesirable to perform *Umra* between the 9th and the 13th of Zil-Hajja.

Pilgrim Road

In the Name of God be the course and the mooring.
Prayer of Nuh as he launched the ark,
and of pilgrims as they set out for Mecca. Quran: Sura
II: 41 Hud

I come with many sins
From a far land ...
O God ! this Sanctuary is Thy Sacred Place.
Prayer on entering the gates of Mecca

Once at least in a lifetime, every Muslim capable of doing so is supposed to pack his bag, leave his home and take the road for Mecca; Mecca, to which his thoughts have turned every day since in childhood he learned to pray. Over a million people go there each year, most of them during the month of pilgrimage. In 1980, the total had risen to 1,900,000 and about half of these came from outside Saudi Arabia. The Saudi government keeps a register of pilgrims from other countries. In 1968 these were 318,507; in 1969, 406,895. In 1974, out of a total of 1,484,975, the number from outside Arabia was 918,777.

Much of this human torrent flows through Jadda, with its modern airport and deep-water harbour. More and more come by air: 5 3 2,000 in 1979, 571,000 in 1980. This involves handling up to 50,000 arrivals a day during the short and hectic period just before the Hajj. To meet this challenge Jadda's immense airport, dedicated in April 1981, includes a special Hajj Terminal, imaginatively constructed like a huge tent. Here the pilgrims can enter, wait to meet their guides, and find transport by road on the final stage of their journey to Mecca.

Every contrast of colour and costume, class and race is to be seen, but to enter Mecca all are dressed alike in two sheets of unsewn white cloth. External trappings and all things superficial are laid aside. King and peasant, descendant of the Prophet and newest African convert, all are equal in this demonstration of brotherhood — and sisterhood. Women, never veiled on pilgrimage, take full part.

The King moves from Riyadh to lead the pilgrimage and entertain rulers and ambassadors of Muslim states. Informal discussions on policy and action are an important element. The Saudi Arabian government moves its headquarters to Mecca, and a considerable part of the oil wealth of the country has gone into modernising the arrangements for the reception of so vast a crowd.

Health precautions have turned what used to be a hazardous journey into a still rigorous but comparatively safe undertaking. Strict quarantine regulations, hospitals and mobile clinics, water supplies, drinking taps by roads along which almost a million must walk in a day: all these help the health record, and there have been no serious epidemics in recent years.

In the 1970's, a programme of building completed the expansion of the Great Mosque itself, so that 300,000 pilgrims can gather in its court at one time, each with a clear view of the square-built, black-draped building at its centre, the Kaaba. Tradition dates the worship of God here back to the days of Ibrahim.

No non-Muslim may enter Mecca. Soon after the day when the Prophet re-entered the city and cleansed the sanctuary of its idols - and before his own Pilgrimage of Farewell - it was closed to any but followers of Islam.

Father Ibrahim : The pilgrimage rites recall two events: the story of Ibrahim and the Farewell Pilgrimage made by the Prophet shortly before his death. The Patriarch and Prophet Ibrahim travelled the desert caravan routes linking the centres of early civilisation: the same routes along which, through the past fourteen centuries, millions of pilgrims have passed - destination Mecca. More important, he travelled the road from the worship of many gods to that of the One Creator. The stories of his family, of his break with idols and his finding faith in the God, Allah, are told in the Quran.

Muhammad regarded himself as the restorer of the pure faith in One God first pioneered by Ibrahim, the spiritual father of the three great monotheistic faiths, as well as the ancestor of the Jews and of many Arabs; cousins whose destiny has been closely linked in history ever since. According to Meccan tradition, the sanctuary there was first built by Ibrahim and his son Ismail. To reach Mecca from Damascus took later pilgrim caravans forty days. Hebron, where Ibrahim settled and where his tomb is venerated by Muslim, Jew and Christian alike, is nearer still. The journey to Mecca would not be a long one for such a traveller.

There, it is said, he took Hagar when she was turned out by Sarah. Her frenzied search for water was rewarded by the bubbling up of a spring, Zam Zam, from which every pilgrim drinks. Her desperate wanderings are recalled in the running to and fro of pilgrimsbetween the two hillsides of Marwa and Safa. The climax of the Pilgrimage is the Feast of Sacrifice *(Eid-ul-Adha).* This is in honour of Ibrahim's willingness to sacrifice his son. If they can afford it, Muslim families all over the world kill a sheep or other animal at this time, and give part of the meat to the poor.

Significance of Hajj : The Arabic word *Hajj* means "to set out for a definite purpose". Specifically, it refers to the pilgrimage to the city of Mecca. A *Haji* is one who has performed the Pilgrimage. An Islamic Correspondence Course, edited by Haji Riadh El-Drouble and issued by Minaret House, London, devotes one unit to the Hajj. The story of Ibrahim and his readiness to sacrifice his son is quoted from the Quran. Many, but not all, Muslim commentators think that the son in the story is Ismail, but the text might refer either to him or to Ishaq.

The spirit of Hajj is the spirit of total sacrifice: sacrifice of personal comforts, worldly pleasures, acquisition of wealth, companionship of relatives and friends, vanities of dress and personal appearance, pride relating to birth, national origin, accomplishments, work or social status.

This sacrifice of self was attained to the highest degree by the Prophet Ibrahim (peace be on him) who is known as "The Friend of God" *(Khalil Allah)*. The story of his sacrifice is narrated in the Quran in the following manner:

(Ibrahim said) "O my Lord! Grant me a righteous (son)." So We gave him the good news of a boy ready to suffer and forbear. Then, when the son reached (the age of serious) work with him, he said, "O my son! I see in vision that I offer you in sacrifice: now see what is your view."

The son said: "O my father! Do as you are commanded. You will find me, if God so wills, one practising patience and constancy." So when they had both submitted their wills (to God), and he (Ibrahim) had laid him (Ismail) prostrate on his forehead (for sacrifice), We called out to him: "O Ibrahim! You have already fulfilled the vision."

> *Thus indeed do We reward those who do right. For this was obviously a trial. And We ransomed him with a great sacrifice. And We left (this blessing) for him among generations (to come) in later times: "Peace and salutaion to Ibrahim!"* *Quran: Sura 37: 100-109* The Ranks

Although the events to which this narrative refers occurred many centuries ago ... the spirit of submission to God cannot be illustrated for us in any clearer manner.

"Hajj" also signifies the brotherhood of all Muslims, demonstrated in this greatest of all international assemblies ... (It) reminds Muslims of the forthcoming assembly on the Day of Judgement ... and also of the birth, rise and expansion of Islam, the overthrow of idolatry, the establishment of the worship of one God, and the difficulties and accomplishments of the Prophet Muhammad (peace be on him) and the early Muslims.

Motives for the Pilgrimage : Since 1960 the number of pilgrims from outside Arabia has more than trebled. Modern means of transport facilitate but cannot fully explain this increase.

What draws the pilgrims? Here are answers from a number of Muslims. The leader of twenty thousand Iranian pilgrims: Abul Fazl Hazeghi, educator and parliamentarian:

> *The purpose of the Pilgrimage is to clean the heart. A pilgrim has to set right anything wrong between him*

> *and another person, to make his will and to pay his debts. When he leaves home he should be free of debt, hate, bitterness, resentment, impurity.*

Personally, I had three times the honour to take about twenty thousand pilgrims from Iran to Mecca. I have seen many people getting a new direction of life - completely different; some of them paying a large part of their wealth to be used for people's welfare, for the building of mosques, hospitals, clinics, etc. I was witness to many restorations between man and man, sect and sect, removing all kinds of misunderstanding and creating new friendships.

A professor:

> *I have been several times to Mecca. I went with one idea, and came back with another. I looked forward to seeing the places where the Prophet lived and worked. I found more than that: the vast concourse of people from many lands, all the same, all equal; and their yearning for God, as all move round the Kaaba, hundreds of thousands of us together.*

A former prime minister:

> *I have been three times - twice for the Hajj. The simplicity of it is inspiring. But Muslims miss something of what it could be. It could be a conference at which everything of importance to Muslims is dealt with. The Prophet used it in this way. At his last pilgrimage, he made a great speech which is a charter for all Muslims.*

An Egyptian lady:

> *It is like a rehearsal for Resurrection Day - everybody equal, all kinds of people together, the whole of humanity before God.*

An article addressed to London students faces the difficulties encountered by pilgrims. Mecca has its dust and flies, its colds and coughs, its taxi-drivers and water sellers who are cynics. "Hajj does need preparation and training," says the writer. He urges an imaginative use of television and radio to introduce different groups of Muslims to each other — in place of the sometimes incongruous mingling of sermons and western dance music. He concludes:

> *Hajj has maintained the capacity to lift man from the jumble of his preoccupations and out of the mechanical framework within which he lives. Never is prayer offered with a greater feeling. In the unending flow of*

worshippers around the Kaaba throughout the day and throughout the night, there is satisfaction to the heart, joy to the eye, and mystery to the soul...

The scorched and barren landscape synchronises perfectly with these feelings of the pilgrim and even helps to produce them. It could never have done so were it cool and green and luscious. Yet there is no debasement, but ardour and grandeur. The days of the Hajj are indeed unique days. Would that its great possibilities are realised!

Mecca Airlift : During the pilgrimage season hundreds of planes are chartered to bring pilgrims from every continent. Typical is one that started from Britain, in February 1968.

In the bitter cold of London's wintry dockland, the party gathers at the East London Mosque. It is an illustration both of the breadth of the Muslim world, and of the variety of Britain's multiracial society. Pakistanis and Indians are in the majority. A number of Iranians move together. Somali land, Zanzibar, Kenya and Nigeria are represented among the Africans.

Gayest note on a grey day is the emerald head-scarf of a Nigerian woman. She is one of a party of Nigerian students. Her husband says:

Few months ago nothing was farther frommy mind than the Hajj.

I had lost all faith and grip on life. But my brother's son never stopped coming to see me, and in the end he helped me to make a fresh start.

I am going home in a few months. I began to think, "I cannot take home the bad ways I have learned here," and I decided to clean up my life. Now my mother is coming from Lagos, and we shall meet in Mecca and make the pilgrimage together.

Among the party is an exiled ruler. An old man from Guyana is seen off by his son and daughter-in-law, immigrants to Britain. He has stayed with them for two weeks on his way. It is his first journey and he is nervous, as is an elderly Turk whose womenfolk are comforting him. The wife of the caretaker of the mosque encourages the lonely, and sees that everyone has the necessary documents. She is Welsh. She became a Muslim twenty-seven years ago and has, she says, prayed the regular five times a day ever since. Her warm heart, common sense, box of medicines and knowledge of Mecca will stand the others in good stead. Youngest of the party is a fifteen-year-old schoolgirl, travelling with her mother and her father, who has a business in Lancashire.

The women wait in a room above the mosque. Five coaches are at the door. Before they leave, the Call to Prayer is sounded, sheets are rapidly laid on the floor, and all pray. One woman starts to sing -reciting the verses of the Quran which her Urdu pilgrimage book recommends.

Bags and people are piled into the coaches, and they are away. Tomorrow morning they will be in Jadda, the next day in Mecca.

Discipline of Hajj : In a talk to would-be pilgrims in London, it was said, "There is no beauty in the Holy Land. You go to please God, not yourself." While the hardship is now lessened, the Pilgrimage remains a severe physical ordeal. The lunar months of the Muslim calendar come round at different seasons of the year, and the Hajj often takes place in intense summer heat. Any loss of temper or any altercation destroys its value.

There are many books designed to help pilgrims find their way through the month they spend in Arabia. A recent one comes from Dr Hassan Hathout, Egyptian doctor. It is a commonsense document, combining advice on health and diet with spiritual background. Dr Hathout stresses the permaent gain in tolerance and self-restraint.

The journey of Hajj is not easy. It is a taxing process and I do not speak in terms of the distance you cover from Home to Hajj. Coming together with a few hundred thousand people within a limited span of time and space, having to perform the same rites, entailing mass movements in a limited time from one place to another, is an ordeal. Yet the main cause of difficulty is the human one. These people have many different backgrounds and customs, do not speak the same language, and yet they are gathered into this colossal human mass. One can imagine that endless situations would arise all loaded with nervous tension and intolerance. Yet strong "brakes" are placed on any tendency to nervousness or intolerance - it is a criterion of pilgrimage to be pure and tolerant. The Quran says: "The Hajj season comprises the specified months. He who proposes to do Hajj in them must abstain from obscenity, wickedness and ill-tempered disputes during Hajj."

However provoked, you should remain gentle and tolerant. This attitude of peace and forgiveness is imposed by your own self - and you do not pretend to be tolerant, but you feel you really are. This is indeed a great exercise in self-restraint and self-exploration for you will sometimes be surprised to discover your tremendous faculties for love and patience, thus unearthing treasures you can count on in your future life.

Some of us who are highly sophisticated, especially those with western upbringing, do time and again ... voice many complaints ... (but) it seems to me that one of the aims of Hajj is to put the one Nation together in the one pot and make them mix and mingle ... The privileged cast away their arrogance and pride because they know it is a sin to be harsh to your brother or be scornful of him ... It is democracy in practice - and it is democracy in love - under God . It is true that some Muslims live in circumstances precluding them from attaining the standard that would please. Instead of being angry with them we should be angry for them.

Prophet's Farewell Pilgrimage : One of the great events of Islamic history took place during Muhammad's last pilgrimage, shortly before his death. He addressed his followers in a speech that was the climax of his mission. This speech, made in dialogue with his hearers, has come down as a summary of his message. Every biographer of the Prophet describes the event, and every pilgrim recalls it as he follows the course of the Hajj in the Prophet's footsteps.

The crowd, an estimated one hundred thousand, gathered at Arafat, a few miles outside Mecca, as it does today. Muhammad rode the same favourite camel, Al Kaswa, that had carried him as a fugitive from Mecca to Medina ten years earlier.

By his side was Bilal, the negro ex-slave whose great voice had won the honour of giving the first call to prayer on behalf of the Prophet. His voice, picked up by others through the crowd, was the relay-system by which the words of Muhammad reached the whole assembly.

Then came the last verse of the Quran to be revealed:

> *This day have I perfected your religion for you, completed My favour upon you, and have chosen for you Islam as your religion.* *Quran: Sura 5: 4* The Table
>
> *In the course of this address, the Prophet called for the wiping out of vendettas- starting with a blood-feud in his own family as an example. This may be compared with Moses' farewell speech to the men and women of the Exodus, when he said, "Vengeance is mine, saith the Lord, I will repay."* *(Deuteronomy 32:35)*

Among many summaries of this speech, here is one designed for teaching children and students. It comes from *An Easy History of the Prophet of Islam,* published in Lahore.

1. All the customs and practices of the pagan age are abolished.
2. All compensation for bloodshed of the old days is abolished: and on behalf of my family I declare illegal the indemnity for the blood of Ibn Rabia ibn Harith [murdered cousin of the Prophet].

3. All usuries of the past are wiped out.
4. Fear God in respect of women. You, men, have your rights over your wives and they have their rights over you.
5. As regards your slaves, be fair to them. Give them to eat what you eat and to wear what you wear.
6. Your blood and your properties are as sacred for one another as are this day, this month and this place.
7. Each Muslim is a brother of another. All Muslims form one brotherhood.
8. An Arab has no superiority over a non-Arab, nor has a non-Arab over an Arab. You are all born of Adam, and Adam was made out of clay.
9. Whoever is entrusted with a thing belonging to another must deliver his trust to its owner.
10. The debtors must pay their debts.
11. I leave behind one thing, and you will never go astray if you hold it fast, and that is the Book of God.

Three Holy Cities: Mecca, Medina and Al-Quds (Jerusalem) **:** Mecca, Medina and Jerusalem are all holy places to the Muslim. Almost every pilgrim to Mecca also visits Medina (2,25 miles northwest of Mecca), where the Prophet Muhammad lived for ten years and was buried.

Through the centuries, pilgrims to Mecca have regarded a visit to Jerusalem as a completion of their pilgrimage. The city is known in Arabic as Baitul-Maqdis (the Holy House), or Al-Qds.

There uslim and Christian pilgrims have sought the same holy places. When the end of the Hajj has coincided with Easter, large numbers of pilgrims of both faiths have often mingled in the streets. The writer was among them in 1966, the year before the Six Day War.

The Christian shrines were visited by the Muslim pilgrims. One party from Iraq were heard in disappointed argument because a service prevented them from entering the cave in the Church of the Nativity in Baitulaham where by tradition Jesus was born. They had just been to Hebron, to the ancient mosque which marks the tomb of Ibrahim. From some countries, there were pilgrim parties of both faiths: from Nigeria, for instance, and Yugoslavia. The parked coaches from the latter country might carry either Christians or Muslims.

The streets of the Old City were brightly lit, the shops open all night. Many homes had been opened to house the thousands from Syria and Egypt who, with the Cypriots, formed the mass of Christian pilgrims. Alongside these Christian homes were those with gay pictures chalked on the doors to welcome home Hajis. *Hajj mabrur wa dhanab maghfur*. "Pilgrimage made and sins forgiven." Less edifying were the second-hand clothes markets outside Herod's Gate and at the coach park, where Europe's old coats were finding their way to remote villages and Bedouin camps.

For the Muslims, all these things were incidental to the visit to Al-Masjid al-Aqsa, the Farthest Mosque, revered by the Prophet; the place towards which his prayers were first directed, and the starting point of his great mystical experience, the journey into heaven, during which he received the revelation about the five daily times of prayer. This event is known as the "Night of Ascent", and is said to have inspired Dante. About one fifth of the area of the Old City is taken up with the courts of the Noble Sanctuary, Al-Haram al-Sharif, with its large congregational Mosque, Al-Aqsa, to the south, and in the centre the marvel of the Dome of the Rock. In 1966, repairs and restoration had just been completed. The fresh gold on the dome dominated the landscape and the city. A tall crane still stood by its side, and the little Dome of the Chain awaited repair, its condition a measure of the extent of the work done on the larger structure.

Every Muslim child knows the story of the Arab capture of Jerusalem. In AD 638 the Patriarch in the beleaguered city offered to surrender it, but only to the Caliph 'Umar in person. 'Umar, simply dressed, entered the city and said his prayers not in, but near, the Church of the Holy Sepulchre, so that his followers might not be tempted to take it over. The treaty he made is regarded as a model of tolerance. This and the parallel story of the reconquest of the city by Saladin (Salah ad-din) after a century of Christian occupation are viewed in sharp contrast with the bloodshed and slaughter associated with the Frankish armies in 1099 when the Crusaders took the city.

The Dome of the Rock, first of the great architectural achievements of Islam, was finished by the ninth caliph, Abdul Malik, in the year AD 691. In its thirteen centuries of life, it has been fortunate in its restorations. Each, including the most recent, has kept to the character of the building and has enhanced its beauty. As with other great works of art, it has a perfection which is, in its own sphere, unsurpassed.

The care of Al-Aqsa and the Noble Sanctuary is the trust of a group of families whose tenure goes back eight hundred years, though many were exiled after 1967. They were installed by Saladin after he recaptured Jerusalem from the Crusaders in AD 1189. Khatibs, Hussainis and Nashashibis have lived in the houses overlooking the

Noble Sanctuary ever since, and generation has followed generation in its service. Some have been there longer still. Khalidis - the family of the great general Khalid ibn Walid have resided in the city since AD 638. More recent comers are Shihabis, who arrived from Lebanon three centuries ago. To them are entrusted the Prophet's cloak and pen, precious relics which are shown to the faithful each year on the Night of Ascent, Muhammad's mystical journey to heaven.

In the Dome of the Rock, human skill and artistry surround something unique in its rugged simplicity. The stretch of bare rock beneath the dome is a stark reminder of a Greatness no image can evoke, which commands the total submission of man's every gift and talent. The rock is linked with Ibrahim. Centuries after his time, David bought it, and Solomon built his temple here. In these courts Jesus walked and taught. No place on earth has been the focus of so much faith and so much hope. It is central to all three of the great monotheistic faiths. They have a basic kinship stemming from Father Ibrahim. Cooperation between Jews, Christians and Muslims was the hope of the Prophet Muhammad. He was disappointed, but his respect for others who believe and obey God is deeply rooted in the Muslim mind.

Special Status of Friday

- Though Friday, according to Islam, is the best day on which the sun has ever risen, and the lord of days, it is not the Islamic sabbath, because sabbath does not exist in Islam.
- A Muslim should bathe or purify himself with 'wudu' as perfectly as possible before going to prayer. Though bathing is not obligatory, it has a more cleansing effect; though 'wudu' is good, bathing is more excellent.
- Best clothes should be worn and perfume applied, if this is available, or pleasant-smelling oil should be put on the hair.
- A tooth stick or toothbrush should be used to ensure that the mouth is clean and has a pleasant odour. This is more important on Fridays before leaving for prayer than on other days.
- Before leaving for prayer, nails should be cut and cleaned, and one should ensure that clothes are clean and beard and moustache tidy.
- The Friday prayer in congregation is a necessary duty for every Muslim, with certain exceptions, e.g. children, women, invalids and those too ill to perform prayer.
- If there is more than one mosque available, it is yet better to say the Friday prayer together at one mosque.

- Going as early as possible to the mosque on Friday is recommended. Walking to the mosque, if this is possible, and not riding is also more worthy.
- On entering the mosque, the rules of behaviour in the mosque must be observed.
- Care should be taken to avoid annoying others in the mosque; for example, squeezing between two men or stepping on others.
- Most mosques on Fridays become full of worshippers. No individual has the right to make another get up and then move into his place. He should politely ask those present to make room for him.
- While in the mosque, the worshipper must avoid any sitting position which could cause him to drowse, to sleep, or which would invalidate his 'wudu'.
- If a worshipper should find himself dozing, he should try to change his place. In this case, he should change places with his neighbour.
- A worshipper should avoid taking any position that would uncover his body between the navel and the knees.
- The Prophet Muhammad forbade worshippers to sit together in a circle in the mosque before Friday prayer, because this hinders straight rows, and reduces the available space.
- Facing the imam while he is giving khutbah from the minbar (pulpit) is polite conduct.
- When the imam asks God's blessings, etc. for the Muslims, he should not raise his hands in an attitude of supplication.
- When the Friday prayer is finished worshippers should not rush to leave the mosque, or crowd the exits.
- As mentioned above, a sabbath does not exist in Islam, therefore, it is not required that a Muslim abandons working during the whole of Friday. What is required, is to stop working during prayer time.
- A worshipper should listen to the imam as soon as he starts his khutbah and keep silent until he finishes. To attend prayer with a frivolous attitude is against the aim of the Friday prayer.
- It is undesirable to fast on Friday alone; to fast on Friday, however, in conjunction with Thursday or Saturday is allowed.
- It is neither necessary nor required to abandon travel on Friday.
- Friday is a good occasion to remember the Prophet, peace be on him, and invoke a blessing on him by saying: Allahuma Salli

ala Muhammad wa ala ali Muhammad (O God, bless Muhammad and Muhammad's family).

- Reading the Quranic chapter of Al-Kahf every Friday is recommended.

Khutbah at Friday Prayer

- The imam should avoid the custom of always wearing black clothes on Fridays.
- As soon as the imam ascends the minbar he salutes the worshippers, just before he sits or immediately after.
- The imam should face the worshippers while he is delivering the khutbah.
- Topics discussed in the khutbah should be related to current, relevant issues.
- The Friday khutbah is of two parts in each of which the imam must speak while standing; in the interval between he must sit for a short while on the minbar.
- The voice of the imam should be clear, but he should not shout in order to be heard. His language should be simple and understandable.
- The imam should not interrupt his khutbah in order to greet someone or to make an announcement of any kind.
- The imam should not make his khutbah or his prayer lengthy. Each must be of moderate length. In fact, the shortness of the khutbah is a sign of the imam's understanding and knowledge of Islam.
- The second part of the khutbah should not be devoid of informtion.
- The khutbah is a message and not a performance. The imam should avoid being conspicuously eloquent or poetic; he should also avoid speaking in a voice or in a manner which tends towards musicality.
- The imam's raising his hands in the khutbah while saying 'dua' for the Muslims is not recommended. It is enough that he poins with his forefinger.
- The imam should prepare his khutbah beforehand; his 'dua' should preferably be spontaneous and not memorized.
- The imam should not begin the actual prayer until he has convinced himself that the rows of worshippers are straight.

Position of Mosque

The mosque is where Muslims should pray five times every day, where they seek refuge from the troubles of this world, from its everlasting daily demands, its complications and its vanities.

Design

- A mosque should be built in every residential district.
- The design of the mosque should be characterized by simplicity, as must its furnishings.
- The mosque should be devoid of any lavish kind of ornamentation, representation of anything, pictures or images.
- Extravagance in spending large sums of money to build luxurious mosques should be avoided.
- Members of the Muslim society should neither vie with one another about the virtues or beauties of any particular mosque nor compete in building ostentatious mosques.
- Attaching pieces of gold of silver to any part of the mosque or its furnishings is forbidden.
- The carpets and walls of the mosque should be devoid of a multiplicity of colours for that distracts the concentration of the worshippers.
- Writing on the walls of the mosque, inside or outside, including Quranic verses or God's attributes, should be avoided. The names of the Prophet and the first four rightly-guided Caliphs likewise should not be written.
- The minbar should not be placed in the middle of the mosque. Its height should not exceed three steps.
- Every mosque should have two entrances, one for men and one for women.
- Lavatories should be sited as far from the mosque as practicable, and from the fountains or basins for ritual ablution.
- Raising flags inside the mosque is an innovation.

Cleanliness and Tidiness : The mosque deserves to be the cleanest place on earth. Therefore:

- Muslims must be sure before entering the mosque that their body and clothes are clean and do not smell bad.
- Filth must be removed from shoes and the shoes removed before entering the mosque.

- Although it is not forbidden to eat anything in the mosque, it is not a place for taking meals and drinks.
- Whoever brings in or causes dirt in the mosque has a duty to clean it up and remove it. It is not the duty solely of the mosque caretaker to keep the mosque clean and tidy; it is also the responsibility of every Muslim entering the mosque and seeing any uncleanliness, to remove this from the mosque.
- The mosque should be sprayed or sprinkled with perfume to give a pleasant odour.

Regular Worshipping

The Holy Prophet [S.A.W.] observed that Allah has affirmed as follows:

> *"My creatures! Each one of you is misguided, save the one whom I guide. So seek guidance only from Me so that I may instruct you. My people! Each one of you is famished, save the one whom I feed. So apply to Me only for subsistence, so that I may grant you livelihood. My slaves! Each one of you is naked, save the one whom I dress with an apparel, so beseech clothing from Me so that I may dress you with garments. My bondmen! You commit sins day and night and I can forgive all sins. So seek forgiveness from Me so that I may forgive you your sins."* *(Sahih Muslim)*

1. Never lose hope of acceptance by Allah of your repentance and petition for forgiveness. Whatever the magnitude of your sins, purify your soul by offering repentance and be hopeful of Allah's mercy, Despair is the characteristic of unbelievers, It is the distinctive trait of the believers that they repent the most and nder no circumstances do they lose hope of Allah's clemency. It is disastrous to succumb to dismay and lose hope of Allah's Mercy and clemency considering the magnitude of sins.

   The most outstanding quality of the favourites of Allah is that they do not stick to the wrong and guilt but admit their fault clearly and unconditionally. They are never supposed to be above faults and omissions, but when they commit any fault and realise the wrong done, they do all within their means to beg forgiveness from Allah and to purify themselves of that fault and misdeed.

   "And those who when they do an evil thing or wrong them selves remmber Allah and implore forgiveness for

their sins. Who forgiveth sins save Allah only? - and will not knowingly repeat (the wrong) they did." *(3: 135)*

And Allah affirms in another verse:

"Lo! those who ward off (evil) when a glamour from the evil troubleth them they do but remember (Allah's guidance) and behold them seers." *(7: 201)*

And the Holy Prophet [S.A.W.] observed:

"All human beings without exception are sinful, but the best sinners are those who repent the most." (Tirmidhi)

In the Holy Quran, Allah ha mentioned it as a distinct virtue of the believers that they offer penances before Allah at dawn and repent and seek His Forgiveness and Allah has urged the believers that they should rest assured that Allah shall cover their sins with His Forgiveness and Clemency, for He i All Forgiving and the Most Affectionate towards His creatures.

"Ask pardon of your Lord and then turn unto Him (repentant). Lo! m Lord is Merciful, Loving." *(11: 90)*

2. Always be hopeful of Allah's lessings and rest assured that however great your sins may be, Allah's Munificene is wider and all-encompassing. When a person who has committed a greater volume of sins than the surf of the sea feels ashamed and offers sincere penance before Allah, He listens to his entreaties and grants him refuge under His Mercy.

   "O My slaves who have been prodigal to their own heart! Despair not of the Mercy of Allah who forgiveth all sin. Lo! He is the Forgiving the Merciful. Turn unto Him repentant; and surrender unto Him befor there come unto you the doom, when ye cannot be helpe." *(39: 53, 54)*

3. Whenever you feel shame and remorse and at whtever stage of your life, consider this feeling and realisation a special favour of Allah and be sure that the doors are always open for repentance. Allah accepts repentance of His slaves as long as they are alive. However, when they are at the threshold of death and are about to pass over to the next world, the time for offering repentance expires. The Holy Prophet [S.A.W.] observed:

   "Allah accepts the repentance of His slaves, but only before the slave has breathed his last." *(Tirmidhi)*

The brothers of HadratYusuf [A.S.] pushed him into a dark well and felt sure that he was dead. In other words, they stood guilty of the murder of a Prophet. They soaked Hadrat Yusufs shirt in blood and presented it as a positive evidence of his death to their father Hadrat Yaqub [A.S.]. They assured him that a wolf had devoured Hadrat Yusuf [A.S.] Many years after the commission of this grave offence when the sense of guilt prevailed upon them, they went to their father remorsefully and requested him: "ear father, pray to Allah on our behalf and intercede with Him t grant us forgiveness." The Messenger of Allah Hadrat Yaqub [A.S.] did not disappoint his sons by confronting them with the question: "Your offence is grave. Many years have elapsed since you committed this heinous crime, why ask for forgieness now?" Instead he undertook to offer a prayer to Allah that He should grant them salvation and assured them that Allah would certainly forgive them for Allah is the Most Forbearing and Most Compassionate.

> *"They said. O our father! Ask forgiveness of our sins for us, for Lo! we are sinful."* *(12: 97)*
>
> *"He said: I shall ask forgiveness for you of my Lord. Lo! He is the Forgiving, the Merciful."* *(12: 98)*

The Holy Prophet [S.A.W.] told a strange tale to his Companions [R.A.A.] with a view to save them from falling a prey to dismay. The tale contains the moral that whenever at any stage of his life a believer feels ashamed of hs misdeeds and he sincerely entreats Allah to forgive him, Allah shall bestow upon hm salvation and He shall never refuse him His favour.

> *The Holy Prophet [S.A.W.] observed: "There was a man in ancient days who had committed ninety-nine murders. He enquired from people: "Who is the greatest scholar of the time?" The people gave him thename of a Allah-fearing monk. The man approached the monk and sid. "Respected Sir, I am guilty of niney-nine murders. Can my repentance and petition for forgiveness be accepted?" The monk replied: "No, you stand no chances for forgiveness." In utter dismay the man killed the monk too. Now he had completed a century of murders. He again went round asking the people as to who was the greatest religious scholar on the earth. The people gave him the name of another monk. The man approached the monk to offer repentance. He related his problem in detail and enquired from him: Sir, I have committed a hundred murders Tell me, can my repenance be accepted?" The monk replied: Why not? Nothing stand in the way of acceptance of your repentance. Go to such and such country. You will find a few venerable slaves*

of Allah engaged in prayer and devotions to Him. Join them and devote yourself to the worship of Allah and never retun to your homeland, as this place is no more virtually suitable for you (In other words, it is impossible for you to remain firm upon your vow of repentance and to strive to reform yourself while living in this place)." The man set out according to the directions of the monk. He had hardly covered half the distance when death overtook him. Now the angels of grace and the angels of torment fell into a dispute. The angels of grace argued, "This man repented of his sins and went a long way to offer submission to Allah." The angels of torment countered: "No, he has not yet performed a single act of virtue-thus the argumentation between the angels went on. In the meantime an angel appeared in the shape of a human being. The angels requested him to settle their dispute. He gave his verdict: "Measure he distance on both sides and determine which side is nearer; the place from where he set out r the place where was he going." When the angels measured the distance on both the sides, it came out that the destination was nearer as compared to the distance he had so far covered. Thus Allah had in fact forgiven him. *(Bukhari, Muslim)*

4. Confess your sins only before Allah; beseech Him only for forgiveness; express your sense of humility, helplessness and guilt only before Him. Humility and prostration is a tribute which you should pay only to Allah. The unfortunate one, who pays this tribute of humility and prostration t other human beings who are as helpless and humble before Allah as he himself, becomes insolvent and is left with nothing to pay as tribute to Allah. Such a man is condemned to disgrace and ignominy. He goes to everybody in search of honour and respect but he gets none.

Allah affirms:

"Thy Lord is the Forgiver, Full of Mercy. If He took them to task now for what they earn, He would hasten on the doom for them; but there is an appointed term from which they will find no escape." *(18: 58)*

The Quran alarms:

"And He it is Who accepts the repentance from His bondmen, and ardoneth the evil deeds and knoweth what ye do." *(42: 25)*

In fact, one must himself e convinced that there is only one way to salvation and whoever is denied that approach, is condemned to ignominy and destitution for ever. The befitting attitude of mind in a beliver is that whatever the degree of his offence he should only offer penitence to Allah and shed tears of shame only before Him. There is one except Allah Who only has the authority to grant pardon. So much so that even ifsomeone tries to propitiate the Prophet excluding Allah, he will be deprived of favour before Allah, and will be discarded outight. The Prophet of Allah [S.A.W.] is also a slave of Allah soliciting His favour and mercy. The Prophet has been appointed to the exalted office by virtue of his surpassing humility among the creatures of Allah and he makes greater penances to Allah in comparison with others.

The Holy Prophet [S.A.W.] observed:

> *"O People! Seek forgiveness of Allah for your sins and return to Him. Look at me. I offer prayers to Allah for salvation hundreds of times in a day."* *(Muslim)*

Concerning the hypocrites Allah affirms:

> *"They swear unto you, that ye may accept them, Though ye accept them. Allah verily accepteth not wrong doing folk"* *(9: 96)*

Theterrible episode of Hadrat Kaab b. Malik [R.A.A.] as related in the oly Quran gives us a lesson that man should suffer hardships and endure all trials, but he should never think of abandoning ubmission to Allah. The trials that come inthe way of Islam and the maximum pain and suffering hehas to bear in the way of Allah ae means to purify and illumine the life of man and to elevate his rank. This humiliation is the sure means of securing eternal prestige and he who abandns submission to Allah and seeks digniy elsewhere shall find it nowhere. Such a man will meet with disgrace everywhere and no eye on earthor in the sky shall regard him with respect.

> *"And to the three also (dd he turn in mercy) who were left behind, when the earth, vast as it is was straitend for them and their own souls were straitened for them till they bethought them thatthere is no refuge from Allah save towards Him. Then turned He unto them in mercy that they (too) might turn (repentant unto Him). Lo! Allah! He is the Relenting, the Merciful."* *(9: 118)*

The three referred to above are Hadrat Kaab bin Malik Hadrat Murarah ibn Rab' and Hadrat Halala b. Umayyah [R.A.A.]. The example of their penitence serves as a beacon light for the believes as long as the world exists. Hadrat Kaab b. Malik [R.A.A.] who had lost his eyesight in old age and used to walk with the help of his son, had himself related the instructive eisode of his exemplary penitence to his son which has been preserved in the Books of Tradition.

"When the preparations were being made for the battle of Tabuk and the Holy Prophet [S.A.W.] used to call upon the people to join the war I regularly attended all his meetings. Whenever I heard him speak, I made a resolve that I would join the war. However, on returning home I relapsed into lziness. I thought there was plenty of time yet and I had all the provisions of the journey. Moreover, I was in ood health and could afford the best mount. There was nothing that could delay me in joining the battle. In this mood, I continued to postpone my departure until all holy warriors had reached the field of battle and I lingered on in Medina entrapped in indecision and lethargy. "Soon the reports began to pour in that the Holy Prophet [S.A.W.] was returning and one day I heard that he had arrived in Medina and was staying as usual in the mosque. So I went to the mosque. On arrival I found that the hypocrites were trying to convince the Holy Prophet [S.A.W.] of the genuineness of their excuses on oaths. The Holy Prophet [S.A.W.] heard their insincere speeches and indicated his acceptance of their lame excuses by observing 'May Allah forgive you'.

"When my turn came, the Holy Prophet [S.A.W.] enquired: 'Say, what prevented you from coming'? I saw that his smile had a trace of annoyance, so I spoke the truth. "O Messenger of Allah [S.A.W.]! As it happened I had no excuse. I was healthy and prosperous and possessed the mount. It was my lethargy and negligence which deprived me of this privilege. "On hearing me speak the truth, the Holy Prophet [S.A.W.] observed: "Well, then, go and wait the verdict from Allah." I got up and went among the people of my tribe. The people of my tribe railed at me and said: "Why did you not offer some plausible excuse. You have always been in the forefront in the service of Islam." However, when I found that two other friends of mine had also told the truth, I felt at ease and determined to hold firmly to the truth.

"Afterwards, the Holy Prophet [S.A.W.] issued a general proclamation that no one should peak to us. As soon as this proclamation was issued forth, the attitudes in Medina suddenly changed for me. I became a helpless stranger among my own kith and kin. No one in the society exchanged greeings or entered into a conversation with me. One day, I felt extremely depressed and went to a childhood friend and cousin Abu Qatada [R.A.A.]. I offered him salam, but he did not reciprocate. I, then, said: "Abu Qatada! I ask you in the name of Allah, tell me, am I wanting in lovefor Allah and His Messenger [S.A.W.]."

Qatada [R.A.A.] remained silent. I repeated my question, but he made no answer. When I asked him in the name of Allah for the third time, he said: "Allah and His Messenger [S.A.W.] know better." My heart overflowed with a surge of emotion and I burst into tears and returned home with the burden of my grief enhanced.

It was during those days that a Syrian trader in the bazar delivered to me a letter from the monarch of Ghassan. The Christian monarch had written: "It has come to our knowledge that your chief is subjecting you to extreme repression. You are not a lowly person. We know the worth of a man like you. Come to us. We shall treat you as befits your status and rank." As soon as I read the letter, my tongue uttered: "Here is another calamity that has befallen me." And I threw the letter into the hearth. "Forty days had passedin this state when a courier of the Holy rophet [S.A.W.] delivered his command that I should separate from my wife also. I enquired: "Shall I divorce her?" The answer came: "No, just live eparately from her." I despatched mywife to the home of her parents and told her: "Now, wait for the verdict from Allah."

"On the fiftieth day after dawn prayers, I was sitting on the roof of my house highly dejected, stricken with extreme grief and considering life as no longer bearable, when suddenly someone shouted to me: 'Kaab! Congratulations'. On hearing this, I understood that the hour of my deliverance had come and fell in prostration to my Allah. Later people rushed towards me. They came in crowds and congratulated me. I rose and went straight to the presence of the Holy Prophet [S.A.W.]. I saw his august face glowing with happiness. When I moved forward and greeted him, the Prophet [S.A.W.] observed: "Kaab! Congratulations! This is the happiest day of your life."I submitted: "Prophet of Allah [S.A.W.], is this clemency a favour from you or from Allah?" The Holy Prophet [S.A.W.] observed: "This is a favour from Allah" and then recited the verses of *Surah Taubah* (9)."

5. Do not delay in offering repentance. obody knows when his life will end, and the next moment will bring death to him or his life shall continue. Always remember your fast approaching end and continue to cleanse the impurity of sins from your heart and soul and mind and speech.

The Holy Prophet [S.A.W.] observed:

"Allah extends His mercy during the night so that the person ho committed a sin during the day should return to Him in the night. Allah extends His mercy during the day so that the person who has committed a sin during

the night may return to his Lord in the day time and see His forgiveness until the sun rises from the east."

(Muslim)

The expression 'Allah extends His mercy' means that Allah beckons His sinfl slaves towards Himself and desires to cover their sins wih His blessings. If the person has committed a sin under the pressue of a temporary impulse, he should immediately turn towards his kind and All-Forgiving Allah and should lose no time, for sin begets sin. The Satan constantly lies in ambush for the human being and never misses an opportunity to lead man astray.

6. Offer repentance with such true and deep sincerity of heart that the entire course of your life is altered and after repentane you may appear an entirely different man.

Allah decrees:

"O ye who believe! Turn unto Allah in sincere repentance! It may be tat your Lord will remit from you your evil deeds and bring you into Gardens underneath which rivers flow on the day when Allah will not abase the Prophet and those who believe with him." *(66: 8)*

In other words, offer such sicere and true repentance that not a race of any temptation to return to the sin remains in your heart or mind. Such a repentance has three or four ingredients. If the sin relates to a transgression of Allah's right, repentance should have three elements:

(i) Man should be sncerely ashamed of his sins.

(ii) Man should firmly resolve to avoid sin in future.

(iii) And man should put his heart and soul in the task of reforming and embellishing his life.

If a man has committed a sin which involves the violation of a human right, repentance should consist of a fourth element also:

(iv) Man should restre the right of another human being or seek orgiveness of the person whose right he has violated.

This is the repentance which really cleanses the man of all his sins. His soul is cleared of sins and adorne with pious deeds, is presented before Allah and is awarded a dwelling place in His Paradise.

The Holy Prophet [S.A.W.] observed:

"When man commits a sin, his heart is stained with a dark spot. Now if he:

(i) renounces the sin;
(ii) is ashamed of his sin and seeks salvation;
(iii) and turns to Allah with a firm determination to avoid sin in future;

Allah illumines his heart. But if he again commits sin, the dark spot is enlarged until it covers the whole of his heart. This is the rust about which Allah affirms in His Book:

> *"Nay, but that which they have earned is rust upon their hearts."* *(83 : 14)*

7. Take a firm resolve to remain true to your repentance and be vigilant day and night that the commitments you have made before Allah are duly fulfilled. Test the firmness of your resolve by constant efforts to purify and reform yourself. If despite all your efforts to guard against evil, you slip and commit an offence, do not lose hope even thn. On the contrary seek refuge in the Mercy of Allah and offer fervent prayers to him: "O Creator! I am weak and infirm. Do not banish me in disgrace from Your threshold. For, I can seek asylum nowhere except in Your Mercy."

Repentance of a wrong-doer invite the pleasure of Allah. Taubah (Repentance) literally mans 'return, to turn to'. When thoughts and emotions go astray and one gets entrapped in the quicksand of sin, his connection with Allah is severed an he is so far removed from Allah as if he is lost to Allah. And when such a man returns and turns to Allah in utter shame for his sins, it is as if a lost slave has come back to his master. This situation has been graphically descrbed by the Holy Prophet [S.A.W.] in the following eloquent allegory:

> *"If one of you loses his camel in a waterless desert with all his provisions of food and water laden on the lost camel and having vainly searched for the camel in all directions of the desert he depairs of his life and lies down under a tree awaiting death and in this state he suddenly beholds his camel laden with all the provisions standing by his side, imagine then his happiness! - the happiness of your Lord and Creator ar surpasses the happiness of this man when His lost slave returns and having gone astray resumes allegiance to Him."*
>
> *(Tirmidhi)*

On another occasion, the Holy Prophet [.A.W.] elucidated Etiquette of Life in Islam th same fact by means of anoher impressive allegory:

Some prisoners of war wre brought before the Holy Prophet. [S.A.W.] The group included a woman who had lost her infant. The maternal instinct so overpowered the woman that she found no peace or rest unless she picked up and breast-fed any baby she found near her. On seeing the woman in such state the Holy Prophet [S.A.W.] enquired from the Companions [R.A.A.]: "Can you imagine that this woman will fling her baby into fire with her own hands?" The Companions submitted: "O Messenger of Allah [S.A.W.]! Leaving apart the matter of throwing the child herself, she would stake her life to save the child if it were falling by itself." The Prophet [S.A.W.] thereupon observed:

"Allah is by far even more Compassionate and Kind to His slaves than this woman is considerate towards her child."

8. Offer repentance to and seek forgiveness of Allah continuously. There are countless offences which a man commits from morning till evening; sometimes man is not even conscious of these transgressions. Do not imagine that repentance is called for only when a capital sin has been committed; man needs to repent and pray for his salvation at all times, because he is liable to make a slip at every step. The Holy Prophet [S.A.W.] himself used to repent and pray for his salvation seventy or even hundred times in a day.
   (Bukhari, Muslim)
9. Do not look down upon a sinner who repents and reforms his life. Hadrat 'Iran b. al-Haseen [R.A.A.] has reported an incident of the time of the Holy Prophet [S.A.W.]: "A woman of the tribe of Juhainah presented herself before the Holy Prophet [S.A.W.]. She had bcome pregnant as a result of an unlawful relation. She submitted: "O Messenger of Allah [S.A.W.]'. I deserve punishment for adultery. Enforce the Shariah in my cse and punish me." The Holy Prophet [S.A.W.] sent for the guardian of this woman and observed to him: "Treat this woman well and when she has delivered the child, bring her to me." When the woman returned after the delivery of her child, the Holy Prophet [S.A.W.] commanded that her garments should be tied fast around her body (so that the garments may not slip off during stoning and her physical veil may not be torn off) and when this had been done, the Holy Prophet [S.A.W.] ordered that she should be stoned to death. The order was carried out.

The Holy Prophet [S.A.W.] later offered funeral prayers for her. Hadrat 'Umar [R.A.A.] submitted to the Holy Prophet [S.A.W.]: "O Messenger of Allah [S.A.W.]! This woman committed the offence of adultery and you are saying funeral prayers for her." The Holy Prophet [S.A.W.] thereupon obsered: "She repented and offered repentance of such magnitude that if it were portioned among seventy men of Medina, it would secure their salvation. Did you see any one better than the one who presented the gift of life to Allah?"

10. Say the 'finest prayer' to Allah. The Holy Prophet [S.A.W.] observed to Hadrat Shaddad ibn Aus [R.A.A.] 'This is the *Sayyed-ul-Istaghfar'* ('the finest prayer').

    "Allah! Thou is my Creator! There is no deity except Thee. Thou created me and I am Thy slave. I shall remain faithful to the pledge of devotion which I have given to Thee to the best of my capability. I seek asylum with Thee against the fearful consequences of my sins. I acknowledge all the blessings Thou hast conferred on me and I confess that I am a sinner - Hence, O My reator, Forgive my sins. Who else except Thee will forgive my sins?" *(Bukhari, Muslim)*

Five Time Prayers : Pray to Allah only. Do not call upon any one else except Allah to fulfil your needs. Prayer is the essence of worship and worship should be rendered to Allah alone.

The Holy Quran affirms:

> *"Unto Him is the real prayer. Those unto whom they pray beside Allah espond to them not at all, save as (is te response to) one who stretches forth his hand, towards water (asking) that it may come to his mouth and it will never reach it. The payer of disbeliever goeth (far) astray." (13: 14)*

In other words all powers to fulfil prayers and to dispose of things lie in the hands of Allah. All powers vest in Him and no power lies with any one else. All are dependent upon Him. There is none except Him Who hears the petitions of human beings and fulfils their prayers.

> *"O mankind! Ye are the poor in your relation to Allah. And Allah! He is the Absolute, the Owner of Praise."*
> *(35:15)*

The Holy Prophet [S.A.W.] observed:

> *"Allah ffirms, 'My creatures! I have declared tyranny unawful for Me. So you should also consider acts of*

oppression and excess on each other as forbiden. My slaves! Each of you is misguided, except the one whom I guide on the right path. So seek guidnce from Me alone, so that I may guide you aright. My people! Each of you is hungry, except the one whom I feed. Hence call upon Me for sustenance, so that I may provide for your livelihood. My servants! Each of you is naked, except the one whom I have blessed with garments. So entreat Me to confer dress on you and I shal provide you clothing. My worshippers! You commit sins in the night as well as in the day and I shall forgive all sins"! (Sahib Muslim)The Holy Prophet [S.A.W.] also observed: "Man should call upon Allah alone to provide for all his eeds, so muh so that even if a shoelace is broken, man should pray to Allah to provide a shoelace, and if e needs salt, he should beseech Allah to send it to him." (Tirmidhi)

The Implication is that man ought to turn to Allah for the fulfilment of his most insignificant and ordinary needs. None except Allah can hear the prayers and none except Him can fulfil wants.

2. Ask Allah for only that which is lawful and good. To beseech Allah's help for the execution of unlawful purposes and sinful acts is the height of impertinence, immodesty and irreverence. To pray to Allah for the fulfilment of unlawful and forbidden desires and to make vows for such desires is to perpetrate the basest joke on religion. Similarly, do not offer prayers to Allah to change those realities which He has determined once for all and which are now unalterable. For example, a short man should nt pray to Allah to make him tall, nor should a tall man pray to Allah to make him short; nor indeed shoul a man pray to Allah for eternal youth so that he may never experiene old age etc.

The Holy Quran affirms:

"And set your faces upright (towards Him) a every place of worship, and call upon Him, making religion pure for Him (only)." 7: 29)

He, who would present his needs before Allah, should not take to he path of infidelity and pray for the fulfilment of unlawful desire, but should display good character and virtuous passions and beseech Allah for the fulfilment of lawful wants.

3. Say praye with profound sincerity and a righteous disposition and with the conviction that Allah Whom you beseech is perfectly aware of your condition and is Most Considerate

towardsyou; it is He alone who hears the petitions of His servants and fulfils their prayers. Always offer a pure prayer unmixed with all taint of exhbition, display, deception or polytheism.

The Holy Qurn affirms:

"Call ye then Allah devoting your obedience wolly to Him." *(40: 14)*

And Surah Baqarah bears the command:

"And when My servants question thee concerning Me, then surely I am nigh. I answer the prayer of the supplicant when he crieth unto Me. So let them hear My call and let them trust in Me, in order that they ay be led alright." *(2: 186)*

4. Offer prayer with perfect concentration and devotion of mind and heart and with a positive conviction of Allah's favour. Instead of azing at the enormity of your sins, look towards the unlimited mercy, kindness and the countless bounties and blessings of Allah. The praer of an inattentive man whose thoughts are not concentrated on Allah and who is only mumbling a few words halfheartedly at a whim without anticipating the favour of Allah is vain.

The Tradition relates:

"Offer prayer with the firm conviction of Allah's favour. Allah does not accept a prayer sent forth by an inatentive heart." *(Tirmidhi)*

5. Say prayer in utmost humility with awe and fear of Allah. Your heart should be astir with the awesome majesty, grandeur and power of Allah and fear of Allah should be obvious from your physical posture. Your head should be bent and eyes downcast. Your voice should be muffled, limbs limp, eyes damp with tears and the whole demeanour should present a picture of helpless misery before Allah. The Holy Prophet [S.A.W.] on beholding a man stroking his beard during worship, observed: "Had he the fear of Allah in his heart, his body too would have been ovrcome by it."

In point of fact while praying a man should tremble with the realsation of his destitution and helpless misery and with the fear that if he were repulsed from the threhold of Allah, he would not find refuge anywhere. He should have deep awareness of the fact tha he possesses nothing of his own; everything he has is a bounty from Allah; if Allah withholds, no other power in the world can besto anything on him. Allah is the Master of everything; He alone holds the treasure f everything; man s only a miserable beggar.

The Holy Quran commands:

> *"Call your Lord with humility."*
>
> *The dignity of worship consists in the servant calling upon his Creator in desperate humility and in a lowly manner so that his heart and intellect, eotions and feelings and all parts of his body should be bent in homage to Him and the servant's soul and body should ear evidence to his destitution and plea for help.*

6. Say prayer in a muted, faint voice. Do present your petition before Allah in a desperate manner, but never display your desperation and misery openly. Man should display his humility, lowiness and the plea of misery only before Allah.

There is no doubt that sometimes you may say prayers in a loud voice, but only in privacy, or amid a congregtion so tht the others may say 'Amin'. Generally, however, you should say prayer quetly in muffled tones and take full care that your expression of misery and destitution and your supplication is not just a show intended for other people.

> *"And do thou (O Muhammad) remember thy Lord within thyself humbly and with awe below thy breath at morning and evening. And be thou not of the neglectful." (7: 205)*

The Holy Quran praises the beauty of the worship offered by Hadrat Zakriya [A.S.] in these words:

> *"When he cried unto his Lord a cry in secret." (19: 3)*

7. You should execute some pious deed before saying prayer. For instance, make some acrifice, give alms, feed the hungry one or offer supererogatory worship or observe a fast. In case, Allah forbid, you land in some trouble, offer prayer to Alah reminding Him of all these pious deeds which you have performed with true sincerity of heart for His sake only.

The Holy Quran says:

> *"Pure utterances ascend towards Him only and pious deed propel them to higher altitudes." (35: 10)*

The Holy Prophet [S.A.W.] once related the incident of three men who were entrapped in a cave during a very dark night. They prayed to Allah reminding Him of their truly sincere deeds and Allah rescued them from the calamity. It so happened that during a dark night a group of three men took refuge in a cave. As Allah willed, a rock slided down the hill and falling over the mouth of the cave closed the passage completely. It was a massive rock and was too heavy for them to push aside and clear the passage. On consultation among themselves, they resolved to pray to Allah reminding Him of their truly sincere deeds in aticipation of His Favour to rescue them from this calamiy. In accordance with this resolution, one of them related his pious deed as follows:

> *I used to take goats for grazing in the forest and earned my living by means of this occupation. On returning from the forest I used to offer milk first to my old parents and then to my children. One day, I arrived late. My old parents had gone to sleep. The children were awake and hungy. But I could not bear to feed the children before m parents had taken the milk, nor did I wish to put them to inconvenience by waking them up. So I stood all night at the head f their beds holding the cup of milk in my hand. The children clung to my feet and cried for milk all the night, but I remained unmoved and stood there until night gave way to morning.*

"O Allah! I performed this deed for Your sake only. Remove this rock frm the mouth of the cave in recompense for my deed." And Allah caused the rock to move aside just so much as to let in a view of the sky. The second man spoke thus: I put some labourers to work and paid wages to all of them except one man who went away without receiving payment for his labour. A short while later when the man returned to claim his wage I said to him: "All these cows, goats and servants are yours. Take them where you will." He said: "For Allah's sake, don't cut joke with me." I answered: "This is not a joke. All this is yours. I invested the money which you had left behind in business. By the Grace of Allah, the business thrived. All this which you see is the profit derived from that business. Take it with an easy mind. All this belongs to you." And that man went away taking everything with him. "Oh Allah! I acted in this wy to earn Your Goodwill alone. Oh Allah! Remove this rock in recompense of my deed." By the gracious will of Allah the rockmoved further away from the mouth of the cave.

The third one narrated the following account of his pious deed: I had a cousin sister for whom I conceived an extraordinary liking. She asked for some money which I supplied. But when I sat close to her to satisfy my need, she said: "Fear Allah and refrain from this act." I rose at once and I pronounced that sum as a gift to her. "Oh Allah! You know perfectly well that I did this to win your favour only. Oh Allah!

Open the mouth of the cave as a reward for this pious deed." Allah removed the rock from the passag of the cave and liberated the three men from this calamity.

8. Along with offering prayers for the fulfilment of pious purposes, try to reform and adorn your life in conformity with the Ordinances of Allah. Avoid all sins and forbidden things. Respect and obsrve the Commands of Allah in all matters and lead a pious life. It is the eight of folly and insolence to eat and drink forbidden thing, clothe yourself out of unlawful gains and fatten your body on illicit earnings and then anticipate acceptance of your prayer. If you wish your prayer may be accepted, your words and action both should conform to the tenets of Islam.

The Hly Prophet [S.A.W.] observed:

"Allah is Pure and He accepts only pure goods. Allah has enjoinedupon the pious the same deeds as He has upon the Messengers. Allah affirms

*"O Messengers! Partake of lawful provisions and perform good acts."*Addressing the pious, Allah enjoins:

"O ye who believe! Partake of those lawful and pure things which We have bestowed on you."

The Holy Prophet [S.A.W.] then referred to the case of a man who travels a long distance and arrives at a sacredspot to pay homage; he is covered all over with dust; he raises both hands towars the sky and says: 'My Lord', 'O My Lord', yet because he partakes of unlawful food and drinks and dresses out of forbidden gains and fattens his body on illicit earnings, how can the prayer of such a contumacious and disobedient person be accepted?

(Sahib. Muslim)

9. Offer prayers regularly. The expression of one's humility, destitution and sense of loyalty to Allah is in itself worship. Allah Himself has commanded His serants to offer prayer to Him. Allah has said: "Whenever the servant calls Me I lsten to him."

Do not get tired of offering prayer. Do not be tied down by the doubt whether your prayer wuld change your destiny or not. The obstinacy or flexibility of fate or the acceptance or rejection of prayer depends on the Will of Allah Who is All-Knowing and All-Wise. All the same, it is the duty of the slave to offer prayer to Him like a beggar and destitute person and not to consider himself independent of Him for a single moment.

The Holy Prophet [S.A.W.] observed:

"The humblest person is the one who is humble in prayer." (Tibrani)

In addition to that the Holy Prophet [S.A.W.] affirmed: "Allah considers nothing as nobler and as more honourable than prayer." (Tirmidhi)

The most luminous trait of the believer is that in distress or ease, pain or pleasue, poverty or prosperity, advesity or luxury—under all souls of condition he turns to Allah ony and presents his needs to Him alone and prays to Him regularly for grace.

The Holy Prophet [S.A.W.] observed:

"The person who does not pray to Allah invokes wrath of Allah." (Tirmidhi)

10. Put complete faith in Allah as to the acceptance of your prayer. Never commit the blunder of rnouncing prayer in desperation if quick results of the acceptance of your prayer are not forthcoming. Concentrate on offering prayer instead of feeling anxious about the acceptance of your prayer.

Hadrat 'Umar [R.A.A.] observed:

"I am not concerned about the acceptance of my prayer. I am only anxious to pray. When the favour of offering a prayer has been granted to e, the acceptance will also be granted."

The Holy Prophet [S.A.W.] observed:

"When a Muslim turns towards Allah to ask for some favour, Allah inevitably supplies his want. Either his wish is granted or Allah adds the thing desired to the balance of rward which the Muslim will receive in the eternal world. On the Day of Judgement, Allah shall summon a pious man to His Presence and enquire from him fac to face: "O My slave! commanded you to pray and promised that I shal grant your prayer. Did you then offer prayer?" The man will submit: "Yes, I offered prayer." Allah will then observe: "I granted whatever prayer you offered. Did you not pray to Me on that day for the alleviation of sorrow and pain which had seized you and I had succoured you." The slave will submit: "True, O Creator." Allah then will observe: "I granted that prayer and fulfilled that desire of yours in the mortal world. But on the other day you were struck by another

calamity and you prayed to Me for succour, but you found none and, thereore, continued to labour underpain and sorrow." The slave will submit: "Yes, it is true beyond dubt, My Creator." Thereupon Allah will observe: "In Paradise many bounties have I reserved for you in reward for that prayer,"-andin the same manner Allah shall ascertain other needs and make a similar observation in regard to all of them."

Afterwards, the Holy Prophet [S.A.W.] observed:

"There shall not be a single prayer offered by a pious person concerning whichAllah will not state. "I granted this prayer of yours in the world and I added that desire of yours to the balance of your reward in eternity." The pious person will ponder then: "Would that none of my prayers had been granted n the mortal world! Hence the servant should continue to pray under all conditions." (Hakim)

11. Observe all external etiquettes, purity and cleanliness at the time of prayer. Keep your heart clear of all evil passions, illicit designs and absurd beliefs.

The Holy Quran affirms:

"Truly, they are the favourites of Allah who repent most and those oters who keep themselves pure and clean."

In Surah Muddaththir, Allah enjoins:

"Thy Lord magnify and thy raiment purify."

12.Offer prayer for others also, but begin with yourself. Seek favour for yourself first and then for others too. The Holy Quran reproduces two prayers offered by Hadrat Ibrahim and Hadrat Nuh [A.S.] which bear the aboe moral:

"My Lord! Make me to establish proper worship and sons of my posterity (also) our Lord! and accept the prayer. Our Lord! Forgive me and my parents and believers on the day when the account is cast." (14: 40, 41)

"My Lord! Forgive me and my parents and him who entereth my house believing, and believing men and believing women." (71: 28)

Hadrat Ubay b. Kaab [R.A.A.) reports:

"Whenever the Holy Prophet [S.A.W.] happened to mention some person, he [S.A.W.] used to offer a prayer

for that person and commenced the prayer by asking Alah's favour for himself first." *(Tirmidhi)*

13. If you are acting as leader in the prayer, you shold always offer prayer on behalf of the whole congregation using plural parts of speech. The prayers which have been reproduced in the Holy Quran generally contain plural parts of speech. The leader in fact is the spokesman for the whole congregation. When he utters a prayer using plurals, the congregation should say 'Amin' at the end of each prayer offered by them.
14. Avoid prejudice and selfishness in prayer. Do not fall into the error of considering the vast and common blessing of Allah as limited and thus praying for the grant of His Grace and Bounty to you especially.

Hadrat Abu Hurrayrah [R.A.A.] relates: "A Beduin entered the mosque of the Prophet [S.A.W.] and said his prayer and then said: "O Allah: Grant your favour to me and to Muhammad [S.A.W.] and to none else besides us." On hearing this, the Holy Prophet [S.A.W.] observed:

"You have narrowed the vast limits of Allah's blessings."
(Bukhari)

15. Avoid formal and conscious rhyming in prayer. Utter your prayer in a simple manner with profound sincerity. Abstain from singing or rhyming. However, it does not matter if by chance your tongue does utter a rhymed speech or an alliteration. A few such prayers as have an informal rhyme and perfect balance in stress are reported to have been uttered by the Holy Prophet [S.A.W.]. For instance, Hadrat Zaid b. Arqam has reported a very comprehensive prayer offered by the Holy Prophet [S..W.]:

   "Allah I seek Thy refuge from the heart which is devoid of Thy fear, from the being that lacks contentment, from the knowledge that is unprofitable and from the prayer which is unacceptable." *(Tirmidhi)*

16. Offerpraise and thanksgiving to the Lord before putting your needs and requirements before Him. Afterwards, say two Rakats of supplementary prayer and say (Darood) 'peace and blessings be on the Holy Prophet' at the beginning and end of your prayer.

The Holy Prophet [S.A.W.] has observed:

"At times when a person seeks the favour of Allah or the assistance of man in connection with some need or

requirement, the needy person should perform ablution, say two Rakats of prayer, offer praise and thanksgiving to Allah and say (Darood) 'peace and blessings of Allah be on the Holy Prophet'. (Afterwards, he should put his need before Allah)." (Tirmidhi)

The Holy Prophet [S.A.W.] affirmed the fact that the praer of a man which is accompanied by praise and thanksgiving to Allah and by the invocation of Allah's peace and blessings on the person of the Holy Prophet is granted the honour of fulfilment. Hadrat Fadala [R.A.A.] narrates: "The Holy Prophet [S.A.W.] was seated in the mosque when a man entered, performed the worship and at the end uttered. Allahummaghfirli (Allah grant me pardon). On hearing this, the Holy Prophet [S.A.W.] said to the man: "You were rather quick in offering the prayer. When the worship is over, you should first of al render praise and thanksgiving to the Allah, invoke peace and blessings upon the Prophet and finally say your prayers. As the Holy Prophet [S.A.W.] was speaking to the person,another man came in, offered worship and at theend, rendered praise to Allah and invoked His peace and blessings upon th Holy Prophet. The Holy Prophet, thereupon, observed to him: "Now say your prayer, it shall be granted." (Tirmidhi)

17. Offer prayer to Alah at all times and at every sep, for He is never tired of hearing the prayers of His slaves. However, traditions reveal to us that there are certain special times and circumstances in which prayers are accepted very soon. Hence, do not miss the opportunity of offering prayer at these hours and cirumstances:

(i) In the stillness of the latter part of night when most people are enjoying sweet slumber, the man who gets up and engages in communion with Allah and places his needs before Allah in sincere humility sall be blessed with special favour of Allah.

"Allah holds court on the sky of the world every night. When the latter part of the night begins Allah observes, "Who calls Me? I will accept his prayer. Who begs? I will fulfil his need. Who asks for salvation? I will grant him salvation." (Tirmidhi)

(ii) Offer the maximum number of prayers in the night of *Shab qadr*, for in auspiciousness this niht is better than a thousand months. Say the following prayer especially:

"Allah: Thou art All-Forgiving. Thou likest showing Mercy the best. Hence Forgive me."

(iii) In the field of Arafat when the 'guests of Allah' assemble there on the 6th Dhul-Hajja. *(Tirmidhi)*

(iv) At particular moment on Friday which falls between the commencement of the sermon and end of the worship or from the time when the 'Asr praer is over till the hour of the Mahrib prayer.

(v) At the hour of announcement of the Prayer-Call ad at thetime when the Holy warriors are being lined up for battle in the field.

The Holy Prophet [S.A.W. has observed:

"Two things are never repulsed from the Court of Allah. One, the prayer offered at the hour of the announcement of Prayer-Call. Second, the prayer uttered at the time of lining up for battle in the field." *(Abu Daud)*

(vi) In the interval between the announcement of the Prayer Call and the Takbir.

"The Holy Propht [S.A.W.] observed:

"The prayer offered in the interval between the Adaan (Prayer-Call) and the Iqamah is never rejected." The illustrious companions [R.A.A.] submitted: O, Prophet of Allah, what should we pray during this period. The Holy Prophet observed: Say this prayer.

"Allah! I implore of Thee forgiveness, kindness and protection in this world and in eternity."

(vii) During the auspicious days of Ramadan and specially at the time of breaking fast. (Bazaz)

(viii) After the performance of obligatory prayers whether you offer prayer individually or in a congregation.

(ix) In the state of prostration.

The Holy Prophet [S.A.W.] has observed: *"In the state of prostration, the slave gains the nearest proximity to his Allah. Hence offer the optimum prayer while you are lying in prostration before Allah."*

(x) When you are seized by a serious calamity or the deepest sorrow and pain. (Hakam)

(xi) When a religious assemblage takes place for the purpose of remembrance and worship of Allah. *(Bukhari, Muslim)*

(xi) When a reading of the Holy Quran is completed. (Tibrani)

18. Offer prayers at the folowing places, especially. On the eve of his departure from Mecca to Basra, Hadrat Hasan Basri [R.T.A.] wrote a letter to the residents of Mecca stating the importance of putting up in Mecca and the favours thereof and also clearly mentioned that prayers offered at the following fifteen places in Mecca are especially accepted by Allah:
    (i) Near the Multazim (ii) Below the Mizab (iii) Inside the Kaaba (iv) Near the fount of Zam Zam (v) At Safa and Mawa (vi) Near Safa and Marwa at the place where 'Sai' is performed (vii) At the rar of the 'Place of Ibrahim' (viii) In 'Arafat (ix) In Muzdalfa (x) In Mina (xi) Near the three Jamarat. *(Hisn Hassin)*

19. Make constant efforts to memorise the same words of rayer to Allah as are contained in the Holy Quran and the Traditions of the Holy Prophet [S.A.W.]. It is clear that no better words of prayer and no better manner of offering prayer can be found than that which Allah taught to His Prophet [S.A.W.] and to His pious slaves [R.A.A.]. Besides there is no speech which can possibly surpass the word taught by Allah and adopted by His Messengers in effect, sweetness, comprehensiveness, grace and acceptability! Th repetition of the prayers taught by the Holy Quran and the Traditions and a thoughtful consideration of their meanings trains and educates one's mind as to what wishes and prayers should a pious person entertain. What deeds are worthy of his striving and what goals should he set for himself. There is no doubt that prayer transcends all barriers of language, style. It is, however, a supplementary Blessing of Allah that He has revealed to us what to ask for and in hat manner by prescribing words of prayer. Moreover, Allah taught the pious what attitude to adopt for achieving grace in religion and in secular matters and what wishes and aspirations should a pious an entertain in his heart. There is no religious or secular need as well as there is no aspect of grace, for which a prayer has not been prescried. It is more propitious, therefore, that you should pray to Allah in those words which are contained in the Holy Quran and the Traditions and you should repeat only those prayers which are incorporated in the Quran or those which were uttered at various times by the Holy Prophet [S.A.W.] himself.

However, until such time as you take into memory the words of the prayers contained in the Holy Quran and the Traditions, you ought at least to reproduce their sense in your prayers.

We reproduce in the following pags some comprehensive prayers from the Holy Quran as well as from the Traditions of the Holy Prophet [S.A.W.]. ou should learn these prayers by heart gradually and then repeat only these prayers afterwards.

Special Prayers

Prayer for Mercy and Forgiveness : Our Allah! We have wronged ourselves. If Thou forgive us not and have not mercy on us, surely we are of the lost. (7.23)

No doubt unless Allah absolves man of his sins and showers endless Mercy on him, man wll go to ruin.

Prayer for Grace in both the Worlds : Our Allah! Give unto us in the world that which is good and in the Hereafter that which is good and guard us from the doom of the Fire.(2: 201)

Prayer for Forbearance and Fortitude : Our Allah! Bestow on as endurance, make our foothold sure, and give us help against the disbelieving folk. *(2*: 250)

Prayer for Protection against the Mischief of the Devil : My Allah! I seek refuge in Thee from suggestions of the evil ones and I seek refuge in Thee, my Lord! lest they be present with me.*(23: 97, 98)*

Prayer for Protection Against the Torment of Hell : Our Allah! Avert from us the doom of hell: Lo! the doom thereof is anguish. Lo! it is wretched as abode andstation. (25: 65, 66)

Prayer for the Correction of Heart : Our Allah! Cause not our hearts to stray after Thou halt guided us, and bstow upon us mercy from Thy presence. Lo! Thou, only Thou art the Bestower.(3: 8)

Prayer for the Purification of Heart : Our Alah! Forgive us and our brethren who were before us in the faith, and place not in our hearts any rancour towards those who believe. Our Allah! Thou art full of pity, Merciful. *(59: 1)*

Prayer for Favourable Turn of Events : "Our Allah! Give mercy from Thy presence and shape for us right conduct in our plight."(18: 10)

Prayer for Salvation : Our Allah! e believe therefore forgive us and have mercy on us for Thou art best of all who show mercy.(23: 109)

Prayer for the Grant of Satisfaction and Peace in the Family : Our Allah! Vouchsafe us comfortof our wives and of our offspring, and make us patterns for (all) those who ward off (evil). (25: 74)

In other words, grant us such a pure and noble life that the pios should take us as a model and emulate our example.

Prayer for Parents : Our Allah! Forgive me and my parents and the believers on the day when the account is cast. (14: 41)

Prayer for Protectin from Trials and Tribulations : Our Allah! Condemn us not if we forget or err: Our Allah! Lay not on us such a burden as Thou didst lay n those before us: Our Allah! Impose on us that which we have not the strength to bear: Pardn us, absolve us and have mercy on us. Thou art our Protector and give us victory over the disbelieving folk. (2: 286

Prayer for Getting Rid of the Disbelievers' Domination : In Allah we put trust. Our Allah! Oh, make us not a lure for the wrongdoing folk. And of Thy mercy, save us from the olk that disbelieve. (10: 85)

Prayer for a Propitious End : Creator of the heavens and the earth Thou art my protecting Friend in the world and the Hereafter. Make me to die submissive (unto Thee), and join me to the righteous.(10: 101)

Our Allah! Lo! We have heard a criercalling unto Faith: Believe ye in your Lord! So we believed Our Lord! Therefore forgive us our sins, and remit from us our evil deeds and make us die the eath of the righteous. Our Allah! And give us hat which Thou hast promised to us by Thy messengers. Confound us not upon th Day of Resurrection. Lo! Thou breakest not the trust. (2: 193, 94)

Some Prayers of the Holy Prophet [S.A.W.] : The Muhaddithin (Reporters of Traditions) have worked hard and devoted whole of their lives in collecting and compiling the books of Tradtions, the prayers whichthe Holy Prophet [S.A.W.] used to offer during journeys and in camp. Along with the prayers incorporated in the Holy Quran, you should also utter these prayers of the Holy Prophet [S.A.W.]. These prayers are not only comprehensive, impressive and propitious, but also teach the correct thinking to the believer as well as the desire and ambitions he should cherish. In fact, a man's real nature is reflected in his desires, especially moments when he is satisfied that no other human being is present and that his murmur can only be heard by his Ceator. Each word of the prayers offered by the Holy Prophet [S.A.W.] in the darkness of the night, in privacy, in the midst and outside the company of the people, is characterised by profound sincerity, devotion and eagerness and one feels that the utterer of such prayers is the most exalted person who is perfectly aware of his status as the servant of Allah and he constantly begs from his Allah as a needy person. Moreover, his eagerness and devotion is constantly increasing in depth and intensity as he continues to offer prayers to Allah. The essence of all his prayers is as follows: "Allah! Draw me closer! Spare me from Thy wrath! Bestow upon me Thy favour! Give me success and grace in Eternity."

Prayers to be Offered in the Morning and Evening : Hadrat 'Uthman b. 'Affan [R.A.A.] narrates: "The Holy Prophet [S.A.W.] observed: No harm can come to a man from anything who utters the following prayer morning and evening":

> *In the name of Allah by virtue of Whose name naught in the heaven nor earth doth hurt and He is the Hearer the Knower.* *(Musnad Ahmad)*

Hadrat 'Abdullah b. 'Umar [R.A.A.] reports: "The Holy Prophet [S.A.W.] used to offer the following prayer in the morning and evening regularly without respite":

> *O Allah! Behold, I beg to Thee peace in ths world and the Hereafter. O Allah! Bhold, I beg of Thee forgiveness and safety in my faith, in my world, in mine household and in my wealth. O Allah! cover my defects and give me pece from my apprehension. O Allah! protect me from my ront and from my rear, from my right and from my left also from above me; and I seek refuge in Thee lest I be surprised from beneath me!* *(Tirmidhi)*

Prayer Against Lethargy and Cowardice : Hadrat Anas b. Malik [R.A.A.] states:

> *"I used to remain in attendance on the Holy Prophet [S.A.W.] and I used to hear him offer this prayer very often:*
>
> *"O Allah! Behol, I seek refuge in Thee from anxiety and grief, from inability and sloth, from faint heartedness and niggardliness, from the burden of indebtedness and the domination of men.* *(Bukhari, Muslim)*

Prayer for the Attainment of Piety and Purity : O Allah! Behold! I beg of Thee, guidance,piety, purity and contentment. This is the most comprehensive prayer. n these four words the Holy Prophet [S.A.W.] has asked for everything that a believer needs.

Prayer for Protection Aainst Degradation in this World and the Hereafter : "Allah! End al our activities in grace and protect us from the torment of degradation in this world and in the Hereafter." (Tibrani)

Prayer to be Offered after Worship : Hadrat Muadh [R.A.A.] states that one day the Holy Prophet [S.A.W.] took my hand and observed: "O Muadh! I love thee', and then proceeded to affirm: "O Muadh! I advise you that you should never miss uttering thefollowing words after each prayer:

"O Allah! help me in remembering Thee, in expressing gratitude to Thee and in worshipping Thee in the best manner."

Will of the Holy Prophet [S.A.W.] : Hadrat Shaddad b. Aus [R.A.A.] states: "The Holy Prophet [S.A.W.] adised me: Shaddad! when you see the worldly people busy in amassing gold and silver, you should gather the blissful treasure by uttering the following words off and on":

"O Allah! Behold, I beg of Thee steadfastness in keeping (Thy) command and firmness of resolution in (pursuing)the right course. I beg of Thee (the feeling of) thankfulness for Thy grace and (ability for) adoring Thee best. I beg of Thee a sound heart and a truthful tongue. I beg of Thee the good of that which Thee knowest, and I seek refuge in Thee from the evil which Thee knowest. I seek Thy forgiveness for all of my wrongs thou knowest. No doubt Thou knowest all that is unknown to us.

(Musnad Ahmad)

Prayer for Forgiveness nd the Favour of Allah : Hadrat Abu Hurrayrah [R.A.A.] states that the Holy Prophet [S.A.W.] while bequeathing a will to Hadrat Salman Farsi [R.A.A.], had observed: "I wish to bequeath a few words to you. Beseech the Most Kind in these words. Rush towards the Most Kind and offer prayer to Him in these words day and night:

"O Allah! Behold! I beg of Thee vigour and health in my faith an effect of faith in my dealings and behaviour and success leading to peace and mercy from Thee; and also security, forgiveness and Thy pleasure."

(Tibrani, Hakam)

Prayer for Purification from Sins : Hadrat Umm Salama [R.A.A.] narrates: "The Holy Prophet [S.A.W.] used to offer the following prayer:

"O Allah! clean my heart from sins, just as you clean white cloth of dirt. O Allah! cause as great a distance between me and my faults, as there is between East and West. *(Muljam Kabir)*

Prayer for the Attainment of Respect Among the People : O Alah! make me patient and thankful to Thee, and make me small in my own eyes, but great in other people's eyes.

A Comprehensive Prayer : Hadrt 'Aishah [R.A.A.] states: "It so happened once that when the Holy Prophet [S.A.W.] came to see me I was engaged in offering worship. The Holy Prophet [S.A.W.] needed m immediately but I was delayed, whereupon the Holy Prophet [S.A.W.] observed: 'Aishah, you should utter brief and comprehensive prayers. When I came to the Holy Prophet [S.A.W.] I submitted: "O Messenger of Allah [S.A.W.]! Teach me a brief and comprehensive prayer." The Holy Prophet [S.A.W.] observed: "You should utter the following prayer:

> *O Allah! I ask of The all the good which is in the present or in the future, and I ask of Theeparadise, and the works and deeds, which would take me nearer to the same, and I seek refuge in Thee from Fire and the works and deeds which would take me nearer to th same. And I ask of Thee that which was sought by Muhammad, and I seek refuge in Thee from that regarding which Muhammad sought Thy Protection, and that the end of all Thy decrees above me should be good."* *(Hakam)*

Prayer for Holding firm to Islam **:** O Allah! maintain my faith in Islam, while I am standing or while I am sitting or while I am lying and let not the enemy, the envious pass sarcastic remarks about me.

Prayer of a new Convert to Islam **:** Hadrat Abu Malik Ashja [R.A.A.] reports: "My father narrated that wheever a person embraced the religion of Islam, the Holy Prophet [S.A.W.] used to teach him Salat and also the following prayer:

> *"O Allah! orgive me, have mercy on me, guide me, grant me peace and give me sustenance."*

Prayer for the Avoidance of Dissensions and Immorality **:** O Allah! I seek refuge in Thee from evil morals, deeds and desires. O Allah! Behold, I seek refuge in Thee from schism, hypocrisy and evil morals.

Invocation of Peace and Blessings on the Holy Prophet [S.A.W.] : Invoke peace and blessings of Allah upon your venerable benefactor Hadrat Muhammad [S.A.W.]. Truly, we can make no recompense for his countless favours and limitlss love and affection. What we can do, however, is to invoke the peace and blessings of Allah on him with the deepest sense of reverence, love, devotion and loyalty to his person. We should pray to Allah, "Creator! Your Messenger [S.A.W.] had to suffer terrible torments in his task of communicating your message to us. He [S.A.W.] took great pains to guide us on the path of righteousness. Creator We can make no return for this favour. We implore You, O Creator! to shower Your boundless benefactions upon the Prophet [S.A.W.], to exalt him i Your favour; to protect his religion from the onslaught of falsehoo; to extend his religion and to bestow upon him a higher rank than all other favourite companions of Yours in the eternal world." The Holy Quran enjoins upon the Muslims:

> *"o! Allah and his angels, shower blessings on the Prophet. O ye who believe! Ask blessings on him and salute him with a worthy salutation."* *(33: 56)*

The Holy Prophet [S.A.W.] observed to Hadrat Ubay bin Kaab [R.A.A.]:

> *"Uby! If you devote all your time to invoking peace and blessings of Allah upon the Prophet, Allah shall take i upon Himself to provide for your sustenance in this world and in eternity."* *(Musnad Ahmad)*

Hadrat Anas b. Malik [R.A.A.] narrates that the Holy Prophet [S.A.W.] observed:

"A person who invokes peace and blessings of Allah on me is recompensed by Allah in the following manner:

> *"Allah showers blessings on him ten times. Allah adds ten virtues and erases ten vices from his record of deeds. And Allah elevates his rank by ten grades."* *(Nasai)*

In addition to this, the Holy Prophet [S.A.W.] affirmed:

> *"The angels continue to invoke the blessings of Allah upon a man as long as he devotes imself to invoking peace and blessing of Allah upon me."*
> *(Ahmad and Ibn Majah)*

The Holy Prophet [S.A.W.] observed:

> *"The man who hears my name mentioned yet fails to invoke the peace and blessings of Allah on me is a miser."*
> *(Tirmidhi)*

The Holy Prophet [S.A.W.] declared the perso most deserving of the hnour of his companionship and attendance in the life Hereafter who invokes the peace and blessings of Allah on him the most.

The Holy Prophet [S.A.W.] observed:

> *"The person who invokes peace and blessings of Allah on me the most, willbe the best deserving my compaionship and attendance on the Da of Judgement."*
> *(Tirmidhi)*

There is a sligt variation in the wordings of the texts of the invocation of peace and blssings of Allah which the Holy Prophet [S.A.W.] taught to the illustrious companions [R.A.A.] on various occasions. You may use any of these texts. The ext which is generally recited in worship and which has been declared as the mostpropitious one by Hadrat 'Abdullah b. 'Abbas [R.A.A.] is as follows:

> *"O Allah! Shower Thy mercy upon Muhammad and the followers of Muhammad, as thou didst shoer Thy mercy upon Ibrahim and the followers of Ibrahim! Behold Thou art Praiseworthy, Glorious! O Allah! shower Thy blessing upon Muhammad and the followers of Muhammad, as Thou didst shower Thy blessings upo Ibrahim and the followers of Ibrahim. Behold, Thou art Praiseworthy, Glorious."* *(Sihah Sitta, Musnad Ahma)*

Hadrat 'Abdullah b. Masud [R.A.A.] observed to the people: "You should invoke peace and blessings of Allah on the Holy Prophet in a proper manner. Who knows this invocation may be presented before the Holy Prophet [.A.W.]?" The people requested him to teach the proper invocation to them. Thereupon he observed: "You should recite the invocation thus:"

> *"Allah! Shower Your favour, blessing and benefactions upon the lord of Prophets, leader of the pious and the seal of Prophets, Muhammad who is Your servant, Yor Messenger of Blessings. Allah, elevate him to an exalted position which may be the envy of his predecessors. Allah! Show Your blessings to Muhammad and the progeny of Muhammad as yo blessed Ibrahim and the progeny of Ibrahim. Truly, You possess the purest attributes and are Great. Allah! Show Your favour to Muhammad and the progeny of Muhammad as You showered favour on Ibrahim and the progeny of Ibrahim. Truly, you possess the purest attributes and are Great."* *(Ibn Majah)*

Hadrat Abu Masud Ansari [.A.A.] narrates: "Once Bashir bin Saad [R.A.A.] submitted to the Holy Prophet [S.A.W.]: In what manner should we invoke peace and blessings of Allah on you? The Holy Prophet [S.A.W.] remained silent for a while and then observed: Say these words:

> *O Allh! shower Thy mercy upon Muhammad and the followers of Muhammad as Thou didst shower Thy mercy upon the followers of Ibrahim! Behold! Thou art Praiseworthy, Glorious. O Allah! shower Thy blessings upon Muhammad and the followers of Muhammad, as Thou didst shower Thy blessings upon Ibrahim in the worlds. Behold Thou art Praiseworthy, Glorious.*

Supplication of Sacrifice : Lay down the animal parallel wit the direction of the Qibla and utter the following prayer first:

Behold I have turne my face earnestly towards Him Who originated the heavens and the earth and I am not of polytheists. Behold, my salat, my offering, my living and my dying are all for Allah,Lord of the worlds. No partners hath He, concerning this I have been bidden and I am of the Muslims O Allah! (I offer this) to you and You gave it to me.

After reciting this prayer, Say *'Bismillahi Allahu Akbar'*. (In the name of Allah Who is Great) and cut the throat of the animal with a sharp-edged knife. Having performed the slaughter read this prayer:

"Allh' Accept this sacrifice offered by me as Thou accepted the sacrifice offered by Thy friend Ibrahim and tht offered by Thy loved one Muhammad. May peace and blessings descend upon both."

Although it is permissible to let someone else perform the slaughter of your sacrificial anial, yet it is better if you perform this act with your own hands. While you perform the slaughter, try to think and feel in the same way as you express through the words you utter at the time of sacrificing the animal i.e., all that we have got belongs to Allah and it is all to be spent in His way only. The act of sacrificing the animal in His name is in submission to His will and if ever required we shall readily sacrifice even our own life in the way of Allah and shall be grateful o Him that He conferred upon us the honour of martyrdom by affording us an opportunity to shed our blood in Hs name.

Aqiqa Prayer : 'Aqiqa' refers to the goat or ram which is sacrificed on behalf of a newborn child on the seventh day aftr his birth.

The Holy Prophet [S.A.W.] observed;

"On the seventh day a name should be prescribed for the child. Its hair and all filth should be removed and sacrifice should be performed on his behalf."

Before sacrificing the animal, first make it lie down parallel with the direction of the Qibla and recite the prayer which is uttered at the slaughter of a sacrificial animal i.e. from his wards say and cut the throat of the animal with a sharp-edged knife and then recite the following prayers:

"O Allah! This is the 'Aqiqah of .... Accept it as Thou accepted the 'Aqiqah offered by Thy loved one Muhammad [S.A.W.] and by Thy friend Ibrahim [A.S.]. The bloodof this sacrifice is ransom for the blood of the

child; its flesh is the ran some for the flesh of the child, its hair are a ransom for the child's hair and its bones are ransom for the child's bones. Alah! Accept it."

The people who possess means must offer sacrifice on behalf of their children. 'Aqiqah is a desirable sacrifice. Two lambs or goats on behalf of the male child and a single goat or lamb on behalf of the female. It is permissible also to sacrifice a single goat on behalf of a boy. However for those who lack means, it is certainly improper to perform the sacrifice by begging loans.

Non-cooked 'Aqiqah meat may be distributed. It is preferable, however, to send cooked meat to the beggars, the poor and your neighbours. On the eve of the *'Aqiqah* of Hadrat Hasan [R A.A.] the Holy Prophet [S.A.W.] instructed: "Send one chopped leg of the animal to the midwife and eat the rest yourself and feed others."(Abu Daud)

Taravih Prayer: The word 'Taravih' isthe plural form of 'Tarviha'. 'Tarviha' denotes the period of rest and relaxation at the end of every four Rakats of prayer. It is in this context that this supplementary prayer of the month of Ramadan is called 'Taravih'. Tarviha, i. e. to pause and relax at the end of every four Rakats of prayer, is a Sunnah.

The following prayer should be recited during *'Tarviha':"Pure is the Ruler and the Sovereign. Pure is the Exalted and the Supreme, the Awesome and the Powerful and the Great Wielder of Authority. Pure is the Immortal Sovereign Who neither sleeps, nor will ever die. Purest and free from all blemishes is our Sustainer Who is the Provider of angels and of Jibbrail.*

Allah! Grant us asylum from the Fire of Hell. O Protector, O Protector, O Protector."

Offer the 'Taravih' prayer in congregation and if possible listen to the recitation of the full text of the Holy Quran during *'Namaz'*. Offer 'Taravih' behind a 'Hafiz' (the one who has memorised the full text of the Holy Quran) who recites the Quran with full reverence, devotion and eagerness in moderate pace and with proper pauses and correct accents so that the listeners do not get tired and the Quran may be recited so clearly as to make every word of it audible and distinct. It is a great injustice with the Holy Quran to read it rapidly without understanding as if you are trying to get rid of a burden. The Book of Allah deserves to be read with a will, devotion and concentration pondering over its meaning and implications and trying to grasp its real sense and spirit.

Similarly the 'Taravih' prayer must be offered with ease and concentration showing no haste and hurry. To perform Ruku and Sajda (Prostration) in rapid succession without knowing what is being uttered amounts to sheer disregard of the objectives of prayer and missing the reish of real taste and enjoyment of worship.

Qunut-i-Nazila : Whenever, Allah forbid, the Muslims are faced with a critical situation and the menace and terror of the enemy has overcome them, they should recite Qunut-i-Nazila during prayers, especially in the course of the dawn prayer (Fajr). In the second Rakat of the morning prayers, after performing the Ruku' recite the following prayer in the standing posture before performing the prostration. Traditions reveal that this prayer was recited during worship by the Holy Prophet [S.A.W.] and his illustrious Companions [R.A.A.] at critical times, they offered this prayer especially during morning worship:

> *O Allah! guide us amongst those whom Thou hast gided aright, and preserve us among those whom thou hast preserved. Include us amongst those whom Thou hast taken under Thy protection. Bless us in that which Thou hast bestowed upon us and protect us from the evil of that which Thou hast ordained, for it is Thou Who ordainest and none can ordain against Thee indeed! Never is he abased whom Thou takest as friend and none is respected whom Thou takest as a foe. Blessed art Thou Our Allah and exalted. We ask repentance from Thee and turn to Thee; O llah! send torment upon the unbelievers, who prevent us from following Thy way and refute Thy messengers, and fight against Thy friends. Allah! grant forgiveness to us and to the Faithful males and females and Muslim men and women and bring reconciliation among them and foster affection (for one another) in their hearts and bless them with conviction and insight and make them firm and unwavering followers of the Holy Prophet [S.A.W.] and enable them to fulfil the pledge You have taken from them; help them against Thy enemies and against their enemies. O Real Deity! hear our prayers an deal us with these people!"*

Prayer for the Fulfilment of a Need : Whenever any need, big or small, arises, you should stand before Allah and offer two Rakahs of supererogatory prayer, (Salat al Hajat).

Afterwards, offer thanksgiving and praise to Allah and invoke peace and blessings upon the Holy Prophet [S.A.W.]. Then utter the following prayer. There is every hope that Allah will not reject your prayer. The Holy Prophet [S.A.W.] observed:

> *"When someone seeks fulfilment f a need from Allah or man, he should first carefully perform abluion, say two Rakats of supererogatory prayer and then offer thanksgiving and praise to the Lord; afterwards, he should invoke peace and blssings of Allah on the Holy Prophet; [S.A.W.] and finally utter this prayer to Allah: "There is no deity save Allah the Clement the Bountiful. Glory be to Allah, Lord of the Magnificent Throne! Praise be to Allah, Lord of the Worlds! I beg of Thee the means of (obtaining) Thy mercy and securing Thy pardon; participation in every righteousness and protection from every sin. Leave no sin of mine unforgiven no anxiety unrelieved and let no need of mine unfulfilled wherewith Thou art pleased. O Thou the Most Merciful of Those who show mercy! (Tirmidhi, Ibn Majah)*

Prayer for Memorsing the Quran : To learn the Holy Quran by heart and to memorise its text for ever you should offer the prayer whic was taught to Hadrat 'Ali [R.A.A.] by the Holy Prophet [S.A.W.].

Hadrat 'Abdullah b. 'Abbas [R.A.A.] reports: "Once we were stting in the company of the Holy Prophet [S.A.W.] when 'Ali [R.A.A.] arrived and complained about his memory: O Messeger of Allah [S.A.W.]! My mind does not retain the verses of the Quran. I cannot remember what I have learnt previously." The Holy Prophet [S.A.W.] observed:

> *"O Abul Hassan! Let me teach you a prayer wich will be of benefit to you and to those whom you will teach this payer and having learnt this praer whatever you commit to memory shall be retined and you shall always remember it." Hadrat 'Ali R.A.A.] submitted: "O Messenger of Allah [S.A.W.]! Do teach me this prayer" Whereupon the Holy Prophet [S.A.W.] observed concerning this prayer: "Say this prayer on Friday night and offer it on three, five or seven Thursday nights in succession. By the Will of Allah, this prayer will prove efficacious, I swear by His Name Who has entrusted me with the Religion of Truth, this prayer by the believers never goes unanswered."*

Continuing his narration, Hadrat 'Abdullah b. 'Abbas [R.A.A.] says: "Five or seven Thursday nights had passed when Hadrat 'Ali [R.A.A.] came to the company of the Holy Prophet [S.A.W.] and submitted: "O

Messenger of Allah [S.A.W.] Before this whenever I memorised four verses, my memory failed me when I tried to I reroduce them. Now, however, the position is that I memorise forty verses and when I wish to reproduce them, it appears as if the Book of Allah is lying open before me. Similarly, I used to hear a tradition and later failed to reproduce it, but now I hear several traditions and retain them so well that I hardly miss a single word while reproducing those traditions." On hearing this, the Holy Prophet Muhammad [S.A.W.] observed:"I swear by the Lord of Kaaba that Abul Hassan is a true believer."

Giving detailed instructions about this prayer, the Holy Prophet [S.A.W.] observed: "Say this prayer on Friday night. When the sons of my brother Yaqub requesed him to pray for their redemption, Ya'qub replied: "Yes, I shall offer a prayer for your redemption shortly." Ya'qub meant that he would pray for their redemption on the next Friday night. So 'Ali! Rise at the hour of 'Tahajjud' on Friday night, for this is the most propitious time for the fulfilment of prayer; one's soul is eager at this time and the heart is fully devoted to Allah. If perchance you are unable to rise in the later part of the night, get up at midnight.

If you can't wake up at midnight, then offer four Rakahs of supererogatory prayer in the first part of the night in the following order: In th first Rakat, recite Surah Fatiha and after this Surah Yaseen; in the second Rakat, recite Surah Fatiha and Surah Ad-Dukhan, in the third Rakat, read Surah Fatiha with Surah Alif Lam Mim Sajdah; and in the fourth Rakat, recite Surah Mulk, after Surah Fatiha. Afterwards, having recited 'Attahiyyat and offered Salam on both sides, offer thanks to Allah and praise Him. Invoke Allah's peace and blessings upon the Holy Prophet and all other Messengers in a proper manner. Implore Him to grant redemption to all the believing men and believing women and offer prayer for the salvation of those brethren who preceded you in faith. And finally say this prayer:

> *"O Allah! Be thou gracious unto me by enabling me to eschew sins altogether as long as Thou sufferest me to live; and have mercy upon me lest I concern myself with ought which is of no consequence to me. And vouchsafe me the aesthetic sight whic will cause Thee to be well pleased with me."*

"O Allah! Originator of the heavens and the earth Lord of Majesty and Glory and of Might is comprehensible! I beseech Thee O Allah' O Beneficent Allah in the name of Thy Majesty and of the Light of Thy countenance to cause mine beau to retain Thy explaint as Thou hast taught to me. And grant that I may recite it in such manner as will cause Thee to be well pleased with me. O Allah, Originator of the heavens and the earth, Lord of Majesty and Bounty and of Might Who is unchallengeable. I beseech Thee O Allah, O Beneficent Allah! i the name of Thy Majesty and of the Light of Thy countenance, to illuminate my sight with Thy scripture, make my tongue fluent with its words to comfort mine heart therewith, to make me fully receptive to it and to wash my body clean with its blessings. For indeed, none aideth me in (attaining) the truth besidesThee and now giveth it unto me besides 'Thee. There is no strength nor power save in Allah, the Exalted, the Magnificent."

Prayer for Gaining Understanding of the Quran : The favourite worship of the pious is to recite the Holy Quran and to meditate and reflect upon its meaning. Love of Qurn is proof of attachment to Allah as it is also a means to establish communion with Allah. The believer obtains spiritual bliss by contemplaing and meditating on the meanings of the Quran and it is through this process only that he secures access to the founts of wisdom contained in the Quran.

The Holy Quran is undoubtedly an easily comprehensible Book. As regards obtainng guidance from it and carrying out its injunction, the teachings of the Holy Quran are very simple, clear and free of all ambigity or complexity ofmeaning. However, to grasp its inner meanings and significance and to derive wisdom from it, it is imperative that you should study the Quran after having fulfilled all the conditions and obligations for gaining comprehension of it; reflect upon its contents with sincere application and never adopt a careless and listless attitude towards the Book, but study it constantly for the rest of your life.

It is uite natural that at certain points during study, you will come across a text upon which you will deliberate long and hard without arriving at any one interpretation which your mind will accept. You will then feel at a loss. But if youare a devoted student of the Quran, don't ever feel dejeted or lose heart, nor should you entertain any impudent notion of levelling criticism upon the Holy Book. And feeling hopeless, don't abandon the practice of deliberating and meditating upon the meanings of the Quran.

On the contrary, you should turn towards Allah with full concentration and reposing complete trust in Him you should seek His aid in the unravelling of this problem. Do not make an impudent bid to make a whimsical exposition of the Quran or to give it an interpretation which conforms to your ideas. Like a true seeker of Truth, stick to the meaning which the text of the Quran makes plain and pray to Allah in extreme humility and with a sense of helplessness: 'O Allah! Eliminate my confusion; make the true meaning manifest to me and let my heart be content with that interpretation and meaning which is really true'. For this purpose, recite the Holy Quran rather loudly but distinctly with pauses in the course of supererogatory prayers at night. Offer the prayer reproduced below. It is hoped from Allah that the prayer will prove efficacious.

The Holy Prophet [S.A.W.] observed: "Any person who offers this prayer while in a state of sorrow and distress, Allah shall alleviate his suffering and bestow upon him felicity and rejoicings."

"Allah! I am Thy slave. I am the son of Thy bondman and the son of Thy bondmaid. My brow is in Thy grip. I am under Thy command. Thy jugement in regard to me is just and fair. In the Name of all Attributes applicable to Thee and all Attributes which Thou hast reserved for Thyself, or those which Thou bast revealed in Thy Book, or have transmitted to one of Thy creatures or have kept them hidden in the treasury of the unseen with Thee in the Name of all these Attributes I implore Thee to makethe Holy Quran the joy of my heart, the light of my bosom, a paacea for my distress and a cure of my sorrows and perplexity."

The narrator of this Tradition Hadrat 'Abdullah ibn Masud [R.A.A.] states that the people submitted to the Holy Prophet [S.A.W.]: "Shall we learn this prayer?" Whereupon the Holy Prophet [S.A.W.] observed: "Any one who hears this prayer, must learn it and memorise it."

Weekl Sermon : The Friday sermon is an extremely effective and disciplined means of arousing Islamic sentiments, keeping the Faith alive and carrying out the duty f remembering Allah constantly and in an orderly manner.

It is a unique religiousinstitution designed to remind the Muslims of their obligations each week in a perfectly natural way and to inculcate in them a sense of the requirements of religion and an impassioned spirit to serve Islam. But you can make an effective use of this institution only when you address the congregation in their vernacular.

As regards the second sermon, it must be delivered in Arabic; however, the first sermon ought to be delivered in a speech which the audience can understand. It is proper for you to prepare a brief but comprehensive address on the requirements of religion in the context of current affairs and try to develop the mind of the people and rouse them to live each week regularly and in a disciplined manner. If for some reason it is not possible for you to prepare an address yourself, you should at least read the Arabic text and deliver its meaningful translation in the vernacular of your audience.

Among the Arabic texts, your best choice is a sermon delivered by the Holy Prophet [S.A.W.] or the illustrious companions [R.A.A.]. Below are reproduced qotations from the authentic speech of the Holy Prophet [S.A.W.]. One of these is the historic sermon which he [S.A.W.] delivered on the first Friday after his migration to Medina. The second address contains an eloquent call to the Muslims to acquire a deep sense of the Holy Quran and to deliberate and ponder over its meanings constantly for it is impossible to hold on to religion without a firm attachment to the Holy Quran.

The First Sermon of the Holy Prophet [S.A.W.] in Medina:

> *"Thanksgiving and Praise be to Allah. I pay Him gratitude. I invoke His aid. I beseech His Forgiveness and seek Guidance from Him; and I put my faith in Him; and I disbelieve Him not and I consider him as my enemy who disbelieve Him. And I bear witness that there is no deity except Allah; He is Alone and has no partner; and I bear testimony that Muhammad [S.A.W.] is the servant of Allah and His Apostle. Allah sent him with guidance, light and exhortation and instituted him as His Messenger at a time when the office of Prophethood had long remained dormant; the light of true knowledge had faded; evil was dominant; society was in a state of upheaval; doom was hanging overhead; and death was hovering over the head of each man. Hence he who believed in the Messenger and obeyed Allah and His Messenger was righteous. And he who defied the both went astray, transgressed limits and fell into shortsightedness and having lost the path of righteousness advanced far into wrong. I instruct you to fear Allah.*
>
> *The best counsel that a Muslim can offer to another Muslim is that a Muslim should persuade the other to make provision for the life Hereafter and urge him t fear Allah. Fear Allah as hath He ordained you to fear Him. Hence no exhortation is better than this, nor can there be a better reminder. The fact is that awe and fear of Allah is the real aid to secure a propitious destiny in the eternal world forthe man who passes his life in constant fear of Mighty and the Exalted. Allah affirms: "My word suffrs*

no change and I neve do the least injustice to any of My people." Hence fear Allah in all the public and private affairs relating to this world or the life Hereafter. Verily Allah redeems the sins of a person who fears His wrath and He enhances the reward of such a person to the maximum degree. And he who constantly fears Him achieves the highest success; and behold, the fear of Allah saves an from His punishment, protects him from His wrath and behold! the fear of Allah makes your faces radiant and lively; it pleases Allah and elevates the man before Allah Almighty.

So, gather virtues of your share and ever fail, or lack in submission to His Commands, especially when He has taught you what is right and what is wrong through His Book and has guided you to the right path. Tis is to diferentiate the truthful from those who are liars. Behave well with the people, as Allah has treated you with kindness. Consider His enemies as your own, ad strive hard in the way of Allah. He has chosen you and has designated you as 'Muslim' so that one who is to perish should meet his doom with manifet reason and logic and one who is to live, should live with manifest reason and all power and authority rests n Allah and Allah one.

So, ever remember and mention Allah and mind your deeds and actions keeing in view the day to come; for the man who sets the matters between him and the Almighty, Allah suffices him in all the matters between Him and the mankind because Allah decides the fate of the mankind an the mankind wields no authority over Him. Allah is the Master of every thing that men pssess; men exercise no power on anything that men possss; men exercise no power on anythng divine; He is Paramount and there rests no power but with Allah."(Al- Tibri, Vol. 12, p. 255)

Advice to Develop Interest in the Quran : "Verily, thanksgiving and praise are due to Allah alone. I offer Him gratitude and praise and beg His aid; and we seek asylum with Him against our misdeeds and wrongs committed byus.

Whomsoever He guideth (and he guideth only those who really look for His guidance) no one can led him astray. Whomsoever He deflects from the right path (and He deflects only those who yearn not the guidance) no one can guide him aright."

I bear witness that there is no deity save Allah. He is Alone. He has no partner.

Verily, he best wod is the Book of Allah. Indeed, successfl is he who adorns his heart with the word of Allah and whom Allah has favoured with Islam and turned him away from paganism and whopreferred the word of Allah over all the human thinking and theories. Verly the word of Allah is the truth, most impressive and most effective. Love him wholoves the word of Allah. Develop real love and attachment with Allah with your heart and soul. Let not the recitation of the word of Allah and remembering Him bore you and let not your hearts beindifferent and adamant to the word of Allah. Worship Allah alone; and attribute none as His partner or associate, fear Hm ever to the extent He should be feared. Confirm your pious deeds by your words also i.e. say what is proper and becoming of you; and love each other for the cause of Allah and in total submission to Him. May Peace and Mercy of Allah be upon you!"

(Ijaz-ul Quran)

The Second Sermon : "The praise is due to Allah, the abundant praise, and benediction and peace be upon His Messenger whom Allah has sent as a witness, warner and an inviter towards Allah with His mandate and as a radiant lightand may peace and abundant peace be on his progeny, followers and compnions.

Thereaftr, O mankind, I exhort you to fear Allah, for verily fear of Allah is supermost virtue and icumbent upon you is the obedience. And verily he, who obeys Allah nd His Messenger, achieves great success, Allah, the Exalted, has declared in His Dignfied Book (the Quran): Verily, Allah and Hisangels invoke Sense of Devotion benediction on the Apostle. So, O ye wo believe, invoke blessings on him and seek abundant peace for him.

Allah! Bestow on our Master and ur Guide Muhammd and on his progeny, followers and his companions who obeyed him in adversity. Allah! Shower Thy perfect pleasure on those who excelled (to affirm faith) amongst the emigrants and the helpers, particularly on the unanimously admitted he most excellent of mankind, next to the Prophets the Amir o the believers, our master, Abu Bakr the most truthful [R.A.A.] and on the Amir f the believers, our master Umar Al Farooq [R.A.A.] and on the Amir of the believrs, our master, Uthman b. Affan [R.A.A.] and on the Amir of te believers, our master, Ali [K.A.W.] and on his two noble sons, the masters of the youth of the inmates of Paradise Hasan and Hussain [R.A.A.] and on their mother, theleader of the ladies of th paradise, Fatima-Zohra [R.A.A.] and on all companions of the Holy Prophet and their successrs [R.A.A.]. Allah! Grant success to those who uhold the way of life taught by the Deen of Muhammad [S.A.W.] and make us amogst them; and humiliate those who humiliate the teachings of Muhammad [S.A.W.] and make us not amongst them. O servants of Allah! May Allah show mercy n you. Verily, Allah enjoins justice and kindness, and giving to kinsfolk, and forbids indecency, abomination and transgression.He exhorts you so that you always remember. Remember Allah, He will remember you (in adversity) Pray unto Him, He will respond to you. And remember Allah the most High, most Excellent, most Dignified most Superior, most Grand and the Greatest."

Celebration on Child's Birth

It is propitious to read a sermon at a wedding ceremony in order to explain the significance of 'Nikah' (marriage contact) in Divine law, and to bring home to the parties the requirements and heavy responsibilities imposed by this contact.

With a view to derive the maximum benefit from the sermon, it is advisable for the preacher to translate the sermon and offer a brief exegesis of the text in the vernacular so that the assembly may fully appreciate the sermon. Tothis end, we reproduce below the text of the Nuptial Sermon along with its translation:

> *"Thanksgiving and praise are due to Allah alone, we seek aid from Him alone; and we beseech forgiveness of our sins from Him only; and we consign orselves to he protection of Allah against te evils of our souls and against all offences: Truly, whomsoever Allah guides on the straight path (and He puts him only on the straight path who sincerely desires towalk along that way), no one can lead him astray. And whomsoever Allah deflects (and He deflecs only him who yearn to be deflected), no one can put him on the straight path. And I bear witness that there is no deity except Allah and I testify that Muhammad [S.A.W.] is the bondman of Allah and His Messenger."*

O Believer! Fear Allah, as He should be duly feared; and die not save you be Muslims.

O mankind! Fear the wrath of your Allah Who created you from a single soul and from it created his spouse; and from then twain bath spread (all over the world) a multitude of men and women. Fear Allah, in Whom you claim your lights from one another and (be careful in observing your duty to) the wombs (that bore you). So! Allah is Watchful over you.

> *O Believer! Fear Allah constantly and utter what is fair and ound. Allah, then, will rectify your deeds and cover up your sins with forgiveness; and whosoever obeys Allah and His Messenger, he indeed hall secure a glorious success.* *(Mishkat)*

The Holy Prophet [S.A.W.] says:

> *"By Alah! I fear Allah more than all of you; I save myself from the wrath of Allah more than do all of you; but I observe fast and sometimes I do not keep fast. I say praers at night and I sleep also; and I also take women in marriage. Hence whosoever turns away from my way, he bears no relation with me."* *(Bukhari)*

Guideline fo Decisions : Do have 'Istikhara' on the eve of such importantevents of life as journey, Nikah (marriage ontract), employment and in commercial matters. 'Istikhara' means 'to beseech goodness and welfare'. Whn your mind is in doubt as to which aspect of an important and lawful problem is propitious for you, you must perform an 'Istikhara' and, then, adopt the course uggested by your heart, taking it was the will of Allah.

Whenever you are confronted with an issue of extraordinary importance and find it difficult to reach the correct dcision and adopt the right course, perform two Rakas of supererogatory prayer at any hour outside the unpropitious and forbidden timings. Afterwards,offer the 'Istikhara' prayer . Hadrat Sad b. Abi Waqqas [R.A.A.] reports that the Holy Prophet [S.A.W.] observed:

> *"t is propitiou for the progeny of Adam to beseech goodness and welfare frm Allah; and it is also propitious for the progeny of Adam to submit to the Will of Allah; and it is most unfortunate for the progeny of Adam if they do not beseech goodness and welfare from Allah and are not happy in the Will of Allah."*
>
> *(Musnad Ahmad)*

The Holy Prophet [S.A.W.] also observed:

> *"One who observes 'Istikhara' is never disappointed; and the one who takes counsel is never put to shame; and the one who observes economy does not have to depend on others."* *(Tibrani)*

Hadrat Jabir [R.A.A.] states: "As the Holy Prophet [S.A.W.] taught us the Quran, so also he [S.A.W.] instructed us to observe 'Istikhara' in every matter. The Holy Prophet [S.A.W.] used t observe: When anone among you is perplexed over an important matter, he should perform two Rakats of supererogtory prayer and then offer this prayer: (Bukhari)

O Allah! I ask of Thee the good hrough Thy knowledge, and ability through Thy power and beg (Thy favours), Thine infinite bounty. For, behold, Thou hast power; I have none. Thou knowest, I know not; and Thou art the great knower of things hidden.

O Allah! If in Thy knowledge this matter be good for my aith, for my livelihood, and for the issue of my affairs, then ordain it for me, an make it easy for me and bless me therewith. But if in Thy knowledge, this matter be bad for my faith, for m livelihood, and for the issue of my afairs, then turn it away from me, and turn me away therefrom and ordain for me the good wherever it be, and cause me to be pleased there with.

The Submission : The Holy Prophet (S.A.W.) has said:

"O believers, adorn your lives with the virtues of service. Cover yourselves with the sheet of the fear of Hereafter, make Hereafter the goal of your life; and be ever prepared to make your abode there. Bear in mind, you have to depart from this world and to present yourselves before Allah."

Only two things will save you there; firstly your good deeds done during your lifetime in this world, and secondly tht source of charity which you might leave behind, after your death.

Devoted Prayers : Ablution and Cleanliness are Prerequisites of prayers, while performing wuzu, clean your teeth with a miswak also. The Holy Prophet (S.A.W.) has said: "The distinuishing sign of my followers on the Doomsday shall be that their foreheads and the limbs washed in ablution shall glow with radiance. Thus, whosoever wishes to enhance his radiance may do so."

Offer Prayers in clean and proper dress. The Holy Quran lays down "O the offsprings of Adam! Go to pray adorned with proper apparel for each prayer. (7 : 31)

Prayers should be Offered Punctually.

(Innas salata Kanat, alal-mominina kitaban mauqoota)

> *"Worship has been made obligatory upon the Muslims with fixed hours."* *(4 : 103)*

Hadrat Abdullah bin Masud (R.A.A.) once asked the Prophet (S.A.W.) "O Prophet of Allah! Which action pleases Allah the most?" The Holy Prophet (S.A.W.) said: "The act most liked by Allah is to offer prayer at its proper time."

> *The Holy Propht (S.A.W.) has also said:*
>
> *"Allah has made five prayers obligatory. One who offers them with submission and humility having performed the ablution at the prescibed time, becomes entitled for salvation by Allah. But one who fails to do so, may gt salvation or may not."* *(Malik)*

Importance of Congregational Prayers : Prayers should always be offered in congregation even if the congregation is missed, the obligatory (farz) (prayers should be offered in the mosque. Sunnah prayers may, however, be offered at home.

> *The Holy Prophet (S.A.W.) has said: "He who offers prayers with the first takbir (i.e. immediately on hearing the call) for forty days consecutively in a congregation, is made safe from both Hell and hypocrisy." (Tirmidhi)*
>
> *And further: "If people come to know the recompense and reward for collective prayers, they would flock to the mosque despite a thousand impediments. The first line of the congregation is like the row of the angels. A two-man party of worshppers is better than one mans and the greater the congregation, the more it is liked by Allah."* *(Au Daud)*

Prayers should be offered with composure and peace of mind. Perform all the forms(postures) of prayer with an undisturbed mind and peacefulness. There should be a resonable pause between the two prostrations (Sajda) and the following prayer is to be recitedduring this interval.

"Allah forgive me and bless me with The Mercy, guide me on the straight path, relieve me of my distress, grant me peace, and arrange for my livelihood."

The Holy Prophet (S.A.W.) has said: "He who offers his prayers properly, is in return blessed by Salat in these words, "May Allah protect thee as thou hast protected me."

He has also said: "The worst kind of theft is the pilferage of prayer." When asked by the companions. "Prophet of Allah, how can one steel prayers?" The Holy Prophet (S.A.W.) said. "By performing imperfect postures in prayers."

How to Pray : Offer prayers with concentration, humility, and submissiveness which may inspire you with the majesty and sublimity of Allah. Unnecessarily moving one's hand or feet, scratching the body, combing beard with fingers, putting finger in the nose, and setting clothes right ar acts of extreme insolence and should be avoided.

Prayers are a Means of Achieving Nearness to Allah : Offer prayers as if you are before Him; or at least imagine that Allah is watching you. The Holy Prophet (S.A.W.) has said:

> *"The servant of Allah is closest to Him when he prostrates himself befor Him. Therefore, when you prostrate yourself, pray fervently." (Muslim)*

You should act upon the teachings learnt in the prayers in your daily life and let its sublimity reflect in your worldly affairs. The Holy Prophet (S.A.W.) has pointed to this aspect through a beautiful mtaphor. He shook a dry twig with some force. All the leaves dropped off. The Holy Prophet (S.A.W.) said: "The sins of persons offering prayers drop off like the eaves of this dry twig." He then recited the following ayat (verse) of the Holy Quran:

> *"And establish prayers on the two points of the day (i.e. morning and sunset) and after some time when night has set in. Verily, good deeds erase misdeeds. Thisis an admonition for those who wish to acquire it. (11:114) (Nasai)*

While offering prayers, the Holy Quran should be recited slowly and clearly. This applies to other utterances during the prayer, which should be recited with appropriate pauses and ith concentration, ardour, and alertness of mind. If prayers are offered ith understanding and care, they become real prayers.

Prayers are to be offred regularly and with punctuality. It is a basic distinguishing feature of the Muslims that they offer their prayers regularly and in time. The Holy Quran says:

> *"(And the believers are those) who guard their prayers,"*

Optional Prayers : Together with obligatory prayers, the worshippers should also offer nafl or optional prayers. These prayers should be offered as much as possible. The Holy Prophet (S.A.W.) has said: "For the person who offers twelve rakats of nafl or optional prayers in addition to the five compulsory prayers, has his house built in the Paradise." (Muslim)

Offer Some Prayers at Home also : Sunnat and Nafl prayers (other than compulsory) should occasionally be offered at home. The Holy Prophet (S.A.W.) has commanded this by saying. "After having offered prayers in the mosque, do offer some prayers at home. Allah will bless your homes on account of such prayers."

The Holy Prophet (S.A.W.) himself used to offer such prayers very often at home.

When leaving your home, for the morning prayers, recite the following supplication:

> *"Allah enlighten my heart, my vision, my hearing; creat light on my right, on my left, on my rear and light in front of me. Enlighten me from above and below. O Allah, bestow upon me light, and make it light for me, fill my muscles, flesh, blood, hair, skin, tongue and my breath with light and make light within myself. Give me; Allah! the great light, and make me all light."*

Supplication to be Recited after Prayers : Hadrat Sauban (R.A.A.) says that the Holy Prophet (S.A.W.) after completing the prayer with the Salam used to say Astaghfirullah (Allah forgive me) thrice and then recited the following supplication:

> *Allah! Thou art peace, and the fountain-head of peace is from Thee. Thou art Blessed, Thou art Great, and Munificent.*

Recitation of Holy Quran : The Quran should be recited with full ardour and keen interest, believing that love for the Quran is love for Allah. The Holy Prophet (S.A.W.) has sad:

> *" The best form of prayer for my Ummah is the recital of the Quran."*

Reward for Reciting the Holy Quran : A Muslim should recite the Quran very often and he should never feel tired or bored by its recitation. According t the Holy Prophet (S.A.W.):

> *"Allah has said that a servant of His who is so engrossed in reciting the Quran that he will not have an opportunity to pray to Himfor his needs, shall be granted more than that which He shall grant to those who ask."(Tirmidhi)*

The Holy Prophet (S.A.W.) said:

> *"Allah's servant gains the maximum proxmity to Him through the reading of the Quran."* *Tirmidhi)*
>
> *In a beautiful simile, the Holy Prophet (S.A.W.) has compared the individual who reads the Quran daily is like a bottle of musk, perfume of which spreads in all thefour directions, while he, who has read the Quran but does not recite t, is like a bottle full of musk which has beensealed."* *(Tirmidhi)*

The Quran should be recited for guidance and inspiration only. It should not be chanted for any other purpose, e.g., for endearing oneself to others or impressing people, or for trying to reate an impression of piety. These traits should be eschewed. The are impure motives and anyone who recites the Quran for such a purpose shall not get guidance from the Quran.

Before Recital, Ensure Absolute Cleanliness **:** Avoid touching the Holy Quran without first having performed ablution nd recite it in clean place.

Manner of Recitation *:* While reciting the Holy Quran, read it with full concentration, ardour and utmost devotion. Allah has said:

> *"The Book we have revealed upon you, is full of blessings; so that (people) may ponder upon it and the wise men may receive instructions and inspiration from the same."*
>
> *(38 : 30)*
>
> **Recite the Holy Quran Distinctly in a Melodious Tone :** *Read the Quran in a measured and deliberate tone, pronouncing each word correctly and distinctly in an easy tone making sentences quite intelligible. The Holy Prophet (S.A.W.) has directed that the reciter should recite the Quran in a pleasing manner, making it charming with his voice and melody.*
>
> *(Abu Daud)*

The Holy Prophet (S.A.W.) recited the Quran pronouncing each word clearly and each ayat (verse) separately. The Holy Prophet (S.A.W.) has said:

> *"The reciter of the Quran shall be commanded on the Day of Judgement to recite the Quran melodiously with the same measured tone an sustained pitch, with which he used to recite the Book in the world, and get elevated*

a step higher as a reward for each ayat. His real abode lies near the last ayat *he had recited."* *(Tirmidhi)*

Tone of Recitation : The pitch to be adopted in recitation should neither be too high nor too low. It sould be intermediate as Allah has set down:

"And offer your prayers neither too loudly nor slowly, instead follow the middle way." *(17 : 110)*

Best Time for Recitation : Although it is always good to recite the Holy Quran, yet the best time to do so is during late midnight with Tahajjud prayers and at dawn, before or after Fajr prayer. Recitation of the Holy Quran at these hours is very gracious and rewarding. The wish of every Muslim should be to achieve this privilege.

Don't Rush Through the Quran : The recitation of the Quran should never he completed within less than three days. The Holy Prophet (S.A.W.) has said: "One who has recited the whole Quran within less than three days, has not comprehended it."

The Holy Quran is not to be Recited Rapidly : It should be read with understanding and meditation. Hadrat Abdullah Bin Abbas (R.A.A.) used to say that it is much better to read short surahs like Al Quraish and Al-Qadr with understanding and comprehension, than rapidly going through long *surahs* like *Al-e-imran* and Al-Baqarah without following them. The Holy Prophet (S.A.W.) once continued to recite only one ayat for the whole night:

"(O Allah) i Thou submitest them to Thy wrath, they are Thy servants. If Thou forgivest them, Thou art Most Powerful and All Wise."

Have due regard for the majesty and divinity of the Holy Quran. And as you care for the visible cleanliness of your person, while reading the Holy Quran, in the same way cleanse your heart of evil thoughts, foul ideas and base motives: A heart that is polluted by evil thoughts and impure motives will neither admit the sublimity of the Holy Quran nor its significance. Hadrat 'Ikramah (R.A.A.), on opening the Holy Quran for recitation, frequently fainted and on regaining consciousness, would say; "This is the word of my Majestic and Dignified Sustainer."

Study Holy Quran in Order to Correct and Remould your Life : The Quran should be studied with the view and the goal that one's life is to be reshaped and remoulded according to the commands contained therein: One should try to wash off wrongs in ones life in the light of the teachings of the Holy Quran. The Holy Quran would show our wrongs to us like a mirror; and now it is for us to cleanse ourselves.

Inspiration from the Holy Quran : While reciting he Holy Quran, one should try to imbibe the effect conveyed by each ayat. When one recites the ayats concerning Allah's compassion, forgiveness, and the eternal gifts of the Paradise, one should feel elated with beer. While reciting ayats pertaining to Allah's wrath and the torture of the Hell, your body should tremble with awe and fear and tears should spill out of your eyes; even your heart should be moved with the emotions of repentance and shame. On reading the accounts of success of the pious Muslims, your face should glow with happiness; and while reading the stories of destruction of nations having gone astray, you should feel sorrow and unhappy. Verses containing warnings and threats of punishments should send a wave of sensation through your body; and verses which bring joyful tidings should make your soul overflow with the spirit of thanksgiving.

Supplication after Recital : After reciting the Holy Quran supplicate to Allah, Hadrat Umar (R.A.A.) has recommended the following prayer after recital:

"O Allah, make me familiar with the wilderness in my grave. O Allah, have mercy upon me for the sake of the great Quran, and make it my leader, light, guide and mercy. O Allah, let me remember what I have forgotten of it, and teach me what I do not follow, and give me capacity to recite it in the parts of night and day and O Lord of the worlds, make it my argument on the Final Day."

Chapter 7

Social Behaviour in Islam

Islamic Society

Islam teaches that God is concerned not only with moral and ethical reform, but also with social emancipation and economic conditions. *Abdul Moghny Said*

Islam strikes a balance between the two extremes of capitalism and socialism. *Muhammad Qutb*

The simultaneous stress on both the material and the spiritual aspects of life is a unique characteristic of the Islamic economic system. This synthesis of the material and the spiritual is what is missing in the other two systems, capitalism and socialism. Both the capitalist and the socialist systems have neglected the spiritual needs of the human personality.

Muhammmd Umar Chapra

Contemporary attempts to base the life of nations on Islamic principls cover a wide range. All are profoundly influenced by the xample of the Prophet and of the early Muslim community in Medina. They are also strongly influenced by reacions to events and trends in the Western world, both capitalist and ommunist. The great adjustments that are taking place in Muslim society are happening at a time when it feels itself under threat from a dominant civilisation which, while no longer politically imperialist, is imposing its norms of behaviour and its materialism on others. Reactions towards the "West" face Muslims with difficult dilemmas. The search goes on for answers to social and world problems that are consonant with Islamic tradition, neither merely reactions to nor adaptations of alien thought.

"The dominant, permanent factor in Muslim countries," says Dr Fathi Uthman, former editor of the *Islamic World Review,* "is Islam as a comprehensive way of life." It is important to realise, he adds, that those who hold this view can be progressive - recognising that not everything "modern" is tied to secularism. The Islamic revival is many-sided, forward-looking as well as traditional.

The tide of renewal in the Muslim world began to flow more than a century ago, with movements such as that of the Wahhabis in Arabia, the Arab awakening in the Near East, and the expansion of Islam south of the Sahara.

The Twentieth Century has seen a war of ideologies — of powerful ideas regarding man and society. Every tide of ideology that has swept through the world during the course of the past decades has had its observers, its critics and sometimes its supporters in the Muslim world. Liberalism and socialism in turn were interpreted in Muslim terms. The atheistic creed of communism has never been acceptable to Muslims, but the Marxist diagnosis of society and history has had its influence in various quarters. Nationalism, though contrary to the Islamic concept of the universal community, the *Ummah,* helped to raise many local and regional loyalties, as well as to inspire the larger vision of Pan-Arabism. Young men — and women also of each succeeding generation pinned their hopes of radical change to one banner or another: often to suffer disillusionment when the promises of their leaders were not fulfilled.

More and more, hopes of profound change on a national and global scale came to focus on a return to the teachings of Islam. Islam itself could be viewed as an ideology, in the sense of a comprehensive system of ideas that embraces the whole of life. Some of many trains of thought and action are indicated here: a view on Arab Socialism; the principles of Islamic banking by one of its pioneers; an insight into the universal nature of science; and how the West is seen. Is it irretrievably decadent, or are its people possible partners in fashioning a new age? The key to all progress is in the renewal of faith.

Origins of Arab Socialism : The Islamic principles on which Arab socialism was based differ fundamentally from dialectical materialism. One of those who contributed to the development of independent Arab socialist thinking is Abdul Moghny Said, until 1975 Under-Secretary in the Ministry of Manpower, Cairo. He is known for his pioneering work in the field of workers' education. In his book, *Arab Socialism,* he traces its origins in the thought and practice of the Quran and the Prophet. The concept of Arab socialism actually existed for many centuries before modern Arab nationalism came upon the scene. Its roots were planted long before Marx. They lie deep in the soil of Islam and in the cultural heritage of the Arabs.All the great monotheistic religions were cradled in these Eastern Mediterranean lands which have always been the home of the Arab people. The impulse towards social emancipation is found in all these religions, but it is perhaps most developed in the precepts of Islam. The Quran makes it clear that, as well as setting up moral standards as a basis of decent behaviour and better human relations, religions must bring help to the poor and improve the livingstandards of the masses. In previous revelations the message was simple: "Do not exploit; be charitable; practise unselfishness." In Islam, for the first time, an economic theory of equal opportunities and fair distribution was outlined.

Without being too theological, it is possible to explore the social and economic implications of Islam and the principles which have influenced contemporary Arab socialist thought... Islam teaches that God is concerned not only with moral and ethical reform, but also with social emancipation and economic conditions.

The Quran provides a basis for a moral interpretation of history; an interpretation which is deeper and broader than that of Karl Marx because it covers both the moral and material aspects, while that of Marx concentrates entirely on the material aspects, being greatly influenced by the materialistic evolutionary philosophies of his time. Religion is not the opium of the people. The great religions aimed at a classless society, where equality, justice and prosperity would prevail. In their principles, and particularly in Islam, which Marx completely ignored, we can trace much that pointed towards socialism.

A New Economic Order : Muslims responsible for the policy of nations - Asian and African as well as Arab — see the teachings of the Quran as having relevance to major questions of economics, and also to the stewardship of money and the distribution of world resources.

Banking is one field where practices based on these teachings have been increasingly explored and expanded. In the 1970's and 1980's numbers of Islamic banks were set up, based on the principles of partnership and the sharing of profit and loss. It is essential that the system should be interest-free, since the Quran specifically forbids usury, and this is generally taken to include any form of interest. But the emphasis is on working out a positive system, not merely on excluding an incentive regarded as wrong. By 1987 there were more than 100 Islamic banks and financial institutions throughout the world, including multinational banking companies. The Islamic Development

Bank (IDB) was established in 1975 by the Organisation of the Islamic Conference (OIC) to undertake long-term financing of development projects.

One of the pioneers of these developments is Prince Muhammad Al-Faisal Al-Saoud, Chairman of the International Association of Islamic Banks. In 1981 he founded the Geneva-based Dar-ul-Mal al-Islami (DMI). The aim is that Islamic banks and interest-based banks should view each other not as competitors but as partners. One of many steps towards this goal was a symposium of bankers held in Baden-Baden, West Germany, in May 1981, organised by the Syma Institute and chaired by Prince Muhammad.

In his inaugural address he outlines some value premises of Islam. (1) The unity *(tauhid)* of thought under God: His power and direction are relevant to every aspect of life. (2) The vice-gerency of man who is God's deputy and who has to act as a trustee: with no extravagance, no waste, but positive utilisation of the available resources. (3) The search for justice, political and social as well as individual. From such a value-framework, he says, the economist will derive a new set of policy conclusions. The thrust of economic analysis will move from what people demand, to what the world needs, and this will be a revolutionary change in economic thinking.

The basic principles of Islamic banking and finance are not new. What is new is only in the application. Our philosophy is based on the Quran in which there are certain things that are given, things which do not bear discussion, because we cannot in any way adjust them. However, there is wide area in which innovation, new approaches and methods can be applied. We feel we can contribute to the solution of some of the problems in the economies of the world today. We are trying to help in relieving the pressures on the Third World by mobilizing the resources of the Islamic countries through Islamic banking. Man has been created as God's surrogate in this world. Therefore he is not a totally free agent in his social and economic interactions. There is a certain code. The question of interest is one thing, but more important is the total integration of morality in the dealings of any human being in any endeavour he undertakes. Economics, as we understand it in its classical form, is the satisfaction of the need for goods and services. With Islam, the definition is slightly different. It is the material satisfaction of the need of sciety according to the role man plays in this world. This entails certain limitations, which make it different from the western concept of total freedom of action.

Trusteeship brings the idea of accountability in this world before humans, and before God in the life hereafter ... We shall have to develop social accounting over against the type of accounting with which we are familiar at the moment... These concepts are not just ethical norms, but have important economic consequences.

In this new approach, we do not claim that we have all the answers or that we have been able to develop all the solutions. We would like to learn from other traditions, and we would like to see others also adopt a more open attitude to the study of the Muslim approach to economics.

Science and Faith : The search for knowledge is a duty in Islam. European scholarship owes a debt to the Muslim world for its earlier leadership in the scientific field. Now, however, "The Muslim World can and should learn from and profit by the West, particularly in the spheres of modern sciences and technology." Muhammad Asad, author of *The Road to Mecca,* is one among many who develop this theme.

Never have the worlds of Islam and the West come so close to one another as today. Cultural imitation, opposed to creativeness, is bound to make a people small... Not that the Muslims could not learn much from the West, especially in the fields of science and technology. But the acquisition of scientific notions and methods is not really "imitation"; and certainly not in the case of a people whose faith commands them to search for knowledge wherever it is to be found. Science is neither Western nor Eastern, for all scientific discoveries are only links in an unending chain of intellectual endeavour which embraces mankind as a whole.

Every scientist builds on the foundations supplied by his predecessors, be they of his own nation or of another; and this process of building, correcting and improving goes on and on, from man to man, from age to age, from civilisation to civilisation, so that the scientific achievements of a particular age or civilisation can never be said to "belong to that age or civilisation." At various times one nation, more vigorous than others, is able to contribute more to the general fund of knowledge; but in the long run the process is shared, and legitimately so, by all. There was a time when the civilisation of the Muslims was more vigorous than the civilisation of Europe. It transmitted to Europe many technological inventions of a revolutionary nature, and more than that: the very principles of that 'scientific method' on which modern science and civilisation are built. Nevertheless, Jabir ibn Huyyan's fundamental discoveries in chemistry did not make chemistry an "Arabian" science; nor can algebra and trigonometry be described as "Muslim" sciences, although the one was evolved by Al-Khwarizmi and the other by Al-Battani, both of whom were Muslims: just as one cannot speak of an "English" theory of Gravity, although the man who formulated it was an Englishman. All such achievements are the common property of the human race. If, therefore, the Muslims adopt, as adopt they must, modern methods in science and technology they will do no more than follow the evolutionary instinct which causes men to avail themselves of other men's experiences.

Change through Renewal : The Islamic concept of change in society is renewal *(tajdid),* as the key to reform *(islah).*

The Prophet did not start with a system, or with large numbers. He began with change in the hearts of men and women - his wife, his closest friends. The idea of reform is not the modern one, which begins with the outward, trying to reform the world but never man himself. Africa south of the Sahara has seen a vigorous expansion of Islam during the nineteenth and twentieth centuries. This renewal of Islam in West Africa may be regarded as "a model of *tajdid",* suggests Dr A. R. Doi, Director of the Center for Legal Studies, Ahmadu Bello University, Zaria. The revered Shehu (Sheikh) Uthumanu Dan Fodio (d. 1817), scholar and preacher in what is now Northern Nigeria, was regarded by his thousands of followers as the Renewer *(mujaddid)* of his age. In one of his many books he speaks of the character of such a reformer. It is related [in a saying of the Prophet] that at the beginning of every century God will send a learned man to the people to renew their faith. The characteristics of this man must be that he commands what is right and forbids what is disapproved of, that he reforms the affairs of the people, and judges between them, and that he assists the truth against vanity and the oppressed against the oppressors, in contrast to the characteristics of the other learned men of his age. The struggle the Shehu declared against rulers he regarded as corrupt began with preaching (the *jihad* of the word). At the risk of his life he took a stand against an injustice, and, his struggle turned into an open revolt (the *jihad* of the sword). With his brother Abdullah and his son Muhammadu Bello he established a state in the new city of Sokoto. This became the centre of a renaissance of poetry, literature and religious study, as well as of prosperous trade. All three were learned and scholarly men: more than a hundred books by them survive. These were concerned with the application of the precepts of Islam to the practical affairs of home, trade ad state, and also with the poems, in Arabic and in the vernacular languages, which helped to make the teachings of Islam live for a population largely illiterate. The memory of Uthumanu Dan Fodio is still a powerful influence among the more than 150 million Muslims in West African countries, and also in the Sudan.

Renewal in this spirit is the aim of the Emir of Kano, HH Al haji Ado Bayero. He sees his responsibilities as extending to the contribution a united Nigeria can make to the world. At the end of Ramadan 1988 he invited chiefs from the south of Nigeria, as well as his northern neighbours, to celebrate the Feast, the Eid-ul-fitr. Together with the

Anglican Bishop of Kano, he spoke of uniting peoples of all creeds on the firm ground of moral rectitude, selflessness, and dedication for the betterment of mankind. In a situation tense with recent religious conflict, he and the Bishop gave joint witness to "religion as an agent of unity rather than of division and destruction." Amid the blare of trumpets and the thuder of hooves as thousands of horsemen thronged the ancient city, a note was sounded of quiet faith for the future.

Islam and the West : Over the past hundred years, a renewal of faith and confidence has come to the Muslim world. The forms of this renewal have been manifold: its expressions range from the personal to the running of states, from individual integrity to steps towards a new economic order, from scientific research to art and poetry. The springs of renewal, or resurgence, in the Muslim world may be discerned in the Quran, in the potency of its teachings and of the basic tenets of Islam. What actually occasioned it, at this time in history, was reaction to the domination of western civilisation, in its political form of imperialism and, more insidiously, in the onslaught of its materialism and secularism.

A reaction had to come. Revulsion against the West was inevitable, and might take controversial forms — not always viewed by Muslims as true to the best in Islam. It was not a reaction against Christianity, but against moral corruption as well as economic and political domination. In face of the threat of a dominant culture, three possible courses present themselves: rejection, surrender or a selective choice, says Sayyid Abul Hasan Ali Nadwi, Rector of the Nadwat al-*Ulama* Islamic University in Lucknow. One of the most widely read authors of his time, he has written more than 40 books - in Arabic, Urdu and English. His insights into the world situation and the demands it makes on Muslims have done much to challenge the fears and raise the hopes, especially of the younger generation.

In his book, *Western Civilisation - Islam and Muslims,* he analyses the choices that face them.

An unrelenting battle of ideas and ideals is taking place throughout the Muslim world- a clash between the Islamic and the Western concepts of life, values and traditions. The past history of the Islamic countries, the indestructible attachment of the Muslim masses everywhere to Islam, the ideals which inspired them in their struggle for freedom - all these things demand that Islamic values alone should have a claim on their leadership. On the other hand, the intellectual make-up, education and political interests of the ruling classes in Muslim countries require that Western forms of life should be pushed forward.

The attitude of rejection and withdrawal is emphatically futile. It is bound to fail. No nation can aspire to maintain its individuality which lacks faith in itself and is plagued with an inferiority complex. All its efforts to hold its ground against a mighty civilisation, which has also become the dominant trend of the time, must ultimately fail.

In contrast there is the philosophy of defeatism, capitulation, servility. Its advocates are ardent, though immature, disciples of the West. Modernism to them means westernisation.

A man who does not make the West his preceptor and relegate himself to the rank of a pupil, but treats it as an associate, [can] make his own contribution. He ought to know that if he has to learn a great deal from the West, the West too has to learn no less from him. His endeavour should be to bring about a synthesis between the material and spiritual forces of the West and East and then to evolve from it a way of life the West may also be compelled to adopt, and which may serve as an inspiration to the most highly advanced nations of the present day world.

"Arousing the Conscience of the West" : Criticism of western ways does not necessarily regard the fight for values as confined to the Muslim world, nor as irretrievably lost in western society. Dr. Fathi Uthman, former editor of the *Islamic World Review,* in a seminar held at the Oxford Centre for Islamic Studies (February 1987), gave points of common hope and advance, providing grounds for cooperation. As the shadow of colonialism recedes, he said, new friendships are arising. Business relationships enable economic problems to be tackled together. And above all within the structure of western society there are many positive initiatives, "arousing the conscience of the West and countering the impression of an imminent collapse of standards and values."

Response to such initiatives of change, recognised in the conduct of Christians encountered in the West, was confirmed by a Muslim Brother from the Sudan. "I have moved from condemnation to the realisation that there are people we can and should work with," he said. "Absolute moral standards provide the area of cooperation to achieve the Will of God."

The Right Path

When you want to understand Islam, where do you go? A learned professor has said that we must go to the dictionary and scholarship, and then to the mosque. Certainly it is necessary to go to these places, but going there alone will be incomplete. Islam is not confined to the mosque - it is a code of conduct and a guidance for everyday life. We have to watch the career of a Muslim who has himself understood the religion of Islam and who practises its principles. Without that watching, the mosque or the textbook will give us only an incomplete understanding.

The Honourable Justice M. M. Ismail, Madras

Islam's conception of life is often put in terms of a road. A road has a beginning and a destination. The individual is somewhere on the road between birth and death. The human race is on the road too -the road from Creation to Judgement.

The millions now turning their faces to Mecca pray many times a day: "Show us the straight way." "Guide us on the straight path." *Al-Fatiha,* the opening chapter *(sura)* of the Quran with its seven verses, is repeated at each of the five times of prayer.

Whole books have been written on these verses. They are the first to be memorised by children, and they are pondered by statesmen. An ex-Prime Minister, asked what was the inspiration behind his success in recent negotiations, went through the Fatiha step by step.

The first volume of one modern "explanatory translation" of the Quran is entirely devoted to this opening chapter. "Let us look at the *Surat Al-Fatiha* as a whole," it says, "and see what type of mind it reflects or tries to build."

"Al-Fatiha": The Opening : In the Name of God, Most Gracious, Most Merciful.

Praise be to God,
The Cherisher and Sustainer of the Worlds;
Most Gracious, Most Merciful; Master of the Day of Judgement.
Thee do we worship, And Thine aid we seek.
Show us the straight way,
The way of those on whom
Thou hast bestowed Thy Grace,
Those whose (portion)
Is not wrath,
And who go not astray.

The Holy Quran, Sura I

Signposts on the Road: The Pillars of Islam : For the traveller who sets out on the road of faith, there are certain signposts or pillars by which to chart his way. The Muslim is taught to mark five such pillars.

The first is hiswitness to the God he serves: the One God, to whom man must submit or surrender totally. The word *Islam* means such surrender, and *Muslim (Muslima)* is the man or woman who thus submits to God. This "witness" *(shahada)* or creed is:

"There is no god but God (Allah)

And Muhammad is the Prophet of God."

The second of the pillars is prayer.

The third is *Zakat*: the giving of a certain proportion of income for the relief of poverty. The fourth is the discipline of fasting - from dawn to sunset during the month of Ramadan. The fifth is the pilgrimage to Mecca - to be performed once in a lifetime by every Muslim able to make the journey.

Of these, the duty which most affects the daily life of the Muslim family is the observance of the five daily times of prayer, starting before sunrise and ending late in the evening. In many of the Muslim homes in which I have stayed, the family are up for the Dawn Prayer that begins the day. It should be performed between dawn and sunrise. My hostess in a Cairo club slipped away to a quiet corner after lunch, so that the midday prayer might not be missed. A cheerful schoolgirl, hurrying in to her home with her books under her arm, went first to pray and then to tea. In the cool of the evening in Bombay's beautiful Hanging Gardens, many of the faithful were praying as the sun set. The midday prayer on Fridays is the weekly congregational gathering. Shos close, business stops. A sermon precedes the prayers, which are performed together without regard to rank. A gallery or aisle in the Mosque is often set apart for women. There are many who do not pray, and many for whom it is a mere repetition of a formula. The following quotations come from some of those to whom prayer is a reality - individuals in widely differing circumstances.

Daily Prayers: In his prayers, a Muslim faces the direction of the city of Mecca. When the time comes, in whatever place he happens to be, he turns towards Mecca and says his prayers. Facing one direction is a symbol of unity of purpose for the millions of Muslims offering their prayers at the same time in the four corners of the earth.

The Muslim says the *Fatiha,* and recites any other portion of the Quran he feels like reciting, because of its particular meaning, or because he happens to remember it. Bowing, and touching the earth with his forehead, he terminates with a formal prayer in which he asks God to bless him and his people "as Thou hast blessed Ibrahim and his people."

The daily prayers are made by practising Muslims individually. A family can join in prayer, or any group which happens to be together. On Fridays, however, the noon prayer should be made collectively.

Voice Within : Prayer reminds man of God and helps him to be receptive to His guidance. The five daily prayers are the best rest intervals for man in our busy and materialistic world. The moral foundations of Islam are standards in which human behaviour can be channelled for the good of the individual as well as for the good of the community as a whole. They are not mere preaching stuff which may not keep step with ever-changing conditions. They form together that which we call "conscience" or the good side of us. The "voice within" reminds us always that God is with us. To believe in God is simply the way to develop this "voice within" by seeking God's remembrance, presence and guidance.

Man can Choose : The trouble we now see in the world - and in the Muslim world -is the result of listening to self-will when we should listen to God.

If we ask, what does God say in such a crisis as we face today, we can turn to the Holy Quran and find a key in the verse, "God does not change the conditio of a people until the people change themselves." Another key is in the *Fatiha,* the prayer we repeat so many times a day. It says, "Guide us in the straight path." This shows us that God wants us to take guidance from Him. If this is so, we have to listen for that guidance. He will not catch us by the ear and drag us along that straight path. We must open our ears to His guidance, which the *Fatiha* makes us ask for.

Man is *ashraf al-makhluqat,* the top of creation, the highest of living beings. We have freedom to think for ourselves, about what is right and what is wrong. If we say everything is under God's control, we imply that He wills evil. You may say a leaf falls to the ground — and God wills it. But with man's actions it is different. He can choose between right and wrong, which lead to heaven and hell. Therefore we need to ask God's guidance along the straight path.

A time of quiet listening and asking for Gods guidance in this way is very important for every Muslim.

Haroun S. Kably,

Plaited Kufic ornamentation

"God gathers mankind for the Day of Judgement"

Advocate, Supreme Court, Delhi, and President, All India Cutchi Memon Community

Thy Lord Hath not Forsaken Thee : Verses may be chosen from the Quran as optional acts of prayer to suit the circumstances of the believer, his joy and sorrow, gratitude and need.

A television programme in Cairo on the Prophet's Birthday (April 1973) included a talk on courage in adversity by the newly-appointed Sheikh al-Azhar, Dr Abdul Halim Mahmud. The chapter of the Quran named *The Glorious Morning Light* (Sura 93) was read. Afterwards a Palestinian lady, a refugee living in Egypt, said:

> *As I knit, I pray - just as Gandhi used to say the name of God as he spun. It is the same with the beads you see in my husband's hand. Men say short prayers as they handle them. One of these is, "Your covering and mercy, oh Lord." It means that the inner life is protected. Whatever the circumstances and defeats outside, the life inside our hearts need not be invaded by evil.*

One part of the Quran which is often used in our prayers when we are disappointed or disheartened is the sura called *Al-Doha, The Glorious Morning Light.* It is said that these verses were revealed to the Prophet in Mecca, after he had received no revelations for some time and his opponents were mocking him.

By the morning hours

And by the night when it is stillest,

Thy Lord hath not forsaken thee nor doth He hate thee,

And verily the Hereafter will be better for thee than the present,

And verily thy Lord will give unto thee so that thou wilt be content.

Did He not find thee an orphan and protect (thee)?

Did He not find thee wandering and direct (thee)?

Did He not find thee destitute and enrich (thee)?

Therefore the orphan oppress not,

Therefore the beggar drive not away,

Therefore of the bounty of thy Lord be thy discourse.

Mrs Fareeza Taji, Palestine and Cairo

Prayers for Forgiveness and Obedience : The following come from a prayer-book in use in the Sudan.

O God! I ask forgiveness for myself and for my father; for all Muslims, both men and women; for all believers, both men and women; for those of them who are alive and those of them who are dead.

Deal with me and with them, whether soon or late, in the faith, in this world and the next, according to what You deserve. Do not deal with us, O Lord ! according to what we deserve. For You are forgiving, patient, generous, bountiful, tender and merciful.

O God ! in Whose hand are all our affairs, put an end to our neglect of You. We have turned away from You, and from Your Commands, and from listening to the good things You say. The crime that has caused this is that we have turned towards people who are no concern of ours. These have drawn us away from the benefit of Your speaking with us, and from our fear of You, in spite of our great need of you.

In this there is nothing but loss.

We pray you to turn our desires towards You. For You alone can rescue us from danger in this world and the next.

From *Al-Ratib,* a book of prayers used by the Imam Muhammad al Mahdi

The Call to Prayer : God is great! God is great!

I testify that there is no god but God!

I testify that Muhammad is God's Prophet!

Come to pray! Come to prosperity!

God is great! There is no god but God!

In the Mosque : Here the believer is a fish in water: the hypocrite is a caged bird.

Inscription on the gate of the Masjid Jami' mosque, Isfahan

The Fast of Ramadan : The Muslim calendar consists of twelve lunar months. Because of this the annual festivals occur at different seasons - thirteen days earlier in each successive year.

The ninth month is the month of fasting, Ramadan. All through it, from the first glimpse of the crescent moon to its reappearance a month later to mark the feast, no food or water may be taken from dawn till sunset. Before light, the sound of a drum is often heard in the street, with its summons to awake and eat in the twilight, before a white thread can be distinguished from a black, and the day's fast begins. Ramadan is a time of discipline — and also of surprising gaiety, of family visits and neighbourly calls for the *iftar* (break-fast) parties in the evenings when the fast is over.

There are various aspects of Ramadan. One is the recollection of the revelation of the Quran, especially on the "Night of Power" or "Night of Destiny", the 26th-27th of the month. The Prophet's victories - the

Battle of Badr and the conquest of Mecca - are celebrated. It is also a time for the healing of quarrels. This is especially associated with the feast at the end of Ramadan. It is customary to greet one's friends by saying, "If I have done you any wrong, please forgive me."

A lady in Djakarta put this into practice. She reached the conclusion that the resentment she held against a friend was in itself wrong — however deeply she felt that she had been injured. She decided to take the opportunity of the feast to set it right on her side. She went to mutual friends and said, "You know how it is between us. Help me." Together they went to the house, and her companions supported her while she apologised for the ill will she had harboured.

The Turkish editor Ahmet Emin Yalman relates a similar incident. God forgives, and so must we. That is the purpose of the Bairams (feasts). Their function is to be an occasion of reconciliation. This is effective. For instance, when I was engaged, there was a division in my fiancee's family. I noticed that a certain relative was never seen in their company, though I did not know the cause. When the next feast came, the family went to call on the man, there was a sweet reconciliation and all was well.

"I must clean my heart," is a phrase often heard in connection with this kind of action. The instruction in the Quran about Ramadan is as follows. It is reproduced from the leaflet sent out for Ramadan 1974 by the Islamic Cultural Centre, London, giving the times of sunrise and sunset in different cities in the United Kingdom, for the benefit of those keeping the Fast.

Ramadan is the (month) in which was sent down the Quran, as a Guide to mankind. Also clear (signs), for guidance and for judgment (between right and wrong). So every one of you who is present (at his home) during mat month should spend it fasting. But if anyone is ill, or on a journey, the prescribed period (should be made up) by days later. God intends every facility for you. He does not want to put you to difficulties. (He wants you) to complete the prescribed period and to glorify Him.

The feast that follows Ramadan lasts three days. It is known as the *'Eid-ul-fitr* (Feast of the Breaking of the Fast).

Payment Due : It is at the end of Ramadan that the yearly payment of alms or poor-tax (*Zakat)* is made. This is defined as "an obligation prescribed by God on those Muslims, men and women, who possess enough means, to distribute a certain percentage of their annual savings or capital in goods or money among the poor and needy." The basic traditional percentage is *2½* per cent. In recent years *Zakat* has played a large part in plans for an Islamic economic order and a tax system in line with Islamic tradition.

Declaration of Human Rights in Islam

The fifteenth century of the Islamic era opened on 9 November 1980 AD, (1 Muharram 1401 AH). The year before and the year following this date were a period of intense activity throughout the Muslim world. Behind the turbulent political conflicts of the time Muslim scholars, writers and economists, as well as many of the rank and file of practising Muslims in different walks of life, were seeking to deepen their understanding of their faith. It was an opportunity, said Dr Inamullah Khan, Secretary General of the World Muslim Congress, "to take stock of the gains and losses of the Muslims in the 1400 years. We should not only talk about our achievements but also our failures and the pitfalls into which we have been falling ... As Islam wants to build an egalitarian and a humanitarian society the two-year Hijra celebration should be for correcting past mistakes in all fields of life, be it educational, cultural, social, not ignoring the very important part that economics play in modern life today."

To bring an eternal message to the attention of mankind involves a continuing battle to clarify its meaning and to purify its expression, in the lives and in the statements of Muslim believers. Two such statements were issued by the Islamic Council of Europe: the *Universal Islamic Declaration,* April 1980, which stressed that "a universal order can be created only on the basis of a universal faith and not by serving the gods of race, colour, territory or wealth"; followed by the *Universal Islamic Declaration of Human Rights,* September 1981, "based on the Quran and the Sunnah and compiled by eminent Muslim scholars, jurists and representatives of Islamic movements and thought."

The Declaration follows the lines of the Declaration of Human Rights, issued in 1948 by the General Assembly of the United Nations. It has 23 clauses:—the Right to Life, to Freedom, to Equality, to Justice, to Fair Trial etc. There is a basic difference of approach. The United Nations Declaration starts with "the recognition of the inherent dignity and of the equal and inalienable rights of all members of the human family." The Muslim Declaration looks to "the Divine source and sanction of these rights." "We, as Muslims, believe ... that each one of us is under a bounden duty to spread the teachings of Islam by word and deed, and indeed in all gentle ways, and to make them effective not only in our individual lives but also in the society around us." The Rights of Minorities are included. "The Quranic principle, 'There is no compulsion in religion', shall govern the religious rights of non-Muslim minorities." The "Right to found a family" (common to both Declarations) is followed by a section on the rights of married women. Explanatory notes point out that throughout the Declaration "person" refers to both the male and female sexes: and also that each of the Rights expressed carries a corresponding duty.

> *"This is a declaration for mankind, a guidance and instruction to those who fear God."*
>
> *Quran: Sura 3: 138 Al-'Imran*

A Note on the Illustrations : The oneness of God and the essential unity of His creation are basic to Islamic art, as they are to all Muslim life and thought. This is reflected in an exactness of mathematical design which gives serenity in architecture and undergirds all the arts.

Light is one: yet when broken by a prism it reveals every shade of colour. The millions of mankind are all equal — all sons of Adam, made of clay - yet in that equality there is scope for the differences of human personality, and never in all history have two individuals been identical. So it is with design: mathematically perfect, yet infinitely varied. This perfection of pattern is given life in different ways: by the flowing lines of the Arabic script, drawn with the master skill of the calligraphed; by the floral designs that recall the "gardens through which rivers flow" so often described in the Quran; by the reshaping of triangle, square, and circle swept, as it were, by the movement of wind or water.

The Right Path

Islam has called itself a 'Natural Religion' which is free from all these impurities

> *"So (O Prophet !) set your face steadily andtruly to the faith. (Establish) Allah's nature on which He has framed mankind. There is no change in what Allah has created; that is the standard religion ; but most among mankind do not understand."* *—(Rum : 30)*

The function of the eye i to see until there is some disturbance in it. The ear hears the sound till it becomes deaf. The function of the nature is to follow the right path, and to rush towards it with such alacrity as the water rushes down from a height, unless it is overcome by corruption and wickedness, which may take its reins in hands and turn it away from the path of righteousness and blessings.

The disturbing things which corrupt nature are sometimes the result of the past centuries or sometimes they are the creation of the lowly environment and habits and customs, or both these things together are responsible for the disturbances. These things are a great danger for the nature of man. They cause a variety of diseases in it. The real Jihad of a reformer is to fight these inhibitions and customs and to weaken their strength. He tries to relieve Nature of these dangers in order that its original purity may be regained and it may be able to fulfil its real responsibility. Islam has given a full clarification of this ethod.

After explaining the natural religion in the above quoted verses, the holy Quran says immediately thereafter:

> *"Turn back in repentance to Him, and fear Him ; Establish regular prayers, and be not you among those who join gods with Allah, those who split up and become sects, each party rejoicing in that which is with itself."*
>
> —*(Rum : 31-32)*

To encourage faith in place of disbelief, righteousness in place of wickedness, to adopt the policy of fearing God, in place of disturbed thoughts in respect of Allah the righteous people's unity of thought and action-these are the manifestations that show that man has remained on the righteous nature.

This has been clarified in the following verse of the Quran:

> *"We indeed created man in the best of moulds, then we have abased him to be the lowest of the low, except such as believe and do righteous deeds."* —*(At-Teen : 4-6)*

What is the best mould or form of man? The understanding of Truth and adopting it, fulfilment of its requirements and meeting of its demands. This is called the attachment to virtuousness and decency, and consideration of these two good qualities in man's individual and collective life is the real achievement. And attempts to make them operative in all the departments of life is the real mould and form.

But there is a very large number of people who do not reach this high level. They remain attahed to the earth only. They follow their own desires, and express disobedience of God's commands. In this way they fall to the lowest level. Quran has called this "Asfala safileen (lowest of the low), to which Allah has thrown such people.

To throw the men of such nature t the lowest level is according to the divine law regarding guidance and transgression. And these laws are true and based on justice. The holy Quran mentions them as under :

> *"And Allah will not mislead a people after He has guided them, to order that He may make clear to them what to fear (and avoid) for Allah has knowledge of all things."*
>
> *(Tauba : 115)*

In Surah Araf this law of guidance and transgression has been mentioned thus

"Those who behave arrogantly on the earth in deterrence of right-them I will turn away from My signs; even if they see all the signs, they will not believe in them ; And If they see the way of right conduct, they will not adopt it as the way of error is the way they will adopt ; for they rejected Our signs, and 'failed to take warning from them." (Aaraf : 146)

Who is it then that remains on the 'best mould' and keeps himself away from the indignities of the world ? In the verses of the Surah At-Teen occurring immediately after those quoted above the answer is given

"Except such as believe and do the righteous deeds."
(At-Teen)

In th foregoing pages we have seen that the outcome of Faith and the Righteous Deeds is the excellence of moral character.

Answer to Evils : Islam's stand vis-a-vis man's pure nature and its strength and firmness has been discussed. As regards itsdealings with the devil-like natures, that has also been made clear. Islam warns mischievous-natured people. It entrusts its rens in the hands of the healthy intellect ; it encourages it to bow down to the pure nature and to surrender itself to Allah.

The prophet has hinted at some of these kinds of natures:

"The son of Adam reaches the old age and two of his habits do not leave him. One is greed and the second is the unending succession of hopes." —(Muslim)

"The worst evil found in man is the frightening cowardice and the undignifying miserliness." —(Abū Daud)

"If the son of Adam is given a valley of gold, he will desire to have another one. And if the other is also given, he will be greedy to have the third one. The hunger of Adam's son will not be satisfied except when his remains are mixed with the dust. And the one who turns to Allah, Allah accepts his repentance." (Bukhari)

The holy Quran has mentioned some of the habits in the Surah Ale Imran:

"Fair in the eyes of men is the love of things they covet, women and sons ; heaped up hards of gold and silver ; horses branded (for blood and excellence) ; and (wealth

of) cattle and well-tilled land. Such are the possessions of this world's life ; but in the nearness to Allah is the best of the goals (to return to)." *—(Al-e-Imran : 14)*

The firt thing Islam wants man to pay attention to is this that to run afte the carnal desires of the self and to follow its unending demands will never satisfy self and make it contented. Truth and right path will not be acceptable to it.

The condition of the self is that when its one desire is satisfied, it immediately demands to have some other desire satisfied. It is always busy in eating, drinking, and having a good time, and greedy with desire to have more and more of everything. It has no hesitation in committing sin and acts of aggression and cruelty. Therefore, Quran has forbidden men to follow the desires that have been considered Haram

"Nor follow you the luts (of our heart), for they will mislead you from the path of Allah; for those who wander astray from the path of Allah, is a penalty grievous, for that they forget the Day of Account." *—(Saad: 26)*

The policy of the infidels and the necessity of opposing it and its importance have been mentioned in these words:

"If the Truth had been in accord with their desires, truly the heavens and the erth and all beings therein would have been in confusion and corruption! Nay, We have sent them their admonition, but they turn away from their admonition." *(Minimum: 71)*

It is necessary that a distinction be made between the forbidden desires of myself and the lawful desires, because some so-called religious people have mixed up these two very dangerously. If man wants to enjoy the goods of the world, then there is nothing wrong in it, but it is a very serious error that this kind of lawful demands and desires have also been included in the list of forbidden, wicked acts.

Its consequence is this that man satisfies his lawful and respectable desires, but his conscience becomes like the conscience of those people who accept crimes as lawful and adopt them willingly. In this way their çonscience becoes a victim of a great error. When he realises that e has committed a mistake, and that sin is an inevitable part of his life, then he commits more serious sins and indulges in the strictly forbidden acts. In other words this time he becomes a criminal and a sinner in the real sense of the word.

The holy Quran has paid special attention to this aspect and has very clearly declared the pure desires of the self and the lawful wishes as proper and lawful, and provided it with a chance to use halal and clean things. It declared any interference of narrowness and inhibition in this respectable and lawful sphere by way of any checks on the self as bad and obscene, because it opens the gate for obscene acts and sinning.

> *"O you people I Eat on earth what is lawful (halal) and clean (tayyib) and do not follow the footsteps of Satan. Indeed, he is an open enemy for yours. He will command you (to do) what is evil and indecent and induce you to say about Allah that which you do not know."*
>
> *—(Al-Baqarh : 168-169)*

It is a fact that to put restrictions on the consumptions of what is lawful (halal) and clean (tayyib) is nothing but levelling false charges against Allah, and this thing amounts to evil and indecency which Satan commands men to do. Islam does not like to repress such natures and inclinations with force and punishment, nor does it want to placate or flatter them, but Islam follows a balanced method which is free of any kind of excess.

Morality Holds the Reins : As the rules and regulations of the healthy nature are secure in faith and reform and they have no connection with heresy and agnosticism, similar is the case of the rebellious natures and habits.

In both the cases only a strong and firm moral character can control it. Where the holy Quran has mentioned man's weakness, his anxiety, his richness and indifference, there it has also made it clear that the remedy of these indignities lies in following the path of religion.

> *"Truly man was created very impatient ; fretful when evil touches him ; and niggardly when good reaches him ; not so those devoted to prayer,those who remain steadfast t their prayer ; and those in whose wealth is recognised right for (the needy) who asks him and who is prevented (for some reason from asking) ; and those who hold to the Truth of th Day of Judgement ; and those who fear the displeasure of their Lord, for the Lord's displeasure is the opposite of peace and tranquillity ; and those who guard their chastity.*
>
> *—(Al-Maarij : 19-19)*

It is common knowledge that good moral character does not develop suddenly. Nor does it become strong and firm in the beginning. It requires consistency and gradualness. And in strengthening it there come many stages.

That is the reason why in its nourishment and growth it is required to perform such acts that have to be repeated. The quality that is developed should have consistency, e.g. prayer, fasting, Hajj, Zakat, and the performance of other forms of worship, confirmation of the Day of the Judgement, and to be fearful of its punishment, etc. When the rebellious natures insist on their acts and are steadfast on their wrong stance, and continue to attempt to traverse the wrong path from time to time, then to check and prevent it no fixed and temporary remedy can be found.

Their transgression and intensity can be brought to the normal level only by such an activist who is more strong and powerful than they and who may be able to bring them to a balanced level. The long and short of the discussion is that Islam respects the human nature and considers its teachings as the voice of that nature. It warns the rebellious natures and reforms their point of view. Those forms of worship which have been made compulsory in Islam are such as strengthen the human nature and turn the wind of desires to the right direction. And these forms of worship do not perform their duties satisfactorily and the desired objective cannot be obtained from them unless they generate the excellent moral character and the tendency to exemplary treatment of others.

Checks and Balances

To generate goodness in someone by coercion and to call him a man of good moral character is not possible. Similarly no faith can be developed in any person by means of force or terrorism. Only personal and intellectual freedom is the sole basis of responsibility and accountability. Islam understands this reality and respects it. It builds up its edifice on the foundation of the excellent moral character.

Where is the need for Islam to use force and coercion to bring man to the right path and to make him run towards righteousness, when it has full confidence in the human nature and is certain that if the obstructions before man are removed then the best generation can be developed ?

Goodness is ingrained in the human nature. It does not mean that it cannot do anything except good, but it means that only good can coordinate with his original nature and offer resistance. The nature wants to attach itself to good only and wants to function in its light, like the bird that after getting free from the cage flies round and round in the sky in ecstasy in accordance with its foremost wish. According to Islam the right method is to break nature's checks and chains. After this when man falls down to the ground, and has no strength to rise and walk, then he should be considered as sick and efforts should be made to treat him. Islam does not order such kind of sick persons to be thrown out of society, provided his existence is not harmful and damaging to others.

Within the limits of this sphere, Islam fights against moral crimes. At first it imagines that every man wants to lead a decent life and wants to live by the sweat of his brow and enjoy luxuries on what he earns from his own labours, that is he does not depend on thefts and looting. Then what thing compels him to take to thieving? In order to provide him for the necessities of life, therefore, Islam says that the necessities and the means should be in such abundant quantities that they may make him indifferent and above taking wrong steps.

This is the responsibility of the society. If it is deficient and compels the individual to steal, then the responsibility for this crime falls on the deficient society, and not on the head of the wrong-committing individual. But if the society provides his requirements, and after this the individual advances in the wrong direction, then the actual condition of the individual should be ascertained before inflicting any penalty (Hudd) on him. Probably there may be such extenuating circumstances that may save him from the punishment. As it is, Islam desires delay in inflicting punishment. The Messenger of Allah his reported to have said : "It is better if the Imam pardons somebody by error than he penalises him by error."

Fixation of Penalties : When after examining the conditions and problems it is ascertained that the individual's nature is bent on rebellion, and that the society which has brought him up and had provided for him is being subjected to his depredations and he wants to repay its kindness with disturbance of peace, then if that society inflicts some penalty on this kind of an individual and wants to cut away that harmful limb, it cannot be criticised or blamed.

The holy Quran has termed a theft deserving the penalty of cutting the hand as the theft of tyranny and corruption, and about such a thief it has stated as under

> *"But if the thief repent after his crime, and amend his conduct, Allah turns to him in forgiveness ; for Allah is Oft-Forgiving, Most Merciful."* —*(Maids : 42)*

The penalty which Islam inflicts is in reality for saving the reformist, welfare, and just society from the damage that a harmful member may cause it. A criminal who repays justice with cruelty and reform with corruption — who would liketo consider him deserving of mercy ?

Appeals to the Hearts : I have mentioned this example merely to show that the penalties for moral crimes have not been fixed with a view to generating forcefully goodness in society, nor does it amount to coerce people to follow the right path.

For Islam the better way is to appeal to the hearts of men, to awaken their sleeping nature, to stir their repressed inclination and desire towards progress and perfection, to return them to the presence of God, and to adopt such a method that would have convincing arguments and the sweetness of love and brotherhood. The moral values should be explained and clarified in such a way that the heart may be convinced that it is necessary to adopt them for attaining the good and the righteous qualities. In such an environment he rule of that law is necessary which hlps in nourishing the human capabilities and in developing excellent habits and good moral character. There is nothing wrong if this useless and profitless limb is cut and thrown away, because in the society we are undertaking farming of various kinds of produce. The purpose is growth and nourishment, whether it may involve the clearance of the wild plants or the thorn bearing shrubs.

The security of the interests of common man and their safety is not a thing of less importance, Therefore, there is no reason for being critical of these penalties which are inflicted by Islam. This thing has been mentioned in the Torah, and all the divine religions have placed emphasis on this.

Responsibility of the Society : According to Islam the society itself plays a very important role in the spread of good or evil that spreads in that society. It (Islam) wants to attain power because it wants, with other things, to form a society in such a way that it may be helpful in encouraging chastity, righteousness, aversion from wickedness, proliferation of good acts, indifference to love for world, steadfastness for the right path and consistency.

The Prophet has told the story of a murderer who wanted to repent for his crimes. He inquired of the address of the greatest learned man of the land. His name was given to him, whom he saw and said

> *"I have committed hundred murders. Is there any chance of repentance for me?" He was told: "What thing can come between you and repentance. Go to a particular place, where some good slaves of Allah reside and are always found worshipping Him. You also join them in worshipping, and do not return to your village, because it is a bad place."* —*(Bukhari)*

In another version, it is narrated that he went to a monk and related his whole story and placed his difficulty before him. The monk told him

> *"You have committed a big mistake. How am I concerned with this ? However, there are two villages. One of them is named 'Nasrah' that is supporter of Allah and the other one is named 'Kaffarah' that is rejector of God. The people of Nasrah perform the deeds of the people of the paradise. Any person who follows other methods cannot stay there. The citizens of Kaffarah perform the deeds of the people of the hell. If you stayed there and worked like those people, then there would be no doubt about the acceptance of your repentance."* —*(Tibrani)*

For this reason Islam says that for the safety of the healthy nature and for the training and reform of the rebellious tendencies the care and vigilance of the environment is necessary, and in the formation of the good moral character it plays a very important role.

We are sure that if all hese aspects are taken care of, then a clean and tidy society can be brought into existence, in which pure qualities and chaste character may be nourished.

Treatment of the Minorities : Every religion has its characteristic symbols, which make it distinct from every other religion.

Undoubtedly there are certain fixed forms of worship in Islam which have been made compulsory for its followers. Besides there are certain values prevalent among the folowers which have no relation with the Non-Muslims. But the moral teachings do not come under this category or within the sphere of this principle. Every Muslim has beZen made responsible to employ good manners in dealing with all the citizens of the land unhesitatingly. For every Muslim it is necessary that he should be truthful in dealing with the Non-Muslims. Similarly good qualities like charity, keeping one's promise, tolerance, decency, generosity, cooperation, etc. are to be brought into play while dealing with Muslims and Non-Muslims alike.

The holy Quran has commanded us not to indulge in such debates with the Jews and the Christians that may encourage mutual enmity, clashes and quarrels. It says:

> *"And do not indulge in disputation with the people of the Book except in a refined way, unless it be with those of them who inflict wrong, and say: 'We believe in the Revelation which came down to us and in that which*

came down to you: Our Allah and your Allah is one; and it is to Him we bow'. *(Ankabut : 46)*

And the followers of Moosa and Isa (Moses and Jesus) were asked, expressing wonder, whether they were indulging in this kind of argumentation and polemics ? "Say: `Do you argue with us about Allah when He is our Lord as well as your Lord ? We are accountable for our deeds and you for yours ; so we are sincerely (dedicated) to Him'." *(Baqarah : 139)*

It is a famous incident of the biography of the Prophet that he owed something to a Jew. The Jew demanded repayment and in a very harsh tone said : "O Son of Abdul Muttalib ! You people unnecessarily delay the repayment of your loans." At that place Hadrat Umar bin Al-Khattab was also present. He decided to teach the Jew, who insulted the Prophet, good manners, and drew his sword from the scabbard. But the Messenger of Allah silenced Umar saying : "I and he deserve better treatment. Teach him to demand his money in a better way and advise me to repay it in a refined manner."

Islam has commanded to deal justly and fairly even if the opponent may be a wrong-doer or an infidel. ,Allah's Messenger has said:

"The payer of the oppessed is answered. If he is wicked and wrong-doer, his ill effects will go against him." (Ahmad)

In another Hadith it is stated : "Even if the oppressed person is an infidel, there is no obstruction between his prayer and its answer. Give up doubful things and adopt those matters in which there may be no doubt." In the light of these authorities and the commands, Islam has advised its followers not to maltreat their ideological and religious opponents.

In connection with the insistence on treating the followers of the other religion kindly, there is one more *Hadith*:

Hadrat Ibn Umar says that a goat was slaughtered in his house. When he came home he inquired whether the gift was sent to the neighbouring Jew or not? He further says : "I have heard the Messenger of Allah as saying 'Jibbrail' had been regularly insistingon me to treat kindly my neighbours, so much so that I surmised that the neighbour would be made a recipient of the inheritance." *(Bukhari)*

Similarly Islam has ordered that its followers should be kind to their relatives, even though they may have rejected this religion which they have made their own. Therefore, following the Truth does not mean that the rights of the relatives may be usurped

> *"And bear them company in this life with justice (and consideration), and follow the way of those who turn to Me (in love); in the end the return of I meaning) of all that you did."* *(Luqman,: 15)*

Need of Morality for the Nation and the Country : This discussion was on the importance of morality at the level of individuals. As regards the importance and need of morality at the public and collective level, Islam says that the progress and the survival of the nations, the nourishment and the development of their civilization and culture, and the consolidation of their power and strength depend on morality. If the people have good and excellent moral character, then all these good qualiies will be found in them, but if their moral character is a lower level, then kingdom and rule will soon end.

"Nations live till their morality lives. When their moral character declines, they also decline." This reality is fully explained in a Hadith in which the Prophet says to the people of his nation that although they have control over the whole of Arabia, and are in a position to decide the fate of the people of the country, as they hold an important position, their power can be maintained on the pillar of morality only.

Anas bin Malik says: "We were sitting in a house where some members of the Ansar and Muhajir were present. The Messenger of Allah came into the room and everybody tried to make room for him near his own seat. Then he proceeded towards the door and stood taking support of the door and said:

> *"The leaders will be from the Quraish, and I have great right on you and they have also a right on you as they would do. When they would be requested to show mercy, they would show mercy. When they would give a judgment, it would be based on justice. And when they would make a covenant, they would honour it. He who does not do like this, there would be on him the curse of Allah, of the angels and of all the people."* —*(Tibrani)*

This *Hadith* unambiguously shows that any person, community, nation or government would be deserving of as much honour and respect as they would be the representatives of the best qualities in this world and would be striving to achieve high objectives.

If a government flaunts the label of Islam and Quran but the people are not satisfied with it, if it does not decide their matters justly, if it is not kind to the needy and does not honour its covenants, then it should be understood that in this government Islam and Quran are merely name, and this government is bereft of Islam's basic values and it deserves to be cursed from every corner of the earth and the skies.

Hadrat Hussain narrates that the Messenger of Allah has said:

> *"When Allah wants to deal kindly with a nation, He entrusts its reins in the hands of the wise men, gives wealth to its generous people ; and when He wants to deal with a nation harshly, he entrusts its wealth to its miserly men."* —*(Abu Daud)*

It is a famous saying of Imam Ibn Taimiyah : "Allah guards the justice-loving government, even if it i the government of the infidels, and destroys the tyrant government, even if it is the government of Muslims."

In the light of the holy Book and the Sunnah, morality is the perfect religion and also the perfect world. If any nation loses its honour in the eyes of Allah or commands no respect among the people, it so happens because of its losing good moral character and becoming deprived of decent and honourable traits.

Celebrating the Feasts : Feasts in Islam are confined to two occasions: Eid-ul-Fitr (Feast at end of Fast) which immediately follows the month of Ramadan, and Eid-ul-Adha (Feast of Sacrifice) which falls on the tenth day of the month of pilgrimage (Dhul-Hijja). Both are occasions to thank God for having allowed individual and community to fulfil their eligious duty.

Observig the Feasts

- Taking a bath on the occasion of the two Feasts is recommended. This can be done any time after midnight preceding the Feast day.
- A Muslim should dress well and wear a pleasant perfume before leaving for the Feast prayers.
- Before going to pray in the morning onthe day of Eid-ul-Fitr, eating some dates, or sweets, is recommended.
- It is preferable not to eat anything on the day of Eid-ul-Adha until performing the Feast prayer in th morning; then one should return home, slaughter an animal, and prepare the Feast meal.
- Walking to the place of the Feast prayer is recommendd unless it is too far away to do so.

- The Feast congregational prayer is usually not performed in the mosque, unless it is raining. To perform it in an open square is recommended.
- It is recommended that the whole Muslim community, with the exception of invalids and the disabled, should gather in the open square for the Feast prayer. This includes menstruating women, who may be present at the occasion but who may not participate in the prayer.
- It is strongly recommended to wait and listen to the Feast khutbah given by the imam.
- When going back to his home after the prayer a Muslim should return by a different road from the one he took when going to the prayer. This will provide him with an opportunity to meet a larger number of Muslims than would otherwise be the case.
- One should take the initiative and congratulate Muslims on this occasion by saying: Taqabbal Allah minna wa minkum (May God accept the work we have done for His sake).
- The rules of conduct and behaviour in the mosque, must be followed here as well.
- Fasting on the day of Eid-ul-Fitr or during the three days following the day of Eid-ul-Adha is forbidden.
- A Muslim should dress his children beautifully, buy them sweets, and help them to celebrate and experience the occasion. This is necessary to help them identify with their Islamic culture.
- A Muslim must avoid doing anything that would annoy his family or dampen their good spirits and spoil their good humour on this occasion.
- Fathers and responsible persons should ensure on such occasions that Islamic law is adhered to, as these Feasts are to thank God and not to indulge in disobedience to Him. Thus, such things as mixing of the sexes, etc. should not occur, although such happy occasions could easily give rise to the wish to do so.

Behaviour on Eid-ul-Adha : Eid-ul-Adha lasts two days after the day of sacrifice, which falls on the tenth day of the lunar Islamic month of Dhul-Hijja.

- It is recommended, whether one is a pilgrim or not, that every family ofer a sacrifice on this occasion. By sacrifice is meant the slaughtering of certain kinds of animals.

- The sacrificial animal should be chosen from healthy stock. An animal whose ear or tongue has been clipped, whose horns have been broken, or who is crippled, should not be selected; the animal should be more than one year old; if sheep, goat, cow or ox, more than two years; and if camel or she-camel, more than five years.
- The sacrificial animal is replaceable by alms equal to the cost of the animal.
- The sacrifice may be a sheep, a goat, a cow, or a camel. A cow or a camel serves for seven people, who share with one another the sacrifice.
- The correct time for slaughtering is upon return from the Feast prayer. Therefore, slaughtering should be avoided before that time, since that will not be considered a sacrifice. If one sacrifice is made before the prayer, another sacrifice may be made after the prayer.
- If a person can slaughter well, then it is recommended that he performs the slaughtering himself, otherwise he should entrust someone to slaughter on his behalf.
- When slaughtering the sacrifice the knife must be sharp, the animal must face towards the Kaaba and God's name must be mentioned, saying: Bismillah, Allah Akbar (In the name of Allah, Allah is most Great).
- A sacrifice may be slaughtered at home, though it is preferable, if possible, to perform the slaughtering in the open square where the prayer was performed.
- Parts of the animal may be eaten or kept by the person making the sacrifice. A large part of it, however, should be given to the poor. Something may also be given to the relatives of the person making the sacrifice.
- The time of slaughtering sacrifices lasts three days including the first day of the feast.
- Selling any part of the sacrificial animal or giving any part of it, including the hide, to the butcher or person who slaughtered it, in payment, is forbidden.

Special Instructions for Eid-ul-Fitr

- Zakat or Sadaqah al-Fitr must be given by every financially able Muslim on the occasion of breaking the fast of the month of Ramadan.

- Zakat al-Fitr should also be given for those who are supported by a Muslim, such as his wife and children.
- Giving the above-mentioned alms to the poor must be done before the Muslims go out to pray the Feast prayer. This will enable the poor to participate in the fetival. However, if one forges to pa Zakat al-Fitr before the prayer, it must be paid as soon as possible afterwards.

Attitude towards Animals

Mercy and Kindness

- Mercy and kindness should characterize all aspects of the treatment of animals.
- Animals should carry loads according to their strength and capability.
- Slaughtering animals should be carried out skilfully and perfectly, so that an animal is not tortured in the process.
- As mentioned in the rules of travelling, when passing with a beast through an area where there is grass and water, a traveller should proceed slowly. When, on the other hand, he is passing through a barren, or desert area, he should proceed quickly.
- Killing non-useful but nevertheless unharmful animals or insects, such as moths or small birds, should be avoided.
- Slaughtering animals who produce milk, eggs, etc. should be postponed for as long as possible.
- Castrating (emasculating) animals or spaying the female is forbidden in Islam.
- Killing some types of creatures should be avoided, unless they become harmful, such as bees, ants, hoopoes and frogs.
- One should not hesitate to kill the following four types of creatures: scorpions, mice, snakes and geckos.
- To refrain from killing snakes out of superstition indicates a weak faith.
- To cross a horse and a donkey in order to produce a mule should be avoided.
- To use gold or silver in an animal's saddle or bridle, or in a dog's line, or to bedeck an animal with silk, is forbidden, for it is a waste of money and betrays arrogance and pride.

- To brand an animal on the face is forbidden. Branding an animal on any other part of its body is allowed, provided no harm is done to it, and branding is confined to necessary limits.
- When beating an animal, striking its face must be avoided.
- To set animals against each other, such as cocks, oxen or sheep, for the sake of fun or for any other reason, is completely forbidden in Islam and considered an act of cruelty.
- It is not allowed to sell or buy an animal which is still in need of its mother. If such a transaction has already been carried out, it must be annulled.
- When hunting birds or animals, hunting young animals still in need of their mothers should be avoided; likewise killing a mother who has young ones should be avoided, as the young ones would then die.
- Hunting animals during hajj or Umrah is forbidden. If it should happen that a Muslim does hunt or kill an animal or bird while performing hajj or Umrah, then it is his duty to make special atonement.
- Animals which feed on filth should be avoided for meat and for riding. Neither should their milk be used until the animals have been confined to clean fodder for a sufficient period.
- If a Muslim owns livestock, birds or animals, then it is his responsibility before God to feed them and to take care of them.
- Using an animal as a target for shooting practise with a gun or bow is forbidden.
- To seek refuge in God from the devil whenever one hears a donkey braying is a recommended act.
- A Muslim should ask God to bless him whenever he hears a rooster crow.
- Every animal is created for a certain purpose such as milking, riding, etc. Therefore, animals should be used according to their purpose.
- Dismembering a dead animal is forbidden.
- One should never curse an animal.
- Animals are of two kinds, clean and unclean. Unclean animals are dogs and pigs. When a dog drinks out of a vessel, it must be washed seven times, using earth once.

- A dog may not be owned by a Muslim except for two reasons: (a) as a watch-dog; (b) as a hunting dog. The place for such dogs, however, is outside the house, not inside.

Essential Elements

Islam has given laws based on the Book of Allah, preached and practiced by the last Messenger of Allah which guarantee the rights of human beings, their life and property, their honour and prestige, security and peace. They guarantee social, religious and political rights to all its citizens, irrespective of race, caste, creed or colour. All enjoy equal rights and equal freedom in an Islamic society. In the way ward society of Arabia, women were treated as animals, life and honour of none were safe. Men buried their daughters alive. No law existed and men bowed before idols. In that society robbery was not considered a crime, trust had no sanctity and a man could lose all his possessions including his wives and children through games of chance. It was Hadrat Muhammad (PBUH) who brought about a marvellous change in the life of such people.

He cast kindness into their hearts and converted robbers into custodians. People constantly fighting among themselves became brothers. They learnt to stand side by side, shoulder to shoulder in a row while praying. It was Hadrat Muhammad (PBUH) who taught that all human beings belong to one brotherhood and that they are all equal He made life easier by his teachings of tolerance of oher people's views and opinions, especially in matters of faith. The Quran says:

"Let there be no compulsion in religion." *(2:256)*

Everyone in the Islamic society is free to practice his religion. This philosophy of religious freedom is further explained in the Holy Quran:

"If it had been the Lord's will
They would all have believed
All who are on earth!
Will you then compel mankind,
against their will to believe!" *(10:99)*

The protection of life and property is fully guaranteed to every citizen in an Islamic society.

"take not life, which Allah hath made sacred, except by way of justice and law:" *(6:151)*

And with regard to property:

"And do not eat up your property among yourselves for vanities, nor use it as bait for the judges, with intent

that ye may eat up wrongfully and knowingly a little of (other) people's property." *(2:188)*

In an Islamic society, wealth should remain in circulation. For this purpose, Islam has established the institution of *Zakat* which is collected from the rich and distributed amongst the poor of the society. *Zakat* is compulsory and, therefore, if one does not pay it, he goes against the commandment of Allah and for him, is prescribed a painful punishment. As regards the acquisition of wealth, Islam encourages all lawful means and condemns the unlawful ones. Muslims are required to earn livelihood by honest means; it regards begging and unemployment as undesirable. Its emphasis is on lawful and legal trade and it considers hoarding, games of chance and gambling as illegal.

Yet another feature of an Islamic society is justice which is to give every deserving person his right. It is the duty of every individual member of the sociey to cooperate with the society towards this end, to the best of his ability. In order to eradicate evil, the Holy Prophet (PBUH) first attacked the basis of corruption. He prohibited all alcoholic drinks and gambling in the Islamic society. He encouraged people to adopt piety, goodness and justice in their individual as well as social dealings. He also discouraged slavery and used all possible methods to get rid of this evil from society.

The social system based on these principles has been working successfully till the present times. In these comprehensive principles, the most balanced Divine Gidance is given to mankind to purify their life and to lay the foundation of a healthy, pious and chaste society in which people can live in peace and happiness. These are the distinctive features of the society set up by Prophet Hadrat Muhammad (PBUH) which provides honour, peace and security to every human being.

Ideal Society

There seem to be four main types of sexual relations, of which we either have a society of pure homosexuals, an entirely promiscuous society, a society in which no sexual relation exists except between husband and wife, or a *laissez-faire* society in which all these forms are tolerated. Are there any rational and objective bases on which we can choose among these types of society ?

Let us start with the easiest one to rule out. If men continue to be moral then a society of pure homosexuals is a self-defeating one, since it severs the enjoyment of sex from its reproductive function. An entirely promiscuous society seems to many to be the best, and in the long run the inevitable form of sexual relations. In such a society, sex, it is thought, ceases to be a problem, since here we shall for the first time combine complete freedom with the deepest enjoyment as well as the procreation of children. This, however, is a mere dream in which one does not see the facts as they are but as one wants them to be. Here are some of the difficulties that beset such a society.

Far from being the natural or ultimately the inevitable, and even if man is viewed as a mere animal, this is a dream which shall never be realised. This is because the human being is basically and biologically a pair-forming species. As the emotional relationship develops between a pair of potential mates it is aided and abetted by the sexual intimacies they share. The pair-formation function of sexual behaviour is so important for our species that nowhere outside the paining phase do sexual activities reach such a high intensity.

The facts are therefore against those who argue that man is basically promiscuous. "It is true that in many cultures economic considerations have led to gross distortion of the pair-forming pattern, but even where this pattern's interference with officially planned 'pseudobonds' has been most vigorously suppressed, with savage penalties and punishments, it has always shown signs of reasserting itself. From ancient times, young lovers who have known that the law may demand no less than their lives if they are caught, have nevertheless found themselves driven to take the risk. Such is the power of this fundamental biological mechanism."

As a dream, a promiscuous society is one where everybody chooses whoever he likes at whatever time he prefers. As a reality it is a society in which sexual deprivation becomes the main problem.

The young and the beautiful are universally more attractive than the plain or the ugly, and the old. And then there are personal tastes as to voice, form, culture, gesture, dress, etc. And if a person fails to find the mate of his or her liking, then even if he or she is physically satisfied, he or she is most likely emotionally deprived. In such a society people are sure to be obsessed with sex, the search for the younger, the more attractive, the what not, becomes a full-time job. If time is a valuable asset, then much of it is unnecessarily wasted in such a society. And this leads inevitably and naturally to the commercialization of this human need, a commercialization which through advertisement, pictures, specialised magazines, the employment of sexually attractive girls and, only very occasionally boys and men, and a hundred other cunning devices, yet increase the obsession with sex.

And the natural outcome of this is a distortion of human values. We do not mean by this anything metaphysically or mysterious. We only mean that in such a society a person's worth will depend on the accident of her or his being of a certain age or having good looks and/or a beautiful body. Girls are rewarded socially, and materially, and even 'crowned', not for anything they achieved but for a thing they had at their hour of birth. By implication the less beautiful girls are punished for no fault of theirs. How manifestly unjust an arrangement, one might say, even cruel !

And the fact of the matter is that a promiscuous society is definitely a cruel one. Even in a normal society, the feeling that one is getting older —and hence less attractive and less wanted therefore—is somewhat annoying, but how much worse it must be in a society where the worth of a person is determined, above all, by the degree of physical attraction, almost to the exclusion of other considerations.

If many criminal tendencies among both the young and the old are discovered to have their origins in broken homes and unstable families, what is going to be the fate of the army of parentless children which a promiscuous society produces? We cannot go here into details of the problems of the mass bringing up of children, but we have pointed to some of the consequences. Contemplating them, some might say : "Well, no-one ever seriously advocated this kind of society. All we stand for is a society where every individual or group of individuals shall have the freedom to lead the kind of sexual life which they prefer. In such a society, married people will live side by side with promiscuous individuals and homosexuals, each appreciating and respecting the ideas and choices of the others and tolerating their behaviour." But, on even a little reflection one will realise that this will not do either. First, because the bad consequence of homosexuality (with the details of which we are not presently concerned) and promiscuity, will not be eradicated by having those who practise them living among married people. All the complications will be there, though on a narrow scale. Secondly, if the consequences are admitted to be harmful, then why encourage, and not lessen, the factors responsible for them ? And, the unfortunate fact is that tolerating homosexuality and promiscuity means encouraging them and pushing more and more people to practising them inasmuch as tolerance leads to others to experiment, and in due course, to come to practise them—as is invariably the case with any other aberrance that is 'tolerated.' The inevitable result will be that the society will become more and more homosexual and promiscuous and it is the married people who will come to be looked upon as 'eccentric', as happened in the case of the people of Prophet Lut (peace be upon him):

> *"And Lut : (Remember) when he said unto his folk : Will you commit abomination such as no other people ever*

did before ? Lo ! you come with lust unto men instead of women. Nay, but you are a wanton folk ! And the answer of hie people was only that they said (one to another) : Turn them out of your township. They are folk, forsooth, who keep pure !" *(7 : 80-82)*

Although wicked people have always been committing this most heinous sin that has given the people of sodom an everlasting notoriety yet it has always been considered a filthy and detestable act. But the only people who have tried to raise it to a moral excellence, were the Greek Philosophers in the ancient world, and the Europeans in the modern world. The latter are doing their utmost to make up the deficiency by making an open propaganda for it, and have succeeded in giving this filthy act a legal sanction. So much so that the legislatures of some countries have legalized it. It does not require elaborate argument to show that homosexuality is a horrible social crime and a heinous sin. For the Creator has made the male and the female of each and every living species different from and complementary to each other for their reproduction. Then this difference in the human species has been created to serve another purpose. This is to urge the two to live together in order to form a family along with their offspring. For this is the foundation of a civilized life for which man has been created. That is why their bodies have been made complementary to attract each other for the satisfaction of sex urges and for the service of the natural function of reproduction of the species. Therefore the one who satisfies this sex urge in an unnatural way becomes guilty of many crimes at one and the same time :

1. Such a one, so to speak, wages a war against the natural and physical functionings of his own organs and those of the victims of his lust. This inevitably produces very harmful effects on their physiques, their minds and their morality.
2. He becomes guilty of treachery and dishonesty against Nature for he enjoys sexual pleasure, without performing the necessary service of his species and civilization and without fulfilling the rights and obligations attached to it.
3. He commits a breach of trust against the society in general for he enjoys all the benefits of the civilized society, but in his turn does not take on himself the responsibilities of the married life and wastes all his powers in the unnatural satisfaction of his sexual desires. This selfish and unworthy attitude is not only useless but also positively harmful to the collective morality. Thus he makes himself unfit for the service of the family and of the human race and produces unnatural feminine characteristics

in, at least, one other male, and opens the way to adultery and moral degradation for at least two women.

By elimination then, and also by implication, the society with the least evil and most good is a society of married people who do not tolerate, but do their best to eradicate, all the causes of homosexuality and promiscuity.

Dhimmi

A dhimmi is a non-Muslim subject of a state governed in accordance with sharia law. Linguistically, the word means "one who's responsibility has been taken". This has to be understood in the context of the definition of state in Islam, which is different from the current definition of citizenship of a state. The dhimma is a theoretical contract based on a widely held Islamic doctrine granting special status to adherents of Judaism, Christianity, and certain other non-Muslim religions ("People of the Book").

Dhimma provides rights of residence in return for taxes. Dhimmi have fewer legal and social rights than Muslims, but more rights than other non-Muslims. However often these limited rights correspond to how in modern democracies, some rights may not be available to some citizens. For example the United States President must be a citizen that was born in the United States They are excused from specifically Muslim duties, and otherwise equal under the laws of property, contract and obligation. Under sharia law, dhimmi status was originally afforded to Jews, Christians, and Sabians. The protected religions later came to include Zoroastrians, Mandaeans, Hindus and Buddhists. Eventually, the largest school of Islamic legal thought applied this term to all non-Muslims living in Islamic lands outside the sacred area surrounding Mecca, Saudi Arabia.

This status therefore applied to millions of people living from Spain and Morocco on the Atlantic Ocean to Indonesia in the Pacific, and from the 7th century CE until modern times. As an example of the distinctions between Muslims, dhimmis, and others, sharia law permits the consumption of pork and alcohol by non-Muslims living in Islamic countries, although they may not be openly displayed.

These same commodities are expressly forbidden to Muslims. As another example of this, sharia law in present-day Saudi Arabia prescribes blood money to be paid for the death of a person caused by another. The amount payable for a Christian or Jew is half that for a male Muslim; but all others are valued at 1/16. However this is a minority view, and the largest school of legal thought in Islam i.e. the

Hanafi school does not make any distinction between a non-Muslim dhimmi and a muslim citizen.

Treatment of Dhimmis

The question of how tolerant Islam was, and is, towards other religions requires a definition of terms. If a lack of discrimination is the criterion for tolerance, one answer will emerge. If a lack of persecution, defined as active and violent repression, is the criterion, the question gets a different answer.

Discrimination against dhimmis was institutionalized in traditional Islamic societies. Persecution, on the other hand, was rare and atypical. The dhimmi communities had their own chiefs and judges, with their own family, personal and religious laws.

Many of the dhimmi restrictions seem to go back to the early days of the Arab conquest, and to have been instituted as security precautions in order to protect occupying military and administrative personnel. Most of the restrictions were social and symbolic in nature.

Various restrictions, such as dress codes, building codes, and limits on openness of worship, were enforced unevenly on the dhimmi populations. A pattern of stricter, then more lax, enforcement developed over time. In times of external threat, or under a more pious ruler, the restrictions would be rigorously enforced for a while – then more lax enforcement would again return.

The major financial disabilities of the dhimmi were the jizya poll tax and the fact dhimmis could not inherit from Muslims. The jurists and scholars of Islamic sharia law called for humane treatment of the dhimmis, however the commentators were more severe.

Unlike the Jews and Muslims of Spain after its reconquest by Catholic Christians, the dhimmis did not have to choose between apostasy, exile and death. Islam has become the dominant religion in much of the world primarily through three avenues. First, a gradual process of religious conversion for material and spiritual reasons. Second, interfaith marriages, which require the children to be raised as Muslims. Third, and more recently, differing rates of population growth among the religious communities. There were no large scale massacres or expulsions of dhimmi populations until the dissolution of the Ottoman Empire, and the resulting emergence of modern secular Turkey, in the 20th century.

Bibliography

Ahmad, Khurshid : *Islam : its Meaning and Message,* Islamic Council of Europe, London, 1976.

Ahmad, R.S. : *Al-Harakat Al-Islamiyya.* Cairo: Sina Linasr. Allport, G. 1958.

Ahmed, S. Akbar : *Discovering Islam: Making Sense of Muslim History and Society.* London: Routledge, 1988.

Alfieri, Binaca Maria : *Islamic Architecture of the Indian Subcontinent,* Lawrence King, New York, 1989.

Ali, Asghar : *Theory and Practise of the Islamic State,* Lahore Pak. Vanguard Books, 1985.

Ali, Maulana M. A. Muhammad : *A Manual of Hadith,* The Ahmadiyya Anjuman Ishaat Islam, Lahore, Grand Rapids: Baker Books, 1999.

Allchin, Bridget : *The Rise of Civilization in India and Pakistan,* Cambridge University Press, New Delhi, 1989.

Arberry, A.J. : *The Islamic Art of Persia,* Goodword Books, New Delhi, 2003.

Arnold, T.W. : *The Islamic Art and Architecture,* Goodword Books, New Delhi, 2003.

Asad, Muhammad : *The Message of the Qurán,* Published by Dar Al-Andalus, Gibralter.

Aurobindo, Sri : *The Foundations of Islamic Culture,* New York, 1973.

Ayoub, Mahmoud: *The Quran and its Interpreters,* Albany: State University of New York Press, 1984.

Barbour, Ian: *Religion and Science: Historical and Contemporary Issues.* San Francisco: Harper San Francisco, 1997.

Beckett, Katharine Scarfe : *Perception of the Islamic Word,* Cambridge University Press, New Delhi, 1992.

Berkey, Jonothan P. : *The Formation of Islam : Religion and Society in the Near East,* Cambridge University Press, New Delhi, 1990.

Bukhsh, S. K. : *Contribution to the History of Islamic Civilization,* Kitab Bhavan, New Delhi, 2000.

Carre, Olivier : *Islam and the State in the World Today,* Manohar Publisher, New Delhi, 1989.

Chaudhri, Sajedul Bar : *The Profile of an Islamic State,* Dhaka, Islamic Foundation Bangladesh, 1984.

Daniel Pipes : *In the Path of God: Islam and Political Power,* New York: Basic Books Inc., 1983.

Enayatullah Mashriqi *: Quranic System of Law,* Akhuwat Publications, Rawalpindi, Pakistan.

Engineer, Asghar Ali : *Islam : Challenge in Twenty-first Century,* Gyan Books Pvt. Ltd., New Delhi, 2004.

Esposito, L. John : *Islam : The Straight Path.* New York: Oxford University Press, 1991.

Fatima, T. : *Islamic Law and Judiciary,* Deep & Deep Publications, New Delhi, 2001.

Fred M. Donner: *The Early Islamic Conquests,* New Jersey: Princeton University Press, 1981.

Glasse, Cyril : *The Concise Encyclopedia of Islam,* San Francisco: Harper & Row, 1989.

Heyworth-Dunne : *Religious and Political Trends in Modern Egypt,* Washington,1950.

Hoodbhoy, Pervez : *Islam and Science: Religious Orthodoxy and the Battle for Rationality,* London: Zed Books, 1991.

Hussain, Ch. Muhammad : *Development Planning in an Islamic State,* Karachi, Royal Book Co., 1987.

Ikram, S.M. : *Muslim Civilization in India,* Oxford, New York, 1981.

Ilyas Ahmad : *The Social Contract and the Islamic State,* Kitab Bhavan, New Delhi, 1981.

Inayat Ullah Khan El-Mashriqi *: God, Man and the Universe,* Akhuwat Publications, Rawalpindi, Pakistan.

Islahi, M.A.A. : *Islamic Faith and its Presentation,* Adam Publishers, New Delhi, 2002.

James, Piscarton : *Islam in the World of National States,* MacMillan, New York, 1982.

John F. *Science and Religion: From Conflict to Conversation.* Mahwah, NJ: Paulist, 1995.

Keddie, Nikki R. : *Roots of Revolution: An Interpretive History of Modern Iran.* New Haven: Yale University Press, 1981.

Khan Ali Ahmad*: The True Translation of the Glorious Qur'an,* Published by World Islamic Mission, Gulberg, Lahore, Pakistan.

Khan, M. Shabbir : *Social Structure and Economic Change in Islam,* Ed. Pub.,

Index

❑❑❑